Web 2.0
The Business Model

Web 2.0
The Business Model

Edited by

Miltiadis D. Lytras
University of Patras, Patras, Greece

Ernesto Damiani
University of Milan, Milan, Italy

Patricia Ordóñez de Pablos
University of Oviedo, Asturias, Spain

 Springer

Editors:

Miltiadis D. Lytras
University of Patras
Research Academic Computer Tech. Inst.
Computer Engineering & Informatics Dept.
Patras, Greece
lytras@ceid.upatras.gr

Ernesto Damiani
Università di Milano
Dipartimento di. Tecnologie
dell'Informazione
via Bramante 65
26013 Crema, Italy
damiani@dti.unimi.it

Patricia Ordóñez de Pablos
Departamento de Administración de Empresas
y Contabilidad
Facultad de Ciencias Económicas
Universidad de Oviedo
Avd del Cristo, s/n
33.071 Oviedo-Asturias, Spain
patriop@uniovi.es

ISBN-13: 978-0-387-85894-4   e-ISBN-13: 978-0-387-85895-1

Library of Congress Control Number: 2008935102

Printed on acid-free paper.

springer.com

To the ORLY dream. Miltos

As Nishapur's poet wrote "[...] The Caravan of Life shall always pass". Patricia

FOREWORD

Web 2.0 is one of the hottest topics nowadays in Information Systems. Currently the main discussion is emphasized on technologies while there is a great demand for editions that will analyze the business models and business perspectives of the new generation web. This book is one of the first attempts to discuss in an integrated way the business implications of Web 2.0 and its linkage to business value.

Web 2.0, refers to a perceived or proposed second generation of Internet-based services—such as social networking sites, wikis, communication tools, mashups and folksonomies—that emphasize on online collaboration and sharing among users.

This book has a clear editing strategy.
- To go beyond the typical discussion of Web 2.0 as an emerging technological primer and to contribute to the literature and practice by summarizing a number of successful business models for business exploitation
- To promote state of the art on Social Web as a milestone enabled by the evolution of Web 2.0
- To provide a reference book for the area with main emphasis to be paid on practical/business aspects.
- To become a reference edition for people (business people, managers, executives, policy makers, government officers, academics and practitioners) thirsty for knowledge on Web2.0 and its business potential

Three are the major pillars of the book:

1. The discussion of the State of the art Research on Web 2.0

Concerning this pillar we will emphasize on three major components of Web 2.0

- Social Networks Analysis
- Recommendation Systems
- Communities Building

Within this general context the following topics are also of priority:

- Design variables and conditions for social networks
- New forms of interaction in social systems
- Blogging as a social activity and approaches to semantic blogs
- New forms of interaction in knowledge sharing and creation systems
- Blogging and enterprise blogs as a new strategic tool
- Collaborative filtering in social settings
- Analysing social interaction for finding knowledge on Web users
- Semantic Desktops
- Social Network Analysis enabled by the Semantic Web
- Learning and Knowledge Communities
- Analysis of Large Online Communities Web Communities of Practice
- Network Analysis for Building Social Networks
- Implicit, Formal, and Powerful Semantics in Communities
- Semantic Social Networks Metadata and Annotation Techniques
- Metadata schema describing individuals and social ties
- Folksonomies, tagging and other collaboration-based categorisation systems
- Wikis, semantic Wikis and other collaborative knowledge creation systems
- Online Social Networking

- Applications of Online Semantic Networks
- Knowledge Management with Semantic Networks

2. **The Analysis of Successful cases of Web 2.0 with a Business Model perspective**

3. **The understanding fo the potential of Web 2.0 for business in different domains**

The final part of the book will provide taxonomy of business models of web 2.0 in the form of Ebusiness Models for Electronic Markets as Timmers proposed them.

The main target groups of this book are:

- Managers / Executives [they will be able to realize the power of Web 2.0 and its business potential]
- Students in Management and IT/CS majors [they will have an excellent source of information covering not only the state of the art theory but also an excellent practical oriented edition with tight linkages to the Practice and Market]
- Politicians / Government Officers / Policy Makers [they will be able to realize the power of Web 2.0 and its potential for E-government / E-Democracy]
- Professors in academia [they will have an excellent/ teaching oriented edition for E-business/ IS / Business Strategy Courses. Exactly this combination and the capacity of the edition to serve, as a reference edition to many different courses on IT/Strategy and Mgmt is a key advantage.

Additionally we don't want to miss this opportunity to say thanks to Springer Publisher, and in particular to Susan Lagerstrom-Fife and Sharon Palleschi, for giving us the opportunity to develop this book. Also thanks for all authors of chapters, for their interest in collaborating in this book.

Finally, before closing this foreword of the book **Web 2.0: The Business Models**, we would like to invite all our colleagues interested in the adoption of Web 2.0 towards the so called Human Web, applications for the Human and The Society, Information Systems &Information Technology, Knowledge Management and E-Learning, Digital Libraries, Digital Culture and Electronic Tourism, E-Business, E-Government and E-Banking, Politics and Policies for the Knowledge Society, Sustainable Development for the Knowledge Society and New Competitive Resources (Culture, Tourism and Services) to pay attention to an important event organised by **OPEN RESEARCH SOCIETY** in 2009: **"The 2nd Athens World Summit on The Knowledge Society"**, September 2009,. Website: http://www.open-knowledge-society.org/summit09.htm

Editors Bios

Dr. Miltiadis D. Lytras

Computer Engineering and Informatics Department

University of Patras

Office Address: Argolidos 40-42, 153-44 Gerakas Attikis, GREECE

Lytras@ceid.upatras.gr

Miltiadis D. Lytras is the President and Founder of Open Research Society, NGO. His research focuses on semantic web, knowledge management and e-learning, with more than 100 publications in these areas. He has co-edited / co-edits, 25 special issues in International Journals (e.g. IEEE Transaction on Knowledge and Data Engineering, IEEE Internet Computing, IEEE Transactions on Education, Computers in Human Behaviour, Interactive Learning Environments, Journal of Knowledge Management, Journal of Computer Assisted Learning, etc) and has authored/[co-]edited 22 books [e.g. Open Source for Knowledge and Learning Management, Ubiquitous and Pervasive Knowledge Management, Intelligent Learning Infrastructures for Knowledge Intensive Organizations, Semantic Web Based Information Systems, China Information technology Hanbook, Real World Applications of Semantic Web and Ontologies, Web 2.0: The Business Model, etc] . He is the founder and officer of the Semantic Web and Information Systems Special Interest Group in the Association for Information Systems (http://www.sigsemis.org). He serves as the (Co) Editor in Chief of 12 international journals [e.g. International Journal of Knowledge and Learning, International Journal of Technology Enhanced Learning, International Journal on Social and Humanistic Computing, International Journal on Semantic Web and Information Systems, International Journal on Digital Culture and Electronic Tourism, International Journal of Electronic Democracy, International Journal of Electronic Banking, International Journal of Electronic Trade etc] while he is associate editor or editorial board member in seven more.

Professor Ernesto Damiani

University of Milan

Department of Computer Technology

Via Bramante, 65, I-26013 Crema (CR), Italy

damiani@dti.unimi.it

Ernesto Damiani is a Professor at the Dept. of Information Technology,University of Milan, where he is the Head of the Ph.D. program in Computer Science and leads the Software Architectures Lab. Prof. Damiani holds/has held visiting positions at several international institutions, including George Mason University (Fairfax, VA, US) and LaTrobe University (Melbourne, Australia). Prof. Damiani is an Adjunct Professor at the Sydney University of Technology (Australia). He has written several books and filed international patents; also, he co-authored more than two hundred research papers on advanced secure service-oriented architectures, open source software and business process design, software reuse and Web data semantics. Prof. Damiani is the Chair of IFIP WG 2.6 on Databases, the Vice-Chair of WG 2.12 Web Data Semantics and the secretary of IFIP WG 2.13 on Open Source Software Development. He is also the Vice Chair of IEEE TC on Industrial Informatics and Associate Editor of the IEEE Transactions on Service Computing. Prof. Damiani coordinates several research projects funded by the European Commission, Italian Ministry of Research and by private companies including Siemens Mobile, Cisco Systems, ST Microelectronics, BT Exact, Engineering, Telecom Italy and others.

Patricia Ordonez De Pablos

University of Oviedo

Dept of Business Administation and Accountability

University of Oviedo

Facultad de Ciencias Economicas

Avd del Cristo, s/n, 33.071 Oviedo-Asturias, SPAIN

patriop@uniovi.es

Patricia Ordóñez de Pablos, is Professor in the Department of Business Administration and Accountability, at the Faculty of Economics of The University of Oviedo (Spain). Her teaching and research interests focus on the areas of strategic management, knowledge management, intellectual capital measuring and reporting, organizational learning and human resources management. She is Executive Editor of the International Journal of Learning and Intellectual and the International Journal of Strategic Change Management as well as EIC of the International Journals of Chinese Culture and Management and IJ of Arab Culture, Management and Sustainable Development.

Contents

Chapter 1: Empirical Analysis of Functional Web 2.0 Environments

R. Todd Stephens, Ph.D.

AT&T Corporation, USA

Abstract

In this chapter, the author addresses the need for a functional framework used to integrate Web 2.0 components into the organization business model. The success of the Internet can be seen within any organization but customers are asking for more interaction with the enterprises they do business with. Simply taking a product or service to the Internet is no longer enough. Web 2.0 provides the basic technology for creating a network of customers who are passionate about the company's product offering. This chapter will also review the framework as it is applied to the Wine Industry where four organizations are reviewed in detail. The framework will provide researchers and organizations a functional view of the value when integrating Web 2.0 technologies into the basic business offering.

1   Introduction

Enterprises are being transformed from an old business model built around the command and control aspects information management to a new one where collaboration and social networking are the essential components in defining a long-term business value. When researchers speak of Web 2.0 applications, they tend to focus on the technology aspects of the environment. However, the real impact of integrating Web 2.0 technologies is in the transformation of the organizational business model. This chapter will focus on the development of a framework for organizations looking to integrate Web 2.0 into the value-add functions of the business. This framework will demonstrate how this technology can be adopted by enterprises already utilizing the web for business transactions and presence.

2   Background

While the web itself is about twenty years old, businesses are still implementing the technology into the fabric of the business model. The background section will focus on defining the building blocks for the framework including defining the basic components of Web 1.0 which focused on the presence and business transaction. The Web 2.0 section will focus on defining the basic building blocks of customer interactions, while the final section will focus on a review the wine industry.

2.1 Web 1.0: Presence and Electronic Commerce

The term Web 1.0 emerged from the research around the development of Web 2.0. Prior to this, researchers commonly referred to Web 1.0 as Electronic Commerce or E-Business. Where as, web 1.0 focused on a read only web interface, Web 2.0 focuses on a read-write interface where value emerges from the contribution of a large volume of users. The Internet initially focused on the command and control of the information itself. Information was controlled by a relative small number of resources but distributed to a large number which spawned the massive growth of the web itself. Like television before it, the web allowed for the broadcasting of information to a large number of users. Initial web sites were built simply to communicate presence or provide information on the business itself. This component includes information like marketing materials, investor relations, employment opportunities, and product information. Some researchers describe the integration of the business transaction as Web 1.5, indicating a separate phase of development. This altered the static information environment and transformed the web into an integral part of the business environment. The World Wide Web (WWW) was conceived at the European Particle Physics Laboratory in Switzerland. Berners-Lee, Cailliau, Luotonen, Nielsen, and Secret (1994) describe the web as "collaborative medium" which would allow information providers in remote sites to share ideas without boundaries. Most businesses have moved toward the web in order to take advantage of the capabilities of the electronic-commerce business model. Moving business functions from a traditional brick and mortar model to an electronic commerce model is not as simple as it might seem. The idea of Web 1.0 revolves around the digital enablement of transactions and processes within the organization, involving information systems under the guidance or control of the firm (Laudon & Traver, 2003).

2.2 Web 2.0: Customer Interaction

While Web 2.0 has been debated by researchers as to who and when the concepts emerged, little argument exists that the technology and demand has arrived. Unlike Web 1.0, this new technology encourages user participation and derives its greatest value when large communities contribute to the content. User generated metadata, information, and designs enable a much richer environment where the value is generated by the volume of users. Sometimes referred to as sharing, collaboration, aggregate knowledge, or community driven content, social software creates the foundation of collective intelligence (Weiss, 2005). Much of the Web 2.0 technology is difficult to nail down an exact definition, the basic truth is that Web 2.0 emphasizes interaction, community, and openness (Millard & Ross, 2006). Along with these characteristics, Smith and Valdes (2005) added simple and lightweight technologies and decentralized processing to the mix. O'Reilly (2005) defined Web 2.0 as a platform, spanning all connected devices; Web 2.0 applications are those that make the most of the intrinsic advantages of that platform: delivering software as a continually-updated service that gets better the more people use it, consuming and remixing data from multiple sources, including individual users, while providing their own data and services in a form that allows remixing by others, creating network effects through an "architecture of participation", and going beyond the page metaphor of Web 1.0 to deliver rich user experiences. While Web 2.0 has many and often confusing definitions most include the concepts of weblogs, wikis, Really Simple Syndication (RSS) functionality, social tagging, mashups, and user defined content.

Weblogs or Blogs

Weblogs or blogs have become so ubiquitous that many people use the term synonymous for a "personal web site" (Blood, 2004). Unlike traditional Hypertext Markup Language (HTML) web pages, blogs offer the ability for the non-programmer to communicate on a regular basis. Traditional HTML style pages required knowledge of style, coding, and design in order to publish content that was basically read only from the consumer's point of view. Weblogs remove much of the constraints by providing a standard user interface that does not require customization. Weblogs originally emerged as a repository for linking but soon evolved to the ability to publish content and allow readers to become content providers. The essence of a blog can be defined by the format which includes small chunks of content referred to as posts, date stamped, reverse chronological order, and content expanded to include links, text and images (Baoill, 2004). The biggest advancement made with Weblogs is the permanence of the content which has a unique Universal Resource Locator (URL). This allows the content to be posted and along with the comments to define a permanent record of information. This is critical in that having a collaborative record that can be indexed by search engines will increase the utility and spread the information to a larger audience.

With the advent of software like Wordpress and Typepad, along with blog service companies like blogger.com, the weblog is fast becoming the communication medium of the new web.

Wikis

A Wiki is a web site that promotes the collaborative creation of content. Wiki pages can be edited by anyone at anytime. Informational content can be created and easily organized within the wiki environment and then reorganized as required (O'Neill, 2005). Wikis are currently in high demand in a large variety of fields, due to their simplicity and flexibility nature. Documentation, reporting, project management, online glossaries, and dictionaries, discussion groups, or general information applications are just a few a examples of where the end user can provide value (Reinhold, 2006). The major difference between a wiki and blog is that the wiki user can alter the original content while the blog user can only add information in the form of comments. While stating that anyone can alter content, some large scale wiki environments have extensive role definitions which define who can perform functions of update, restore, delete, and creation. Wikipedia, like many wiki type projects, have readers, editors, administrators, patrollers, policy makers, subject matter experts, content maintainers, software developers, and system operators (Riehle, 2006). All of which create an environment open to sharing information and knowledge to a large group of users.

RSS Technologies

Originally developed by Netscape, RSS was intended to publish news type information based upon a subscription framework (Lerner, 2004). Many Internet users have experienced the frustration of searching Internet sites for hours at a time to find relevant information. RSS is an XML based content-syndication protocol that allows web sites to share information as well as aggregate information based upon the users needs (Cold, 2006). In the simplest form, RSS shares the metadata about the content without actually delivering the entire information source. An author might publish the title, description, publish date, and copyrights to anyone that subscribes to the feed. The end user is required to have an application called an aggregator in order to receive the information. By having the RSS aggregator application, end users are not required to visit each site in order to obtain information. From an ed user perspective, the RSS technology changes the communication method from a search and discover to a notification model. Users can locate content that is pertinent to their job and subscribe to the communication which enables a much faster communication stream..

Social Tagging

Social tagging describes the collaborative activity of marking shared online content with keywords or tags as a way to organize content for future navigation, filtering, or search (Gibson, Teasley, & Yew, 2006). Traditional information architecture utilized a central taxonomy or classification scheme in order to place information into specific pre-defined bucket or category. The assumption was that trained librarians understood more about information content and context than the average user. While this might have been true for the local library with the utilization of the Dewey Decimal system, the enormous amount of content on the Internet makes this type of system un-manageable. Tagging offers a number of benefits to the end user community. Perhaps the most important feature to the individual is able to bookmark the information in a way that is easier for them to recall at a later date. The benefit of this ability on a personal basis is obvious but what about the impact to the community at large. The idea of social tagging is allowing multiple users to tag content in a way that makes sense to them, by combining these tags, users create an environment where the opinions of the majority define the appropriateness of the tags themselves. The act of creating a collection of popular tags is referred to as a folksonomy which is defined as a folk taxonomy of important and emerging content within the user community (Ahn, Davis, Fake, Fox, Furnas, Golder, Marlow, Naaman, & Schachter, 2006). The vocabulary problem is defined by the fact that different users define content in different ways. The disagreement can lead to missed information or inefficient user interactions (Boyd, Davis, Marlow, & Naaman, 2006). One of the best examples of social tagging is Flickr which allows user to upload images and "tag" them with appropriate metadata keywords. Other users, who view your images, can also tag them with their concept of appropriate keywords. After a critical mass has been reached, the resulting tag collection will identify images correctly and without bias. Other sites like iStockPhoto have also utilized this technology but more along the sales channel versus the community one.

Mashups: Integrating Information

The final Web 2.0 technology describe the efforts around information integration, commonly referred to as "mashups". These applications can be combined to deliver additional value that the individual parts could not on their own. One example is HousingMaps.com that combines the Google mapping application with a real estate listing service on Craiglists.com (Jhingran, 2006). Other examples include Chicagocrime.org who overlays local crime statistics on top of Google Maps so end users can see what crimes were committed recently in the neighborhood. Another site synchronizes Yahoo! Inc.'s real-time traffic data with Google Maps. Much of the work with web services will enable greater extensions of mashups and combine many different businesses and business models. Organizations, like Amazon and Microsoft are embracing the mash-up movement by offering developers easier access to their data and services. Moreover, they're programming their services so that more computing tasks, such as displaying maps onscreen, get done on the users' Personal Computers rather than on their far-flung servers (Hof, 2005).

User Contributed Content

One of the basic themes of Web 2.0 is user contributed information. The value derived from the contributed content comes not from a subject matter expert, but rather from individuals whose small contributions add up. One example of user contributed content is the product review systems like Amazon.com and reputation systems used with ebay.com. A common practice of online merchants is to enable their customers to review or to express opinions on the products they have purchased (Hu & Liu, 2004). Online reviews are a major source of information for consumers and demonstrated enormous implications for a wide range of management activities, such as brand building, customer acquisition and retention, product development, and quality assurance (Hu, Pavlou, & Zhang, 2006). A person's reputation is a valuable piece of information that can be used when deciding whether or not to interact or do business with. A reputation system is a bidirectional medium where buyers post feedback on sellers and vice versa. For example, eBay buyers voluntarily comment on the quality of service, their satisfaction with the item traded, and promptness of shipping. Sellers comment about the prompt payment from buyers, or respond to comments left by the buyer (Christodorescu, Ganapathy, Giffin, Kruger, Rubin, & Wang, 2005). Reputation systems may be categorized in three basic types: ranking, rating, and collaborative. Ranking systems use quantifiable measures of users' behavior to generate and rating. Rating systems use explicit evaluations given by users in order to define a measure of interest or trust. Finally, collaborative filtering systems determine the level of relationship between the two individuals before placing a weight on the information. For example, if a user has reviewed similar items in the past then the relevancy of a new rating will be higher (Davis, Farnham, & Jensen, 2002).

2.3 Wine Industry

This research focused on the retail wine industry to validate the model due to the characteristics of the environment. The wine industry is ideal since the end user is enthusiastic and passionate about the production and consumption of wine. The United States has the third largest aggregate consumption of wine worldwide. California accounted for roughly 90% of the value of the United States wine productions which is down from 2000 when the rate was around 94% (Goodhue, Green, Heien, & Martin, 2008). The industry itself is going though an ongoing consolidation where the top eight companies produce 75% of the wine within the United States. However, the industry does have a long tail of wineries that number around 4,929 which produces over 7,000 brands (McMillan, 2007). This consolidation is creating a problem for smaller wineries to get their wine into the supermarkets and restaurants. In addition, the internet has provided one alternative where individual wineries can sell directly to the consumer. That being said, downward price pressure, increased competition, and the bargaining power of the distribution channels has created a challenging business environment for everyone (Kim & Mauborgne, 2005).

Wineries and consumer sales organizations understand the importance of building their brand in an online environment. Wines, like Yellow Tail, have made significant investments in building their brand with a Web 1.0 environment. However, most sales still come from retail organizations and initial investments in Web 2.0 technologies have been limited but are expanding. Currently there are more than 900 wine oriented blogs with an average readership ranging from 20 to 20,000 (McMillan, 2007). Other alternatives like podcasting and posting videos on YouTube have also started to make an impact but success stories are limited.

As few established organizations have yet integrated emerging technologies into their business models, the longer-term implications are unknown and the future of firms relying mainly on Web 2.0 channels is unclear. Early movers still struggle to develop successful e-commerce initiatives and sustainable digital business models. A closer look at the industry reveals a highly constrained legal environment, uncertainties regarding consumer demand, and an intricate picture of complex relationships (Gebauer & Ginsburg, 2001). This research is going to focus on several organizations that are building communities, integrating Web 2.0 technology, and conducting business with this new medium of communication. The four organizations that will be the focus of this research include Cork'd.com, Wine.com, CalWineries.com, and Snooth.com. Each offers a variety of different levels of Web 2.0 technology.

3 Web 2.0 Integration Framework

The previous section focused on defining the foundation for the development of a framework for implementing Web 2.0 technologies. Having a framework allows organizations to better understand where these technologies fit into the business value chain. This section of the chapter lays out the Web 2.0 Integration Framework currently in use by several different organizations. The framework is not built from an architecture or technology perspective but rather from the business perspective. Figure 1 presents the basic model of implementation, common to all four organizations.

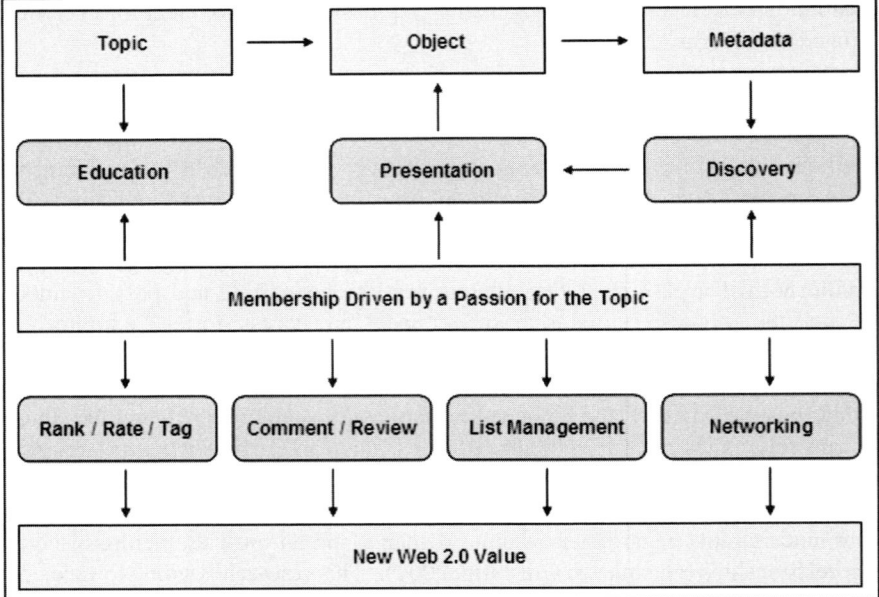

Figure 1: Functional Web 2.0 Model

3.1 Traditional Online Framework

The model produces two basic layers of abstraction: Information Layer (Web 1.0) and the Interaction Layer (Web 2.0). The informational layer includes the first two rows of the model since these represent much of the information provided by a standard Web 1.0 application. The second layer (bottom three rows) is the interaction layer which focuses on the various forms of asynchronous communication mediums that come into play in a Web 2.0 environment. Figure 2 provides a simple view of the business functions utilized in a Web 1.0 based business model as applied to the wine retailer.

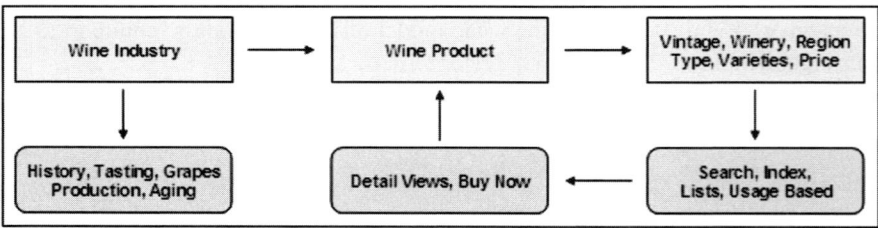

Figure 2: Web 1.0 Framework

Wine Industry and Education

The information section begins with an overview of the wine industry and provides a basic level of understanding. The first area is an educational element of the industry itself which can provide the basic level of understanding or instruction. Without any dialog with the end user, there is no real method of knowing the user's level of knowledge. Some end users have little or no knowledge of the product while others may have a sommelier certification. Therefore, a contextual education is required of the user for which they can either opt-in or opt-out of the communication medium. Consumers regard wine as a complex activity with a significant investment in knowledge and terminology, in particular in the premium categories. In many cases, there is a lack of sufficient product information may deter consumer purchase. By sharing information and providing background information, the wine consumer has not only consumed more wine over the past ten years but also moved to higher quality wines. Moving away from the inexpensive jug wines, consumers are buying more popular premium, super premium, and ultra-premium wines that can cost as high as $15.00 or more. In fact, the super-premium category is the fastest growing segment accounting for 25% of the wine consumption (Goodhue, Green, Heien, & Martin, 2008). Of the four studied organizations, CalWineries provided the best information on the history of wine, the types of grapes, the regions of the world, production methods and aging concepts. They also cross linked to several other social software sites that enhance the education of the wine consumer. Figure 3 provides an image of the CalWineries' education page.

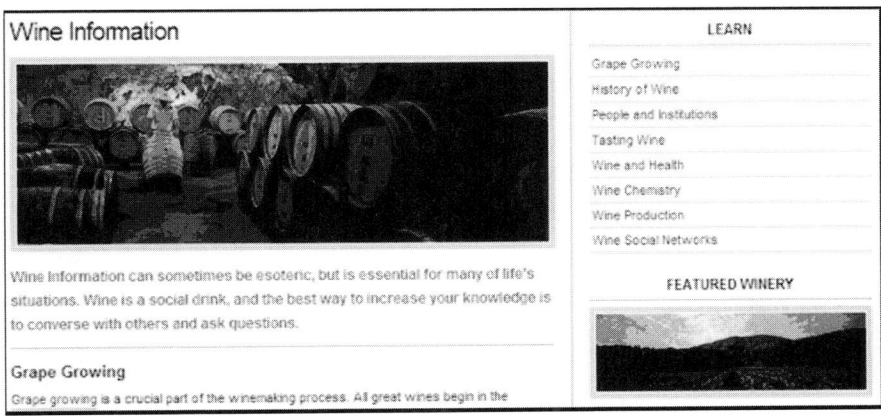

Figure 3: CalWineries Wine Information Portal

The landing page sets the stage for educating the consumer with a sequential delivery of content. Beginning with the process of growing grapes, the site provides the basic context of climate, terrain, planning, pets, and the annual life cycle of the vine. The end user can then move on to the "History of Wine Making" and several other educational pages, including "Wine Social Networks". Additionally, they spotlight specific wineries or wine regions to provide a more local flavor to the information provided. By adding education to the environment, CalWineries becomes an integral part in the overall wine industry. Since one of the main goals of online environments is the generation of traffic, education is an excellent method of generation.

Wine Product and Associated Metadata

The second area of the model focuses on the actual product which in this case is the bottle of wine. From an implementation perspective, we can actually combine the product and the metadata boxes for producing the product description; this is commonly refereed to as the product page. The metadata or product information may also be used to help the end user locate information using a variety of tools such as search engines, tag clouds, or taxonomy based listings. Most technologists came across metadata in the database world where the definition presented was "data about data". Students get their first introduction in the library science world where metadata describes the books, journals and magazines held within the library itself. Metadata can provide abundant information about where an asset is located, what primitive elements make up the asset, how the asset was developed or created, where the asset is physically located, who the steward of the asset is, and, of course, an inventory of what assets exists. Organizations can use this technology and apply it to the product offering. Product pages provide the specific details of the selected item. Different users the product pages to either verify the product selected or help them in deciding which product to choose (Chak, 2003).

Figure 4: Cork'd Product Information

Figure 4 provides an image of the product page within the Cork'd.com environment. The application provides the metadata about the product including the winery where the wine was made, the vintage, the type of wine, the local region, price, and who authored the entry. One interesting aspect of social environments versus traditional electronic commerce sites is the ability of the user to add wines to the inventory. This can be extremely beneficial for micro-wineries. Since anyone in the network can create an entry for the product, this information can serve to build the user's reputation. Other sites will also allow you to tag the wine which is like adding personalized metadata without the system constraints.

Discovery

The key to any environment is the ability to locate the product through a variety of methods. Eismann, McClelland, and Stone (2000) describe the navigation structure as a framework for providing viewers the information required to know where they are and a method of getting where they want to go. In addition, navigation quickly becomes intuitive when you use consistent treatment, placement, weight, and behavior of navigation repository elements. Navigation is a goal-centered and action-oriented activity that revolves around the user experience. A navigation system should be easily learned, consistent, provides visual feedback, appear in context, offer alternatives, and provide an economy of action and time (Fleming, 1998). Snooth.com provides an interactive interface in refining your search results based on the metadata components as well as taxonomy for locating your favorite wine.

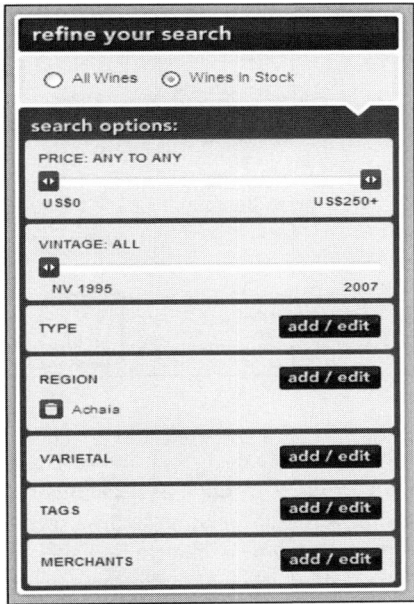

Figure 5: Search and Sitemap from Snooth.com

12

Figure 5 provides two different methods of locating wine in the Snooth environment. The image on the left shows an interactive Ajax tool that reduce the scope of wines found in the inventory. The user can add constraints or use the interactive adjustment bar to filter the result set. With thousands of wines to choose from, having an interactive interface make sit easier on the end user to find, learn, and buy the wine of their choice. The second image presents the taxonomy of the metadata and the associated options in the form of a sitemap. While the page is not really a sitemap by the standard definition, the result is the ability of the consumer to see the bigger picture of how the wines are categorized. With very large product environments, these types of tools can be the difference with end users getting frustrated and leaving the environment before making a purchase.

Business Transactions

The final box is the actual business transaction and online support environment. Business processes like ordering, order tracking, and support should be provided by the online environment. An end user that accesses an electronic commerce site has a specific purpose in mind that generally revolves around a business function. A business function is defined as any activity that can assist a person or organization to achieve the buying or selling of goods with a moderate expectation of quality of the goods and services (Poong, Talha, & Zaman, 2006). In the studied organizations, the purchase of the product was the main business transaction defined. Figure 6 provides the purchase transaction page view for Wine.com.

Figure 6: Wine.com Transaction Environment

Notice several other business transactions like the ability to add notes, review the product, bookmark the page, and add to your wine list. Each of these business transactions are actually integration functions of Web 2.0 technology described in the following section. One of the key findings is that some of the studied sites only linked to a Business-to-Consumer (B2C) transaction services versus actually offering the service themselves. These organizations made profit from either advertising on the site or accepted a small transaction fee from the online retailer; much in the same way Amazon.com offers for their merchant program.

Integration of Web 2.0 Components

As described in the background section, more and more organizations are looking toward Web 2.0 to get closer to the consumer and build communities around the product or service. In many enterprises, the customer is confined to a limited role in the process of development, delivery, and innovation of the business model. Businesses no longer have 20 years to manage the growth cycle and lock out competitors due to intellectual property rights. Take the Apple iPhone as an example. Within three weeks of the product's release, hackers are disabled the AT&T network connection requirement and made changes to the hardware so that the iPhone could be connected to any network. Within three months, China was able to produce the MiniOne which worked on any network and could run more applications (Dartford, 2007). Tapscott (2006) indicates that a power shift is underway in which only those organizations that can harness mass collaboration will survive. The key is to be able to integrate the new technology by building on top of the current infrastructure. This will enable organizations to take advantage of the technology without putting the business at risk. Figure 6 represents the Interaction Layer of the framework as applied to the wine industry.

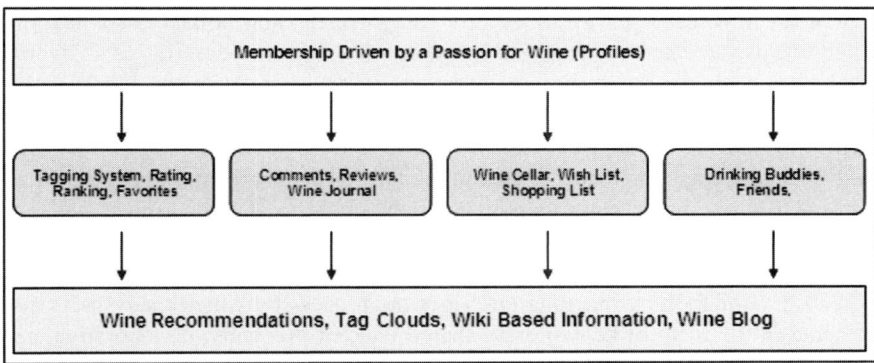

Figure 6: Interaction Layer (Web 2.0)

Membership into the Network

The key component of any Web 2.0 application is finding people who are passionate with the subject or product. In many Web 2.0 services, a contribution rate of less than 1% is common. That is to say that the percentage of people that consume the information is 99% while those that actually contribute is around 1%. Some sites do better than the 1% like Wikipedia which has a reported 4.5% ratio (Kuznetsov, 2006). Li and Bernoff (2008) reported an 18% contribution rate from those that actively participate in social technologies is common. When a user is driven to get involved then mechanisms need to be in place that will support member business functions like user profile creation, profile maintenance, profile feedback, and contributor scoring. Users get involved with social environments for several reasons including: the ability share information or knowledge, increase innovation, or get known as a subject matter expert.

Tagging Systems

The second tier begins to add additional Web 2.0 elements like the ability of tagging information. Tagging can take on many forms such as ranking or rating of the product. In other cases, the information may be added to the end user's favorites as in a preferred wine or winery. These are commonly referred to as recommender systems which provide consumers with personalized recommendations based on their purchase history, past ratings, profile, or interests. These collaborative filtering based recommender systems have been applied to many electronic commerce systems and shown good performance in predicting a list of products a consumer prefers (Kim & Srivastva, 2007).

Tags are an effective means for organizing content within the enterprise. While there may already be metadata tags that allow the end user to define how the product should be categorized from their perspective, the essence of this area is that the end user can add structured information about a product or service. Tagging content creates a taxonomy type structure better known as a folksonomy. Content in a Web2.0 service is usually categorized using collaborative tagging which is a user-created organization based on tags. Tags are descriptive keywords attached to items for the purpose of organization (Khan & Nauman, 2007). Folksonomies represent a growing approach to the problem of classification in the Web. Users can associate freely chosen tags to the resources and in this way they produce knowledge for the entire community. As the work of categorization is performed by the users, folksonomies are democratic, scalable, current, inclusive and have a very low cost; according to many researchers they are a forced move, in response to the uncontrolled growth of the Web (Colombetti, Eynard, & Laniado, 2007). Collaborative tagging describes the process by which many users add metadata in the form of keywords to shared content. Recently, collaborative tagging has grown in popularity on the web, on sites that allow users to tag bookmarks, photographs and other content (Golder & Huberman, 2005). While tagging is emerging, the ability to add unstructured content is also evolving.

Contextual Knowledge

Contextual knowledge moves beyond the simple metadata and provides more of a discussion medium for users to communicate within the community. Collaborative environments operate over unstructured information and can span several business processes and organizational boundaries. Since the need for virtual workspaces emerge when organizational collaboration occurs, the ability to predict demand is nearly impossible. More importantly, when the business need arises for a virtual workspace, the technology cannot wait or the competitive advantage may be lost.

Collaborative workspaces are generally designed for distributed teams which can be defined as groups of people that interact through interdependent tasks guided by common purpose, and work across space, time, and organizational boundaries primarily through electronic means (Maznevski & Chudoba, 2000). In order to be effective in sharing information and working in an online environment, end users need to understand and develop knowledge sharing practices (Becerra-Fernandez & Sabherwal, 2001). Unstructured information can be captured in a wide variety of tools such journals, wikis, discussions, reviews, and content commenting. Contextual knowledge alters the medium from one of classification to one geared toward a discussion.

Information Tracking

The third box represents the emerging trend where end users can actually manage their own information within the online environment. For example, Amazon.com allows you to manage your wish list or bridal directory with online tools provided by the company. In the wine environment, customers can manage their wine lists, keep an inventory of wines in their cellar, or establish a wish list of wines they want to try. This capability is a huge step forward to engage end users in a more innovative way. The process of creating and maintaining personal information is relatively simple. In fact, a list is simply a connection between a product and the user profile. The system creates a one-to-many relationship between the consumer and the product offering. Hence, the idea of tracking my wine purchases over time. Additional elements or metadata can be added like where the wine is stored within the wine cellar. By adding these additional elements, the end user can configure an unlimited number of personal utilities.

Social Networking

Social Networking can be defined as an application that connects people by matching profile information with direct interactions. These connections may be in the form of dating interests, employment status, or political party affiliation (Counts & Geraci, 2005). Social Networking sites provide two basic functions. The first is the ability to create and maintain a profile that serves as an online identity within the environment. The second is the ability to create connections between other people within the network (Joinson, 2008). Social networks are critical to the wine industry since the network increases the passion, awareness, and engagement of the product itself. One of the more innovative uses of the social network is the "Drinking Buddies" within the Corkd.com environment. The value of the network, not only increases the product knowledge, but also allows the user to connect with the organization in a more cost effective manner. Additionally, the organization can provide additional products and services to create a more comprehensive offering.

Web 2.0 Value-Add Components

The ultimate goal of adding the Web 2.0 technologies is to deliver value back to the business in increased sales, improved customer services or lowering the cost of doing business. By combining ranking and rating with comments and feedback, the end user will gain a valuable insight from people like them. One of the most credible sources of information is from "people like me". According to the Edelman (2007), the impact of "people like me" has risen from 20% in 2003 to 68% in 2007. Clearly, the ability to manage the conversation about ones products in an imperative to expanding the business value of an organization. While recommendation type systems have been around, they focused support more on the transaction side versus the customer context side of the equation. Miller (2005) argues that organizations can gain the greatest value from recommender systems by generating recommendations that serve users - the individuals, not commercial sites. Kostan, Riedl & Schafer (2001) have argued that the success of a recommender systems should really be measured by how effectively the system helps its users make decisions, rather than measuring how much profit it generates for a commercial website.

Utilizing the tagging elements of Web 2.0 produces new mechanisms for finding and locating product information. Tag clouds are visually-weighted renditions of collections of words (tags) that can be used to represent the concepts present in large collections of information. Tags may be assigned to products manually or by automatic indexing. The qualities of associations between each tag and the entity it describes, such as frequency or time, are visually represented with variable font sizes and colors (Good, Hentrich, Kuo, & Wilkinson, 2007). By adding new and innovative methods of locating products or support information, tag clouds can drive up sales as well as interest in the product itself.One of the primary purposes of a collaborative tools is to consolidate information and provide an overall view of the topic that the majority of the user can agree. The wiki environment is an ideal environment to create a collaborative environment that is easy to use and easy to maintain. Additionally, a wiki promotes organization learning and provides a rapid form of communication (Hasan & Pfaff, 2006). The business benefit of having an open or collaborative environment for contextual information is the speed and accuracy that emerges when end users begin to take responsibility of the information. Dell is one of the best examples where a company has brought together Web 2.0 components to create a support environment. Tools like blogs, discussions groups, forums, and videos come together to provide the consumer enormous value from the experience of owning a computer.

The final area focused on enabling the business value is the emergence of several wine type blogs within the industry. The business value of a blog is that is provides a mechanism for communicating across a very broad audience. With the addition of aggregators like Technorati, blogs can be used to distribute information to large group of individuals. There are several well known blogs authored by experts like Tyler Colman, Alice Fering, and Joe Dresser. Within the studied organizations, most had an associated wine blog to help communicate the core business message.In order for businesses to invest the resources in developing social software, the business value must be easily identified. Developing and engaging the community is important but if the result fails to deliver an increased value to the business then resources may have been better served in other areas. Other business models may depend on advertising or click-thru rates which can be greatly enhanced with Web 2.0 tools. Much has been written about viral marketing which is basically any strategy that encourages individuals to pass on a marketing message to others, creating the potential for exponential growth in the message's exposure and influence. Organizations can leverage this medium to drive their value and brand message to a large number of users fairly quickly. The key here is the ability to tap into the enthusiasm of the consumers so that they are encouraged to become producers. Each of the four organizations focused on created communities to enable this synergy which then can be translated into real business value.

4　The Future of Web 2.0 Integration

In 1968, Mel Conway (1968) devised the "Conway Law" which states that the structure of systems will reflect the structure of the organization that develops it. Since the majority of organizations are built under the command and control, centralized, and authoritative model, the ability incorporate collaborative technologies will be limited. Integrating these technologies into established business models approaches the problem, not from the top down but rather from the bottom up. The benefit from this approach is to have as little impact as possible to the core business model. However, future businesses will need to be built from the ground up with integrating customer interactions as the core strategy of value generation.

4.1 Future Research Areas

The base problem organizations will have in integrating Web 2.0 technologies is the simple extensions of Web 2.0, like adding an executive blog, are fairly simple and many organizations have garnered the business value of this type of integration. Yet, true transformation into Web 2.0 may be elusive due to the ability to assemble the various pieces which will need to be loosely joined versus hardwired. Examples of these may include Google Services, Mashups, and sharing services. The implementation of these technologies may be simple but the integration into the business model is much more of a challenge. Some organizations are looking into building a corporate presence in Social Networking sites such as MySapce and Facebook. Other organizations are moving into virtual environment like Second Life to establish virtual stores and online support centers. The end result of the Web 2.0 integration may not be as clear cut as Web 1.0 which focused on the presence and business processes. In the Web 2.0 world, we have an indefinite number of possible integrations and services that can be added to the core business model. This uniqueness may very well be the basis for value creation in the near future. Success stories like the wine industry are emerging as more organizations change their business models. Organizations like Lego, Apple, or Nike can generate end user engagement while others may have to be more creative in the development of communities. More research is needed for organizations whose business model revolves around commodities or infrastructure type product lines.

4.2 Conclusions

Much of this chapter was devoted to the integration of the Web 2.0 technology with little attention paid to the end user and the culture transformation that needs to happen. The producer and consumer must work together to create new value as many electronic commerce sites have done with customer reviews and ratings. As collaborative products mature, this type of effort will become common place and set the stage a truly Web 2.0 experience. Web 2.0 allows organizations to listen to their direct customers which create a conversation of value. This type of conversation or communication medium energizes the customer base to be more than just consumers but rather an engaged part of the business.

References

Ahn, L., Davis, M., Fake, C., Fox, K., Furnas, G., Golder, S., Marlow, C., Naaman, M., & Schachter, J. (2006). Why do tagging systems work? Proceedings of the SIGCHI conference on Human Factors in computing systems. Montreal, Canada: The Association of Computing Machinery.

Baoill, A. (2004). Conceptualizing the weblog: Understanding what it is in order to imagine what it can be. Interfacings: Journal of Contemporary Media Studies, 5(2), 1-8.

Becerra-Fernandez, I. & Sabherwal, R. (2001). Organizational Knowledge Management: A Contingency Perspective. Journal of Management Information Systems, 18(1).

Berners-Lee, T., Cailliau, R., Luotonen, A., Nielsen, H.F. & Secret, A. (1994). The World-Wide Web. Communications of the ACM, 37(8), 76-82.

Bernoff, J. & Li, C. (2008): Groundswell: Winning in a world transformed by social technologies; Harvard Business Press, Boston, Massachusetts.

Blood, R. (2004). How blogging software reshapes the online community. Communications of the ACM, 47(12), 53-55.

Boyd, D., Davis, M., Marlow, C., & Naaman, M. (2006). Social networks, networking & virtual communities: HT06, tagging paper, taxonomy, Flickr, academic article, to read. Proceedings of the seventeenth conference on Hypertext and hypermedia. Odense, Denmark: The Association of Computing Machinery.

Chak, A. (2003). Submit Now: Designing Persuasive Web Sites. New Riders Press: Indianapolis, IA.

Christodorescu, M., Ganapathy, V., Giffin, J., Kruger, L., Rubin, S., & Wang, H. (2005). An auctioning reputation system based on anomaly detection. Proceedings of the 12th ACM conference on Computer and communications security. Alexandria, VA: The Association of Computing Machinery.

Cold, S. (2006). Using Really Simple Syndication (RSS) to enhance student research. ACM SIGITE Newsletter. 3(1).

Colombetti, M., Eynard, D. & Laniado, D. (2007). A semantic tool to support navigation in a folksonomy. Hypertext 2007. 153-154

Conway, M. (1968). How Do Committees Invent? Datamation. 14(4), 28-31.

Counts, S. & Geraci, J. (2005) Incorporating co-presence at events into digital social networking. CHI Extended Abstracts 2005: 1308-1311

Dartford, M. (2007). China's iClone. Popular Science. 8(7).

Davis, J., Farnham, S., and Jensen, C. (2002). Finding others online: Reputation systems for social online spaces. Proceedings of the SIGCHI conference on Human factors in computing systems: Changing our world, changing ourselves. Minneapolis, MN: The Association of Computing Machinery.

Edelman (2007). 2007 Edelman Trust Barometer. Retrieved March 12, 2007 from http://www.edelman.com/image/insights/content/FullSupplement.pdf

Eismann, K., McClelland, D., & Stone, T. (2000). Web Design: Studio Secrets. Foster City, CA: IDG Books World Wide.

Fleming, J. (1998). Web Navigation Designing the User Experience. Sebastopol, CA: O'Reilly & Associates.

Judith, G. & Ginsburg, M. (2001). The vines they are e-changing or are they?. Working paper Fisher CITM.

Gibson, F., Teasley, S., & Yew, J. (2006). Learning by tagging: group knowledge formation in a self-organizing learning community. Proceedings of the 7th international conference on Learning sciences. Bloomington, IA: The Association of Computing Machinery.

Good, B., Hentrich, T., Kuo, B., & Wilkinson, M. (2007). Tag clouds for summarizing web search results. Proceedings of the 16th international conference on World Wide Web. Alberta, Canada: The Association of Computing Machinery.

Goodhue, R., Green, R., Heien, D. & Martin, P. (2008). California Wine Industry Evolving to Compete in 21st Century. California Agriculture, 62(1).

Hasan H. & Pfaff, C. (2006). The Wiki: an environment to revolutionize employees' interaction with corporate knowledge. Proceedings of the 20th conference of the computer-human interaction special interest group (CHISIG) of Australia on Computer-human interaction: design: activities, artifacts and environments. Sydney, Australia: The Association of Computing Machinery.

Hof, R. (2005). Mix, Match, And Mutate. Business Week Online. Retrieved October 1, 2006 from http://www.businessweek.com/@@76IH*ocQ34AvyQMA/magazine/content/05_30/b3944108_mz063.htm.

Hu, M, and Liu, B. (2004). Mining and Summarizing Customer Reviews. Proceedings of the 10th Conference on Knowledge Discovery and Data Mining. Seattle, WA: The Association of Computing Machinery.

Hu, N., Pavlou, P., and Zhang, J. (2006). Can online reviews reveal a product's true quality?: empirical findings and analytical modeling of Online word-of-mouth communication. Proceedings of the 7th ACM conference on Electronic commerce. Ann Arbor, MI: The Association of Computing Machinery.

Jhingran, A. (2006). Enterprise information mashups: Integrating information simply. Proceedings of the 32nd international conference on Very large data bases. Seoul, Korea: The Association of Computing Machinery.

Joinson, A. (2008). 'Looking at', 'Looking up' or 'Keeping up with' people? Motives and Uses of Facebook. Proceeding of the twenty-sixth annual SIGCHI conference on Human factors in computing systems. Florence, Italy: The Association of Computing Machinery.

Khan, S. & Nauman, M. (2007). Using Personalized Web Search for Enhancing Common Sense and Folksonomy Based Intelligent Search Systems. Proceedings of the IEEE/WIC/ACM International Conference on Web Intelligence. Washington, DC: Institute of Electrical and Electronics Engineers.

Kim, W. & Mauborgne, R. (2005). Blue Ocean Strategy: How to Create Uncontested Market Space and Make the Competition Irrelevant. Harvard Business School Press. Boston, MA.

Kim, Y. & Srivastva, J. (2007). Impact of social influence in e-commerce decision making. Proceedings of the ninth international conference on Electronic commerce Minneapolis, MN: The Association of Computing Machinery.

Kostan, J., Riedl, J. & Schafer, J. (2001). E-commerce recommendation applications. Data Mining and Knowledge Discovery, 5(1):115–153.

Kuznetsov, S. (2006). Motivations of contributors to Wikipedia. ACM SIGCAS Computers and Society. 36(2).

Laudon, K.C., C.G. Traver (2006): E-Commerce: Business, Technology, Society; Prentice-Hall, Englewood-Cliffs, New Jersey.

Lerner, R. (2006). At the Forge: Creating Mashups. Linux Journal, 147(10).

Maznevski, M. & Chudoba, K. (2000) Bridging space over time: global virtual team dynamics and effectiveness. Organization Science 11 (5): 473-492.

McMillan, R. (2007). State of the Wine Industry. SVB Financial Group Research Paper, Santa Clara, CA.

Millard, D. & Ross, M. (2006). Blogs, wikis & rss: Web 2.0: hypertext by any other name? Proceedings of the seventeenth conference on Hypertext and hypermedia. Odense, Denmark: The Association of Computing Machinery.

O'Neill, M. (2005). Automated use of a wiki for collaborative lecture notes. Proceedings of the 36th SIGCSE technical symposium on Computer science education SIGCSE '05. St. Louis, MO: The Association of Computing Machinery.

Poong, Y., Talha, K. & Zaman, M. (2006). E-commerce today and tomorrow: a truly generalized and active framework for the definition of electronic commerce. Proceedings of the 8th international conference on Electronic commerce: The new e-commerce: innovations for conquering current barriers, obstacles and limitations to conducting successful business on the internet. New Brunswick, Canada: The Association of Computing Machinery.

Reinhold, S. (2006). Wikitrails: Augmenting wiki structure for collaborative, interdisciplinary learning. Proceedings of the 2006 international symposium on Wikis WikiSym '06. Odense, Denmark: The Association of Computing Machinery.

Riehle, D. (2006). How and why wikipedia works: An interview with Angela Beesley, Elisabeth Bauer, and Kizu Naoko. Proceedings of the 2006 international symposium on Wikis WikiSym '06. Odense, Denmark: The Association of Computing Machinery.

Smith, D. & Valdes, R. (2005). Web 2.0: Get ready for the next old thing. Gartner Research Paper. Stamford, CT.

O'Reilly, T. (2005). What Is Web 2.0: Design patterns and business models for the next generation of software. Retrieved July 17, 2006 from http://www.oreillynet.com/pub/a/oreilly/tim/news/2005/09/30/what-is-web-20.html.

Tapscott, D. & Williams, A. (2006). Wikinomics: How Mass Collaboration Changes Everything. Penguin Group: New York, NY.

Weiss, A. (2005). The power of collective intelligence. netWorker, 9(3), 16-23.

Chapter 2. New Forms of Interaction & Knowledge Sharing on Web 2.0

Kathrin Kirchner

Friedrich-Schiller-University Jena, GERMANY

Liana Razmerita

Copenhagen Business School, DENMARK

Frantisek Sudzina

Copenhagen Business School, DENMARK

Abstract

The current focus of knowledge management initiatives in organizations is one of identifying and sharing knowledge more widely. Companies explore new ways to cultivate and exploit knowledge sharing with customers, suppliers and partners (Mentzas et.al. 2007). They try to exploit a richer form of knowledge assets, including blogs, wikis, and social networks using Web 2.0 and focusing on the social, collaborative dimension of the Web. This chapter discusses new forms of managing knowledge according to the literature review and gives concrete examples of how these new forms of managing knowledge are used in enterprises. We conclude with a discussion of the role of Social Web and its associated tools for managing and sharing knowledge in companies and we discuss future associated challenges.

1 Introduction

After a first phase of Knowledge Management (KM) in which companies institutionalized knowledge creation, storage and sharing through internal KM initiatives we talk now about a second phase of knowledge management where companies use the social dimension of Web 2.0 tools including tools like wikis or blogs.

A KM initiative is an important but challenging task as an important number of KM systems failed. Knowledge management supports companies to be more flexible and knowledge-intensive firm (Schultze and Borland 2000). KM implies an intertwining of the various forms of knowledge: tacit, explicit, individual or collective. Nonaka and Konno (2000) define a spiral of knowledge and emphasize the fact that knowledge creation involves an iterative conversion from tacit to explicit in four different modes: socialisation, externalisation, combination and internalisation. Nonaka and Tageuki (1995) emphasize that the social dimension is key for the whole knowledge creation process.

KM practice is often associated with the use of information systems and the effort to codify, share and create knowledge using KM systems. Knowledge sharing and knowledge creation requires time and effort on top of the daily activities of knowledge workers who are the main contributors to the system. It requires a critical mass of active knowledge workers in order to be successful. An active behaviour of the users and adoption of knowledge sharing practices are critical success factors for Knowledge Management solutions (Roda et.al. 2003). Specific challenges for achieving effective KM solutions can be associated with: how to motivate people to create and submit knowledge assets in the system, how to stimulate collaboration and knowledge sharing between knowledge workers irrespective of their location, how to alleviate information overload, how to simplify business processes and work tasks, etc (Razmerita 2007).

The outline of this chapter is as follows: the next section summarizes the findings of the literature review related to knowledge management followed by a discussion of Web 2.0 phenomenon and its implications on Knowledge Management. In the second part of the chapter we introduce case studies and we discuss this second phase of managing knowledge in comparing with the first phase of KM. Finally the paper concludes with our findings and suggestions for successful integration of KM 2.0 in enterprises.

2   Literature Review

The roots of knowledge management go back to the late 1960's (Zand 1969) and 1970's (Rickson 1976). These papers discussed the management of knowledge in organizations and societies. Various scientific disciplines like organizational sciences, human resource management, management information systems, psychology, or sociology played a role in the development of KM research (Maier 2004).

In the late 1980's the term knowledge management has started to expand (Lloyd and Sveiby 1987). Since that time, the number of publications about KM has grown, like (Nonaka and Takeuchi 1995), (Davenport 1995), journals like Journal of Knowledge Management or Knowledge Management Magazine or web portals like www.kmworld.com or www.knowledgeboard.com. Since early 90's KM the field has constantly grown. Trying to understand the evolution of publication related to KM in academic journals over the last years we have mined the Web of Science articles based on keywords like: knowledge management, knowledge sharing, knowledge transfer, knowledge culture, knowledge worker, knowledge base or communities of practice. The bar graph represented in Figure 1 depicts our findings. According to these keywords associated with the articles, the number of items has been constantly growing from 1997 to 2001. After 2001, the number of items remained stable on a rather high level.

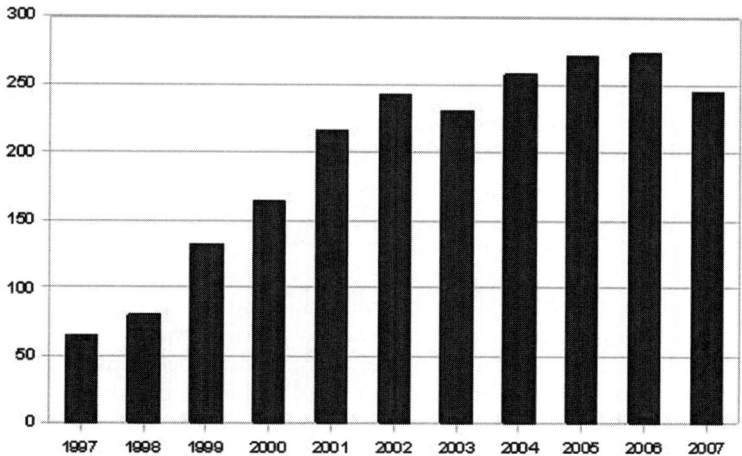

Fig. 1. Number of Web of Science articles with knowledge management, knowledge sharing, knowledge transfer, knowledge culture, knowledge worker, knowledge base or communities of practice in their title

Authors agree that systematic treatment of knowledge-intensive processes in organizations generates benefits. Other papers discuss problems and hindrances of KM. Swan et.al. (1999) state that "practice of KM is frequently reduced in the literature to the implementation of new IT systems for knowledge transfer". Wilson (2002) discusses "the nonsense of knowledge management". He argues that KM is promulgated by consultancy firms and is not part of organizational culture. Several empirical studies about KM and KM systems examined the state of the art of KM in organizations. According to (KPMG 2003) knowledge management has not daily priority and is not integrated in business processes. The Fraunhofer studied (Edler 2002) around 497 German enterprises. Their study emphasized that the internal transfer of knowledge is very important for the firms, but the transfer of knowledge to partner companies is less important. Despite the practical hindrances of knowledge management solutions and its associated criticism the number of articles about KM and intellectual capital has been increasing at the average rate of 50% per annum according to the ABI/Inform Index of mostly Anglo-American literature (Serenko and Bontis 2004).

In a highly interconnected, dynamic world new ways to cultivate and exploit knowledge sharing with customers, suppliers and partners are forcing companies to expand their KM concept and agenda (Mentzas et.al. 2007). We can talk about a second phase of knowledge management where companies try to exploit a much richer form of knowledge assets, including the blogs, wikis, and social networks using Web 2.0 and focusing on the social, collaborative dimension of the Web.

McAfee (2006) speaks of Enterprise 2.0 as a next generation enterprises using Web 2.0 technologies. He states that Web 2.0 usage generates strategic advantages for companies. New communication tools are used, "... new technologies focus not on capturing knowledge itself, but rather on the *practices* and *output* of knowledge workers." According Forrester Research (Young 2008) especially global and big companies use these new Web 2.0 tools whereas surprisingly half of smaller businesses are not even considering enterprise 2.0 applications. Till 2013, social networking will be the biggest priority, and it is a decent substitute for knowledge management applications.

Shimazo and Koike (2007) discuss the influence of Web 2.0 impact on KM and argue that the concept of collective intelligence has the biggest impact. Collective intelligence is defined as the set of all digital information stored in a company including blog data or information in social networks or wikis. Shimazo and Koike define Knowledge Management 2.0 as "a model that places collective intelligence at its core and promotes its use by accelerating the distribution of information." Zettsu and Kiyoki (2006) state that the goal to retrieve web pages "is being replaced by the desire to discover communities of knowledge and acquire collective intelligence". This change of KM from technology-centric to people-centric approach resulted in a "new" KM approach called KM 2.0.

Other papers discuss limitations of the actual social networks and forecast future trends in relation with the booming effect of social networks (Breslin and Decker 2007). Because today's social networks are often boring – people only collect contacts and visit other profiles for curiosity reasons, the Semantic Web will help to represent heterogeneous ties that bind people to each other and connect different social networks.

Besides more theoretical founded literature some studies or trend analyses have been reviewed. McKinsey (2007) found that executives of companies use Web 2.0 tools to communicate with customers, partners and to collaborate inside their company. Bitkom (2007) has forecasted new trends in KM and has argued that with the transformation to Web 2.0 enterprises, social networks, blogs and wikis have become more and more important for KM. Several case studies on this topic are discussed e.g. in (Müller and Dibbern 2006) or (Dearstyne 2007).

3   Case studies

KM 2.0 is discussed in literature as a new people-centric approach in knowledge management with advantages and limitations. We question how KM 2.0 is used in companies today, which industries and department use which tools for which purposes and what are advantages and disadvantages. According to the literature review and interviews with employees from three companies we had to define success factors for KM 2.0 in companies.

Scoble and Israel (2006) state that - despite blogging being a global phenomenon - some companies are actively involved in blogging while others are not. They also indicate a variety of factors, including the availability of technology and reasons of culture; have encouraged blogging in some countries while inhibiting it in others. According to Scoble and Israel (2006, p. 130), blogging is "exploding in the United States, France and Japan but (is) growing slowly in Germany, Russia and China". The most probable reason why some organizations do not encourage employee to blog is a fear that employees might misuse blogs, communicate negative information about the company or exchange confidential information. Murray (2005) suggests that organizations may not like the idea of not being able to control their employees' blogging. Regarding the latter aspect, Conlin and Park (2004) argue that many companies are willing to give up this control aspect because they understand that employee bloggers can develop meaningful relationships with customers.

According to a Backbone Media (2005) survey the top five reasons why employees have created web blogs are: to publish content and ideas (52%), build communities (47%), promote leadership thinking (44%), make information available to customers (36%) and get feedback from customers (23%).

A positive example of successful blog and wiki usage in companies is IBM, where 15% of the employees run their own company-internal or public blogs, half of the employees wrote more than 143,000 entries in 8800 wikis (Schuett 2007). The company encourages their staff to share their knowledge with others and defined blogging guidelines to ensure the high quality of blog contents (IBM 2005). External blogs and wikis bring IBM customers and developers together. All entries are sorted by topic, search functionality is included and new entries can be found easily. Members of the community use their real names, and often introduce themselves (see Figure 2).

**Fig. 2. External blogs on IBM website
(www.ibm.com/developerworks/community/)**

In 2006, IBM organized InnovationJam (www.collaborationjam.com), the largest collaborative online brainstorming session. More than 150,000 people – among them employees, customers and business partners of IBM – took part in online forums that lasted three days (Dearstyne 2007). IBM Work experiences and practical solutions for everyday changes were discussed in different forums. Each forum had a moderator, who had to encourage and keep the discussions focussed. Participators and the moderator could rate ideas. In order to motivate people and to draw people in, posters, web site articles and emails from CEO have been advertised. Best ideas were honoured acknowledged and rewarded after the jam. Behind the scenes a technical team was responsible for supporting participants (Halverson et. al. 2001).

Another case study is Synaxon AG in Germany. Enterprise knowledge is collected in wikis with more than 5200 entries – from partner contracts to job openings, the documentation of all projects or the explanation of technical terms (Fig. 3). Feedback from company employees is positive – all activities are transparent and staff can make suggestions for improvements. All entries have to be signed with the own name (Bergmann 2007).

In addition to Synaxon's wikis are blogs (blog.synaxon.de) and a social network for former and actual employees, partners and students (synaxon.ning.com).

Like in other social networks people related to the company can join and stay in contact.

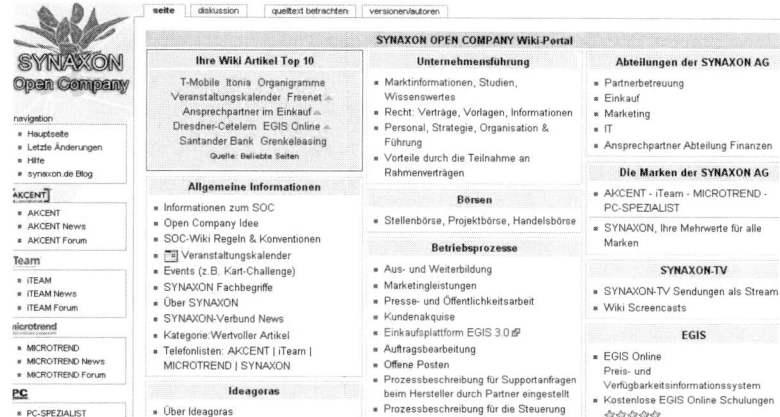

Fig. 3. Wiki of Synaxon AG, Germany (soc.wiki.synaxon.de)

The software company Serena is an international, decentralized company with more than 800 employees working in 14 countries. Serena encourages their employees to use Facebook to get to know each other and collaborate. The management encourages their employees to use social software tools for one hour a week to connect with other employees, customers, family and friends. Besides open communication internal Facebook groups were build were only employees can exchange documents and share corporate information. Each employee uses Facebook approximatively ten minutes a week (Weiss 2008).

Additionally to these use cases we found in literature we interviewed employees from the ICT companies Microsoft, SAS Institute and Motorola in Denmark related to the use of Web 2.0 tools for KM, their experience and associated challenges. Table 1 shows the results of our face-to-face interviews. All three companies use different tools for knowledge management, among them wikis and blogs. The main problems are out-dated knowledge and missing advanced search functionality.

According to six case studies presented here, blogs, wikis and social networks as typical Web 2.0 tools are used for KM. An open company culture and the management support are facilitators for the success of these tools. High quality contributions are assured not only by guidelines but also by reputation and sometimes the rating of the contribution. Regarding the usability of KM 2.0 tools we noticed that sorted entries and a better search functionality should be issues to be considered in further developments.

Table 1. Microsoft, SAS Institute and Motorola Denmark usage of Web 2.0 tools for KM

	Microsoft	SAS Institute	Motorola
Tools used for K M 2.0	Wikis, blogs, Share-Point, SourceDepot	Blogs (user sites – ran by both user groups and SAS Institute), Share-Point	Wikis (Twiki), blogs (Lyceum), Sourceforge
Traditional KM tools	Mailing lists, Intranet tools, MS library for ordering books or downloading electronic books discussion forums, small tools for internal use (e.g. codeplex.com)	Mailing lists (used for everything and more extensively than necessary before KM 2.0 adoption; nowadays used only for urgent matters) and intranets.	Mailing lists (too much spam email sent), Intranets, "idea collection" platform where employees post ideas. These ideas are evaluated by a committee and can be financially rewarded and/or patented.
Integration of KM 2.0 in the company	Everybody has to use SharePoint sites for each team (people can easily find materials describing processes related to a particular team). Wikis and blogs were created spontaneously. During the New Employee Orientation day lists of links for the most useful sites are distributed.	Some "have to" do it, since they are content contributors according to their job responsibilities, others do it voluntarily when they feel that they have something important to say; reading is done on an as-needed basis.	KM 2.0 tools facilitate knowledge sharing and communication across different teams, sites and countries (USA, Europe, Asia). Normally projects involve several sites on different continents. It avoids information overload and mailing spam.
Purposes of usage	The purpose is mainly the internal communication for the development of products and their maintenance and communication with partners. These tools do not intentionally support direct communication with end-users.	Keep track of their success, i.e. what contracts were won and lost, what were the issues, document good experience with e.g. seminars and products, who has been in a group implementing which software in which company. Communication with customers mainly through user sites	Project management, News in the company, Top management communication, etc.
Problems and chal-	Difficulty to find the right piece of informa-	Out-dated knowledge; people would upload	The information must be better structured

lenges	tion and the right KM tool, structure of information and knowledge	something but forget to delete it when it is not relevant anymore	otherwise nobody can find it.

4 Success Factors

KM success is a multidimensional concept. It is defined by capturing the right knowledge, getting the right knowledge to the right user and using this knowledge to improve organizational and/or individual performance. According information systems, success factors like user satisfaction and involvement (Zmud 1979) as well as the system's acceptance and quality (Ives and Olson 1984) are discussed. More recently, DeLone and McLean (1992) proposed an integrated model for information systems success. They defined system and information quality, use, user satisfaction, individual and organizational impact as important success factors. Maier (2004) extended this framework for knowledge management systems and defined three levels – system, service and use (user satisfaction and system use) and impact (on individuals, groups of people and organization). The number of aspects that has to be measured is rather high, for practical usage they have to be limited to the most important ones.

Probability of failure in any new activity, like the introduction of KM 2.0 in companies, is rather high. Based on the literature review, Šajeva (2007) identified five types of barriers for knowledge transfer in organizations:

- individual barriers (fear, lack of motivation, personal characteristics),
- organizational context related barriers (cultural, structural, management-related, strategic management related),
- technological barriers (technical, complemented by organizational and individual aspects),
- project management related barriers,
- and knowledge nature related barriers.

Šajeva suggests promoting trust in order to overcome fear of giving up power and authority, fear of becoming replaceable, fear of reducing job security, and uncertainty about the value of possessed knowledge. Appraisal, care, empowerment, rewards, incentives should leverage lack of motivation and commitment, unwillingness to do intrusive and extra work, and lack of time. Competence leverage, knowledge crew, and training should solve poor communication and interpersonal skills, personal differences, lack of awareness of KM strategies and instruments, and/or lack of social networks.

Collaboration, community of practice, dialogue between colleagues and the development of a knowledge-sharing culture should address lack of trust, low mistake tolerance, closed corporate culture, internal competition, and resistance to change. Organically structured organization should take care of rigid hierarchies, insufficient formal and informal spaces to collaborate, reflect and generate (new) knowledge, constant staff turnover, inflexible company structures, and in-coordination between units. Climate of openness, management sponsorship, knowledge champion, leadership should resolve lack of management commit-ment; management scepticism, top management sponsorship without active, ongo-ing involvement, lack of leadership, insufficient motivational and reward systems. The business objective of implementing a KM, proper KM strategy should disen-tangle KM project as an object for political manoeuvring, lack of a proper KM strategy, lack of specific business objectives, and lack of involvement in decision-making process.

Knowledge repository and proper KM tools should overcome technical prob-lems such as bandwidth limitation. KM tools are too cumbersome or complicated to use, the high cost of maintaining the KM tool, and legacy systems incompatibil-ity. Collaborative platform and training should unravel an over-reliance of KM tools and systems, a mismatch between people's requirements and IT systems, lack of familiarity and experience with new IT system, lack of training regarding employee familiarization of new IT systems, and lack of communication the ad-vantages of new system to employ.

Project management related barriers, such as insufficient time and resources for KM activities, lack of KM user involvement in the project, lack of staff with the required technical and business expertise, conflict management, no systematic ef-fort to track and measure the success of the KM project as it is developed, high in-vestments and incomplete KM program architecture should be overcome by intro-ducing planning, systematic assessments and metrics.

Understanding the nature of knowledge and KM strategies and training should help to get to the bottom of the knowledge nature related barriers, such as uncer-tainty of knowledge, difficulties in extracting knowledge, difficulties in identifica-tion of valuable knowledge, information overload, difficulties in knowledge evaluation, and incorrect knowledge reuse.

An older comprehensive KM critical success factor literature review (Alazmi and Zairi 2003) categorized identified factors into training, sharing, culture, trans-ferring, top-management support, technology infrastructure, creating, knowledge strategy, and knowledge infrastructure. The most often mentioned factors were sharing, technology infrastructure, and top-management support (in 11, 10, and 9 articles respectively).

The main question for companies is how they can benefit from the new possi-bilities of Web 2.0 tools in KM. Based on this additional literature review and the case studies we found the following four groups of success factors (Fig. 4): indi-vidual aspects, technical support, organizational context and management support.

- The key factor of KM 2.0 tools is the *individual aspect* – the extent to which users contribute with their knowledge (O'Reilly 2005). If employees have an intrinsic motivation to use KM 2.0 and take part voluntarily, they will persuade others too. Motivation, trust and perceived usefulness are key issues for indi-

viduals. The rate of KM activity is computed as the number of active participants divided by the number of employees participating in KM activities
(Maier 2004).

The basis of active usage is usability. The tools should be easy to use and provide good search functionality, enable to filter out relevant information (Smolnik, Riempp 2006). The content should have a clear benefit for the users. Otherwise people won't use these tools or irrelevant discussions occur (Pesch
2007). Relevance of content, credibility, and being up-to-date are also important (Smolnik and Riempp 2006). Users want to trust the information they find.
Name of the contributor, frequency of updates, comments of other people or
number of other comments of this contributor make it easier to see if the content of a source is trustworthy (Breslin 2008).

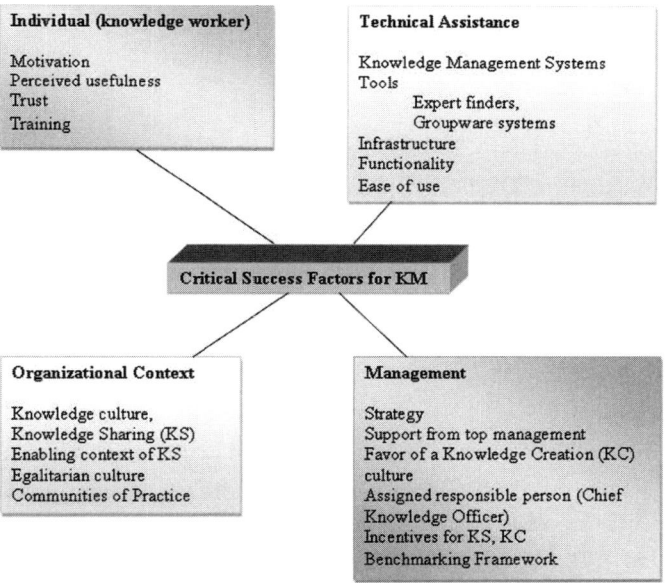

Fig. 4. Critical success factors for KM in Companies

- *Technical factors* including ease of use, usability and functionality are important. Schulzki-Haddouti (2008) lists problems with wiki usage in enterprises.
  Wiki syntax is not simple, so employees could not easily adopt them. It is not
  easy to find the right information in wiki, subtopics are not visible or it is unclear if the needed information is available in another language. Wiki has to be
  administrated regularly in order to stay usable over the years, rights management is not easy to implement.

Employees know social software from their leisure activities; they use social
networks to connect with friends, blogs to write about their holidays or
Wikipedia to inform and share knowledge about interesting topics. So it is eas-

ier for them to use these skills in their work environment than to learn new software tools. If employees have good experiences with Web 2.0 tools in their spare time, they will be likely to adopt them in the office as well.

- An *open communication culture* in companies is very important. The company management has to encourage knowledge exchange between employees. Instead of resisting the sharing of knowledge, people are willing to publish and give their knowledge in order to become an expert. The management should give employees plenty of opportunity and time for using Web 2.0 tools to connect and communicate.
- The management support is related to the organizational context and culture. Conlin and Park (2004) suggest that many *corporate executives encourage employees* to blog because they believe that their employees can create personal relationships with other employees and even with customers. It is good to set guidelines, e.g. that every entry contains identifying information, assign responsible person to monitor content and delete inappropriate entries (Dearstyne 2007).

The use of Web 2.0 tools for knowledge management enable companies to reap large benefits compared with traditional KM system. For promoting products and services, companies can reach much more users and get valuable feedback. Companies have to decide if they build their own blogs, wikis or use existent tools. It depends on the number of employees/customers, because a critical mass of users is necessary (Breslin 2008).

5   Conclusions

This article discussed how companies can benefit from the new possibilities offered by Web 2.0 tools in KM. According McKinsey (2007), companies made investments in Web 2.0 technologies, because they are important for supporting their market position and for addressing customer's demands. Web 2.0 tools can improve organizational and/or individual performance, but they also encounter a series of problems.

Based on our findings professionals and academics may get a better understanding of the role of Web 2.0 tools for managing knowledge. We showed six case studies – three from literature review and three from face-to-face interviews - how this new KM 2.0 tools are currently used in a number in companies presented as case studies and we suggest how people can be motivated to use them and what policies are necessary.

Practical solutions concerning the strategic use of knowledge and its management is dependent on the organizational context (Ciborra and Andreu 2001). The authors of the paper agree that the organizational context is important for selecting different systems and different forms of managing knowledge and this is also applicable for KM 2.0. The case studies are mostly IT businesses and we draw the preliminary conclusion that the early adopters of the KM 2.0 are mainly IT businesses.

While we talk about Web 2.0, some foresee already Web 3.0 arriving. According to Cronk (2007), while Web 2.0 relies on professional writers, photographers, programmers, or community organizers, Web 3.0 is about making tools available to anyone to report on events, capture life on film, create new applications, and even change the world. The term "Web 3.0" was first coined by John Markoff of the New York Times in 2006, while it first appeared prominently in January 2006 in a blog article written by Zeldman (2006). According to Spivack (2006), Web 3.0 is the third decade of the Web (2010–2020) during which he suggests several major complementary technology trends will reach new levels of maturity simultaneously including:

- transformation of the Web from a network of separately siloed applications and content repositories to a more seamless and interoperable whole;
- ubiquitous connectivity, broadband adoption, mobile Internet access and mobile devices;
- network computing, software-as-a-service business models, Web services interoperability, distributed computing, grid computing and cloud computing;
- open technologies, open APIs and protocols, open data formats, open-source software platforms and open data (e.g. Creative Commons, Open Data License);
- open identity, OpenID, open reputation, roaming portable identity and personal data;
- intelligent web-based on Semantic Web technologies such as RDF, OWL, SWIRL, SPARQL, GRDDL, semantic application platforms and statement-based data stores;
- distributed databases, the "World Wide Database" enabled by Semantic Web technologies;
- intelligent applications, natural language processing, machine learning, machine reasoning, autonomous agents.

Semantic Web technologies will enhance Web 2.0 tools and its associated data with semantic annotations and semantic knowledge representations, thus enabling a better automatic processing of data which in turn will enhance search mechanisms, management of the tacit knowledge and the overall efficiency of the actual KM tools. The benefits of semantic blogging (Cayzer 2004), semantic wikis or semantic Wikipedia (Oren et.al. 2006; Volkel et.al. 2006), semantic-enhanced social networks (Breslin and Decker 2007) , semantic-enhanced KM (Maedche et.al. 2003) and semantic-enhanced user support (Razmerita 2005) are already acknowledged by a large community of academics and practitioners working within this area. In few years the KM 3.0 term will probably proliferate associated with a next generation of semantic-enhanced KM tools.

References

Alazmi, M., Zairi, M. (2003) Knowledge management critical success factors. Total Quality Management, 14 (2), 199-204

Bergmann, J. (2007) Die gläserne Firma. brand eins (3), 109-115

Bitkom (2007) Wichtige Trends im Wissensmanagement 2007 bis 2011

Backbone Media (2005) Survey. blogsurvey.blackbonemedia.com/archives/2005/06/_not_a_factor.html

Breslin, J. G. (2008) Social network service for enterprise use, http://socialmedia.net/2008/02/04/social-networking-services-for-enterprise-use-2/

Breslin, J. G., Decker, S. (2007) The Future of Social Networks on the Internet: The Need for Semantics. IEEE Internet Computing Magazine, 11 (6), 86-90

Cayzer, S. (2004). Semantic blogging and decentralized knowledge management. *Commun. ACM, 47*(12), 47-52

Ciborra, C. U., Andreu, R. (2001) Sharing knowledge across boundaries. Journal of Information Technology, 16(2), 73-81

Conlin, M., Park, A. (2004) Blogging With The Boss's Blessing, *Business Week*, (June 28), 96-98

Cronk, H. (2007) Pushing Towards Web 3.0 Organizing Tools. Social Policy, 38 (1), pp. 27-34

Davenport, T. H. (1995) Think Tank: The Future of Knowledge Management. *CIO, 9* (6), 30-31

Dearstyne, B. W. (2007). Add Added Blogs, Mashups, & Wikis Oh, My! The information management journal, 41 (4), 24-33

DeLone, W. H., McLean, E. R. (1992) Information Systems Success: The Quest for the Dependent Variable. Information Systems Research, 3 (1), 60-95

Edler, J. (2003) Knowledge Management in German Industry. Fraunhofer Institute, Karlsruhe

Halverson, C., Newswanger, J., Erickson, T., Wolf, T., Kellogg, W., Laff, M. and Malkin, P. (2001) World Jam: Supporting Talk Among 50,000+. Poster on Seventh European Conference on Computer Supported Cooperative Work, Bonn

IBM Corporation (2005) IBM Blogging Policies and Guidelines, http://www.snellspace.com/IBM_Blogging_Policy_and_Guidelines.pdf

Ives, B., Olson, M. H. (1984) User Involvement and MIS Success: A Review of Research. Management Science, 30 (5), 586-603

KPMG Consulting (2003) Insights from KMPG's European Knowledge Management Survey 2002/2003

Lloyd, T., Sveiby, K. E. (1987) Managing Knowhow. London: Bloomsbury Publishing PLC

Maedche, A., Motik, B., Stojanovic, L. (2003) Managing multiple and distributed ontologies on the Semantic Web. *VLDB Journal, 12*(4), 286-302

Maier, R. (2004) Knowledge Management Systems. Berlin: Springer

McAffee, A. P. (2006) Enterprise 2.0: The dawn of emergent collaboration. MITSloan Management Review, 47 (3), 21-28

McKinsey (2007) How businesses are using Web 2.0: A McKinsey Global Survey

Mentzas, G., Kafentzis, K., Georgolios, P. (2007) Knowledge services on the semantic web. Communications of the ACM, 50 (10), 53-58

Mueller, C., Dibbern, P. (2006) Selbstorganisiertes Wissensmanagement in Unternehmen auf Basis der Wiki-Technologie – ein Anwendungsfall. HMD - Praxis der Wirtschaftsinformatik, 43 (252), 45-54

Murray, D. (2005) Who's Afraid of Employee Blogs?, The Ragan Report, November 14, 1-2

Nonaka, I., Takeuchi, H. (1995) The knowledge-creating company: How Japanese Companies Create the Dynamics of Innovation. New York: Oxford University Press

Nonaka, I., Toyama, R., Konno, N. (2000). SECI, ba and leadership: a unified model of dynamic knowledge creation. *Long Range Planning, 33*(1), 5-34

O'Reilly, T. (2005) What Is Web 2.0. Design Patterns and Business Models for the Next Generation of Software, http://www.oreillynet.com/pub/a/oreilly/tim/news/2005/09/30/what-is-web-20.html

Oren, E., Volkel, M., Breslin, J. G., Decker, S. (2006) Semantic wikis for personal knowledge management. In Proceedings of Database and Expert Systems Applications, Vol. 4080, 509-518

Pesch, U. (2007) Web 2.0. PERSONALmagazin (12), 22

Razmerita, L. (2005) *Exploiting Semantics and User Modeling for Enhanced User Support,* Paper presented at the HCI International (Human Computer Interaction) Conference, Las Vegas, USA

Razmerita, L. (2007) Ontology based user modelling. In Sharman, R., Kishore, R.and Ramesh, R. (Ed.), Ontologies. A Handbook of Principles, Concepts and Applications in Information Systems (Vol.14, 635-664). Boston, MA: Springer Science+Business Media, LLC

Rickson, R. E. (1976) Knowledge Management in Industrial Society and Environment Quality. Human Organization, 35 (3), 239-251

Roda, C., Angehrn, A., Nabeth, T., Razmerita, L. (2003) Using conversational agents to support the adoption of knowledge sharing practices. *Interacting with Computers, Elsevier, 15*(1), 57-89

Schuett, P. (2007) Blogs und Wikis erfolgreich im Unternehmen einsetzen. Computerzeitung, 05.06.2007

Schultze, U., Boland, R., J. (2000) Knowledge management technology and the reproduction of knowledge work practices. The Journal of Strategic Information Systems, 9(2), 193-212

Schulzki-Haddouti, C. (2008). 8 Argumente gegen den Einsatz von Wikis in Unternehmen, http://blog.kooptech.de/2008/04/8-argumente-gegen-den-einsatz-von-wikis-in-unternehmen/#comment-67

Scoble, R. and Israel, S. (2006). Naked Conversations. Hoboken (NJ): John Wiley & Sons

Serenko, A. and Bontis, N. (2004) Meta-Review of Knowledge Management and Intellectual Capital Literature: Citation Impact and Research Productivity Rankings. Knowledge and Process Management, 11 (3), 185-198

Shimazu, H.and Koike, S. (2007) KM2.0: Business knowledge sharing in the Web 2.0 age. NEC TECHNICAL JOURNAL, 2 (2), 50-54

Smolnik, S.and Riempp, G. (2006) Nutzenpotenziale, Erfolgsfaktoren und Leistungsindikatoren von Social Software für das organisationale Wissensmanagement. HMD - Praxis der Wirtschaftsinformatik, 43 (252), 17-26

Spivack, N. (2006) The Third-Generation Web is Coming, http://www.kurzweilai.net/meme/frame.html?main=/articles/art0689.html?m%3D3

Swan, J., Newell, S., Scarbrough, H.and Hislop, D. (1999) Knowledge management and innovation: networks and networking. Journal of Knowledge Management, 3 (4), 262 - 275

Šajeva, S. (2007) An Investigation of Critical Barriers to Effective Knowledge Management. Social Sciences/Socialiniai Mokslai, 58 (4), 20-27

Volkel, M., Markus, K., Vrandecic, D., Haller, H., Studer, R. (2006) *Semantic Wikipedia.* Paper presented at the Proceedings of the 15th international conference on World Wide Web

Weiss, H. (2008) Bei Serena ist jeden Freitag Facebook-Tag. Computerzeitung 12, 14

Wilson, T. D. (2002) The nonsense of 'knowledge management'. Information Research, 8 (1)

Young, O. (2008) Global Enterprise Web 2.0 Market Forecast: 2007 To 2013, Forrester Research

Zand, D. E. (1969) Managing the Knowledge Organization. In Drucker, P. (Ed.), Preparing Tomorrow's Business Leaders Today (pp. 112-136). Englewood Cliffs (NJ): Prentice Hall

Zeldman, J. (2006) Web 3.0, http://www.alistapart.com/articles/web3point0

Zettsu, K. and Kiyoki, Y. (2006) Towards knowledge management based on harnessing collective intelligence on the web. MANAGING KNOWLEDGE IN A WORLD OF NETWORKS, PROCEEDINGS, 4248, 350-357

Zmud, R. W. (1979) Individual Differences and MIS Success: A Review of the Empirical Literature. Management Science, 25 (10), 966-979

Chapter 3: Web 2.0 Business Models as Decentralized Value Creation Systems

Christian Briggs

Indiana University School of Informatics, USA

Abstract

The advent of Web 2.0 has brought with it new business models that are serious departures from any that have existed since the Industrial Revolution. This chapter attempts to provide a means of understanding the differences between pre-Web, Web 1.0 and Web 2.0 business models by focusing on each one's value creation system.

1   Introduction

The Industrial Revolution saw the advent of technical capabilities and social norms that made centralized value creation the golden standard for the competitive business. Though there is still a great deal of debate about the factors that brought about the Industrial Revolution, it is generally agreed that centralization and specialization were the keys to competitive advantage, and was therefore the philosophy at the center of many business models which still exist today. From its beginning, Web 2.0 has had quite the opposite effect, providing capabilities and fostering social norms that allow large groups of temporally and geographically-scattered people to self-organize and to co-create value in a decentralized manner. Consequently, new business models have begun to emerge that leverage this tendency toward decentralization to varying degrees and in different ways.There are many ways to begin to make sense of the new business models that have emerged on and around the Web over the course of the last 10 years. In this chapter, we will focus on the highly-decentralized nature of Web 2.0 business models by situating them within the lineage of recent business models, and by looking at the change over time through the lens of value creation, with an eye toward understanding the practical implications and opportunities of these models for current and future web-based businesses.

2 The Connection Between Value Creation & Web 2.0 Business Models

At its heart, an organization's choice of any business model, Web 2.0 or otherwise, is highly dependent on the way that it conceptualizes the notion of value creation. Though this business model/value creation relationship is a complex one, if we focus on the way that businesses choose and execute their business models based on their conception of value's *locus*, its *creator* and its *scarcity,* the landscape of Web 2.0 business models will be considerably easier to understand.

2.1 Value

We will begin here with the standard definition of value found in the Merriam-Webster's Online Dictionary (Merriam-Webster, 2008), which defines value as: "relative worth, utility, or importance." Starting from this definition, we can then assume that *value creation* is – at least within the setting of a business model – the creation of the relative worth, utility or importance in a product or service such that the utility or importance can then be exchanged within a market for some sort of gain.

2.2 Value as a Inherent in the Product Itself vs. Value as a System of Relations Around the Product

Though we started with a relatively simple initial definition of value, in order to better understand the shift in business models occurring in Web 2.0, we will first need to explore a little deeper two general approaches to understanding value. They are:

1. Value is inherent in the product itself (modern)
2. Value is a system of relations around the product (postmodern)

Though there is not a clearly defined line between these two approaches, for the purposes of our discussion here the distinction will help us to better understand some of the origins of Web 2.0 business models. despite the fact that the everyday man seems anecdotally to have become relatively likely to adopt a more postmodern view of the value of art or of other cultural objects over the last few decades, his work practice has been less likely to follow suit. In other words, while at home he may be willing to believe that the meaning of the work is determined not by the author, but instead by the reader, when he enters his workplace he is more likely to believe that the value of that product is created by the designer, and that the designed value inheres within the product itself. As an example of the modernist approach, the Ford Model T automobile was most likely to have been considered to have a hypothetical (if difficult to determine) value that existed even before it was given market value. This value was created by the designers, the process engineers, and to a smaller degree (according to Ford's writings, at least) by the assembly line workers. Though I am oversimplifying a very complex philosophical argument here, the modernist, established and still-practiced approach to understanding and facilitating value creation tends to conceive of value as inhering in the product itself. We can see evidence of this in the importance that many business models place on internal research, design and development, in order to create as much inherent value in the product as possible before exchanging it with the customer. If we look closely at the basic definition of value, however, the concept of value does not appear to be suitable to a modernist interpretation. In the definition given earlier for example, value is defined as "relative worth," which implies that value, by its very nature, is a system, since relativity implies that the value of something emerges out of at least one relationship.

System Defined

A simple and powerful definition of "system" comes from Cybernetician George Klir, who constructed a symbolic representation that very generally describes the nature of a system. It is $S=(T|R)$, or to translate it into plain english, any system (S) is the relationship between its things (T) and their relations (R) (Klir, 2001). Another way to say this is that, for any given system, if one were to remove a thing or a relation between two things within any given system, the system would either change its nature, or it would cease to be a system.

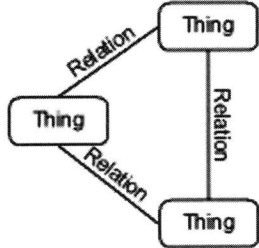

Fig 1. A System is made up of Things and Relations between them

In the case of value, therefore, the fact that it is defined as "*relative* worth, utility or importance" means that the existence of value depends on the existence of at least two *things* which have some sort of *relationship* between them. In other words, value is a system. While the concept of value existing as a function of the relationship between many parts has been well-explored in the excellent work of Verna Allee et al. on "value networks," (Allee, 2003) I would like to lean, for our analysis, on the more philosophically-inspired "systems" concept of George Klir and other systems thinkers, which places a heavy emphasis on the importance of understanding the boundaries – functional or otherwise – of a given system. In the highly-decentralized world of Web 2.0, the difficulty of determining what is or is not part of a given *value creation system* can be great. As an example of a value creation system, let us consider the relationship between a product, a group of users of that product and the person who produced the product. If we take out or modify any of the things or relations in the system, the entire system would change, as would the value. Additionally, if we were given only one part of the system – the product for example - it would be impossible to extrapolate fully from that single element the nature of the entire value creation system. In essence, in a *value creation system*, the value, instead of inhering in the product itself, emerges as a function of all of the factors involved.

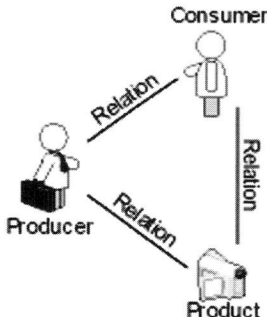

Fig 2. Value is made up of Things and Relations between them

While this point may seem a bit obvious, we will soon see that while pre-Web 2.0 businesses have largely treated the systemic nature of value as external to their sphere of influence, Web 2.0 models have begun to make it a core part of their business models.

2.3 The Locus/Creator/Scarcity Lens

So far, we have determined that:
1. There is a strong connection between an organization's conception of value and the business model it chooses
2. Value is a system

Our next step will be to begin to better understand actual Web 2.0 business models in light of these two assertions with the help of a simple lens, which will focus on a business model's operationalization of:

1. The Locus of Value – where value of a product is believed to exist
2. The Creator of Value – who or what is believed to be the agent of value creation
3. The Scarcity of the Product – how much of the product is produced and reproduced. For a much deeper treatment of this concept, I would recommend reading Yochai Benkler's *Wealth of Networks* , which is included in this chapter's references.

To illustrate the use of this lens (which I will from here on refer to as the Locus/Creator/Scarcity Lens), we return to the example of the Ford Motor Company in the early 1900's. The Ford business model was clearly based on simplicity, and the scientific, orderly and linear integration of small jobs in a hyper-efficient assembly line in order to maximize efficiency, quality and to reduce error as much as possible. If we look closely at this business model and apply the Locus/Creator/Scarcity Lens to our observations, we find that, in terms of the Model T automobile, Ford's primary *locus* of value was within the car itself, and within the processes by which it was created. To state this another way, the primary Locus of Value for the Model T was *not* the personalized nature of the product or the customer-centric attitude, the lack of which were betrayed by Ford's assertion that "Any customer can have a car painted any colour that he wants so long as it is black." (Ford, 1922). Using this lens, we also find that the primary *creators* of value around the Model T were the industrial design and process experts. A high degree of value was *not* created by the assembly line worker who, in Ford's highly-regulated and hyper-efficient process, were subject to the "..reduction of the necessity for thought on the part of the worker and the reduction of his movements to a minimum." (Ford, 1922)

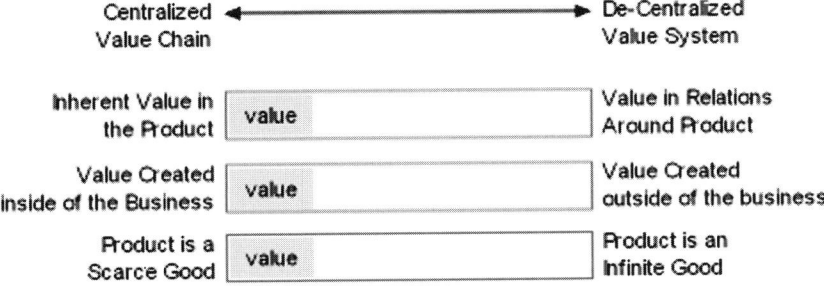

Fig 3. The early Ford Motor Company when viewed through the Locus/Creator/Scarcity Lens.

Finally, our lens helps to reveal that Ford conceived of its product as quite scarce – in that it was not easy for a customer to buy, copy, and share a car with a friend. Based on these observations, then, the value bars in figure 3 above for the Ford Motor Company are located quite far to the left – which reveals the highly-centralized nature of the Ford Motor Company's business model. While this is a simple and obvious example, the hope is that this lens will help now help to shed some light on less-obvious examples in the Web 1.0 and 2.0 arenas.

2.4 Value Creation Pre-Internet

As we've discussed already, regardless of the common person's conception of value in her personal life, her business practices tend to approach its creation – both explicitly and implicitly – as a sort of chain, where one side of the business / consumer equation creates inherent value, which is then exchanged in the market for the passive consumer's money. Perhaps the main reason these business models have persisted in spite of the changing beliefs of those who work within them is their practicality. The linear model of value creation has worked quite efficiently for many years as a way to understand and to facilitate value creation in a world which favored the centralized business.

In the 1980's, this approach was made explicit with the advent of Michael Porter's concept of the "Value Chain" (Porter, 1985), roughly interpreted in Figure 4 for illustrative purposes, which posits that the primary creator of value is the producer or business, and the locus of value is primarily within the product that is produced. Implicit in this theory is the idea that the locus of value creation is on the producer-side of the chain (including its business partners), away from the customer. This will be an important point to remember as we begin to consider the Web 2.0 transition from value chains to value creation systems.

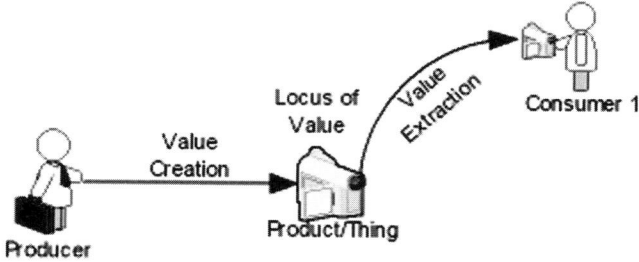

Fig 4. The Pre-Web Value Chain.

The value chain concept has had important implications in the formation of business models. Once a business determines or determines that the locus of value is the product itself, and that the creator of that value is the business and that the scarcity of their goods are high, the business will attempt to improve its competitive advantage in the market by funneling its resources inward toward the development of the "perfect product" through research, product design, and market research, and development. It will also begin to place much of the responsibility of value creation on professionally trained designers, whose job it is to create the maximal value. In the traditional value chain model, the concept of value or value creation existing or occurring outside of the firm is not an explicit part of the model. Additionally, when the good produced is seen as essentially scarce, the business will typically try to extract value based on high cost, as well as aggressive legal efforts to inhibit unauthorized copying, selling or re-selling of the product.

2.5 Value Creation in Web 1.0

With the advent of the public Internet, or Web 1.0, in the early 1990's, the promise of new business opportunities loomed large. Not only could information travel to more people more quickly and more cost-effectively, but it could also be used to create large amounts of business value in the form of e-commerce. With all of the novelty of Web 1.0, however, most of the business models that emerged were similar to those of the pre-internet world (based on the idea of a value chain). The locus of value was still in the product, the creator(s) of value were still the business, and the goods produced were still treated as though they were scarce. Figure 5 depicts the Web 1.0 model visually.

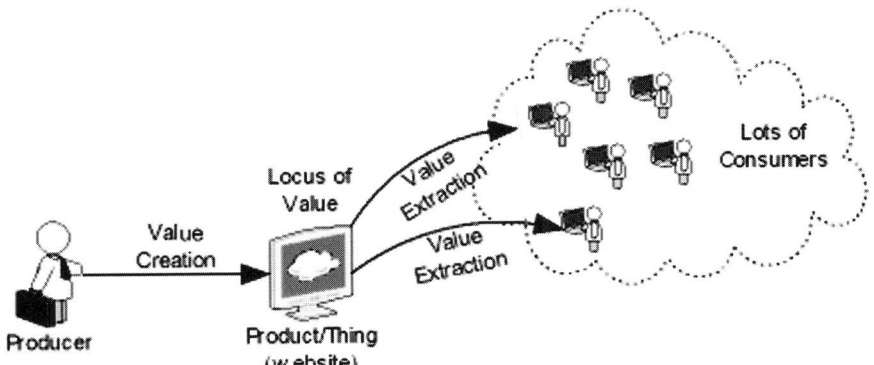

Fig 5. The Web 1.0 Value Chain Looked a Lot Like its Pre-Web Predecessor.

The Publishing House Value Chain

In 1994, I was working as a Technical Editor at a publishing firm – one of the older technical publishing houses in the market at the time. For many years it had published a number of magazines for computer enthusiasts, gamers, shoppers, IT directors, etc. In 1994, however, the firm – and more specifically our small interactive division of the firm – was deeply involved in the first movement toward the new Web 1.0 world, which promised (at the time) that the company's magazine content would now be instantly available to millions of people worldwide. With all of the novelty that this new world provided as we pushed our content to the Internet, our business model remained mostly the same. This becomes quite apparent when viewing it through the locus/creator/scarcity lens, which highlights the fact that the content was still seen as the locus of value. The creators of value too had remained the same. They were the authors, editors, and in this new world, our little interactive division which hand-translated Quark files into HTML for eventual exchange with our passive customers. Additionally, though the marginal cost of a new reader/viewer had essentially dropped to zero (a new reader of *digital* content essentially costs the company nothing, unlike a reader of *print* content, for which the company would have to pay additional printing/shipping charges), the company was still treating the content as scarce – going to great lengths to secure access to the website through online subscription forms and security measures. In Figure 6 below, the publishing house's position on our three elements of value creation are quite similar to that of the Ford Motor Company.

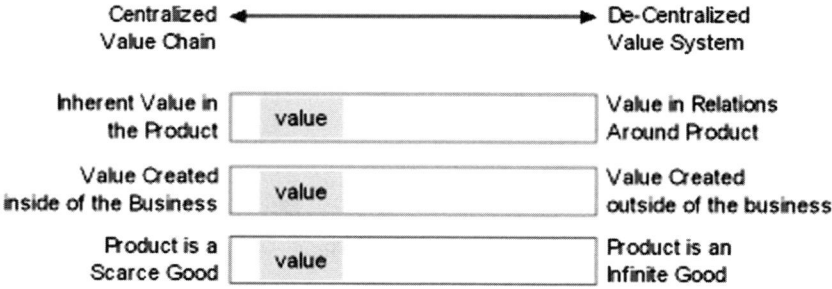

Fig 6. The Publisher's business model looks very similar to pre-Web business models when viewed through the Locus/Creator/Scarcity Lens.

The publisher in 1994 still conceived of value creation as a chain and not as a system. But that was about to change.

2.6 Value Creation in Web 2.0

Though it is nearly impossible to draw a firm line of demarcation between the time of Web 1.0 and that of 2.0, if we begin to look at businesses and their business models using the locus/creator/scarcity framework, we can start to see some of the main differences that began to emerge some time in the late 1990's and early 2000's. Some of these differences are a direct result of internet technology and the socialization to use it, and some are indirectly related to other societal and market forces which bled over into the Web 2.0 space. For now, I will focus primarily on the Web 2.0 world. During this time, a curious thing began to happen, starting with the growth of open source software like Linux, and continuing on with the advent of easy-to-use, self-publishing formats such as blogs and wikis. The locus of value creation in new business models began to shift away from the product itself, and toward the relationships that the product had with the consumer and with other products. It also began to shift to the relationships that people around a product forged with each other. Additionally, businesses began to question whether or not the parts of their product or service they had previously considered scarce were or should be scarce. Figure 7 below is a simplified depiction of this somewhat more complicated system of value creation.

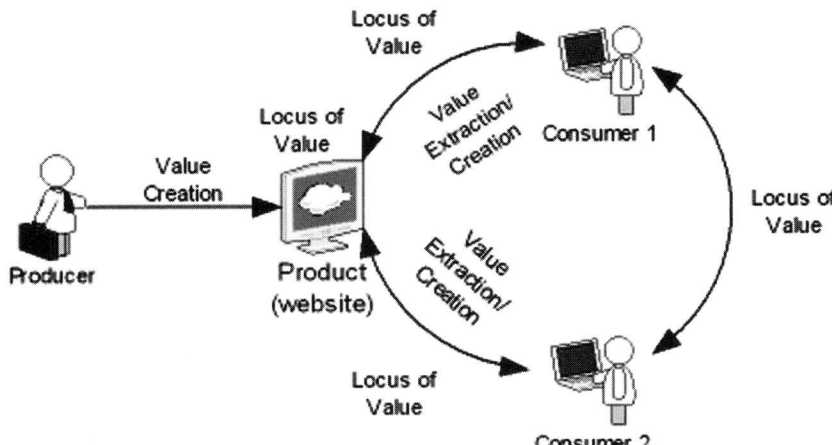

Fig 7. The Web 2.0 Value Creation System is Quite Different From Previous Models

The MySpace Value Creation System

As a stark example of this Web 2.0 shift in business models with respect to value creation, let us look at MySpace.com. Some time in 2007 I was approached by a U.S. research firm, who was working with one of their clients who wanted to understand what factors had contributed to the then-astronomic rise in the popularity of MySpace. The client was hoping to understand the loci of value in the massive network, as well as the key creators of that value. At the point at which I began talking with the research firm, the bulk of their exploration had been accomplished with measures of MySpace that were intended to find the inherent value in the system by looking at its aesthetics and its usability. For some products or spaces, such an inquiry might have yielded at least some insights into its value, but for MySace, such inquiries resulted in completely counter-intuitive findings. Despite its wild success, the research firm's work revealed that MySpace had very poor usability. In addition, the aesthetics of the site were found to be even less appealing than many of its closest, unsuccessful competitors. In fact, none of their research seemed to explain why (at that time) close to 65 million users had created user accounts.

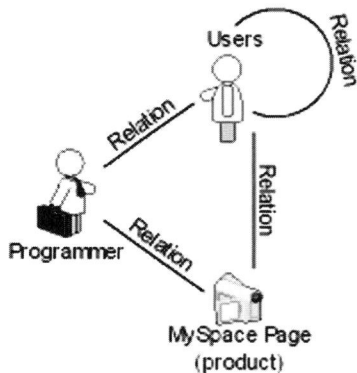

Fig 8. The MySpace Value Creation System.

An understanding of this phenomenon, of course, becomes much more clear when we apply the locus/creator/scarcity lens to the MySpace business model. It becomes quickly evident that MySpace is a highly-decentralized value creation system, and is therefore difficult to understand from a value chain perspective. Evidence of this can be further seen if we perform a small experiment – a la George Klir – to take away one or another element of the system to see if it is, in fact, a system. The results are clear. Removal of any of the pieces of the value creation system would significantly lessen its value. If we were to remove the users from the value creation system, for example, the system's value would plummet, since MySpace relies on its users to create all of its content. Likewise, if we were to remove the MySpace pages from the value creation system, the value of the system would also plummet, since 65 million users would have no way to connect with one another (within the MySpace domain). MySpace's value is very much a system, and therefore its business model must properly account for the creation of that value if it is to survive.

When we view MySpace through the locus/creator/scarcity lens (see figure 9 below), the stark difference between its business model and those of its antecedents is clear. MySpace is a highly decentralized value network. Not only does the value reside in the *relations* between the company, the technology and the users, but that value is created mainly outside of the company by the users, whose content and actions provide value to each other and to the company. Additionally, the fact that MySpace gives away the bulk of its accounts for free signifies that the company does not see its product (in this case user pages) as scarce.

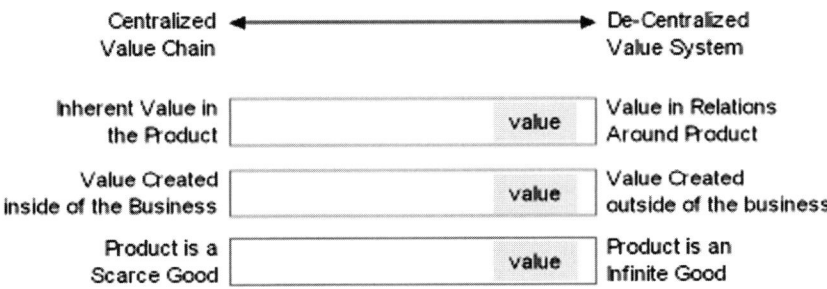

Fig 9. The MySpace business model marks a significant departure from pre-Web and Web 1.0 business models when viewed through the Locus/Creator/Scarcity Lens.

3   Why the Change?

An important part of understanding a shift in media and in its use is the understanding of its functional qualities which both enable and are enabled by the humans that interact with it. In the case of Web 2.0, for example, the medium itself – its technologies, the ways that it handles data, etc. – is an important part of what distinguishes it from Web 1.0, and from other forms of media. Also, the people who affect, and are affected by, the medium within our current culture – their adoption, their linguistic conventions, their technological adeptness – are an important part of what distinguishes Web 2.0 from 1.0.

3.1 Lingua Franca for Content Creation

History seems to show a common trend that when a medium begins to take hold, it is often due to the development of a lingua franca or a common language that allows everyday people to create their own content or to communicate using the new medium. In the history of the written word for example, and more specifically in the history of books, we can see this at work. In the Middle Ages, the production of printed works was accomplished only by the educated and the highly-skilled few within the population, who had the writing tools, the literacy and the time to produce content. Since there was only a small amount of printed matter within the society at the time, the social motivation to become literate was likely not very high. With the advent of the printing press, however, the mass production of content was possible, and the lingua franca of print was thrust to the forefront of the world, and became so widespread and important that, according to some scholars such as Alexis DeTocqueville, it "..enables him [every man] to summon all his fellow countrymen and all his fellow men to his assistance. Printing has accelerated the progress of equality, and it is also one of its best correctives." (Tocqueville, 1835)

Where Web 1.0 provided the technology – roughly analagous to the printing press – that allowed the wide and rapid dissemination of lots of information , Web 2.0 has been characterized by the development of a lingua franca – roughly analagous to the literacy and skills of using the printing press – that has allowed the common man to both effectively read and also to create his own content. Where in the Web 1.0 era much of the discussion was about the percentage of the public who could view content on the internet, Web 2.0 discussions have shifted to account for the percentage of the public who create their own content on the web, which, according to a 2008 study conducted by Deloitte and Touche, is around 45%. (Deloitte, 2008)

3.2 Speed of Content Creation, Co-Creation and Dissemination

Another important aspect of Web 2.0 is the speed at which content is created and disseminated. Where in Web 1.0 the speed at which content, created in advance by a business, could be disseminated was high, the creation of the content itself was still accomplished mostly by the same people that had created it in the pre-internet world: the experts. In the Web 2.0 world, the tools as well as the lingua franca of interaction and content creation has radically increased the rate at which content can be created by large groups of "non-experts." Through the use of mechanisms like tagging, subscription (email and RSS), wikis, blogs, email, chat and a host of others, large groups of people are now able – and socialized to – create and co-create content online. As a simple example of the difference here between Web 1.0 and 2.0, Encyclopedia Britannica which went online in 1994 and currently has 120,000 articles (Encyclopedia Britannica, 2008), is created by paid experts (1.0). Wikipedia, which launched in 2001, currently has 2,400,380 articles (Wikipedia, 2008), is created by unpaid non-experts.

3.3 Group Decision Making

Another important aspect of Web 2.0 is the collection of mechanisms that have made group decisionmaking easy, prevalent and entertaining. In the design of Web 2.0 sites today, it is just about considered standard practice to include some sort of rating/commenting system that allows the user to rate or to comment on a piece of content. While at first this may seem a trivial thing, when enough users become socialized to participate often in this way, entire business models can eventually be built on this. Digg.com, for example, allows its users to post links to internet news items and to rate each other's links. The final product is therefore a list of the top-community-ranked news items for the entire community to see.

4 Implications for Current Web-based Businesses

The implications for the change in business models with the advent of Web 2.0 are many. As the business environment continues to evolve and to increase the number of decentralized models, it will be imperative that any Web-based business be able to understand, appropriate and innovate on these models within their own business when necessary. It will also be imperative that any Web-based business possess the ability to understand the necessity (or not!) for adaptation to a new business model.

4.1 Assessing the Need for Value Creation Systems

Before jumping onto the Web 2.0 bandwagon and completely decentralizing an entire business's model, it is imperative that it first assess the necessity of change. A good starting point will be to analyze the existing business model through the locus/creator/scarcity model to first understand the current state of affairs. How decentralized is it already – and if so, along which dimension of the lens?

Surveying the Current Value Situation

1. Find the locus of value in the existing business model. What are people actually paying for? If the value is centered on the product itself, are there latent loci of value creation that might be worth exploring? Currently a number of Web-based businesses, for example, are exposing their data publicly and for free through API's (Application Programming Interface) to create value outside of their core product.
2. Find the creators of value in the existing business model. Is it the designers and coders only (highly-centralized model), or does the group of creators include customers and partners of the business? Many Web 2.0 businesses are beginning to allow their customers to design, create and promote products as part of their business model.
3. Examine the business's pricing strategies to see if it sees its products as an infinite or a scarce resource. Is the business charging a fee to download digital music and creating security measures to prevent free the sharing of content? It most likely sees its products as scarce. Many Web 2.0 businesses give away their infinite resources for free (like a free account on a website, for example), but charge for the finite resources (like spending an hour speaking with a support representative)

4.2 Moving Toward a Value Creation System Approach

If potentially positive opportunities are discovered for decentralizing the value creation activities of the business, the next challenge is to figure out how/when to manage the change. Usually, there is no need to change the entire business model at once. Instead, a partial value creation system approach is possible, and even preferable.

Starting With a Partial Value Creation System Approach

With the exception of companies like MySpace which started up in the Web 2.0 era, the best approach is usually to phase in a decentralization effort, which may or may not end up in a fully-decentralized business model. Reuters, for example, while still charging a fee for the commercial use of its content (a scarce resource tactic), has recently released an API through their Reuters Labs site, which allows a non-commercial interest pull and use their data (an infinite resource tactic). By making the data available to outside users and non-commercial programmers, they are expanding their community of value creators to include people outside of the company, without forfeiting the continuing value of their centralized content creation efforts.

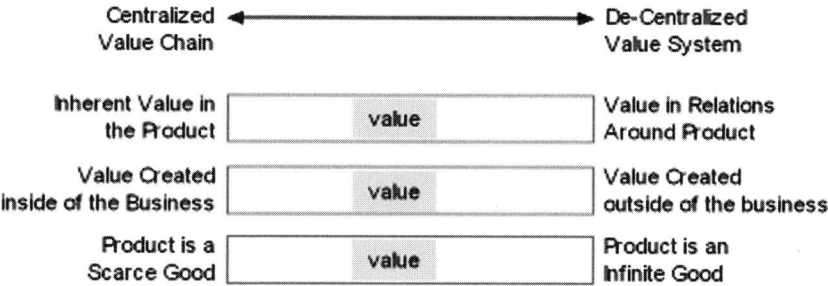

Fig 10. The Reuters business model is somewhere between centralized and de-centralized

Table 1 below includes some other common ways that Web 2.0 businesses are partially or fully decentralizing their value creation activities.

Table 1: Current Means for Decentralizing Web 2.0 Value Creation

Company	Description of Means
Twitter, Yahoo!, Google, YouTube	Have released API's which allow outside commercial and non-commercial developers to execute functions as well as to pull and push data to and from their systems.
Facebook, Salesforce, MySpace	Have created platforms which allow outside commercial and non-commercial developers to build entire applications within the system.
Digg, OhMyNews, Wikipedia	Have allowed users to create a large amount of the content within the system
CrowdSpring, Threadless, Widgetbox	Have allowed users to self-organize to create products individually or in groups through the system

5   Implications for Future Web-based Businesses

While the future of Web business models is of course uncertain, if we examine the corrolary media histories of the past, it does seem to occur that the most media and the business models that they create begin in a rather centralized fashion and then become decentralized through social and technical factors. Books, for example, were at first hand-written by elite learned scribes, then by large, centralized publishing firms. Now it is possible for any person to self-publish a print novel with relative ease and for a relatively low cost. There are likely to be even more novel and perhaps radical examples of value creation systems that will emerge in the coming years. Given the current upward trajectory of device ubiquity, end-user literacy, online participation in content creation, socializing, commerce and collective action, it appears that business models will continue to develop decentralized value creation systems as a means of competitive advantage.

References

Allee, V. The Future of Knowledge: Increasing Prosperity through Value Networks, Butterworth-Heinemann 2003
Benkler, Y. The Wealth of Networks: How Social Production Transforms Markets and Freedom. Yale Press, 2006.
Christensen, C. The Innovator's Dilemma: The Revolutionary Book that Will Change the Way You Do Business (Collins Business Essentials) 1997
Ford, H., & Crowther, S. (1922). My Life and Work.
Klir, George. Facets of Systems Science. Plenum Press, New York. Second Edition: Kluwer/Plenum, New York, 2001.
Media Democracy | Future of Media | Consumer Electonics Show | Survey - Deloitte LLP. . Retrieved June 5, 2008, from http://www.deloitte.com/dtt/article/0%2C1002%2Ccid%25253D182990%2C00.html.
Merriam-Webster Online Dictionary: http://www.merriam-webster.com/dictionary/value. Accessed July 24, 2008.
Porter, M. Competitive Advantage: Creating and Sustaining Superior Performance. Free Press, New York, 1985.
Prahalad, C.K. and Ramaswamy, V. The Future of Competition: Co-creating Unique Value with Customers. 2004.
Tocqueville, Alexis. [1835] 1988. Democracy in America. Ed. J. P. Mayer. New York: Harper Perennial.
Von Hippel, Eric, The Democratization of Innovation, The MIT Press, Cambridge, Massachusetts, 2005
Why try Britannica Online? A. . Retrieved June 5, 2008, from http://www.britannica.com/premium.
Wikipedia, the free encyclopedia. Retrieved June 5, 2008, from http://en.wikipedia.org/wiki/Main_Page.

Chapter 4. Open Innovation Communities…or should it be "Networks"?

Margarida Cardoso, João Vidal Carvalho, Isabel Ramos

University of Minho, PORTUGAL

Abstract

Open innovation appears now as an effective strategy to provide organizations with access to a wider range of ideas in the worldwide market of ideas, thus reducing the costs associated with R&D. In the context of open innovation, the concepts of both community and network have been introduced to describe the Solvers (creative people and organizations that propose solutions), the Seekers (organizations seeking solutions for their specific innovation problems) and the Brokers (organizations that mediate the interaction between Solvers and Seekers). The objectives of this chapter are twofold: (1) to explore the assumptions and practices supporting the concepts of community and network;(2) to provide a description of the open innovation phenomenon, and in particular, its expression on the web. The chapter describes the concept, the dynamics and the technology associated open innovation strategies and business models.

1   Introduction

We live in a complex world subjected to economic and social turbulence. In globalized world, people and organizations are interconnected in such a way that successes and failures of some may have huge impact in the lives of many other people and organizations.

People and organizations produce huge amounts of information and knowledge, which is easily delivered worldwide through various means, namely the web. No one can really deal with most of the information and knowledge available. Therefore, collaboration is now more important than ever, since groups can be clever than each of their members. Groups capture, store and process more information; groups can produce more sophisticated thinking and action.

Consumers have now access a global market where they can find all kinds of products and different offers of the same product. To stay competitive, organizations are required to innovate at a faster pace to meet ever changing consumer needs and preferences. Close innovation has traditionally enabled organizations to find indoor the ideas and technologies required to create new products or add value to existing ones. However, close innovation requires important investments and does not guarantee the creativity necessary to constant innovation.

Open innovation appears now as an effective strategy to provide organizations with access to a wider range of ideas in the worldwide market of ideas, thus reducing the costs associated with R&D.

In the context of open innovation, the concepts of both community and network have been introduced to describe the Solvers (creative people and organizations that propose solutions), the Seekers (organizations seeking solutions for their specific innovation problems) and the Brokers (organizations that mediate the interaction between Solvers and Seekers.

The objectives of this chapter are twofold:
1. To explore the assumptions and practices supporting the concepts of community and network;
2. To provide a description of the open innovation phenomenon, and in particular, its expression on the web.

Section 2 of the chapter presents the concepts of community and network and the assumptions that support them; section 3describes open innovation: concept, principles, web businesses and future research; chapter 4 discusses what changes if we see open innovation as a strategy implying a community or a network.

2 Community dynamics

Though many times put together, the concepts of community and network can be parted. Dal Fiore reffers to the difference between the tension that occurs within a community, towards homogeneization and conservation, something that makes it a space of belonging; and the network implying a tension towards differentiation, creative communication and also a space for competing (Dal Fiore 2007) or instead, being just a more adequate notion to larger scale social realities (Mitchell 1974). In the limit, community can even be read as a vague and somehow irresponsability-driven term, and might be replaced by commitment, a more concrete and desirable social notion (Fernback 2007). The author equates a whole new loss of sense of the term community, which really gained this doubtfulness time ago in the anthropological perspective. It's also worth noticing that glocalization induces this same problem, because it creates in fact a need for a shifting perspective, both global and local, as Wellman's glocalized networks call for - glocalization meaning extensive global but also local interactions which have always existed and frame communities (Wellman 2005).

On the other way, community can be considered a distributed communication system or systems, considering distributed communities which account for dispersion and individualization (nodes), and also using the Internet to compose itself

(Gochenour 2006). Nevertheless Wellman (2002) defines community as a network of interpersonal ties and adds to the concept the particulars of social identity. He holds partially to a notion of geographical proximity that induces a neighborhood-centered perspective, though ties can be kept through long distances - and here, of course, enters the Internet and other ways of communication. Peripheral participation referred, for instances, to communities of practice (Lave and Wenger 1991) sure calls for the transcendence of boundaries (Lundkvist 2004).

2.1 Communities and online communities

Place might be considered some sort of materialization of powers, where processes occur and ideologies get settled. On the opposite, space means the context where each individual or group can materialize its choices (Wood and Smith 2005). These notions relate to cyberspace as we know there are spaces that become places, where some kind of control is exerted and intentional communities, unified by some sort of common ground, develop their relations.

So communities can be first of all imagined (Anderson 2005), because those who belong to the community may not know each other face to face, but tend to imagine a common sense of belonging. There can be a spatial materialization for an imagined community and it is possible to establish an identity with it and all those believed to be connected with it, as it is the case for a nation (Anderson 2005). The fact that this community is taken as a kind of horizontal and profound group, strengthens the concept and the multiple contexts in which it is applied (Anderson 2005). This kind of community becomes obviously reinforced if subject to the intervention of some kind of mediated communication. Examples like newspapers or television - or electronic platforms, for the matter - help us understand how the ideas get exchanged and most of all shared, what makes them attain a common version accepted by an entire whole social group. This gives way to what is nowadays called a virtual community, meaning mediated interactions between the members of a group (participants) which have in common some motivating interests. Calling for more than a set of relationships (though online ones), it implies a common public space (or place) and a group of individuals that create identifications with and share it, interacting in real time or just leaving messages. A ground for experimentation where identity can be surpassed (through avatars or anonymity), an interaction context and some sort of a settlement greater that oneself can be enough motivation for the sharing implied. Communities allocate characteristics like interactivity, participant variety, a common space, and some sort of sustained membership, a sense of belonging that desirably can keep it working.

Based on a theory of reasoned action' approach, augmented with extrinsic motivators, Bock et al. (2005) hold that a felt need for extrinsic rewards might diminish a knowledge sharing attitude; people are driven by reciprocity, and self-worthiness is intensified together with the subjective norm of knowledge sharing;

a favorable organizational climate (fairness, innovativeness and affiliation) is very influential on that referred subjective norms, and also weights on individual knowledge sharing intentions and behaviors (Bock et al. 2005). Hislop (2005) refers to a wide spectrum of factors that influence on the will to share knowledge, like potential for conflict (inter-group or inter-personal), status (Nan 1999), sense of equity, interpersonal trust, and others, and above all, the author expresses the need to pay attention to the socio-cultural context and act accordingly. Most of all, collective and mutual trust matter (Ahonen and Lietsala 2007), which might be considered a cultural aspect (Gassmann and Enkel 2004). Knowledge is accepted as a capacity of human beings (Wang and Rubinstein-Montano 2003), meaning some degree of trust is essential to human interaction, implying cooperation and interdependence. The authors conclude that trust has a significant impact on the value of knowledge shared (Wang and Rubinstein-Montano 2003). But other needs must be attended, like the support of group creativity (Ahonen and Lietsala 2007). Energy, time and capabilities are a must to nurture a community, of course (Ahonen and Lietsala 2007), but it becomes possible either to involve in specific tasks or just to handle a general look after weak signals (Ahonen and Lietsala 2007).

Co-opting interactionist concepts of focus (attention) and nimbus (an object's presence) Daneshgar (2005) establishes a difference between objects that constitute actual contextual knowledge in virtual communities, and objects that make possible to the community member to interact within that context. The author explains that there are five levels of awareness – relevant information to a participant in a specific process - when one is interacting in an online community, meaning the first just contextual knowledge about what should be done, without making an actor able to be involved in any kind of sharing transaction. In the next level, awareness now means the actor has some kind of specialized knowledge about what is needed on that specific environment. In a third level the actor will possess knowledge about all the roles involved in the online community. Next level four, the actor will know about all interactions that occur within the community context and finally, at level five, the actor will have specialized knowledge about the objects that make possible to understand other objects and interactions on the whole. He/ she know about what everyone does, and how tasks are performed, and even who collaborates with whom (directly or indirectly).

Considering there are crucial aspects to usage continuance after the adoption of a web platform, or any, for the matter, Limayem et al. (2007) refer to the habit factor, including such different aspects as satisfaction, frequency of past behaviors, stability of context, and usability. Authors propose habit moderates (suppresses) intention is such way it decreases its weight on web platforms continuous usage, what calls our attention on the possibility of experiences over new platforms. Collaboration includes several important factors that have been studied through different lenses, like the structuration theory (Giddens 1984; Evans and Brooks 2005). Collaboration relates to interaction in time and space, professional identity and also on its construction, (Evans and Brooks 2005). Time becomes an important issue as it provides sense and gives content to produced knowledge (Hassan

2003), and though being metaphorically annihilated by some authors it persists as well as it's relevance, due to the fact that it gains new significance with globalization (and networks), but also when referring to individual and group memory, because it's possible to wonder if they're not multi-time layered (Adam 2008). In fact, knowledge conversion processes, meaning the affection of one individual by other's experience and knowledge (directly or based on knowledge artifacts), are time-settled (Massey and Montoya-Weiss 2006). This, together with individual temporal behavior (and culture), has direct implications towards IS/ social media and knowledge conversion, in a parallel or sequential interaction basis.

2.2 Networks

The network concept might have entered social sciences through urban complex grounds, opposing the previous notion of community inherent to anthropological original studies in small-scale societies (Mitchell 1974). Attention is called upon the fact that usually authors either choose a morphological approach or an interactional one. Morphology can include several aspects, considering connectedness, density, anchorage, reachability. Interaction includes content, directedness, durability, intensity and frequency (Mitchell 1974). Sometimes, too, authors mingle criteria to obtain specific and more expressive operational constructs. Mitchell gives particular attention to content, which includes communication contents, transaction (or exchange) and normative content (relational).

A social network is something that affects the flow and quality of information (Granovetter 1973; Granovetter 2004; Ahonen and Lietsala 2007; Perkmann and Walsh 2007) that means also the need for coordination mechanisms (Gassmann and Enkel 2005). Sources of reward but also punishment (Granovetter 2004; Ahonen and Lietsala 2007), networks are based on social capital, first of all (Bourdieu 2001; Nan 2001) and establish layers of intellectual capital (Törrö 2007) - somehow a parallel with the sociotechnical model of Bressand and Distler (1995), which includes a layer one, for infrastructure (physical support for communication); a layer two, for infostructure, formal symbolic communication rules; and finally a layer three, for infoculture, the background taken-for-granted knowledge (Lehaney et al. 2004). These networks integrate ideas, and one must consider that the acceptance of an idea is part of its comprehension (DiMaggio 2007), and so being the comprehension of related knowledge and technology. Trust is an important factor (Granovetter 2004; Ahonen and Lietsala 2007), and most of all a network is embedded in an interconnection of networks. This means that an additional layer is built in the organization.

Gassmann and Enkel (2005) make an in-depth study of 230 networks to know their management mechanisms: through this study they come to know that firms gain if they integrate networks' work in their R&D, because they become able to capture knowledge from the outside to the organization. The network might also facilitate a company's transition from a rigid structure to a flexible one (see Gassmann and Enkel 2005, for a comprehensive enunciation of a network's structural elements). Networks can also be defined as social processes or configurations, as Perkmann and Walsh (2007) state.

What are the properties of a network? Tacit and explicit knowledge flow easily (Lambooy 2004). Also, if we consider knowledge as a socially embedded process (Brown and Duguid 1991; Perkmann and Walsh 2007) then knowledge shared will be relevant. But, as Ursula Schneider says, knowledge is treated like a resource or a production factor for firms, and in fact capabilities (interaction between knowledge and its specific application), are more useful than that (Schneider 2007). Other network proprieties are important, as formality of content, intensity, frequency of contact, durability of relationships, and the fact that a network deals either with radical or incremental innovation (Lambooy 2004; Oerlemans et al. 1998); minding this, complexity of innovation is also an important factor (Oerlemans et al. 1998).

Culture can be seen as a set of complex and variable rule-like structures that can constitute resources (Bourdieu 2001; DiMaggio 1997). Network culture means sharing, as Maxwell (2006) says, while referring specifically to a norm of sharing in the open source community, But cultural actions also imply reciprocity and shared patterns of interaction (Nieto and Santamaría 2007) and here it might be noticed that networks are relationship-based, in the sense that they promote the production of a social identity, just like communities, through a specific sociability, support, flows of information, and even a sense of belonging (Wellman 2005; Törrö 2007). The various definitions of culture don't conceal the fact that there's a common ground that may cause conflict showing the difference between groups and their symbolic systems (Bourdieu 2001).

2.3 Thinking and action in community

Social presence theory relates to the exact point where we perceive others as real people and our mutual interactions as relationships (Short et al. 1976). Mediated communication is as much efficace as it allows people to have a certain amount of social presence. This theory becomes important because of the quantity of nonverbal information needed to establish substancially this perception (Wood and Smith 2005). Postmes et al. (1998) try to assess real online relationships through the social identification/ deindividuation (SIDE) theory. The model stands on a basis of group identification through mediated communication, considering that in a certain way people let go of the coherence they should be supposed to sought for, and adapt to those group descriminators, as substitutes of the nonverbal component they cannot access being online. This becomes something of a loss of identity (at least in a conventional way), what psychologists call deindiviation (loss of the individuality in favour of group identity) – typical of the mobs.

Cognition depends on immediate social relationships but also on networks, group memberships and self-identities. One must coordinate his/ her identity either through immediate social context or in a larger network of relationships, which can assume four types, as referred by Thomsen et al. (2007). These frames of relationships include interactions like Communal Sharing, Authority Ranking (in fact, some physical aspects of space contribute to our mental representations about authority and social power), Equality Matching and what the authors call an utilitarian Market Pricing. Now, could we propose a fifth one, mediated distortion?

Cognition paradigms might be referred to as embedded, distributed or extended (cognition but also interrelated memory). There is a common ground which considers some sort of hybridization, meaning interaction between brain and environment – related to complex human set-ups and cognition processes that include people and things (Barnier et al. 2008). This also means there is an extension of the information processing behond the brain activity. An intersection of embodied and distributed cognition occurs, because functions aren't only abstract. This means the externalization of processes to influence and get influenced (Smith 2008). Bearing in mind that human cognition also takes place framed by other people (Smith 2008) then groups and teams become relevant assuming some sort of durkheiminan social division of cognitive labour (DiMaggio 1997). Distributed cognition is a particularly useful concept if we think about memory and related processes like encoding/ storage/ retrieval, which normally involve more than one individual (Barnier et al. 2008).

The difference between group and individual thinking is more a matter of degree, and the group may increase biases shown by one individual (Brown 2000). That will be based particularly on what the group already thinks or co-opts. Minding this, "(...) external influence is (...) primarily negative, the relentless intrusion of the social into malleable individual memory" (Barnier et al. 2008: 35) – what comes to be obviously a fail-to-do-justice view because memory is most of all relational. It's worthwhile referring here to the paradox of memory: past structures come to the present, but the present selects which past remains as a legacy... and above all, history and facts keep being retold. Practices of memory as forms to keep its past present (Jedlowski 2001) call our attention to two important factors: one, the group as a frame for memory (Halbwachs 1968); a second one, when does memory become information? This leads to the following theoretical approaches to memory. The first searches to understand the amount of correct information. Important factors induce variation, which are the collaboration type, inducing collaborative recall (Weldon and Bellinger 1997), the nature of the group and roles assumed (Goffman 1993), all crucial elements for a better group memory performance (extensively: nature of the group, collaboration, size of the group, nature of the stimuli). The objectives are: accuracy, establishing relationships, making good impressions, developing intimacy, and teaching/ informing. Transactive memory means "a set of individual memory systems in combination with the communication that takes place between individuals." (Wegner 987: 186). After all, storing information about who knows what. Of course this must be a systemic approach, in the way that shared recollections are more than the sum of individual ones (transactive systems with emergent properties).

Costs and benefits of remembering in groups may involve group influence, fate of memories, and be a function of the group memory. If the group is more robust, then the transactive memory mechanisms will work better. This implies that in an open innovation context, meaning a large community contribution, the groups can be less robust. So, transactive memory mechanisms will possibly work worse. Open innovation will probably mean that there'll be a collective loss (on transactive memory) but some collective gain (on search and solving problems, see next section.). As Maxwell (2006) says, collective value is built together with participants' self-interest and benefit. Collaborative groups recall more than individuals but less than nominal groups, as Barnier et al. refer. Also, "Some distributed systems are one-offs." (Barnier et al. 2008: 37).

3 Open Innovation

Chesbrough and Schwartz (2007) define open innovation as the "(...) use of purposive inflows and outflows of knowledge to accelerate internal innovation, and expand the markets for external use of innovation, respectively", (Chesbrough and Schwartz 2007: 55). More specifically, firms can include the following archetypes of core processes, when addering to an open innovation process: outside-in or inside-out processes, or a coupled one (Gassmann and Enkel 2005).

The open innovation paradigm implies co-development partnerships, developing a mutual working relationship (versus the traditional defensive business strategy), and using external sources of knowledge. These partnerships might look for the delivery of a new product, technology, or service, to reduce R&D expenses (Chesbrough and Schwartz 2007), to expand the innovation output and its impact, and even to open new markets otherwise inaccessible.

As Törrö holds, the open innovation paradigm means firms practice the sourcing of external competences, use networks as an external resource pool and these means they can benefit from global intellectual capital brokering (Törrö 2007). Lettl (2007) holds that involvement of the right users is a market capability. These firms have, mostly, internal R&D strategies that influence partnership with university-based research (Bercovitz and Feldman 2007, though limited by a small study sample). Becker and Zirpoli (2007) also mention the boundaries of the firm in the open innovation process. A strong relationship between the existence of a firm innovation strategy and the interaction with universities is surely important (Bercovitz and Feldman 2007). Some factors favorable to the existence of university partners (Bercovitz and Feldman 2007) are the perceived ability to fully appropriate results due to different objectives, what puts appropriability as a partnership motivation; and also patenting results. This is changing, though, because of the growing assertion of property rights. Other factors important to choose an innovation partner are the limited risk of competition and the central role of universities in an innovation system.

Partners possibly will have to implement a new business model, considering a common objective for the partnership (for example, to increase profitability or expand market access) (Becker and Zirpoli 2007; Lettl 2007). Becker and Zirpoli (2007) refer that, surprisingly, firms are adapting business models and value chains to open innovation demands. R&D capabilities of both firms should be assessed (Lettl 2007) and classified, between core, critical or contextual categories (Becker and Zirpoli 2007). Core mean, usually, key sources, sparingly shared; critical capabilities are those essential for a product's success and finally, contextual are the ones which aren't essential to one of the partners, yet essential or core to the other, maybe smaller partner. Business model alignment usual problems can be mis-assessment of the objectives, mis-judgement of the criticality of capabilities, lack of alignment - alignment including complementarity, too - and this should be a reason to carefully determine the degree of business model alignment and to manage the partnership caring for future needs (Huang et al. 2002; Lettl 2007).

Before we can start discussing this subject, it is important to stress that the open innovation concept, as referred by Chesbrough, is not new (Christensen et al. 2005). Cohen and Levinthal (1990) had already developed the concept around the competencies developed by R&D labs to manage internal innovation as well as to reach out and integrate external ideas, science and other external knowledge and creativity. Rosenberg (1982), Lundvall (1992), Pavitt (1998) and Von Hippel (1988) among several other authors also contributed for the concept by exploring its interactive, multidisciplinary and inter-organizational nature of innovative learning. In his book "Open innovation: the new imperative for creating and profiting from Technology", Chesbrough (2003) added to those prior formulations, a more focused and systematic study of the corporative practices to effectively manage the external processes of innovation. Chesbrough highlighted the role of open innovation to enable high-tech companies to absorb technological innovation faster and cheaper, changing from an introverted and proprietary paradigm to a more extroverted and open one.

More recent studies in innovation have stressed the growing relevance of external sources of knowledge and creativity (Perkmann and Walsh 2007). These studies have showed that more than trusting their R&D labs, organizations should devote more efforts in open innovation (Chesbrough and Crowther 2006). This means that innovation can be considered the result of knowledge networks connecting several organizations instead of a function within one organization (Coombs et al. 2003; Powell et al. 1996).

In the same sense, the concept of interactive innovation was implemented to understand the non-linear, terative and multi-agent nature of the innovation processes (Kline 1985; Lundvall 1988; Von Hippel 1988).

Parallel to the organizational concern to keep the growth of their structure, they are also required to trust in external sources for the innovation processes' input (Törrö 2007). Collaboration with suppliers is already an important part of the innovation strategy of large organizations. Simultaneously, the traditional outsourcing of innovation, in which the full responsibility for part of the innovation process is transferred to another organization, is growing in popularity. The trend is, however, to form extensive networks in order to reach external competencies.

Thus, the challenge is now to identify and contact individuals and organizations worldwide in order to gather ideas and solutions to eventualy choose the one that can complement the innovation process of the organization (Bowonder et al. 2005; Moitra and Krishnamoorthy 2004; Perrons and Platts 2004; Fowles and Clark 2005; Quinn 2000; Chesbrough 2003a).

Laursen and Salter (2006) have explored the relationship between the openning of the organization to its external environment with the innovation performance. They have concluded that the organizations that are opened to external sources of innovation, or with external inquiry channels, have a higher level of innovation performance. By studying British industrial companies, the authors showed that these companies kept systematic strategies to search various channels and in doing so they were able to get ideas and resources that enabled them to identify and explore opportunities for innovation. This study follows the work of Cohen and Leventhal (1990), who argue that the ability to explore external knowledge is a key element of the innovation performance.

With the aim of promoting the internalization of the organization, the open innovation strategy can induce an improvement in the performance of the innovation processes. Kafouros et al. (2007) suggest that organizations need to have some internationalization maturity, being active in various markets, to be able to successfully innovate.

While lately there is a growing interest in open innovation, little empirical evidence exists on how it is implemented in organizations. As implied by Gassmann (2006), there are still many gaps in the research on open innovation. In line with this understanding, several researchers have stressed the need for further research to study and critically analyse focued topics relevant to understand the phenomenon. Katila (2002) and Laursen and Salter (2006), suggest that a deeper understanding of the ways the organizations structure their inquiry of external ideas needs to be developed. Simultaneously, little is known about open innovation from the point of view of organizations that profit from selling their own intellecttual capital (Chesbrough and Crowther 2006).

More specifically, European organizations show competitive problems due to the low investments in innovation (Vigier 2007). Structural factors such as weak connections between science and industry often explain low levels of knowledge creation. It is believed that only by promoting innovation, including open innovation, will it be possible to go over that deficit, and in that way, to improve competitiveness and market leadership.

63

3.1 Open Innovation: concept and principles

The central idea that sustains the concept created by Henry Chesbrough and presented in his book *Open innovation: The New Imperative for Creating and Profiting from Technology*, is that of globally distributed knowledge and that organizations do not have the enough resources to trust only in internal innovation (Chesbrough 2003). This new concept stresses the limitations the close model of innovation predominant in the last few decades and which limited the R&D processes to the knowledge generated within the organization. Organizations implementing the close model make substantial investments in large R&D Labs to create the conditions for the emergence of knowledge and creativity.

Close and Open innovation models are illustrated in figure 1:

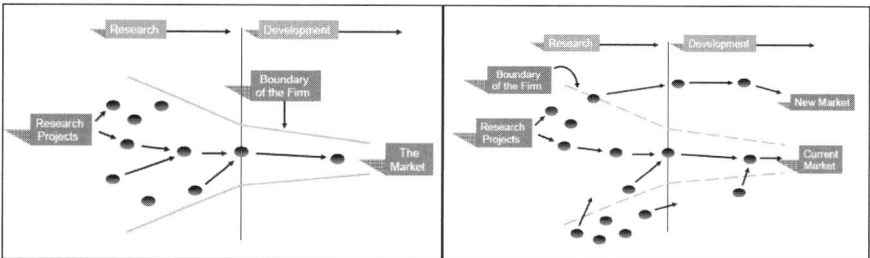

Fig 1: Close innovation e open innovation innovation (Chesbrough 2003)

The open innovation model praise the knowledge flow through the organization boundaries to enable the accelerated development of internal innovations (i.e., supported by the licensing of technologies developed by others), and to expand the use of technologies internally developed that could become underused.

Based on an empirical study of 124 companies, Gassmann and Enkel (2004) identified three open innovation core processes: (1) outside-in process: enriching of the organizational knowledge base by integrating suppliers, clients, and other external sources of knowledge; (2) inside-out process: exploring external markets to sell internal ideas. (3) coupled process: a mix between the outside-in and inside-out processes workingin partnership with other organizations. The following figure illustrates two perspectives of the three processes of the model, identified by Gassmann e Enkel.

64

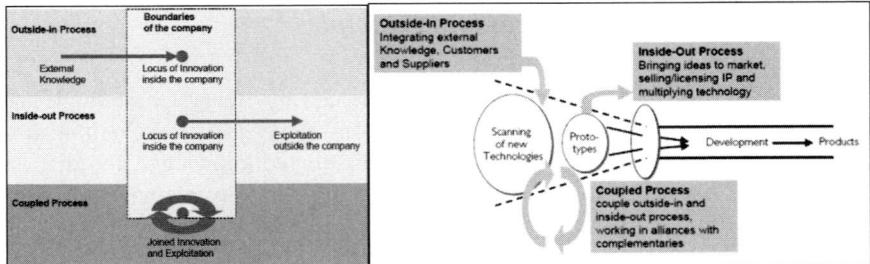

Fig 2: Two perspectives about the three processes of the model identified by Gassmann e Enkel (2004)

The main challenge in adopting the open innovation model is in finding the right people and in fostering the collaboritive work with the aim of integrating scientific discoveries in a innovative way. The resistance attitudes resulting from devaluing the ideas and solutions not developed internally is an important factor hindering the adoption of an open innovation strategy (Chesbrough et al. 2006).

3.2 Collaboration in the context of Open Innovation

Collaborative networks are crucial for the overall open innovation concept. Some studies show their importance in the improvement of companies' innovation performance. Nieto and Santamaria research (2007) shows how different types of collaborative networks contribute to the upgrading and innovation of industrial products. Using longitudinal research data about Spanish industrial companies, results show that a collaborative network is of crucial importance to reach a higher degree of innovation in specific products. Collaboration with suppliers, customers and other firms has a positive impact in innovation, while the collaboration with competitors has a negative impact. This study also puts in evidence that the main positive impact on innovation comes from collaborative networks holding different types of participants.

Perkmann and Walsh (2007) explore characteristics of collaborative relationships between universities and industry through an open innovation perspective. Authors present a model, distinguishing university-industry partnerships from other mechanisms such as technology transfer or just human mobility processes. Research is centered in the analysis of the role of some practices such as collaborative research, university-industry centers of research or academic consultancy. Evidence suggests that such university-business relationships are practiced extensively in a productive way, despite the existing differences between industry and scientific disciplines.

Michaelides e Kehoe (2007) go deeper presenting a methodology to draw collaborative networks in the context of open innovation. Their study shows the benefits of using an information system design methodology (ISDM) to build a research community permanently online, incorporating flexible processes and promoting Open Innovation through new ideas and diffusion of new research results. The methodology is shown on the IPGC community prototype. This methodology is based on focused development stages concerning the definition of a social community and approaching specific organizational issues and process. As Roberts suggests (2006), specific and significant topics existing in one community, could be attractive to new users inspiring them to re-visit. In fact, interesting and useful material is vital to keep conversations going on.

Authors hold that successful online communities demand regular problem monitoring and change to meet its members' needs (Michaelides and Kehoe 2007; Snyder 2000). Additionally, Web 2.0' asynchronous tools must ensure personal publication applications like blogs, as well as RSS (real simple syndication), to enable members to subscribe information sources, allowing filters to select that information. Podcasts, asynchronous messages and event video-conference must also be included.

Nevertheless the conclusions extracted from their work, authors recognize this research faces some challenges because the open innovation model is now rising and many characteristics remain to be discovered. One of the challenges is related to poor IT applications to support knowledge communities. In these communities distributed knowledge flows simultaneously through many actors, and aspect that is poorly support by IT applications.

3.3 Open Innovation on the web 2.0: examples

There is a growing interest in the innovation brokering markets (Arora et al. 2002; Chesbrough and Crowther 2006). The number of companies that mediate the capital intellectual transactions and provide to their clients a new approach to implement inbound and outbound open innovation is growing.

Organizations must integrate a set of specific competencies and capabilities that efficiently manage ideas and suggestions. Brokering companies (brokers) have emerged to deal with a growing demand for creativity and solutions: the new market of ideas. Brokers have strong presence in the Web through intelligent platforms that facilitate the innovation management and implement security mechanisms that ensure the confidentiality of exchanged information and the anonymity of seekers and solvers. These companies act as intermediaries that make available a set of services supporting innovation for their company clients (seekers) (Chesbrough 2003). These platforms are part of the Web 2.0 and are integrating concepts and technologies of the so called Web 3.0.

The Web 2.0 is a term used to designate the second generation of communities and services on the Web. These communities and services integrate technologies such as blogs, wikis, RSS feeds and Ajax resources. The Web 2.0 solutions represent an huge potential for new ways of producing and multiplying intellectual capital and of sharing knowledge in the context of online communities. Web 2.0 tools include IT applications such as:

- Desktop settled videoconference applications together with instant messaging and other collaboration tools to assist collaborative work and real time communication;
- Online publishers allow brainstorming sessions between users in different places;
- Collaborative applications to share people's and group's views over products and to exchange information;
- Places for online meeting and online agendas;
- Automation of communication process between people and groups, making joint projects possible (workgroups);
- Management of contacts and relationships;
- Customization of access to each member/ company;
- Online training actions;
- Indexation/ tagging of contents to make easier the search and its reading;
- Process automation for community communication and ongoing externalization of tacit knowledge, through collaboration tools allowing access to specialized contents;
- Applications to facilitate the spreading of an organization's intellectual production;
- Collective or individual calendars;
- Document management.

The permanent goal will be to develop personalized and flexible services, allowing the exchange of multidisciplinary information and the leveraging of intellectual capital for the companies. These web platforms allow communication improvement, centralizing information and the co-construction of knowledge in simple and easy-to-manage environments.

Some companies, as Innocentive, yet2.com, Nine Sigma, IdeaWicket, Idea-Connection and YourEncore are key examples of open innovation as a management model, creating a global market for scientific knowledge, where everyone can contribute with her/his own developed technology. Innocentive, for example, connects a global network of Seekers and Solvers, allowing companies to spot and hire necessary skills in order to deal with complex technical challenges, something that might be difficult to find internally.

NineSigma: Procter & Gamble contributed to create NineSigma, one of the companies which connect organizations with scientific and technology problems to other firms, universities, government and private laboratories and consulting firms in order to develop specific solutions. If someone can help P&G solve a problem, for example something related to low temperature washing, then Nine-Sigma provides a technological summary describing the problem and sends it through the solution suppliers world network, in order to get the best solution.

Anyone can submit a non-confidential proposal to NineSigma, and the company will share it with the contracting firm. If the company likes the proposal, Nine-

Sigma connects both partners and the project is developed from then on. Nine-Sigma has already distributed technological summaries to more than 700,000 people and as a result finished 100 projects. Remarkably 45% of them gave way to new partnerships.

InnoCentive: Established by Eli Lilly, InnoCentive is much alike NineSigma. But instead of connecting companies and partners who look for the solution of wide problems in many science disciplines, InnoCentive works with more defined and specific scientific problems. It was created in 2001, binding universities and other organizations as well as other non-profit organizations, to break the innovation barrier. Innocentive is a global network that connects companies and collaborative bright minds - currently more than 125,000. Challenges come in the open, so new solutions can be caught up. Its functioning is simple and themes are divided into Science, Engineering and Project, Chemistry, Mathematics and Computer Science, day-to-day sciences, and Business and Entrepreneurship. Each area includes several subjects and best solutions get a reward. The values of rewards vary accordingly to the intricacy of the problem. Solutions become public in project rooms, where each user gains access to a more detailed briefing. Once registered, the user starts to receive interesting challenges by email, RSS and similar tools.

YourEncore: Created in 2003, the firm has been helping to speed up external innovation for other companies, as way to increase their growth. YourEncore connects customer firms with retired scientists and engineers in order to benefit from their knowledge. The company supplies these services to interested companies through a safe and confidential enterprise environment. When using YourEncore, companies can bring indoor highly experienced people and new ways of thinking of other organizations and industries. This seems to be a rather powerful model because firms are able to cut back costs and risks, through interdisciplinary approaches and solutions to specific problems.

Through YourEncore, it is possible to hire a retired engineer with very relevant skills, for a specific short-term project. Currently, it connects about 800 scientists and engineers who are connoisseurs in several knowledge disciplines like life sciences, feeding and consumption-related sciences, materials, aerospace industries and defense.

Ideawicket.com has recently launched its `Open Innovation Vestibule'. The site seeks to become a place where innovators and corporations can connect to exchange their innovation requirements. It is a platform for innovators to showcase and share their creations with the world. Ideawicket.com has been launched by Ideawicket Innovations Private Limited and is based in New Delhi, India. It sees consumers and laypersons becoming the instrumental force behind the development of new products, processes and experiences.

Ideawicket enables people to share their innovative ideas, designs and techniques with others. Users can post solutions for everyday products, processes and services that save time, cost and space, increase productivity and efficiency, foster

easier communication, improve consumer experience, are socially and ecological-
ly responsible, delight the senses or enhance quality of life.

Innovators can also provide information about their solutions such as market,
cost and time analysis, user benefits and intellectual property information. The
portal also offers networking features like private messaging, sharing content with
friends, posting comments, keeping the material 'private' or 'public', uploading
images and adding video feeds.

Yet2.com: Established in 1999, yet2.com focuses on bringing together technology' buyers and sellers looking to make the most of their investments.

While NineSigma and InnoCentive focus on helping companies and their technological problems, Yet2.com mediates technology transfer inside and outside governmental companies, universities and laboratories. Yet2.com is an online market
for copyright exchange. It works with customers providing descriptive summaries
on technologies sought for or rather offering them for licensing or purchase, and
distributes these summaries for a global network of companies, laboratories and
institutions. Interested members contact Yet2.com and ask to be introduced to potential customers. Once introduced, negotiation goes on between the two.

IdeaConnection: This web service was launched by Online Date Services, Ltd.
The problem-solving and multidisciplinary design innovation website allows
people worldwide, from amateurs to experts, to connect and collaborate. In this
way, the service facilitates individual and corporate innovation, ideas, and solutions by offering access to an international pool of thinkers. It is designed for use
by anyone seeking a solution to a problem. The problem can be simple or complex.

The business model is as follows: when a problem is posted, a sum of money is
deposited. The solution seeker then reviews the problem solvers cv's online and
selects and invites one or more people to collaborate to solve the problem. Funds
are distributed to the participants upon a successful solution.

3.4 Open Innovation: future steps

The innovation process approach is related with the way companies choose to
search for new ideas with business potential. New innovation models suggest that
many companies have adapted their way of working, choosing open strategies of
research and connecting a vast set of actors and sources to help them reach and
support innovation (Laursen and Salter 2006).

Eventually, open innovation set up in organizations implies a change in innovation sources. This means a new model will be standing on structures, processes
and adequate technologies, allowing a whole new set of innovation in and outsourcing. From top to bottom, organization and all external contexts will make
available contents based on new perspectives, creating a "global market" of ideas
and inherent value surplus to the firms (Duarte 2007).

However, while this model stays blurred, any perspective on it must be global, involving actors in a distant and distributed innovation environment (West et al. 2006). The model needs detailed studies for innovation activities through all organizational levels of analysis (individual, group, organization, community, etc.).

Therefore, academic and practitioner work has to be developed in order to contribute for the maturity of this new paradigm.

Open Innovation borders or limits aren't clear yet. To identify limits to this paradigm is somehow a crucial activity, studying theories associated to the phenomena associated with open innovation.

Some questions and problems must be raised in future research, as follows:

- Which are the more adequate ways to put into practice Open Innovation? On which companies? Based on which organizational structures? Will open Innovation be more adequate for High-Tech or Low-Tech companies?
- Where will open innovation be more practicable in the future? Will it be more strictly conditioned by intellectual property rules?
- Is there a cycle in the open innovation model? Must the model be restored after technology discontinuity?
- How can we motivate actors to share their knowledge? Is there any advantage in sharing?
- What are the impacts on open business models of using the terms community or network to designate the set of players involved in the business?

Most research studies on open innovation were carried through case studies, focusing companies or individual projects. But to increase knowledge, it will be necessary to develop research on more extensive sources of data and to analyze and test different hypothesis related to open innovation.

While the majority of studies present successful examples of open innovation, other studies should focus on companies' problems and constraints to implement open innovation. These cases could, for example, demonstrate problems when R&D technological opportunities are missed (West et al. 2006).

Other studies could also explore transnational open innovation practice. It would be good to know if this strategy is really efficient when different cultural backgrounds are at stake; or rather if these cultural differences would affect the Open business model performance in a multinational company.

Now that the world evolves from electronic business to ubiquitous computing (Weiser 1991), new chances face open innovation. Dodgson et al. (2005) state that IT supplies ubiquitous digital infrastructure to safe information and data storage and transfer, making it easier to exchange information and knowledge. Based on these concerns, Schmitt et al. (2006) describe how to draw an Open Object Information Infrastructure (OOII) in order to make possible Open Innovation through ubiquitous computation. Potential benefits are presented with the first prototype called Federative Library. Authors hold that this approach introduces an infrastructure that significantly induces a climate of innovation, promoting a new and innovative environment for applications and services development. However, they acknowledge the prototype needs continuous development and further detailed analysis.

Considering the fast Web 2.0 development, some problems might show up to those who develop open innovation platforms and look for best practices and services. In fact, these professionals cannot neglect risks associated to the use of developing services, still little consolidated. It will be necessary to keep on exploring, researching and analyzing the advantages and limitations of Web 2.0 in such a way as to find answers that match an open innovation environment. Is there enough knowledge about the ways organizations use services to manage seekers and solvers needs?

It is very important to understand the implications of using the Web 2.0 and to have close look on the evolution of IT. These evolutions can bring new opportunities for open innovation platforms but there are concerns that must be addressed: the power of the crowd becomes more and more important as the Web makes it easier to build new communities; the user content development becomes increasingly important, though it defies conventional thought on who has the knowledge; the reputation, security and privacy of data generated on Web 2.0; finally, the transfer of copyright of enormous amounts of data and its generation by individuals and firms.

Some questions about IT will come to the forefront:

- How will Web 2.0 services be integrated with more traditional technologies (databases and portals), in order to make research easier?
- How to bind Web 2.0 and the development of mobile devices and ubiquous computing?
- How should organizations put into action social software related services? How should firms integrate Web 2.0 services and their own IS?
- How will businesses answer to the need for interface development in order to ease interactivity with solvers?
- What technologies of the so called Web 3.0 should be integrated in platforms supporting open innovation?

4 Conclusions

The chapter describes the concept, the dynamics and the technology associated open innovation strategies and business models. It starts by presenting the main ideas, principles and practices behind the concepts of community and network. Those two concepts are often used interchangeably when open innovation is referred. However, they imply different ways of relating, both emotionally and structurally. Therefore, we consider relevant that the concepts are clarified and that implications for open innovation are researched.

In the second part of the chapter, the open innovation concept is described, some examples of web services are presented, the supporting technology is summarized. Open innovation is a rapid growing movement to which more and more companies are adhering. This calls for more research that can improve our knowledge on the strategies, business models and relevant technologies involved. Some of the most relevant research questions are described in the chapter. The authors are starting several projects in the area, addressing the social dynamics of open innovation (communities or networks), the study of brokering business models, and the improvements to web platforms brought about by the Web 3.0 technologies.

References

Adam B (2008) The timescapes challenge: engagement with the invisible temporal. Leeds Talk Prose Timescapes Challenge 250208. http://www.cardiff.ac.uk/ socsi/resources/ Leeds%20talk%20prose%20Timescapes%20Challenge%20250208.pdf/. Accessed 14 May 2008

Ahonen M, Lietsala K (2007) Managing service ideas and suggestions - information systems in innovation brokering, Innovation in Services, Conference Proceedings. Tekes, Berkeley CA

Anderson B (2005) Comunidades imaginadas; reflexões sobre a origem e a expansão do nacionalismo. Edições 70, Lisboa

Arora A, Fosfuri A, Gambardella A (2002) Markets for Technology. The Economics of Innovation and Corporate Strategy. MIT Press, Cambridge, MA

Barnier A, Sutton J, Harris C, Wilson RA (2008) A conceptual and empirical framework for the social distribution of cognition. The case of memory. Leslie Marsh (Action Ed.) Cogn Sys Res 9: 33-51.

Becker M, Zirpoli F (2007) Organizing open innovation: the role of competences, modularity, and performance integration, Academy of Management Proceedings, 2007, http://program.aomonline.org/2007/submission.asp?mode= ShowSes-sion & SessionID= 1841. Accessed 24 Jan 2008

Bercovitz J, Feldman M P (2008) Fishing upstream: firm innovation strategy and university research alliances. Res Policy 36: 930-948

Bock G-W, Zmud R W, Kim Y-G, Lee J-N (2005) Behavioural intention formation in knowledge sharing: examining the roles of extrinsic motivators, social-psychological forces and organizational climate. Manag Inf Sys Q 29 (1): 87-111

Bourdieu P (2001) Razões práticas: Sobre a teoria da acção. Celta, Lisboa

Bowonder B, Racherla JK, Mastakar NV, Krishan S (2005) R&D spending patterns of global firms. Res Technol Manag 48 (5): 51-59

Bressand A and Distler C (1995) La planète relationelle. Flamarion, Paris

Brown J S, Duguid P (2000) The social life of information. McGraw-Hill, New York

Brown R (2000) Social identity theory: past achievements, current problems and future challenges. Eur J Soc Psychol 30: 745-778

Chesbrough H (2003) The era of open innovation. MIT Sloan Manag Rev 44 (3): 35-41

Chesbrough H (2003a) Open innovation: The New Imperative for Creating and Profiting from Technology. Harvard Business School Press, Boston, MA

Chesbrough H, Schwartz K (2007) Innovating business models with co-development partnerships. Res Technol Manag 50 (1): 55-59

Chesbrough H, Vanhaverbeke W, West J (2006) Open innovation: researching a new paradigm. Oxford University Press, Oxford

Chesbrough H, Crowther A K (2006) Beyond high tech: early adopters of open innovation in other industries. R&D Manag 36 (4): 229-236.

Cho H, Lee J-S, Stefanone M, Gay G (2005) Development of computer-suported collaborative social networks in a distributed learning community. Behav Inf Technol 24 (6): 435-447

Christensen J, Olesen M, Kjaer J (2005) The industrial dynamics of open innovation – Evidence from the Transformation of Consumer Electronics. Res Policy 34 (10): 1533-1549

Cohen WM, Levinthal DA (1990) Absorptive capacity: A new perspective on learning and innovation. Adm Sci Q 35 (1): 128-152

Coombs R, Harvey M, Tether BS (2003) Analysing distributed processes of provision and innovation. Ind Corp Chang 12: 1125–1155

Daneshgar F (2005) Awareness matters in virtual communities: an awareness ontology, In: Montano B, Innovations of knowledge management. IRM Press, Hershey

DiMaggio P (1997) Culture and congnition. Annu Rev Socio 23: 263-287

Dodgson M, Gann D, Salter A (2005) Think, play, do. Oxford University Press, Oxford

Duarte M (2007) Valor que vem de for a. Jornal de Negócios, Outubro 2007

Evans J, Brooks L (2005) Understanding collaboration using new technologies: a structurational perspective. The Inf Soc 20: 215-220.

Fernback J (2007) Beyond the diluted community concept: a symbolic interactionist on online social relations. New Media Soc 9 (1): 49-69, http://nms.sagepub.com. Accessed 21 Apr 2008

Fiore F (2007) Communities versus networks: the implications on innovations of social change. Am Behav Sci 50: 857-866.

Fowles S, Clark W (2005) Innovation networks: good ideas from everywhere in the world. Strat Leader 33 (4): 46-50

Gassmann, O (2006) Opening up the innovation process: towards an agenda. R&D Manag 36 (3): 223-228

Gassmann O, Enkel E (2004) Towards a theory of open innovation: three core process archetypes. Proceedings of the R&D Management Conference (RAMDA), Lisbon. http://de.scientificcommons.org/2287. Accessed 26 Apr 2008

Gassmann O, Enkel E (2005) Management mechanisms of network layers in MNE. Presented at the European Academy of Management (EURAM) 2005 Conference, Munich. http://www.scientificcommons.org/836. Accessed 26 Apr 2008

Giddens A (1984) The constitution of society: outline of the theory of structuration. Polity Press, Cambridge

Goffman E (1993) A apresentação do eu na vida de todos os dias. Relógio d'Água, Lisboa

Granovetter M (1973) The strenght of weak ties. Am J Socio 78: 1360-1380. http://www.stanford.edu/dept/soc/people/mgranovetter/. Accessed 25 Apr 2008

Granovetter M (2004) The impact of social structure on economic outcomes. J Econ Persp 19 (1): 33-50

Halbwachs M (1968) La mémoire collective. PUF, Paris

Hassan R (2003) Network time and the new knowledge epoch. Time & Soc 12 (2-3): 225-241. http://tas.sagepub.com/cgi/content/abstract/12/2-3/225. Accessed 24 Mar 2008

Hislop D (2005) Knowledge management in organizations: A critical introduction. Oxford University Press, Oxford

Huang J C, Newell S, Galliers R D (2002) Inter-organizational communities of practice, A research paper submitted to the Third Conference on Organizational Knowledge, Learning, and Capabilities, 5-6 Apr, Athens

Jedlowski P (2001) Memory and sociology: Themes and issues, Time & Soc 10: 29-44. http://tas.sagepub.com/cgi/content/abstract/10/1/29. Accessed 24 March 2008

Kafouros M, Buckley P, Sharp J, Wang C (2007) The role of internationalization in explaining innovation performance. Technovation 28 (1-2): 63-74

Katila, R (2002) New product search over time: Past ideas in their prime? Acad Manag J 45 (5): 995-1010

Kline SJ (1985) Innovation is not a linear process. Res Manag 28 (4): 36–45

Lambooy JG (2004) The transmission of knowledge, emerging networks, and the role of universities: an evolutionary approach. Eur Plan Stud 12 (5): 643-657

Laursen K, Salter A (2006) Open for innovation: The role of openness in explaining innovation performance among U.K. manufacturing firms. Strat Manag J 27 (2): 131-150

Lave J, Wenger E (1991) Situated learning: legitimate peripheral participation. Cambridge University Press, Cambridge

Lehaney B, Clarke S, Coakes E, Jack G (ed.) (2004) Beyond knowledge management. Idea Group Publishing, London

Lettl C (2007) User involvement competence for radical innovation, J Eng Technol Manag 24: 53-75. www.elsevier.com/locate/jengtecman. Accessed 23 Feb 2008

Limayem M, Hirt S G, Cheung C M K (2007) How habit limits the predictive power of intention: The case of information systems continuance. Manag Inf Sys Q 31 (4): 705-737

Lundkvist A (2004) User networks as sources of innovation. In: Hildreth P, Kimble C (ed) Knowlegde networks: innovation through communities of pratice. Idea Group, Hershey

Lundvall B (1992) National Systems of Innovation. Towards A Theory of Innovations and Interactive Learning. Pinter, London

Lundvall B (1988) Innovation as an interactive process: from user–producer interaction to the national system of innovation. In: Dosi G, Freeman C, Silverberg G, Soete L (ed) Technical Change and Economic Theory. Pinter, London

Massey A P, Montoya-Weiss M M (2006) Unraveling the temporal fabric of knowledge conversion: A model of media selection and use. Manag Inf Sys Q 30 (1): 99-114

Maxwell E (2006) Open standards, open source and open innovation: Harnessing the benefits of openness. Innov 1 (3): 119-176

Michaelides R, Kehoe D (2007) Internet Communities and Open innovation: an Information System Design Methodology", In 6th IEEE International Conference on Computer and Information Science (ICIS) 2007,IEEE-CS, Melbourne, Australia, 11-13 July

Mitchell J C (1974) Social Networks. Annu Rev Anthr 3: 279-99.

Moitra D, Krishnamoorthy MB (2004) Global innovation exchange. Res Technol Manag 47 (4): 32-38

Nan Lin (1999) Social networks and status attainment, Annu Rev Socio 25: 467-487

Nan Lin (2001) Social capital: A theory of social structure and action. Cambridge University Press, Cambridge

Nieto M J, Santamaría L (2007) The importance of diverse collaborative networks for the novelty of product innovation, Technovation 27: 367-377. www.elsevier.com/ locate/technovation. Accessed 24 Jan 2008

Oerlemans LAG, Meeus MTH, Boekema FWM (1998) Do networks matter for innovation? The usefulness of the economic network approach in analysing innovation. Tijdschr Econ Soc Geogr 89 (3): 298-309

Pavitt K (1998) Technologies, products and organization in the innovating firm: what Adam Smith tells us and Joseph Schumpeter doesn't, Ind Corp Chang 7 (3): 433–452

Perkmann M, Walsh K (2007) Relationship-based university-industry links and Open innovation: towards a research agenda. Int J Manag Rev 9 (4): 259-280

Perrons R, Platts K (2004) The role of clockspeed in outsourcing decisions for new technologies: insights from the prisoner's dilemma. Ind Manag + Data Sys 104 (7): 624-632

Postmes T, Spears R, Lea M (1998) Breaking of buinding social boundaries? SIDE-Effects of computer mediated communication. Comm Res 25 (6): 689-715.

Powell WW, Koput KW, Smith-Doerr L (1996) Interorganizational collaboration and the locus of innovation: networks of learning in biotechnology. Adm Sci Q 41(1): 116-145

Quinn JB (2000) Outsourcing innovation: The new engine of growth. Sloan Manag Rev 41 (4): 13-28

Rosenberg N (1982) Inside the Black Box: Technology and Economics. Cambridge University Press, Cambridge

Schmitt C, Fischbach K, Schoder D (2006) Enabling open innovation in a world of ubiquitous computing, ACM International Conference Proceeding Series, 181, Proceedings of the 1st international workshop on Advanced data processing in ubiquitous computing. ADPUC 2006

Schneider U (2007) Coping with the concept of knowledge. Manag Learn 38 (5): 613-633.

Short JA, Williams E, Christie B (1976) The social psychology of telecommunications. John Wiley & Sons, New York

Smith E R (2008) Social relationships and groups: new insights on embodied and distributed cognition, Leslie Marsh (ed.) Cogn Sys Res 9: 24-32. www.elsevier.com/ locate/cogsys. Accessed 30 March 2008

Snyder J (2000) E-Community Platform Ups Site Stickiness, InfoWorld 22 (24): 78

Thomsen L, Sidanius J, Fiske AP (2007) Interpersonal leveling, independence, and self-enhancement: a comparison between Denmark and the US, and a relational practice framework for cultural psychology. Eur J Soc Psychol. 37: 445–469, www.interscience.wiley.com. Accessed 28 Mar 2008

Törrö M (2007) Global intellectual capital brokering - Facilitating the emergence of innovations through network mediation, VTT Publications 631, Finland. http://www.vtt.fi/ inf/pdf/publications/2007/P631.pdf. Accessed 21 Mar 2008

Vigier P (2007) Towards a citizen-driven innovation system in Europe. Innovation: Eur J Soc Sci Res 20 (3): 131-202. http://dx.doi.org/10.1080/13511610701707359. Accessed 14 Dec 2007

Von Hippel E (1988) The Sources of Innovation: Oxford University Press, New York

Wang R, Rubenstein-Montano B (2003) The value of trust in knowledge sharing. In: Coakes E (ed.) Knowledge management: current issues and challenges. Idea Group, London

Wegner D M (1987) Transactive memory: a contemporary analysis of group mind. In: Mullen B, Goethals G R (ed) Theories of group behaviour. Springer-Verlag, NY

Weiser M (1991) The computer of the 21st century. Sci Am 265 (3): 94–104

Weldon M S, Bellinger K D (1997) Collective memory: collaborative and individual processes in remembering. J Exp Psychol: eLearning Mem Cogn 23: 1160-1175

Wellman B (2005) Community: From neighborhood to network. Comm ACM 48 (10): 53-55

Wellman, B (2002) Little boxes, globalization, and networked individualism. Center for Urban & Community Studies, University of Toronto, Toronto. http:// www.chass.utoronto.ca/~wellman/publications. Accessed 25 Apr 2008

West E, Vanhaverbeke W, Chesbrough H (2006) Open innovation: a research agenda. In: Chesbrough H, Vanhaverbeke W, West J (ed), Open innovation: Researching a New Paradigm. Oxford University Press, Oxford

Wood A F, Smith M (2005) Online communication: Linking technology, identity, and culture. Lawrence Erlbaum Associates, New Jersey

Zhu Z, Chen J (2006) Open innovation and Technological Learning in China, Engineering Management Conference, 2006 IEEE International

Chapter 5: A Model for Business Innovation in the Web 2.0 World

Nicole Radziwill (nicole.radziwill@gmail.com)

Network Roundtable at the University of Virginia – Charlottesville, VA, USA
National Radio Astronomy Observatory – Charlottesville, VA, USA

Ron DuPlain (ron.duplain@gmail.com)

ThoughtView Ltd. – Charlottesville, VA, USA
National Radio Astronomy Observatory – Charlottesville, VA, USA

Abstract

"How can Web 2.0 tools be used to catalyze innovation at my company?" Business models are changing rapidly, and companies must adapt to survive. Using a conceptual model of quality and innovation, this chapter examines how and why managers can use participative networking technologies to innovate, and then provides a roadmap for how to do it. The limitations of current technologies and the impacts of these limitations on future innovation are also explored.

1   What is Innovation?

To understand how Web 2.0 technologies can be used to innovate, the concept of innovation must first be illuminated. Innovation is the practice of making new concepts and ideas *relevant and useful* to individuals and communities of people. This contrasts with the process of invention, through which new ideas are generated while the linkages between these new ideas and existing ideas are simultaneously uncovered. Innovation defines the context of use, while invention does not. The products of innovation are fundamentally ideas, characterized by novelty, utility and relevance. However, the distinctive feature of innovation is that these ideas, once connected with a particular context of use, at once capture the potential to add value to systems, people, processes and even other ideas. Although new mechanisms for value creation can be unlocked through the innovation process, value is created when new products, services and processes are designed, through the integration of knowledge and the understanding of the capabilities of the organization that is poised to deliver that value. As a result, innovation is critically dependent not only on the people *doing* the innovating, but also on the networks of people *connected* to those innovators, whose influences inform and impact the process of discovery.

To examine this point, Hargadon (2003) looked at innovation from the historical context, seeking to understand how the interpersonal networks of innovators in the past have influenced critical advances. In one example, he describes the case of the incandescent light bulb. The innovation is largely attributed to Thomas Edison, who perfected the technology and made it possible for the product to be marketed and achieve widespread use. However, the contributions of Moses Farmer (who had devised a similar light as early as 1859) and Joseph Swann (whose experiments between 1850 and 1870 contributed to Edison's final design) were equally crucial. The dependence of Edison's incandescent light on the work of his predecessors is notable, but without linking that new technology to a context of use and helping people tap its utility, innovation may never have taken shape. This example shows that Edison did not act as the "lone genius" – but instead, mastered the dynamics of pulling together information from the network of people, objects, and ideas to make his light bulb a commercial success.

What happens once this information is available and assembled, and it is time to use it to link an invention to the context of use that will make it an innovation? Henderson & Clark (1990) proposed one model that illustrates the types of changes that can come together to form various degrees of innovation, from incremental to radical. A diagram of this model, shown in Figure 1, characterizes innovation in two dimensions: the effect of the innovation on "core concepts," and the effect of the innovation on the system through the links between these core concepts and "components".

Figure 1: One representation of the Henderson-Clark model of innovation.

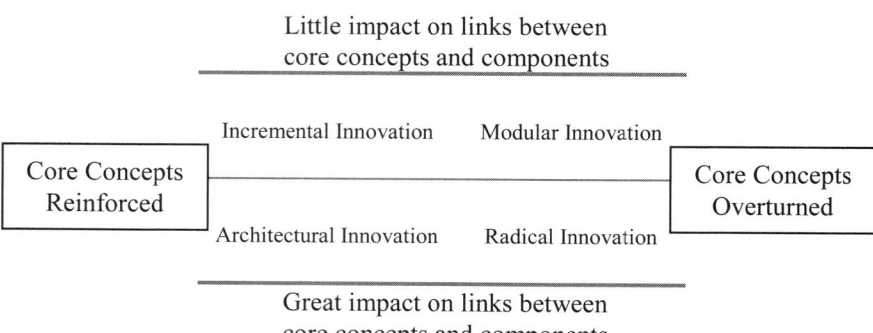

In the Henderson-Clark model, components have two distinctions: they represent fundamental design concepts, and they perform functions that are well defined. An example of a component is an automotive engine. This component is integrated with other components that manage distinct functions (e.g. transmission, brakes, steering) through a shared architecture that ultimately defines the vehicle you drive. The two key questions posed by the Henderson-Clark model to assess the impact of an innovation are: How much do the components change? How much do the changes in the components impact overall changes in the system?

By examining these two dimensions of innovation, four classifications of innovation arise which are distinguished from one another by the *degree of impact on the system*. These can be illuminated using the car example:

- **Incremental innovation**: Both core concepts and architectures remain the same. The introduction of the cup holder, climate control, and in-car entertainment systems can be considered incremental innovations.

- **Modular innovation**: Core concepts shift, but architecture remains the same or nearly the same. Changing from a manual transmission to an automatic transmission is an example of a modular innovation: one core concept is radically changed, but the gearbox function and the way the vehicle interfaces with the gearbox are essentially the same.

- **Architectural innovation**: Core concepts are preserved, but the way in which they are linked together changes. The introduction of the Sport Utility Vehicle (SUV), with large vehicles manufactured to drive like a car, represented an architectural innovation.

- **Radical innovation**: In this paradigm of innovation, both the components and the architecture change. A wheel-less hovercraft that could respond to its driver in all the same ways traditional cars do would be a radical innovation.

According to Hamel (2007), there are four levels of innovation that can be pursued and achieved by a company. In addition to innovating with respect to the business model itself, in which new approaches and technologies are combined to create unprecedented supply chains and new value webs, there are also opportunities for operational, product, and management innovations. **Operational innovations** involve streamlining and reengineering processes and procedures. **Product and service innovation** brings new features to existing products, create new offerings, and extend business into new markets. **Management innovation** involves finding answers to structuring the workplace so that new challenges, such as those posed by increasing globalization, an expanding global knowledge network, and shifting assumptions surrounding traditional trade-offs, can be effectively addressed. The Henderson-Clark model and Hamel's categories can be used together to help understand how to innovate in the Web 2.0 world.

2   The Continuum of Quality and Innovation

Understanding how these models for innovation can be applied in the context of Web 2.0 first requires understanding one of the key challenges of modern companies. Many organizations today *struggle to find a balance* between the efficiency that comes from implementing quality systems and managing for quality, and the creativity that must be cultivated within an organization to innovate for future competitiveness. Both quality and innovation are required ingredients for organizational sustainability. Over the past century, there have been many definitions of quality. Juran (1988) defined quality as "fitness for use," a product-centric definition which implies the notion of customer satisfaction within a specific context of use. The zero defects principle embraced by Crosby (1979) means that both products and processes must be *designed* to be defect free.

Despite the range of definitions, the goals underlying the pursuit of quality are the same: reducing variation, eliminating waste and rework, preventing human error, preventing defects, improving productivity, and increasing efficiency and effectiveness (Okes & Westcott 2003). Unfortunately, all of these definitions seem to leave one or more aspects of quality out, especially when the role of innovation is considered. For example, conformance to requirements is less useful if the requirements rapidly shift or are incomplete, and zero defects is a laudable goal for traditional manufacturing systems where processes are well known, but a less useful measure for unstructured problems where the definition of a defect could itself be emergent.

But quality and innovation are both fundamentally concerned with achieving excellence, and this is the distinction upon which managers should reflect as they develop their organization's innovation agenda. The following points summarize the relationship between invention, innovation, and quality:

- Invention is the process that *creates* ideas,
- Innovation makes those ideas *relevant to people and social groups*,
- The practice of design *transforms* the concepts so that they become actionable, meaning that the innovations can be built, manufactured and/or delivered to the interested parties, and
- Quality systems and continuous improvement enable *delivery* of the promises and potentials embodied by invention.

Achieving quality requires specific organizational and operational capabilities at one point in time, whereas innovation requires meeting future needs, and so identifying how current capabilities can either extend or transform to support quality at a later time is essential. Consumers are becoming progressively more sophisticated, with ever-increasing demands that translate into higher standards for quality, so organizations must strive to achieve high quality now. At the same time, they must build their internal organizational capabilities as well as their product and service offerings, anticipating and delivering to meet emerging and future needs. Although consumers are typically tolerant of lower quality for newly introduced innovative products, this tolerance fades with each new product generation. For example, consumers still bought Microsoft Windows Vista at its introduction despite high system requirements and issues with video handling and security. The ultra-lightweight MacBook Air continued to be on the market despite overheating and display quality issues. Also, the first generation iPods were market winners even though many considered the design to be cumbersome.

Customer perceptions of quality can not only be fickle, but also have far-reaching impacts. Mitra and Golder (2006) reported on a study of 241 different consumer products over 12 years, and found that "high reputation brands are rewarded three years quicker for an increase in quality and punished one year slower for a decrease in quality compared to low-reputation brands." For more durable products, such as automobiles, these researchers found that it could take up to 7 years for a substantial improvement in product quality to be perceived by the marketplace. Because Mitra has shown that prior expectations formed by a customer definitively influence the perceived quality of future products, this suggests that quality might influence how a customer will perceive emerging innovations. A reputation for quality can define and influence the market potential for innovations that reach the consumer.

An organization *must* pursue quality and innovation concurrently to be both effective and competitive. To focus on one without the other constrains an organization to live only in the present, or only in the future – and to be successful and competitive, an organization must strengthen its capabilities today while envisioning how its capabilities must adapt to the needs of tomorrow. Quality and process improvement efforts can complement innovation by reinforcing a consumer's perception of quality, thus facilitating the diffusion of innovations through the market and reducing the barrier for an individual to adopt and use an innovative product or service. Quality improvement activities (e.g. benchmarking, process improvement) can also *generate* the ideas that spawn breakthrough innovations.

To pursue quality and innovation simultaneously, it is important to conceptualize both as part of a dynamic process. Combining Schumpeter's (1942) outline of technological change as the combined process of invention, innovation and diffusion of technologies with the notion of technology transfer, and aligning this with Mitra's (2003) model for understanding how quality influences consumer perception and market performance, provides such a basis for understanding. Figure 1 illustrates this. For example, this representation shows that the antecedents of quality – the things that need to be in place in order for delivering quality to be possible – are driven by invention and innovation. An example of this would be how the continuous improvement processes implemented in organizations (e.g. performance evaluations, productivity improvement goals) can directly influence the way in which innovation is embraced by the corporate culture. The determinants of quality are those factors that enable a company to produce to specifications and with minimal variation, which can either make or break the prospects for technology transfer: if something cannot be consistently produced in a cost-effective way, it is unlikely that it will find a way into the marketplace.

The critical conclusion that can be drawn from Figure 1 is that *socially-oriented networks play a critical role in the pursuit of both quality and innovation*, and it is by providing a means to characterize and leverage these social networks that Web 2.0 technologies can provide an innovative advantage. Idea networks, for example, describe the linkages between concepts held by one or more people within a network of collaborators. Information networks describe the connections between individuals that are in place to share or disseminate knowledge. Energy or affect networks describe connections between people that either generate or inhibit enthusiasm and creativity. Media networks, supply chains and distribution networks also represent connections between suppliers, producers and consumers that are essential for the wide diffusion of innovative products, services, and technologies. Social networks also play a role, because people often learn from and listen to the knowledge and recommendations provided by their friends. Extensive information about social networks can be found in Cross and Parker (2004).

Figure 1: Combining Schumpeter's (1942) stages of innovation with Mitra's (2003) model for quality as a dynamic process reveals the roles that networks can play to facilitate innovation.

Relationship to Quality (from Mitra, 2003)	Antecedents of Quality		Determinants of Quality	Consequences of Quality
Stage of Technological Change	**Invention**	**Innovation**	**Technology Transfer**	**Diffusion**
New Ideas In →	Ideas combined & recombined / Ideas blended with experiences	Concepts linked with a context of use, and evaluated for viability	Operational systems prepared to deliver artifacts of innovation	Artifacts of Innovation Out (Products, Tools, Methods, Services) →
Capabilities that are integrated at this stage:	Internal and External Expertise	Organizational Strategy, Knowledge of External Environment, Design Capabilities	Production and Operations Capabilities, incl. Quality & Process Management	Value Proposition
Integration of capabilities determines:	Potential for Added Value	Utility, Applicability, Relevance of New Concept, Quality Requirements	Organization's Productivity, Effectiveness, Efficiency	Profitability, Customer Acquisition/Retention, Sales, Market Share, User Share
Types of networks involved:	Idea Networks, Information Networks, Social Networks	Information Networks, Energy/Affect Networks	Information Networks	Social Networks, Media Networks, Supply Chains, Distribution Channels
Typical network size (people involved):	1-10	10-100	100-1,000+	1,000-1,000,000+

3 The Relevance of Pervasive and Participative Computing

Pervasive computing, often called ubiquitous or mobile computing, describes a platform of computing that is part of everyday life -- those devices and technologies that are taken for granted, almost as though they are not computers or technologies at all. "They weave themselves into the fabric of everyday life until they are indistinguishable from it." (Weiser 1991) Participative computing connects people to other people, which can be enabled by the infrastructure provided by pervasive computing. Both concepts are essential ingredients in business innovation using Web 2.0 technologies.

3.1 Pervasive Computing

Previously relegated to laboratories and academic environments, pervasive computers have made their way into the pockets, purses, briefcases, and glove boxes of everyday people in the form of mobile phones, PDAs, laptops, and GPS navigators. (Cuff, Hanson, and Kang 2008) These devices often have similar, familiar interfaces to e-mail services, web pages, and other web-based services.

Pervasive computers connect individuals to their information. Mobile phones buzz with SMS (text message) reminders, PDAs beep with appointment reminders synced from laptop task managers, and Blackberries blink when new messages hit the inbox. While some are overwhelmed of the idea of always being connected, Weiser (1991) claims that "ubiquitous computers will help overcome the problem of information overload." Through pervasive computing, individuals can access information over time, in an on-demand or pull fashion, and can access the requested information from a wide selection of devices.

A decade ago, knowledge workers could only access an electronic knowledge base and e-mail while at the office on the local network. Today, organizations use pervasive computing to connect employees and clients to encrypted documents over secure web services and to e-mail through IMAP and web-based mail services. These services become increasingly pervasive as they migrate to text messages and tailored smart phone applications. What once could only be accessed by a few people in a few places can now be accessed by anyone virtually anywhere.

3.2 Participative Computing

Participative defines Web 2.0. "Web 2.0 is participatory, collaborative, inclusive, creator/user-centric, unsettled, and very information-intensive." (Dearstyne, 2007). Participative computing encapsulates these concepts and describes a computing platform – a participative network – which accomplishes the following three goals:

- engages users
- encourages interaction on multiple levels, and
- increases value through increased participation

Web 2.0 and participative computing are more than a collection of flashy web tricks. Asynchronous JavaScript and XML (AJAX, later called Ajax) provides a means for users' web browsers to asynchronously communicate with web servers to keep up-to-date without reloading an entire page within the browser. After its debut, Ajax became a very popular technique for web design, but it alone doesn't define participative computing. Instead, it simply enables users to more readily participate. Through Ajax, a user can open a web browser and over time, a web page can, in effect, update itself in the user's browser. This enables tools like instant messengers, collaborative drawing tools, and interactive photo albums to naturally live in a vanilla web browser. The Facebook web application (http://www.facebook.com) vividly illustrates how participative networks draw value through user participation. At its core, Facebook allows users to create profile pages about themselves (like a traditional college yearbook – sometimes called a facebook), to join networks which correspond to a school or a location, and to find and connection with friends. A user can set privacy limits on a profile, limiting access to accepted friends or to an entire network, leaving all others the permission to view just the name, thumbnail and general location of the user.

Imagine what little value Facebook would have to a user if that user if he or she were the only participant. The result would be a single thumbnail with a terse name and location. Even this might not be visible from a web browser without a valid Facebook login! Instead, Facebook draws significant value for itself and its users by growing its user base with new features and support for more social network locations. Users also grow the user base themselves through word-of-mouth advertising. In turn, the value of the entire network increases for all members. This pattern is sometimes referred to as Metcalfe's Law, after the researcher who originally discovered the relationship in telecommunications networks. Returning to the Facebook example, users are able to connect with more people when those individuals participate in the network, while Facebook is able to build stronger ad revenue. Facebook and its users engage in a mutually beneficial relationship.

The participative value of Facebook substantially increased when it launched its Facebook application framework, through which web developers could build custom add-on applications into the Facebook infrastructure. As a result, Facebook grew from a single web application to a wide collection of applications which take advantage of Facebook's participative computing network. By cultivating interdependence with its user community, Facebook is continually strengthening its potential for success over the long term (assuming that the company resolves its strategy for revenue generation).

3.3 From Pervasive to Participative Computing

Pervasive computing provides broad access to services, and participative computing connects people through those services. Google illustrated how pervasive applications can become participative when it launched its e-mail, talk, calendar, and document tools, collectively named Google Apps.

Through pervasive services, users could access their e-mail, calendar, and documents from any device connected to the Internet, but through Google Apps, users could send instant messages to other Gmail (e-mail) users, share events through Google Calendar, and collaborate on articles, papers, and spreadsheets with Google Docs. Traditionally, these services were mutually exclusive; Google Apps integrated these services and added participative value. A Google Apps user can easily share these services with every other Google Apps user. Because of this, Google Apps originally grew its user base by encouraging users to invite personal contacts to use the Google tools. Many similar services have followed suit.

Among participative computing networks, Facebook and Google Apps were early to include specialized interfaces for mobile devices, creating convenient pervasive experiences for their users and enabling active participation for users on the go. Through pervasive *and* participative computing networks, users can conveniently and reliable connect to information and each other from virtually anywhere through a heterogeneous collection of interfaces.

4   Using Web 2.0 to Stimulate Innovation

Web 2.0 technologies support participative computing; that is, unlike previous web technologies, these new utilities make it much easier for individuals to publish and share information, often in real time. Because Web 2.0 technologies stimulate and encourage interaction, and because pervasive computing technologies make it possible for people to interact with their networks and their computer systems more easily, the combined power of pervasive and participative computing should be acknowledged as a company seeks to innovate through Web 2.0. Web 2.0 technologies not only support innovation, but in fact the full process of technological change. These relationships, and how similar practices have been followed in other industries and throughout history, are summarized in Table 2. Several of the Web 2.0 technologies simply provide ways to streamline approaches to generating new ideas, processes, products and services – many of which have been practiced with success for years.

Table 2: Relevance of Web 2.0 technologies to innovation.

Web 2.0 Technology	Contribution to Innovation & Technological Change	Cultural/Historical Analog
Mashups	Enables "recombinant innovation" where two or more ideas are united to create a unique, synergistic concept	Elvis blends bluegrass, country and R&B to devise some of America's earliest "rock" music in the 1950's; Hollywood remakes foreign films with American actors (Hargadon 2003); In 2008, GEICO insurance and Mrs. Butterworth co-brand a television commercial.
Social bookmarking/ tagging	Enables recombinant innovation by providing a mechanism to more effectively label new content on the web with keywords, and identify linkages between ideas	Librarians, for decades, have been using tagging to describe new books according to the Dewey Decimal system and the processes of "copy cataloging" and "original cataloging" – which are functionally identical to social bookmarking.
Social networking Online Communities	Allows individuals to build, sustain, and monitor their networks of people, facilitating the invention process and diffusion of innovations	Kostoff (2006) recognizes two forms of innovation: literature-based, and workshop-based. Conferences that gather together people with shared interests are forms of workshop-based innovation. Both approaches require communities to be operable.
Blogs Wikis	Both blogs and wikis provide a platform to support invention and recombinant innovation, by providing a place for people to record their thoughts and opinions for present-day or future integration. This is no different than how collaboration on documents has been done in the past; wikis in particular provide a more streamlined platform	People keep journals, diaries, notes, and travelogues. Collaboration on documents has a long history, for example, the Declaration of Independence in the eighteenth century.
Syndication	Facilitates enhanced decision making by speeding the dissemination of information about pre-selected topics to people who want it; Web 2.0 technologies expand the concept so that anyone can syndicate and anyone can receive the information transmitted	Reuters, Associated Press, national television corporations (such as ABC, NBC, CBS) are historical examples; multi-level marketing and franchising also share some similarities, since these concepts involve expanding product and brand awareness using social networks.

5 Innovation with Web 2.x and Beyond

Despite the breadth of opportunities that Web 2.0 technologies make available for business innovation at the operational, product/service, and management levels, there are still many inherent limitations. The "next generation" of technologies, which we refer to as "Web 2.x", may address some of these issues. In the meantime, it is important for business innovators to recognize that simply integrating these new capabilities into a business will not provide instant success. Despite this fundamental challenge, managers can still improve their chances for success with Web 2.0 by understanding how their specific goals relate to the stages of technological change and their related social network types. The following methodology provides one approach, based on the innovation models from the literature, to guide the way.

5.1 A Methodology for Innovation with Web 2.0 Technologies

Because networks are so critical to innovation with Web 2.0, the decision process to form a solution for innovation involves first determining which networks are essential to the stage of technological change that you are primarily concerned with. The next phase involves identifying ways to develop, grow and sustain those networks by blending the implementation of pervasive technologies with participative technologies.

1. First, select a particular operational process, product or service, or management issue that you believe could benefit from a Web 2.0 enabled innovation solution. (If you have several candidates, it will be necessary for you to step through this process multiple times, as the technology solution to stimulate innovation may be different for each area.)

2. What stage of technological change are you, as a manager, concerned with right now in this area? It is possible that you need to stimulate one of the processes *adjacent* to innovation to stimulate innovation. Do you want to generate ideas (invention), or do you actually need to identify a context of use to unite those ideas with the people or groups who will benefit from them (innovation)? Do you need to find new, innovative ways to produce, release or deploy new product or service offerings (technology transfer)? Or, are you looking for better ways to use technology to expand your reach in the market, or to improve customer service (diffusion of innovations)?

3. Once the targeted stage of technological change for your operational process, product, service or management challenge is identified, the next step is to identify the *networks* associated with that stage. For example, from Figure 1, the innovation stage is associated with information networks (where people are connected to one another if they are valuable sources of information for one another), and energy or affect networks (where people are connected as a result of how much they stimulate creativity and enthusiasm within each other) typically having between 10 and 100 members. The goal for a manager is to identify which networks are important, and determine ways to build the network, grow its membership, and sustain interest.

4. Next, technology interventions to build, grow and sustain the network should be explored. What *technology components* support this network? What *architectures* support this network? Which components and architectures are effective in meeting the goals of developing the network, and which are not effective (or less effective)?

5. Based on this analysis, do the components or the architecture need to change to meet the goals of developing the network? Do both the components and the architecture need to change? These questions should be posed with both participative (Web 2.0) technologies and pervasive technologies in mind. The devices used to connect people to their information – as well as to provide information access, visualization, and data mining - are just as important as the mechanisms to connect the members of the network to each other.

6. When you know whether the components, the architecture, or both need to change to support the development of the relevant network, then you will be able to use the Henderson-Clark model to determine whether you are proposing incremental, modular, architectural or radical innovation. This is important as it will help you gauge the magnitude of the change management effort that will be required as an innovation is brought to life.

5.2 Limitations of Web 2.0

Participative technologies are, at their very essence, socially driven. No matter how advanced, powerful, or easy-to-use a Web 2.0 application is, if people don't use it, then it fails to deliver value as a participative product. That is to say, building a perfect Web 2.0 application isn't a technical problem so much as it is social problem -- the same social problem of active engagement which has frustrated leaders for centuries. Even though a person who believes that Web 2.0 bypasses this issue or is otherwise immune to it would be succumbing to a form of techno-utopianism; such "twopointopians" are not uncommon and managers should guard against embracing such viewpoints. What is the best approach to solving this problem? Weiser and Gold launched the ubiquitous computing program at IBM in 1988, wanting to "put computing back in its place, to reposition it into the environmental background, to concentrate on human to human interfaces and less on human to computer ones" (Weiser & Gold 1999). Those who invest in or develop participative computing networks will do well to focus on human-to-human interactions before considering human-to-computer interactions. Thus, Web 2.0 development spans information technology, social psychology, organizational analysis, and related disciplines.

Figure 2: A six-question methodology for innovating with Web 2.0 technologies and beyond.

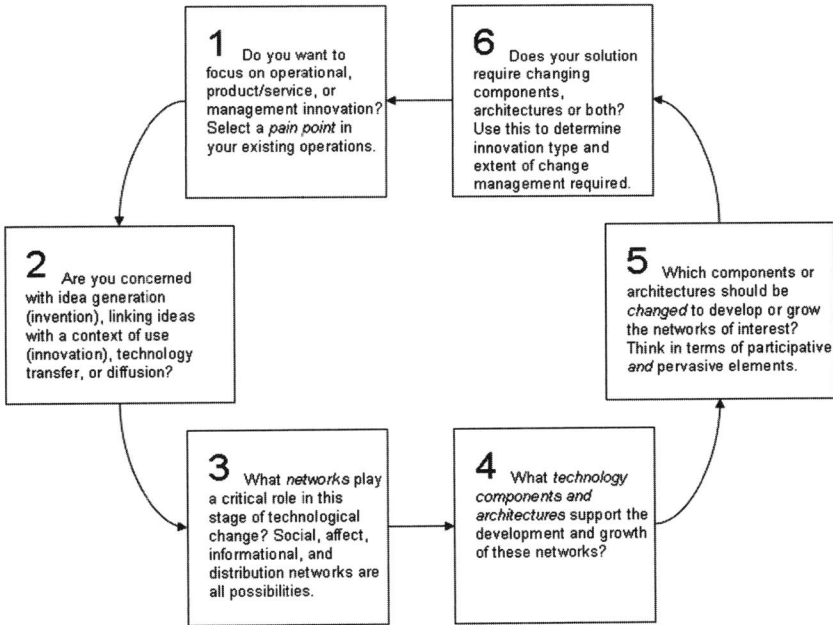

5.3 Web 2.x and Beyond

Pervasive and participative capacities of computing networks are likely to increase as the state of web design and implementation becomes comfortable with Web 2.0. At this point, incremental and modular innovations with the Web 2.0 technologies as a basis will lead to similar, yet more advanced, "Web 2.x" technologies. For example, the Ajax of Web 2.0 could incrementally and modularly shift into alternative application techniques (e.g., see web articles and discussions on "Ajax" and "Comet"). Later versions of Web 2.x (or even architectural innovations with the technology, which will lead to "Web 3.0") may not look or function anything like Web 2.0. As mobile devices become increasingly common, and as the infrastructure connecting these devices shifts, the future of advanced web technologies will certainly hold major architectural and radical changes.

Web 2.x technologies and beyond promise *more pervasive access to services and networks with new forms of participation*. Custom mobile device applications, such as those which debuted on the iPhone and the Blackberry, may move into the forefront of participative networks, leaving the web browser of yesterday to become just another alternative in the myriad of interface choices available for users. In the late 1990's, one of the major challenges encountered by organizations was the integration of established and emerging "customer touchpoints" – including the telephone, fax, e-mail and the web. In the future, companies will seek to accommodate a new variety of touchpoints, different types of technologies, and the prospect for cultivating interdependence between companies and customers will emerge. It is an exciting time for technology innovation.

References

Crosby, P. (1979) Quality is free. New York: McGraw-Hill.

Cross, R. L & Parker, A. (2004). The hidden power of social networks: understanding how work really gets done in organizations. Cambridge, MA: Harvard Business School press.

Cuff, D., Hansen, M. & Kang, J. (2008). Urban sensing: out of the woods. Communications of the ACM, 51(3), 24-33.

Dearstyne, B.W. (2007). Blogs, mashups & wikis, oh my! *Information Management Journal*, July/August 2007, 24-33.

Hamel, G. (2007). The future of management. Cambridge, MA: Harvard Business School press.

Hargadon, A. (2003). How breakthroughs happen: the surprising truth about how companies innovate. Cambridge, MA: Harvard Business School press.

Henderson, R. M., & Clark, K. B. 1990. Architectural innovation: The reconfiguration of existing product technologies and the failure of established firms. Administrative Science Quarterly, 35: 9-30.

Juran, J.M. & Gryna, F. (1988) Juran's Quality Control Handbook. New York: McGraw-Hill.

Kostoff, R. N. (2006) Systematic acceleration of radical discovery and innovation in science and technology. *Technological Forecasting and Social Change*, 73(8), 923-936.

Mitra, D. (2003). An econometric analysis of the carryover effects of quality on consumer

Mitra, D. and Golder, P.N. (2006) How does objective quality affect perceived quality? Short-term effects, long-term effects, and asymmetries. *Marketing Science*, 25(3), 230-247.

Okes, D. & Westcott, R.T. (2000). The certified quality manager handbook. Milwaukee, WI: Quality Press.

Schumpeter, J. (1942) Capitalism, socialism and democracy. New York: Harper Perennial.

Weiser, M. (1991). The computer for the 21st century. *Scientific American*, Sept. 1991, 94.

Weiser, M. & Gold, R. (1999). The origins of ubiquitous computing research at PARC in the late 1980's. *IBM Systems Journal*, 38(4), 693-697.

Chapter 6. Doing business by selling free services

Jose Luis Marín de la Iglesia

Gateway S.C.S. S.L., Paseo Zorrilla 89-1A, 47007, Valladolid, Spain, josmar@gateway-scs.es

Jose Emilio Labra Gayo

Department of Computer Science, University of Oviedo, C/Calvo Sotelo, S/N, 33007, Oviedo, Spain, labra@uniovi.es

Abstract   With the advent of the web 2.0 trend, there have appeared a great variety of services that are offered as free. Although the appearance of free services is not new, we consider that the popularity of these services in the Web 2.0 world is a relevant fact that has to be analyzed from an economic point of view. In this chapter we will give an overview of some of the business models that are present behind those services, like freemium, advertising, work exchange and mass collaboration. We will also present a case study, called EuroAlert, which contains a combination of the above models.

1   Introduction

Although it is not easy to provide a precise definition of Web 2.0, it is clear that there is a trend of web applications which are different from traditional web portals. Web 2.0 is more commonly characterized by a set of features that are shared by some web applications. The eight core patterns which have been characterized in [Musser, 07] can be summarized as:

- *Harnessing collective intelligence,* where the network effects of the architecture of participation produce software that gets better when more people uses it.
- *Importance of Data,* which means that the main value of these applications is the data sources that are managed in a unique, hard-to-recreate way.
- *Innovation in assembly,* the use of data and services which can be remixed by means of APIs, enabling the appearance of applications that create new opportunities and markets.

- *Rich user experiences,* that go beyond the traditional web-page metaphor obtaining rich user experiences combining desktop and online software.
- *Software above the Level of a Single Device,* means that some of these applications offer new experiences using Internet-connected devices
- *Perpetual beta,* which means that these applications break the old models of software development and adoption in favour of online, continuously updated software as a service models.
- *Leveraging the long tail.* Following [Anderson 06], most of these applications capture niche markets profitably through the low costs of production, distribution and access enabled by the Internet.
- *Lightweight models and cost-effective scalability.* The availability of lightweight software development models makes it easier to create new software products where the main singularity is marked by the quality of the innovation.

Apart of those core patterns, it is noticeable that under the Web 2.0 umbrella, some web applications have been very successful making money by offering services that are apparently free to end users. In this paper, we review these business models and offer a case study called EuroAlert which can be seen as a typical Web 2.0 business that follows a mixture of those models.

2   Web 2.0 Business Models: Leveraging the power of Free services

One of the most amazing things of this "web 2.0 era" is the appearance that every service you consume is for free. Once you enter the web you start using really complex-to-develop and high-maintenance applications and the subscription fees never show up in your credit card. Think for a moment in the bandwidth cost involved in running video sharing services like YouTube or the hosting bill that Wikipedia must be paying to provide the service for free for the millions of users that consume (or create) the articles daily. They do not even display ads with the content.

Of course you are paying a flat rate data plan to your network provider every month, but that seems to be everything. You may argue that there must be some kind of money flow you are not aware of but fortunately one of the foundation principles of the internet is network neutrality so there is not cost transfer between carriers and application providers (at least for the moment).

Main business models can be described as the exchange of money for services or products from the customer to the service provider or product retailer. That is the way a supermarket or a buffet of lawyers work and make their money. Of course there are promotions, trial periods, price shifting models and other well-kown practices in which businesses make money by giving away some things expecting you will buy others. But you will find very difficult to name a single company that provides you a service for free, and forever. There is not much sense in giving away things in traditional economies.

The internet, and most precisely the web, is changing some of the most important rules in traditional economics and some companies have proven very profitable by selling their services at zero. As this statement has not apparently much sense we will try to describe what are the four most important ways of giving away really valuable services for free and still make money, in some cases lots of it.

2.1 Advertising: like in Web 1.0 and the analog world?

In very few words, this well known business model is based on the building of an audience, or better to say in internet terms, a community, to which advertisers will want to offer their products or services. A company gets the attention and, even better, the participation of users by giving away high quality services in the form of tools, contents, applications or whatever you manage to prove useful for them. So it's not a two way exchange (between customer and provider), there is a third party (advertiser) who pays to participate in the exchange of free services.

You can argue that there is nothing new to the television or radio stations business model. When in the mid 90's the web started to be a place where everybody wanted to do business, although very few succeeded, advertising was the main tool companies tried to make money with. But as everybody knows the 2000 bubble burst proved this new economy model was a failure and most companies went bankrupt. Some of them had gone public recently, others were well established old economy corporations who made risky bets on the new internet promises, and other were small start-ups trying to rise some venture capital looking for a chance to go public. What all of them had in common was that they did not understand the power of the web and their approach was to import the practices and models of the mainstream media. Obviously it did not work for most of them and for a few years it seemed there was not a clear way to make money in this "new media" they considered the web was.

But as Google and others have taught us by their extremely successful figures and stunning growth rates, it was just a matter of finding how to, not that advertising was not made for the web. Although Google did not invent the concept of text-ads and cost-per-click, they must take the credit for making it succeed (Adwords) and then build the biggest Ad-Network (Adsense) in the Internet. They proved the model was right and Google became a major player in the internet, and in the toughest time, by giving away great applications and services at no cost for users, but running ads on them.

By now lots of companies are creating and experimenting with innovative ways to make money around publicity, like pay-per-post, pay-per-action or pay-per-connection among others. The rise of social networks, video sharing applications and other new services require new approaches that are now being imagined to attract and make valuable the growing expend of advertisers in the online world. We do not intend to discuss in depth contextual advertising or pay-per-click as concepts, but we think it is important to notice that the building of this ad-networks have lowered the barriers for both advertisers and publishers in such a way that a much bigger market has been created.

Lots of free internet services are now making their money by selling the participation of advertisers in their communities, as other tried in the 90s and failed. What is really new and makes the difference in this web 2.0 scenery is that every small local business can buy ads at a very small prize. And that every individual can monetize his small niche blog by selling ad space and it will make good money if his content is valuable.

2.2 Freemium: Premium users pay your bill

This business model is built around the existence of two types of users, a large base that consume the service for free and a small percentage who pay a subscription for the most advanced features of the service. In other words, the margin the companies get from the premium users pays the bill for the ones who consume the service for free. Of course this is a rough simplification of complex sceneries where you can find lots of combinations of multiple tiers of subscriptions with different levels of access to contents or services.

There are lots of examples like the LinkedIn social network, photo sharing services like Picassa or Flickr, or the famous and nearly impossible to replicate Craiglist classifieds. It is important to say that this business model is not equivalent to those models, mainly in the software industry, where you are granted with a trial period where you can evaluate the features and then you are required to pay a license if you want to continue using it. In the Freemium scheme, free users can get the service for free and forever, and the quality of service is good enough for most of the users that will never consider paying for the advanced service because they do not need it. Companies are also comfortable because the small percentage of users that will convert into premium, and pay the few dollars a year the average subscription is worth, is enough for a profitable business model.

This is one of the most common business models in the Web 2.0 world and one of those which also failed in the pre-bubble burst so we must take a closer look. There has not been a significant change in the way the model is being implemented in the Web 2.0 wave. There are not innovative approaches like in the advertising model we discussed previously, which make a difference. But there have been very significant changes in technology and society that have contributed to the success of a new generation of services that are doing good business in the web.

First of all we have the low price of average subscriptions that usually are in the range of a few dollars a year (20 to 100). This is mainly due to the drop of the costs involved in running the services, which now are much lower than a decade ago. Bandwidth, storage and processing are progressively becoming a cheaper raw material for digital services. So costs per user are really low when we go to the scale of thousands or millions of users, and thus to the subscription fees that can be charged.

The other significant change is that now there are thousands or millions of potential users for lots of internet services or applications. Most business plans in the 90s where not realistic in the reach they expected to achieve just because there was not a broad enough user base for them. Since then, a new generation that grew up with a laptop connected to the internet during high school and college is now in the market and they are consumers with the skills to use these web 2.0 services and, as digital natives, their lifestyle demands and needs them.

2.3 Work exchange: Free services in exchange of some work

In this business model, when you are using the service you are creating value for the company who provides it for free. Sometimes, it is a conscious act like when you vote in a news aggregator and you contribute with your knowledge, your experience or your opinion. Other times, it is the sole action in which you use it what is valuable enough not to charge you for the service. It is like you are doing some work for the company in exchange for the free use of the service.

There are especially curious examples like the Google-411 service, which is free with no limits. Directory assistance services are usually very expensive and companies charge high minute fees for each inquiry you do. Google is providing it at no cost and apparently they are not using their profitable advertising business model to subsidize it. The reason beyond is that the real value for them is the act in which each user is adding to their database unique ways of pronouncing and requiring information about businesses, addresses, etc. This information is really important for them, in order to improve their voice recognition technologies. They are compensating the users by providing a free directory assistance service because otherwise it would be very difficult to compile that data. Of course the model works when the companies obtain higher value in this way than charging the users for the service.

Slightly different, but in the same category we can discuss user generated content services like news aggregators. If you think in the model of services like the popular Digg, the community gets for free the most interesting stories without browsing thousands of online media sites in exchange for voting and sharing their preferred stories. If nobody takes the work of sending stories and voting those proposed by other members, the service would not exist. The "work" of each user is creating value for the service and the owner of the platform monetizes by selling ad space, sponsorships or any other way the community tacitly agrees. The final user benefits being better informed than reading a single source. For most people it is a fair exchange but the main question involved in this type of platforms for participation that are run by some one else who is profiting is if the revenue should be split to compensate the creators of the best contents. Some platforms provide affiliate programs to stimulate and incentive the participation of the community of users.

2.4 Mass Collaboration: Free because costs are nearly nothing

Around Web 2.0 platforms arises communities of users that agree in creating something (generally contents or software) by giving away their work with the condition that the service will remain free to everybody. In these categories we can include amazing results of mass collaboration like the Wikipedia and hundreds of open source projects of different size and quality, some of them outperforming in features and reliability its commercial equivalents.

Wikipedia is surely the best and biggest example to describe this model in which apparently there is no money involved. Everything related to mass collaboration started around software sharing and peer production practices, although the scale of people involved have reached new horizons with the Wikipedia project.

Software coders were the pioneers in leveraging the power of the new communication improvements that came with the spread of the internet to collaborate in creating better programs. Most of today's well-known open source software projects were started even before the Web 1.0 time, some even before the internet became commercial. And the new tools in the Web 1.0 time helped spreading ideas about peer production and pushed the foundation of dozens of communities around the idea of creating new and free software.

During this Web 2.0 wave most of the practices used and improved by developers to run their projects were transferred to other ways of creating things, from an encyclopaedia to a journal, written by volunteers. Of course, most of the tools used in these projects are open source, thus maintained for free. So we find people creating value for free in the web 2.0 with the tools that others agreed to create also for free.

When some people argue that this kind of behaviour sounds as unfair competition they should think in the broad and great innovation consequences of the sharing of software, knowledge or just data. In the case of Wikipedia the major cost of production would be the work of volunteers, sometimes really qualified ones, which do it for free. Hosting costs and the minimum staff of Wikimedia Foundation is supported with donations raised in a few campaigns a year. The value the users obtain by the existence of this incredible resource is impossible to measure, but surely this "gift economy" [Anderson 2008] is generating a huge amount in varied forms.

Although Open Source business models fit into this category the discussion would need a whole chapter. Open Source software is usually free of charge, there is not a license cost attached, but lots of companies like Red Hat, have founded successful businesses by charging users for support, deployment or customization services.

2.5 Subsidizing at a global scale

As you see there is no magic in the web, not even in the Web 2.0 and all is about cross-subsides, but not between products like in traditional economies. It is not that you are buying any other product when you enjoy your email service for free. Somebody else is subsidizing the "no cost" for you, not your other acquisitions like when you a get a 3x2 promotion at the supermarket. As a summary this table tries to simplify the scheme in which this four business models work:

Model	Cost	Who pays	Why
Freemium	0	Premium users	Better features
Advertising	0	Advertisers	Attention of community to its products or services.
Work exchange	0	Service provider or sponsor	Getting value from users
Mass Collaboration	0	Donators	Altruism
		Volunteers	Self-promotion
			Interest

We have not talked yet about the most obvious and controversial Web 2.0 business model, the one that involves the music and film industry. This is because we are not seeing a clear new business model there. Surely, entertainment industry is being deeply affected by changes in production and distribution costs driven by technology advances. We think zero-marginal cost consequences is not a business model itself as Chris Anderson documents in his taxonomy, but a factor that influences heavily the way the price has to be determined. As is well known in economy, price is usually more influenced by consumer psychology than by costs of production. When something can be copied and distributed at virtually no cost, what is the right prize? 1$ per DRMed song or free like RadioHead did recently? Anyway this discussion could last an entire book and it is not the purpose of this chapter.

Models around free software should be studied apart, although the distribution costs are affected the same way as in the music industry, the cost of production is very different and there are also evolution and maintenance costs involved.

3 A case study: EuroAlert.net

We will use Euroalert.net as an instrumental case study [Stake, 1994] in order to provide insight into the issues described in theory about Web 2.0 business models. While the main concepts of the four business models selected have been discussed with a few examples of very famous "pure" web 2.0 services or companies like Wikipedia, Flickr or Youtube, in this section we will provide a smaller service.

We have two main reasons why we have chosen Euroalert.net to develop this case study. First of all it is representative for three of the four business models described in theory and it is planning to launch features based on the fourth. Secondly, it is owned by a very small sized company, which is one of the trends of Web 2.0 where small innovators have an opportunity to compete with the big guys.

3.1 Free information and contents about the European Union

Euroalert.net (ISSN 1988-3382) is an internet property of Gateway S.C.S. S.L. that has been providing specialised contents and information about the European Union for nearly ten years. During this period, the business model which has been used by the company who owns the service to monetize has varied notably. As a result of years of experience Euroalert.net holds more knowledge and provides more sophisticated services in this Web 2.0 era than ever before and tries to leverage the "power of free" in various forms to make a profitable business model.

The main contents offered for free in Spanish and in English to users from all around the world are daily news about European Union affairs, the compilation of all initiatives and calls for proposals to get founds for projects, and the calls for tenders and commercial opportunities published in the Official Journal.

Additionally Euroalert.net provides EuroalertSearch, a specialised search engine about EU related resources in the Internet, and a weekly newsletter with a summary of the most important information published during the week. All of the above are for free. Publishing reliable information daily in two languages is a really big effort for a small company, so there is no sense in giving it away for free for its thousands of users if it could not be monetized somehow.

3.2 From printed magazine to free digital web 2.0 services

At the end of the 90s, while the internet in Spain was walking from the academic environments to the commercial world, Euroalert was a fortnightly paper magazine. It was edited by a small company that carefully printed, folded and delivered to subscribers by ordinary mail. It was some kind of craftsmanship. That was the first business model applied, direct sell to subscribers. Of course, its print run was very small and it was geographically concentrated.

When internet gained users, the subscribers demanded immediate information and Euroalert turned into a digital publication were users did not have to wait for the two-week editorial cycle. They could log in and benefit from daily updates, just as any typical Web 1.0 information portal. That was a big step and a significant cut in costs and thus in subscription fees. The number of users also increased significantly and the evolution of the business model proved successful in the new digital world.

In 2007 Euroalert.net indexed into major search engines its ten year archive, launched an international version updated daily in English and became a free service for everybody. That was a big bet for a small company that resigned the subscription incomes and started to give away one of its most valuable assets, its carefully compiled archive of European Union information. Of course there was a reason behind this apparently strange move so we will now describe the four web 2.0 models applied to monetize the service in the next few pages.

3.3 In exchange of some work

First Euroalert.net opened an API with some tools and small applications, widgets in Web 2.0 language, than can be easily installed in other web sites or blogs to communicate with Euroalert services. The Euroalert.net community, carefully built during last ten years, embraced the new vision with curiosity and installed the widgets, mashing up with their own sites. When a website or blog installs a Euroalert.net widget, it improves the service provided to their users by offering specialised and better updated contents or complex services like euroalertSearch.

In exchange of giving away the contents, coding and updating the API and the widgets, and providing support, Euroalert.net obtains two valuable things from the work of the users. First the spread of the brand as the Euroalert logo is attached to many more sites related to the community of users interested in European Union affairs, who are in fact the main clients of the subscription services. The second and more valuable thing is the learning that the Euroalert.net team gets from the use of the free service. The questions and issues received by the support team and the feedback for the marketing team when they communicate the free service is a very valuable asset to improve the commercial version of the widget, for which euroalert.net charges a fee. Another advantage is, of course, that a percentage of the users become subscribers when their needs grow.

3.4 Freemium

The commercial version of the widget that displays automatically European Union information in other websites and blogs by communicating to the API provides extended features, and subscribers are charged with a small monthly fee. In this version, called Euroalert One Web Full Content, there is no branding and the subscriber displays the complete content inside his website. This way Euroalert is transparent to the final user and the subscriber takes credit of the valuable information displayed as all the links are internal to the widget. The Freemium approach is the major source of revenue for Euroalert.net and the way the free services are possible, thanks to the users that pay the subscription.

The scale lets subscribers being more competitive buying the licenses for displaying the contents than creating and updating them by themselves. As an example, in the case of calls for tenders and commercial opportunities at European Union, Euroalert provides daily updates of this information that are highly valuable for lots of companies. At least one person in the average subscriber company, before using Euroalert services, daily browsed the official journals in order to extract the opportunities relevant to their organisations and then sent them internally to the people who must decide if it is worth to apply. The process is quite inefficient as many people and several forwarded emails are involved so the value proposition of Euroalert One Web Full Content is welcomed once it is showed to organisations.And as a matter of scale the price of subscriptions is very low so companies automatically become more competitive by installing in their intranets, filtering the information and targeting to the specific persons who must make the decisions. Additionally the final person can see the information at the moment they go into the office and not several hours or days after, and the organization save the resources they were expending in browsing and filtering the information. Other times the client is an association that provides the same service for its affiliates as they are not big enough to get the service individually.

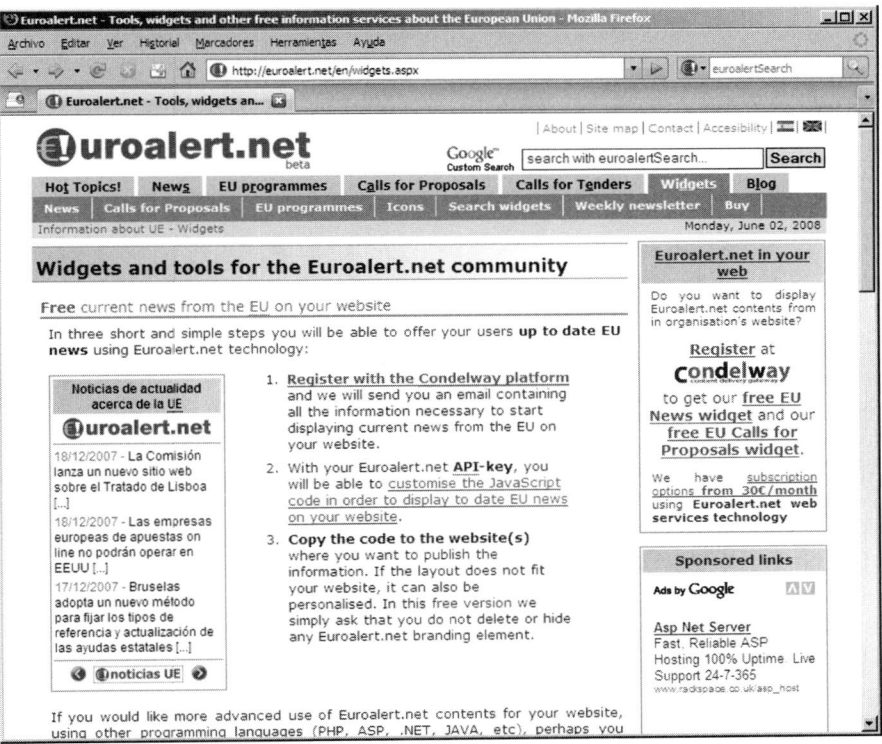

3.5 Advertising and Sponsorship

As every niche community Euroalert.net is very appealing to advertisers so it sells the advertising space to monetize as described in theory. At launch Euroalert.net affiliated to a broadly spread ad-network as Google's Adsense so it was possible to start selling ads even when the number of visits was very low. Although this networks conversion rates are lower than direct ad selling, it is really difficult for a small website to negotiate specific sponsorship contracts when they do not have the attention of a good number of users to trade with. Once the site becomes relevant to a community, sponsors usually come by themselves to buy the attention built.

Euroalert.net combines both ways of monetizing ad space, both general ad-networks and specific sponsorship contracts, usually from projects financed by the European Union that must disseminate results. The only condition to accept them in Euroalert is that ads must be both non intrusive and highly relevant to users. In this way, it is possible to maximize the revenue because users do not think of ads as something disturbing but helpful as they are able to know products and services relevant to them.

3.6 Mass collaboration

At this moment Euroalert does not provide any feature that fits formally into this category as described in theory. We can consider a primitive form of mass collaboration the case when a user sends a story to editors in order to promote their projects, activities with the aim of getting some attention from people interested in European Union affairs. This way Euroalert benefits from free highly relevant contents that monetizes by the three previously described models.

Anyway, as a demand of the community, Euroalert.net is planning to go more social and is developing features to create user generated contents that otherwise would not be viable and that are highly relevant to the community. For example Euroalert.net is now developing a directory of European Union projects where consortiums can fill in and update their information in order to promote their activities. All this information will also be free for users so the creators get free publicity and Euroalert.net more relevant contents than can be monetized with other business models.

This is the less developed model to the moment but the one with higher possibilities as it is only limited but by the imagination and the ability to catch the community, of course offering them something to win.

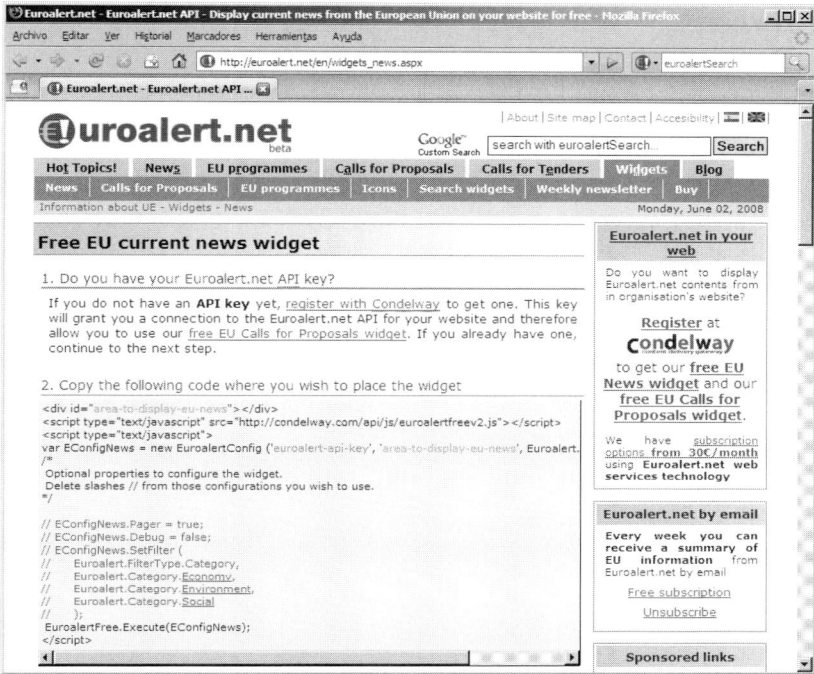

4   Conclusions

In this paper we have reviewed the four main business models of Web 2.0 applications. It may seem surprising that companies are gaining money by delivering services at no-cost for the final users. However, it is a reality that has mainly emerged with the Web 2.0 trend and it is necessary to know the intricacies of this subject.

As a case study, the Euroalert.net service offers a hybrid business model that combines the main ones. It opened an API in order to interoperate with other internet services and distribute its contents via widgets and web services. The service is run by a small company and offers free services for common users, while it charges subscribers with small fees. We consider that most of the Web 2.0 services offer a similar approach to be profitable while offering a free service to end users.

In the near future, Euroalert is planning to launch services that will improve the application of the fourth business model, by providing new community and participation services that are under development at this moment.

References

Anderson, Chris (2006) The Long Tail: Why the Future of Business Is Selling Less of More. New York: Hyperion. ISBN 1-4013-0237

Anderson, Chris (2008) Free! Wired Magazine URL: http://www.wired.com/techbiz/it/magazine/16-03/ff_free

Batelle, John (2005) The Search: How Google and Its Rivals Rewrote the Rules of Business and Transformed Our Culture. London: Portfolio. ISBN 1-59184-088-0

Chesbrough, Henry (2006) Open Business Models: How to thrieve in the new innovation landscape. Boston:Havard Business School Press. ISBN: 1-4221-0427-3

Lessig, Lawrence (2006) Code version 2.0. New York: Basic Books. ISBN 0-465-03914-6

Musser, John (2007) Web 2.0: Principles and best practices. O'Reilly Radar

Stake R.E. (1994) in Handbook of Qualitative Research, edited by Denzin N.K. & Lincoln Y.S. (1994), Sage London

Tapscott, Don / Williams Anthony D. (2006) Wikinomics: How mass collaboration changes everything. London: Portfolio. ISBN 978-1-59184-138-8

Chapter 7. Webstrategy Formulation:
Benefiting from web 2.0 concepts to deliver business values

Senoaji Wijaya

Institute of Information and Computing Sciences, Utrecht University, The Netherlands

Marco R. Spruit

Institute of Information and Computing Sciences, Utrecht University, The Netherlands

Wim J. Scheper

Strategy, Finance, and Operations, Deloitte Consulting, The Netherlands

Institute of Information and Computing Sciences, Utrecht University, The Netherlands

Abstract

With the accelerating growth of internet users, an increasingly rising level of globalization, distributed work environments, knowledge-based economies, and collaborative business models, it becomes clear that there is currently a high and growing number of organizations that demand a proper webstrategy. The emergence of web 2.0 technologies has led many internet companies, such as Google, Amazon, Wikipedia, and Facebook, to successfully adjust their webstrategy by adopting web 2.0 concepts to sustain their competitive advantage and reach their objectives. This has raised an interest for more traditional organizations to benefit from web 2.0 concepts in order to enhance their competitive advantage. This chapter discusses the effective webstrategy formulation based on the web 2.0 concepts in (O'Reilly 2005) and the differing requirements, characteristics, and objectives in different types of organizations. This research categorizes organizations into Customer Intimacy, Operational Excellence, and Product Leadership, according to the Value Disciplines model in (Treacy and Wiersema 1993).

Keywords: web 2.0, webstrategy, framework, mass collaboration, globalization, business model, value disciplines

1 Introduction

The growth of internet usage has been increasing tremendously in the past years. Illustratively, Internet World Stats (2007) reports that there are approximately 1.25 billion internet users in the world., 210.5 million internet users in the United States, 493.1 million internet users within European Union countries, and 459.5 million internet users in Asia. Also, a significant number (73.3%) of the entire population in the Netherlands makes use of internet technology. These statistics show the importance of the internet which connects billions of people, that there is a big potential market in there (the internet community itself) and is one of the triggers of the emergence of internet businesses nowadays. This accelerating growth shows the opportunity to enhance one's businesses through a good webstrategy.

Many new internet companies have been developed in recent years. Some are really successful, while others are still struggling to attract users by providing their unique selling points. Most of the successful internet companies tend to build and grow a web community. The increasing importance of business communities confirms that there is a shift in business models from a traditional hierarchical system and competition into more collaboration and social networking, which are considered to be two of the most important web 2.0 concepts (Benkler 2006, Chesbrough 2006, Tapscott and Williams 2006).

Web 2.0 is defined as "the philosophy of mutually maximizing collective intelligence and added values for each participant by formalized and dynamic information sharing and creation" (Hoegg et al. 2006: page 13). Web 2.0 revolves around seven key concepts introduced by O'Reilly (2005), which are intensively used in this chapter. Next to web 2.0 concepts, the term "web 2.0 features" is also used occasionally in this chapter. While the concepts can be referred to as high level web 2.0 principles, the features are referred as web 2.0 technologies or functionalities in the context of this work. Examples of web 2.0 features are wikis, weblogs, user ratings, RSS feeds, and podcasting. The seven web 2.0 key concepts are discussed in section 5.

Many practitioners are currently debating and exploring the subject of web 2.0 and its implications for all kinds of reasons. An interesting and currently much highlighted prospect for web 2.0 is to aid organizations to enhance their businesses by sustaining their competitive advantage (Gilchrist 2007). Web 2.0 has been successfully adopted by many of the successful internet companies, such as YouTube, Amazon, Wikipedia, and Facebook. They are able to grow and maintain their big web communities by applying web 2.0 concepts in their webstrategy (O'Reilly 2005). Therefore, the following research question arises: "*how can more traditional organizations benefit from web 2.0 concepts?*".

This chapter investigates this research question regarding the formulation of webstrategy benefiting from web 2.0 on any type of organization. The next section elaborates on the business IT alignment to show the importance of IT role and its alignment in the business to create values. Section 3 explains the organizational development to globalization and a knowledge-based economy, which includes the significance of information and knowledge for value creation in this twenty-first century. In respond to this, the business model adaptation is necessary. The collaborative business model is introduced in section 4, where the need of peer-production and knowledge sharing is discussed. Then, the webstrategy framework's composition and its operation in effective webstrategy formulation are explained in section 5. Finally in section 6, conclusions are presented.

2 Business IT Alignment

Ever since the emergence of Information Technologies (IT), organizations have been having difficulties in finding evidence of tangible assets that are delivered by IT to the organization's performance (Brynjolfsson and Hitt 2000). Research findings over past decades indicate that there is inconsistent evidence that IT leads to significant increases in productivity (Brynjolfsson 1993). For example, Bordoloi et al. (1998, 2000), Cook (1999), and Kauffman (1989) show that an increased IT investment results in lack of productivity. Explanations for these research findings include management failure to leverage IT's potential (Dos Santos and Sussman 2000), ineffective implementation (Dehning and Stratopoulos 2000), incomplete measurement of performance (Bharadwaj et al. 1999), and the presence of a time lag between IT investments and performance effects (Barua et al. 1995, Patnayakuni et al. 1996).

Nonetheless, it is believed that IT with its relation to other business dimensions helps to sustain and enhance performance, as well as augment a firm's competitive advantage. In search for the solutions of this IT productivity paradox, Scheper (2002) developed the Business IT Alignment (BITA) model. This model, states that:

- The business domain contains more dimensions than just strategy and organizational processes. Those dimensions are Strategy & Policy, Organization & Processes, Information Technology, Monitoring & Control, and People & Culture.
- Business IT alignment is about multi-dimensional alignment and adaptation
- A model should contain elements that are measurable as performance indicators

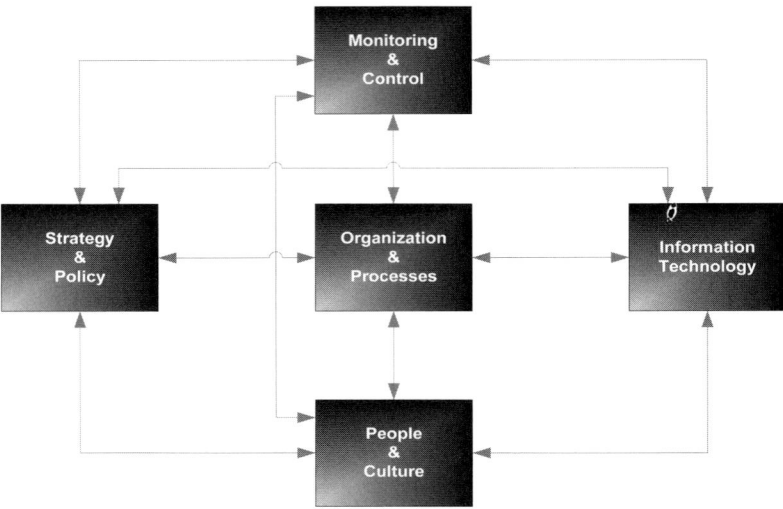

Fig. 2.1 The Business IT Alignment Model (Scheper 2002)

The hypothesis states that the maturities of all business dimensions are equally measured and the multi-dimensional balance between business maturities is basically measured by a factor called (business-IT) alignment. Then it is expected that organizations with higher alignment scores significantly outperform their competitors and improve their performance over time (Beukers et al. 2005, Scheper 2002). Scheper (2002) has confirmed this hypothesis by conducting a benchmark study over 265 organizations in The Netherlands. The result is supported by Batenburg and Versendaal (2004, 2006), who emphasize that the performance of an organization is positively related to the maturity of all dimensions and the alignment of these five maturities. Furthermore, the deployment of new IT systems is often a trigger for improving the business (Peppard and Ward 1999, 2003).

3 Organizational Developments

Organizations nowadays have to adapt to and deal with fast-paced changes in order to effectively continue pursuing their business objectives. In order to do so, effective and efficient information flows within and from the environment into the organization is required. This is supported by Harris (2002) who asserts that organizational and communicative processes involve ongoing changes in order to organize activities. This specifically counts for organizations operating in this twenty-first-century business environment. The fast-changing pace of today's dynamic environment pressures organizations to adapt to these changes by reconsidering its structures, processes, and relationships with its clients, competitors, and partners.

This implicates that organizational and communicative processes need to be adapted as well (Gallois et al. 2004).

Notable changes that have been identified up until now, and which are deeply connected to web 2.0 concepts, include the following observations:

- Globalization is continuously rising. More and more, organizations need to be able to operate in an increasingly complex environment (Chesbrough 2006, Daft 2004, Tapscott and Williams 2006)
- The movement towards a distributed work environment is greater than ever before (Brown et al. 2001, Dennis and Kinney 1998, Kakihara and Sorenson 2002)
- There is a shift towards a knowledge-based economy in which knowledge and information are the primary sources of value creation (Jashapara 2004, Nurmi 1998)

These continuous changes drive organizations to adapt their business model whenever necessary. The globalization, the movement towards a distributed work environment, and the shift towards a knowledge-based economy in which knowledge and information are considered to be the most important aspects of an organization's capital, have tickled the interests of many researchers and practitioners on the benefit and implementation of web 2.0 concepts in every type of organizational context.

3.1 *Globalization and Distributed Work Environment*

Recent technological advances, such as the emergence of the internet and other computer networks that connect billions of people, have pushed organizations toward the globalization era and enabled them to operate in an increasingly complex working environment. They are now able to provide their products and services to one global market. In order to outperform their competitors, organizations should think globally and work collaboratively with their chain partners (Tapscott and Williams 2006). This means that the environment and the work for organizations are becoming more complex and require greater coordination and interaction (Gallois et al. 2004). Thus, the right processes and structures to gain maximum benefits while minimizing the disadvantages are desired (Daft 2004). These processes and structures are more likely organized in a flat design and consist of employees that are highly empowered and involved in the business activities.

Using advanced technologies which support globalization and the increasing necessity, individuals and organizations are more willing and have more abilities to be mobile. This mobility development influences not only organizations but also the entire society (Kakihara and Sorenson 2002), and is supported with the emergence of advanced information and communication technologies which have enabled organization's employees to work together while being spatially and temporally decoupled from one another (Garud et al. 1999). From this point, employees and organizations are required to develop the 24x7 and flexible work culture, which means that the employees can work and collaborate at any time and from anywhere, and therefore, the right set of IT resources are needed. One of the effective solutions is by having the web as a single universal platform that ties everything together and that is accessible at anytime from anywhere. As a result, the changes in the organization's requirements to maintain a high level of communication are inevitable (Nurmi 1998). Web 2.0 concepts, as one of the IT resources, can be employed to help enable such an organizational environment.

3.2 Knowledge-Based Theory of the Firm

Knowledge is considered to be a special strategic resource that does not depreciate in the way traditional economic productive factors do. This kind of resource is intangible and dynamic (Bontis and Curado 2006). The Resource-Based View (RBV) of the firm has been introduced as a theory that examines the resources and capabilities necessary to generate above-normal rates of return and sustainable competitive advantage (Oliver 1997). Barney (1991) argues that the resources leading to competitive advantage must be scarce, valuable, durable, and difficult to imitate. The origin of all tangible resources lies outside the organization, therefore, the competitive advantage of an organization will most likely come from the intangible organization-specific knowledge that allows it to uniquely add value to the resources, procured from outside (Spender 1996).

Knowledge-Based Theory of the firm is an extension of the RBV of the firm, which provides a strong theoretical underpinning for the organization learning and intellectual capital researchers. This theory suggests that knowledge-based resources or intangible assets are the most important assets for realizing competitive advantages (Grant 1996).

3.3 Knowledge-Based Economy

Drucker (1992) defines a knowledge-based economy as an economical situation in which information and knowledge are largely recognized as important capitals of the industries. This new economy is also recognized as the information economy (Benkler 2006). The shift from post-industrial economy to this new economy can already be seen in this global market that requires organizations to adapt knowledge and organizational capabilities in their long-term strategies (Grant 1996). Organizations might choose market mechanisms to coordinate production and services rather than hierarchical governance (Penz and Sinkovics

2005, Williamson 1979). Moreover, in this economy, the development of information and communication technologies has taken a huge leap. Information is digitized and the revolution of communication technologies has led to many developments where knowledge is captured, organized, stored, shared and evaluated. Knowledge is considered an increasingly important source of wealth creation and competitive advantage for organizations (Chesbrough 2006, Donaldson 2001, Tapscott and Williams 2006). From this perspective, it should come as no surprise that knowledge-intensive organizations continue to emerge ever more frequently.

3.4   Web 2.0 Implications

The organizational development and new economy have been discussed in the previous sections. These facts have tickled our curiosity on how web 2.0 concepts can serve organizations in this knowledge economy and globalization era. In this era organizations require to accommodate the increasing needs of collaborative efforts, because coordination of their activities eventually determine their own success. The web 2.0 in itself emphasizes on user collaboration and participation, as well as using the web as a single universal platform to facilitate the organization's activities that enable collaboration at anytime from anywhere (O'Reilly 2005). Thus, an effective web 2.0 solution may help organizations to provide these needs.

4   The Business Model

A business model is a method of doing business by which a company can sustain itself and generate revenue (Rappa 2005). However, Hoegg et al. (2006) argue that this definition does not provide insights into the components of business models and, thus, does not provide a foundation for a systematical analysis of the activities of an organization. According to Timmers (1998), a business model is an architecture for the products, services and information flows, including a description of various business actors and their roles, a description of the potential benefits for the various business actor, and a description of the sources of revenues.

Chesbrough (2006) supports this definition by describing a business model as a useful framework to link and convert ideas and technologies into economic values. He asserts that every company of any size has a business model, whether that model is articulated or not. Alongside other things, a business model performs two important functions: *value creation* and *value capture* (Chesbrough 2003, 2006). Value creation is performed by defining a series of various activities throughout which values are created. The organization, then, develops the model of the products and/or services based on the values that are captured from a portion of these activities.

4.1 Business Model Adaptation

In order to thrive in this twenty-first century with its globalization and knowledge-based economy, the value creation and value capturing activities (generally the business model) of the organizations are required to be adapted and improved (Chesbrough 2006).

A business model not only has to be developed, but it also has to be managed and improved overtime. However, the activities of managing and improving a business model are considered risky and uncertain, especially when a business model has been around for decades within an organization. This is due to the fact that changes made in the business model may lead to additional risks. Nevertheless, there are leading organizations that have been able to foster change in their business models. This is usually done by responding to major shifts in the markets or by benchmarking the best practices of successful competitors (Chesbrough 2006). Thus, business model improvement or adaptation is proven possible, yet, how and where to improve their business models should be studied and discovered further according to their particular situation.

4.2 Collaborative Business Model

When we hear the word "collaboration", some of us might think of the image where several individuals sitting together, having a good discussion and working together to achieve their objectives. However, collaboration in the current context means something significantly different. This type of collaboration aims at harnessing collective intelligence through peer-production, in a more effective and efficient way than ever before (Tapscott and Williams 2006). This peer-production concept is starting to displace the traditional corporation hierarchies as the main system of wealth creation in the economy.

The most recent business model improvement in today's business environment is to involve key suppliers and customers in the value creation and value capturing activities as the business partners of the organization, entering into a relationship where both technical and business risks are shared (Batenburg and Rutten 2003, Chesbrough 2006). This improvement is shifting the economy from the industrial information economy, which typified information production since about two decades ago until recently, into a "networked information economy" (Benkler 2006). The remarkable characteristic of a networked information economy is that decentralized individual action, carried out through participation, plays a much more important role than it ever did in the industrial information economy. This has led to the facts that many of the resources for effective information production and communication are now owned by and available to much bigger communities and provide more possibilities of mass collaboration than they were and ever did before (Benkler 2006, Tapscott and Williams 2006). The individual freedom to cooperate with the others in creating economic value is no longer limited to certain geographical area and timeframe.

Furthermore, the collaborative business model is characterized by the following: (Benkler 2006)

- Nonproprietary information is becoming more common and important in the information production.
- The use of continuously expanding computer network that connects billions of people from everywhere, which provides a platform where the aggregate effect of individual action produces the coordinate effect of a new and rich information environment.
- The rise of the effective and large scale cooperative peer-production of information, knowledge and culture.

These characteristics fit very well with the characteristic of the open business model that is described by Chesbrough (2006). Being "open" means that the organizations require to open up their business models to let more external ideas and technology flow in from outside the organization and allow more internal information and knowledge to flow from the organization. By using external ideas in their own business and letting other organizations use their ideas, the growth of innovation becomes faster than ever with lower cost and shared risks. This is also supported by the new competitive concepts such as openness, peering, sharing, and acting globally (Tapscott and Williams 2006).

In this age of collaboration, communities of individuals and small producers are allowed to cocreate products, share their views and information in many ways. Communication and collaboration patterns, as well as information consumption and production are reshaped (Hoegg et al. 2006, Kolbitsch and Maurer 2006). Tens of millions of people are blogging nowadays and individuals are willing to contribute to social media, such as Wikipedia, YouTube, and Flickr, or to be a part of social network communities like MySpace. Table 4.1 illustrates the accelerating number of contributors and articles in Wikipedia, the free encyclopedia, since January 2001.

Table 4.1 Contributors to Wikipedia, January 2001 – June 2005 (Benkler 2006)

	Jan. 2001	Jan. 2002	Jan. 2003	Jan. 2004	July 2004	June 2005
Contributors*	10	472	2,188	9,653	25,011	48,721
Active contributors**	9	212	846	3,228	8,442	16,945
Very active contributors***	0	31	190	692	1,639	3,016
No. of English language articles	25	16,000	101,000	190,000	320,000	630,000
No. of articles, all languages	25	19,000	138,000	490,000	862,000	1,600,000

* Contributed at least 10 times; ** at least 5 times in last month; *** more than 100 times in last month

The rapid growth of the number of user contributions shows that individuals are reacting positively on the shift toward collaboration. Thus, some pioneering organizations have tried to adopt the collaborative business models and successfully thrive in this networked information economy. For example, Procter & Gamble has successfully developed a program called "Connect and Develop", which licenses in or acquires products from other companies. They also have been using the service of a web community in "InnoCentive" network where approximately one hundred and twenty thousand scientists around the world are ready to solve R&D problems with cash rewards (Tapscott and Williams 2006). InnoCentive is an open innovation marketplace that stimulates anyone from anywhere to contribute or cocreate innovations and new economic values by sharing their ideas, inventions, and knowledge (InnoCentive 2008).

5 Webstrategy

The emergence of the Internet and the World Wide Web have significantly contributed to a fundamental change in views on how economic conditions and business practices work (Penz and Sinkovics 2005). With the accelerating growth of internet users, a rise of globalization, distributed work environments, knowledge-based economies, and collaborative business models, it becomes clear that there is currently a high and growing number of organizations that demand a proper webstrategy. This demand has been increasing over time, as a high number of organizations did not even know what they were getting from the internet and how the internet would influence their business, even after launching their websites or web-enabled applications (Curry and Tetzeli 1996).

A proper webstrategy should allow the organizations to collaborate with their business partners and massive number of individuals (internally and externally), thus, assure them in gaining collective knowledge to sustain their competitive advantage and enhance their businesses. The current research aims to assist these organizations to formulate the proper webstrategy for their business industry.

5.1 Webstrategy Definition

How do we define a webstrategy? In order to define the term 'webstrategy', we may want to know how strategy is described. The word derives from the Greek word *stratēgos*, which derives from two words: *stratos* (army) and *ago* (leading). Wikipedia (2008) defines strategy as "*a long term plan of action designed to achieve a particular goal, most often "winning"*". Another definition is quoted from The American Heritage Dictionary which defines strategy as "*a plan of ac-*

tion resulting from strategy or intended to accomplish a specific goal". Moreover, James Brian Quinn in *The Strategy Process: Concepts and Contexts* indicates strategy as *"the pattern or plan that integrates an organization's major goals, policies, and action sequences into a cohesive whole"*.

Strategy is applicable on different scopes and environments, such as war, business, marketing, and even in the web environment. From the strategy definitions mentioned above, we define webstrategy within the context of this research as *"The plan of action, involving important elements, revolving around a web environment with regard to web 2.0 concepts, designed and implemented in order to achieve organization's business goals)"*. The important elements include:

- Goal (Ohmae 1982, Porter 1980)
- Clients (Haggie and Kingston 2003, Ohmae 1982)
- Products (Haggie and Kingston 2003)
- Time (Haggie and Kingston 2003)
- Resources (Haggie and Kingston 2003, Porter 1980)
- Tools/channels (Haggie and Kingston 2003, Porter 1980)

5.2 Webstrategy Formulation

We believe that the different types of organizations with differing requirements, characteristics, and objectives require a different webstrategy. Therefore, an effective webstrategy formulation is necessary to be performed. In the next sections, we categorize the organizations, and present our webstrategy framework including the key supporting tools. This framework is meant to assist in formulating a good webstrategy according to the organization type and the important elements involved.

5.2.1 Organization Typology

Organizations can be classified into several categories. Many organization typologies have been introduced over the years, such as beneficiary approach (Blau and Scott 1962), control and power (Etzioni 1961), technology structure (Thompson 1967), business process (Wiig 1997), organizational structures (Mintzberg 1980), and environmental approach (Jurkovich 1974). Therefore, it is important to select the appropriate organization typology. For this purpose, we have defined two main criteria:

1. The typology must have a clear distinction on the goal or strategy for each of the organization types

2. Each organization type in the typology must have strong and distinct characteristics from one another, to which web 2.0 concepts can be addressed in order to support them

Based on these criteria, the "Value Disciplines" typology introduced by Treacy and Wiersema (1993) was selected. Value Disciplines categorizes organizations into three types: Customer Intimacy, Operational Excellence, and Product Leadership. Table 5.1 provides the organization's characteristics for each organization type (Haggie and Kingston 2003, Treacy and Wiersema 1995).

Table 5.1 The characteristics of each organization type (Haggie and Kingston 2003, Treacy and Wiersema 1995)

Organization Type	Characteristics
Customer Intimacy	- Build bonds with customers - Understand customers - Tailor its products and services - Customer loyalty is the greatest asset
Operational Excellence	- Improve operational quality - Improve efficiency - Ease of purchase - Low prices - Hassle-free services
Product Leadership	- Keep innovating - Creation of new knowledge - Require highly creative environment and culture - Ability to bring/commercialize new ideas to market quickly - Have state-of-the-art products or services

Treacy and Wiersema (1995) argues that there is no company today can succeed by trying to be all things to all markets. But instead, the unique value that it alone can deliver to the markets must be found and excelled. It is certainly conceivable that organizations may be associated with more than 1 value disciplines. Direct explanation on this statement is that the organizations do not abandon the other two disciplines when they choose to excel in a value discipline. These organizations only choose a dimension of value on which to stake their market reputation over the long term (Treacy and Wiersema 1995). Thus, there is only one value focus an organization would excel at in order to differentiate them from their competitors. Matching the organization's characteristics with the list provided in table 5.1 would help to identify the organization type easily.

5.2.2 Webstrategy Framework

The differing requirements of different organization types have led us to think about how a webstrategy would be best formulated for the specific organization's situation. In order to perform an effective webstrategy formulation and web 2.0 adoption, we have developed a webstrategy framework. The purpose of the webstrategy framework is to assess the current (as-is) webstrategy of an organization, give the direction of the desired (to-be) webstrategy of the organization, and finally provide advices regarding possible improvements and propose a new effective webstrategy. These phases are executed according to the organization's situation and maturity revolving around the important elements of webstrategy and compared to their competitors. These important elements are goal, clients, products, time, resources, and tools/channels.

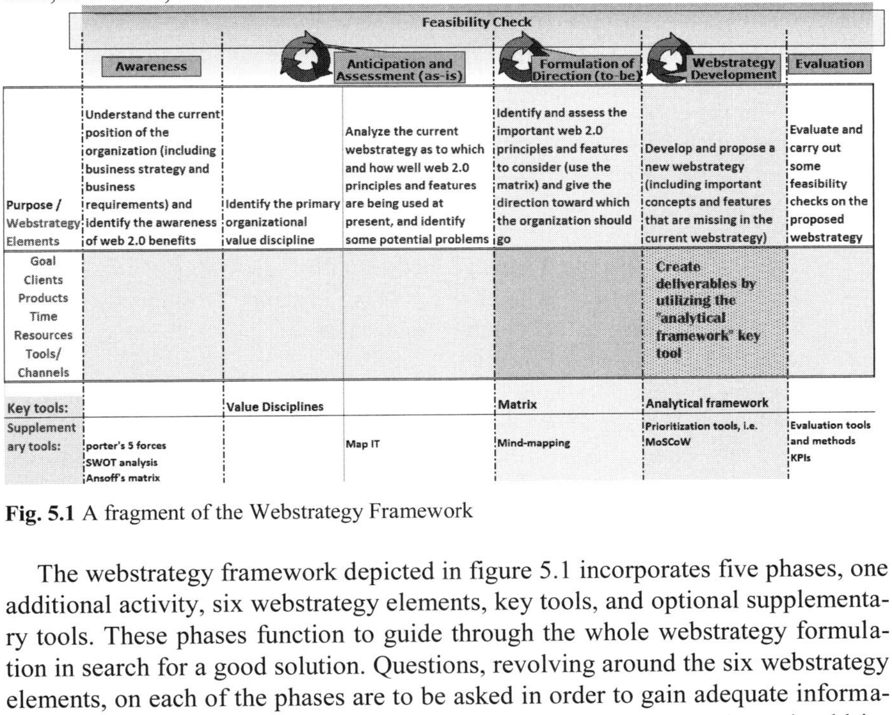

Feasibility Check					
	Awareness	Anticipation and Assessment (as-is)	Formulation of Direction (to-be)	Webstrategy Development	Evaluation
Purpose / Webstrategy Elements	Understand the current position of the organization (including business strategy and business requirements) and identify the awareness of web 2.0 benefits	Identify the primary organizational value discipline / Analyze the current webstrategy as to which and how well web 2.0 principles and features are being used at present, and identify some potential problems	Identify and assess the important web 2.0 principles and features to consider (use the matrix) and give the direction toward which the organization should go	Develop and propose a new webstrategy (including important concepts and features that are missing in the current webstrategy)	Evaluate and carry out some feasibility checks on the proposed webstrategy
Goal Clients Products Time Resources Tools/ Channels				Create deliverables by utilizing the "analytical framework" key tool	
Key tools:		Value Disciplines	Matrix	Analytical framework	
Supplement ary tools:	porter's 5 forces SWOT analysis Ansoff's matrix	Map IT	Mind-mapping	Prioritization tools, i.e. MoSCoW	Evaluation tools and methods KPIs

Fig. 5.1 A fragment of the Webstrategy Framework

The webstrategy framework depicted in figure 5.1 incorporates five phases, one additional activity, six webstrategy elements, key tools, and optional supplementary tools. These phases function to guide through the whole webstrategy formulation in search for a good solution. Questions, revolving around the six webstrategy elements, on each of the phases are to be asked in order to gain adequate information to formulate an effective webstrategy. Moreover, these questions should include internal and external aspects (Ohmae 1982, Porter 1980). The webstrategy formulation phases are:

- **Awareness:** In this phase, information about the current position of the organization should be gathered. This includes their business strategy, business requirements, the industry trends, as well as their awareness regarding web 2.0 benefits. The maturity of the organization compared to its competitors is also included. Some example questions which may be asked are:

– What is the goal of the organization?
– Who are the clients of the organization?
– Does the organization want to enhance its existing market and/or product?
– Is the organization aware of web 2.0 benefits to enhance its businesses?
– What are the current trends in the industry?
– What are the major movements of the organization's competitors?
– What channels are mostly being used by the clients?

- **Anticipation and Assessment (as-is):** The purpose of this phase is, firstly, to categorize the type of the organization by identifying their value discipline. Secondly, the current webstrategy and as-is situation of the organization should be assessed, as to which and how well web 2.0 concepts and features are being used at present, and lastly, the potential problems should be identified. The example questions to be asked include:

  – Is the goal of the organization very hard to achieve without an excellent efficiency within its business processes?
  – Would the organization fail to survive if it did not have excellent relationships with or information about its customers?
  – Does the organization constantly require new knowledge in order to keep innovating?
  – What are the characteristics of the organization?
  – Is the current webstrategy goal aligned with the organizational goal?
  – Does the organization invite its consumers to become prosumers (consumers who produce), to be involved and collaborate or add value to their business? If so, to what extent?
  – Does the organization have GUI-style web applications with Rich Internet Application functionalities to encourage clients to use them?
  – Does the organization currently use or lease data from other organizations or providers?
  – Does the organization have any web applications that can be reached from multiple devices? If so, what applications are they?

- **Formulation of Direction (to-be):** After gathering the information in the first two phases, based on the organization type, the desired situation is formulated toward which the organization should improve their webstrategy. This direction is provided by the "Matrix", one of the key tools provided to support the utilization of this webstrategy framework. The development of this matrix, and the matrix itself are elaborated upon in section 5.2.2.1. Some example questions which may be asked include:

  – To what extent should the web 2.0 concepts be implemented in order to effectively obtain added value from users participation?
  – In order to implement the web 2.0 features listed on the matrix successfully, what knowledge must be obtained and what changes must be performed?

- **Webstrategy Development:** In this phase, the new webstrategy is formulated and proposed to the organization. The important web 2.0 concepts and features that should be emphasized and applied in the webstrategy, but are missing or not getting enough attention in the current webstrategy, are listed. Instead of asking questions, we suggest to create deliverables according to and by using the "Analytical Framework" key tool. During the development of the webstrategy, the alignment with the organization maturity, strategy, processes, goals, capabilities, culture, products, resources, human capitals, skills, knowledge, and industry trends should be taken into consideration to develop an effective and efficient webstrategy (Batenburg and Versendaal 2004, 2006; Beukers et al. 2005; Scheper 2002). The design of the analytical framework is further elaborated in section 5.2.2.2.

- **Evaluation:** Evaluation and final feasibility checks on the proposed webstrategy are performed in the Evaluation phase. Usually this phase is executed after the new webstrategy is implemented. Questions which may be asked to evaluate the proposed webstrategy are:

  - Is the proposed webstrategy well aligned with the business strategy of the organization?
  - Does the proposed webstrategy deliver what it was intended to, and is it able to help the organization to achieve its objectives?
  - Does the proposed webstrategy adequately provide the users a platform to collaborate and add value to the organization?
  - Are the proposed changes acceptable for the organization's employees and clients?
  - Is the proposed webstrategy able to improve the advertising and marketing performance of the products?

In the webstrategy framework shown in figure 5.1, we can see the one additional activity that is performed throughout the whole webstrategy formulation process:

- **Feasibility Check:** The webstrategy framework we developed suggests that feasibility check should be performed continuously throughout the whole process. This is done in order to identify potential problems early in the process, thus, saving time from analyzing and formulating ineffective or inefficient webstrategy. Therefore, in every phase, the feasibility with respect to the following aspects should be checked:

  - Is it within the organization's budget?
  - Does the organization have adequate resources and capabilities?
  - Is it aligned with the organizational goal and the business strategy?
  - Is the organization or the products mature enough?
  - Does the organization have enough human capital, skills and knowledge required?
  - Is it timely feasible?

- Are the employees and clients supportive toward the changes?
- Are the business requirements and web requirements positively addressed?

With the six webstrategy elements, five phases, and the feasibility check activity explained, it leaves us with the last chunk of the webstrategy framework, "tools". The tools are categorized into two parts, which are key tools and supplementary tools. These tools are meant to be used to support the utilization of the framework. The **supplementary tools** are optional and can be used to support information gathering and the completion of particular phase. Examples of supplementary tools include Porter's five forces, SWOT analysis, Ansoff's matrix, MapIT, Mind-mapping, MoSCoW prioritization tool, and Key Performance Indicators (KPIs). Unlike the supplementary tools, the **key tools** are strictly attached to and must be used along with the webstrategy framework.

5.2.2.1 Key Tool: The Matrix

Web 2.0 is not a single philosophy or technology, rather many that should be considered (Manafy 2006). Hoegg et al. (2006) presents the fundament of web 2.0 as collective intelligence maximization, transparency of the information creation and sharing process, and network effects. Next to these, more terms can be found in literature to denote web 2.0: social software (Bächle 2006), peer production (Schonfeld 2006), social networking communities (Breslin et al. 2004), folksonomies and shared media (Mathes 2004), and web logs (Bachnik et al. 2005, Baoill 2004, Gill 2004, Hara et al. 2005, Kumar et al. 2004). However, these terms are leaning toward higher level concepts that are enunciated by O'Reilly (2005). The seven key concepts of web 2.0 according to O'Reilly (2005) are:

1. **The Web as Platform**
   The term "desktop" has evolved to "webtop", where the web is used as a single universal platform that connects and accommodates organizations and individuals to have web 2.0 services. Both, web browsers and web servers turn out to be commodities, and value moved up the stack to services delivered over the web platform (Gilchrist 2007, O'Reilly 2005).
2. **Harnessing Collective Intelligence**
   The interactive exchange of information and the continuous development and maintenance of a group opinion, which results in a commonly accepted opinion and content (Hoegg et al. 2006). An application should be able to encourage user participation and uniquely leverage the ability of the participants to improve the product or content (Baumann 2006, Manafy 2006, O'Reilly 2005).
3. **Data is the Next Intel Inside**
   Knowledge is power and data is treated as a core competence. Database is valuable, growing organically in value if constructed and used correctly (Baumann 2006, O'Reilly 2005).

4. **End of the Software Release Cycle**
Software is delivered as a service rather than as a product, it must be main-tained, reviewed, and improved on a daily basis. This leads to the need to treat users as co-developers, where some sites are in an almost "perpetual beta" con-dition (Gilchrist 2007, O'Reilly 2005).

5. **Lightweight Programming Models**
Programming models should allow for loosely coupled systems, allowing syn-dication rather than mere coordination (Gilchrist 2007, O'Reilly 2005). There-fore, remixability, web services, and mash-ups play an important role.

6. **Software Above the Level of a Single Device**
Software for devices other than computers (multi-channel). Applications are independent of the devices used to access them, and mobile applications are not degraded versions of what happens on the PC (Baumann 2006, Gilchrist 2007, O'Reilly 2005).

7. **Rich User Experiences**
Web 2.0 gives users an experience closer to desktop applications than tradi-tional static web pages (Manafy 2006, O'Reilly 2005). Rich Internet Applica-tion (RIA) is important for user satisfaction by bringing desktop abilities into the web browsers.

This matrix is one of the key tools involved in the webstrategy framework, which will be used in the Formulation of Direction phase. The purpose of this ma-trix is to give the direction of which web 2.0 concepts an organization should fo-cus on. Note that this matrix is not meant to develop a universal webstrategy for each organization type. Instead, its main purpose is to provide a meaningful and accountable direction. The actual webstrategy is developed based on the analysis of this direction and the information specific to the organization's situation (*see 5.2.2.2*). The direction provided in this matrix consists of the different significance and effectiveness levels of each web 2.0 key concept for an organization to sustain or even enhance its competitive advantage, depending on the type of the organiza-tion.

5.2.2.1.1 Methodology

The matrix was developed with two different dimensions. The characteristics of each organization type on one dimension (y-axis), and seven web 2.0 key concepts on another dimension (x-axis), where in each cell contains a numerical value be-tween $1 - 5$.

Table 5.2 Matrix composition

Organization Types and its Characteristics	Web 2.0 Key Concepts						
	1	2	3	4	5	6	7
Customer Intimacy							
- *Build bonds with customers*	c1						

- *Understand customers*	c2							
- *Tailor its products and services*	c3							
- *Customer loyalty is the greatest asset*	c4							
Operational Excellence								
- *Improve operational quality*								
- *Improve efficiency*								
- *Ease of purchase*								
- *Low prices*								
- *Hassle-free services*								
Product Leadership								
- *Keep innovating*								
- *Creation of new knowledge*								
- *Require highly creative environment and culture*								
- *Ability to bring/commercialize new ideas to market quickly*								
- *Have state-of-the-art products or services*								

In order to fill in this matrix, 12 expert interviews have been conducted with web 2.0 experts. Even though the 12 experts have various experience, specialization and industry focus, all of them have strong interest and good understanding, knowledge, and experience on web 2.0 projects. The composition of the respondents according to their job functions are as follows:

- Business Analyst: 1 respondent
- Consultant: 2 respondents
- Senior Consultant: 1 respondent
- Manager: 4 respondents
- Senior Manager: 3 respondents
- Assistant professor: 1 respondent

The duration of each expert interview was ranging between 90 and 120 minutes. During the interview, additional information was provided to ensure that the concepts being discussed were exactly and correctly understood by both the experts (interviewees) and the researcher (interviewer). During this session, the experts were required to complete this matrix by giving an importance score of each concept toward every characteristic of each organization type. The relationship between the concept and the characteristic is *'how important is this concept for helping the particular organization type to realize or support the corresponding characteristic?'*. The score ranges between 1 – 5, where 1 indicates 'least important' and 5 is interpreted as 'extremely important'.

The analysis was performed in two ways by investigating the *averages* and the *frequencies*. The analysis on average values was performed by taking into consideration the standard deviations and potential outliers. The steps taken are:

1. The sum scores of the characteristics of each organization type per concept are calculated for every respondent. Since the number of characteristics, and thus the sum of maximum scores, of the customer intimacy organization is not the same as the other two types, therefore, the calculation is done in percentage in order to make comparable measurements among the 3 organization types, i.e. $(c1+c2+c3+c4)/(c1_{max}+c2_{max}+c3_{max}+c4_{max}) * 100$.
2. From the previous calculations, the average scores of the sum, of the 12 respondents, on each concept per organization type are calculated to draw the final result. The higher the average score, the more important the concept is.

The second analysis is focusing on the frequency. The steps taken are:

1. The average scores of the characteristics of each organization type per concept are calculated for every respondent.
2. The average scores are categorized into 1-2, 2-3, 3-4, and 4-5, and certain points are assigned to each category. The points assigned to the categories are 1 point, 2 points, 3 points, and 4 points respectively.
3. The frequency of the average scores in all categories are analyzed by calculating the points that each concept obtained on each organization type. The higher the point, the more important the concept is.

The two different analyses are performed. In order to have a reliable outcome, the results from both analyses are expected to draw the same conclusion.

5.2.2.1.2 Results

After the data collection and data analysis on the averages, taking into account the standard deviations which were relatively low (smaller than half of the mean values), are completed, the results show that concept (6) "software above the level of a single device" and (2) "harnessing collective intelligence" turned out to be the most important concepts for customer intimacy organization to sustain its competitive advantage and deliver business values. Harnessing collective ideas of what the customers really need, as well as an excellent quality of information about the customers, can be very crucial for this type of organization. These would allow the organization to understand their customers better and be able to tailor its products and services according to the customers' needs, thus improve customer loyalty. By allowing the customers to access and use their web applications from multiple devices, the harnessing collective intelligence activities will be maximized. This allows the organization to get inputs from users who would not have been able to contribute if the software was only accessible through one device. Some experts also argue that multi-channeling, together with "rich user experiences" (7) concept such as RIA (Rich Internet Application), would improve the user-friendliness of the applications, which will lead the organization to build bonds by having more returning customers and improve customer loyalty.

Furthermore, concepts (4) "end of software release cycle" and (5) "lightweight programming models" were found to be the least important concepts when focusing on the webstrategy of customer intimacy organizations in order to deliver business values.

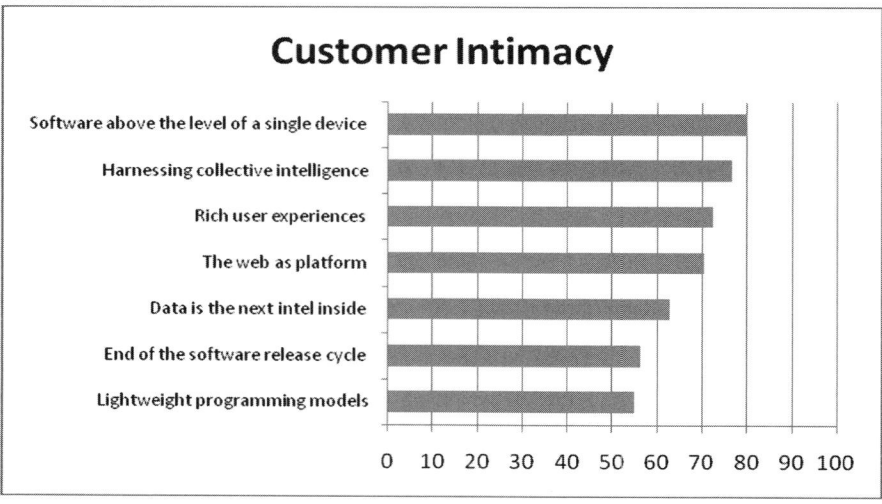

Fig. 5.2 The importance of web 2.0 concepts for customer intimacy organizations

While concept (6) "software above the level of a single device" turns out to be one of the most important web 2.0 concepts for operational excellence organizations, concept (1) "the web as platform" scores slightly higher according to the experts. The two concepts directly and significantly support all of the main characteristics of operational excellence organizations, and hence, sustain their competitive advantage. Operational quality, efficiency and hassle-free services can be improved by using the web as a single universal platform where most of the business activities take place. This excellent operational efficiency sometimes allows this type of organization to skip the middle-man in reaching its customers or to obtain other benefits, which results in low prices. The direct contact between manufacturer and the customers is mostly done on the web, this is where the "software above the level of a single device" concept becomes important. By providing more possibilities to have this type of contact (or to access the web applications) through multiple devices, the ease of purchase and hassle-free services are significantly improved. Customers who are not always sitting in front of their computers can now purchase or obtain services through their mobile phones, PDAs, or other devices from anywhere at any given time.

Furthermore, the result also shows that the five remaining web 2.0 concepts are almost equally important to be implemented in the webstrategy for the prosperity of operational excellence organizations.

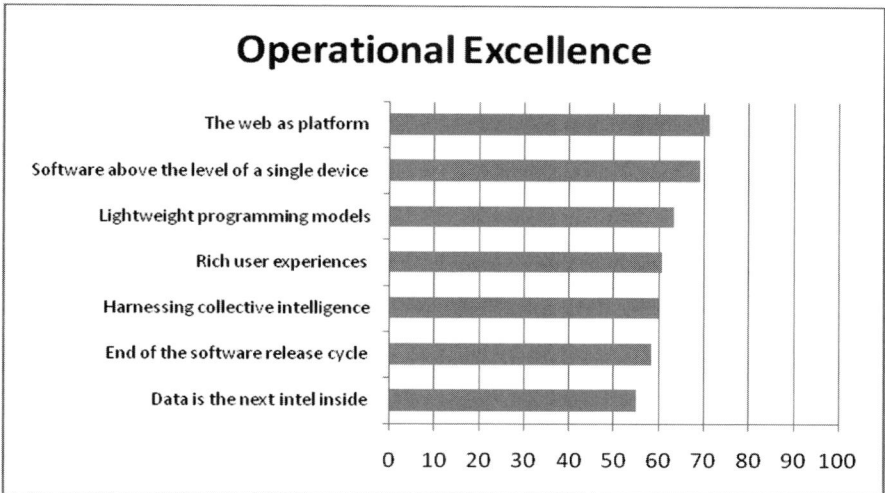

Fig. 5.3 The importance of web 2.0 concepts for operational excellence organizations

Product leadership organizations require constant innovation, new knowledge, and a creative environment. According to the experts, concept (2) "harnessing collective intelligence" directly addresses these three characteristics. The example of P&G and InnoCentive as described in section 4.2 shows how these concepts may help build a highly creative environment that allows constant creation of good quality of innovation and new knowledge. Moreover, the experts believe that concept (5) "lightweight programming models" is an important concept to support the development of state-of-the-art products, along with "harnessing collective intelligence". Lightweight programming models allow the organization to be agile and quickly adjust their software and products according to the latest trends and innovation in the market. Figure 5.4 below also shows that concept (4) "end of the software release cycle" is indeed one of the most important web 2.0 concepts for product leadership organizations. By focusing on this concept in its webstrategy, this type of organization would be able to improve its ability to bring and commercialize the new ideas or products to the market quickly, and thus receive early feedback from the consumers.

According to the analysis, concept (3) "data is the next intel inside" appears to have the least significance, compared to the other web 2.0 concepts, to be implemented in the webstrategy of product leadership organizations to sustain competitive advantage and deliver business values.

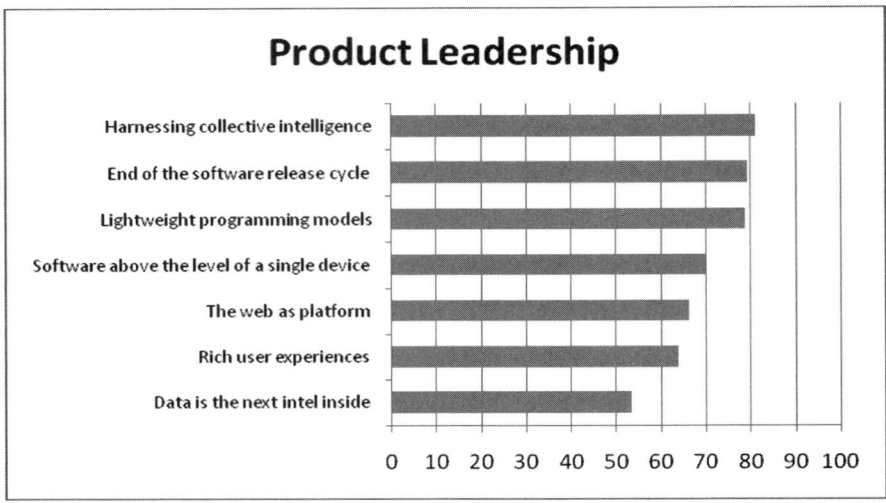

Fig. 5.4 The importance of web 2.0 concepts for product leadership organizations

Next to the average analysis, a frequency analysis has been conducted. The results of this frequency analysis positively support the results of the average analysis, thus the same conclusion was drawn.

- "Software above the level of a single device" and "harnessing collective intelligence" are the most important web 2.0 concepts to deliver business values for customer intimacy organizations.
- "The web as platform" and "software above the level of a single device" are the most important web 2.0 concepts to deliver business values for operational excellence organizations.
- "Harnessing collective intelligence", "end of the software release cycle" and "lightweight programming models" are the most important web 2.0 concepts to deliver business values for product leadership organizations.

Table 5.3 The results of the frequency analysis

Organization Types	Web 2.0 Key Concepts (Frequency)						
(Average Score Categorization)	1	2	3	4	5	6	7
Customer Intimacy							
1-2 (x1 point)	1	0	1	0	3	0	0
2-3 (x2 points)	1	1	3	9	2	0	1
3-4 (x3 points)	6	3	5	2	5	6	6
4-5 (x4 points)	4	8	3	1	2	6	5
Total Points	37	43*	34	28	30	42*	40
Operational Excellence							
1-2 (x1 point)	0	1	0	0	0	0	1

2-3 (x2 points)	2	3	6	7	3	3	5
3-4 (x3 points)	5	6	4	3	8	4	4
4-5 (x4 points)	5	2	2	2	1	5	2
Total Points	39*	33	32	31	34	38*	31
Product Leadership							
1-2 (x1 point)	0	0	2	0	0	0	1
2-3 (x2 points)	1	1	4	0	0	2	5
3-4 (x3 points)	10	5	5	6	4	8	4
4-5 (x4 points)	1	6	1	6	8	2	2
Total Points	36	41*	29	42*	44*	36	31

* The most important web 2.0 concept for corresponding organization type.

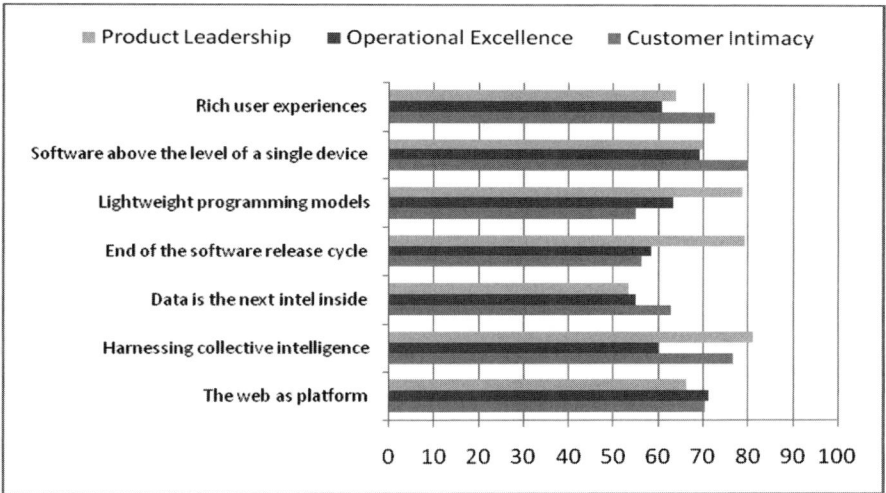

Fig. 5.5 The overall overview of each web 2.0 concept for all organization types

Figure 5.5 presents an overview of the importance of each web 2.0 concept to different types of organizations. It shows that according to the experts, "harnessing collective intelligence" (2) is a very important concept for the success of customer intimacy and product leadership organizations. Next to this, "end of the software release cycle" (4) and "lightweight programming models" (5) concepts appear to be valued the most by product leadership organizations compared to the other types of organizations. Expectedly, "software above the level of a single device" (6) and "rich user experiences" (7) are shown to deliver most values for customer intimacy organizations. Moreover, the result of the research suggests that "the web as platform" (1) and "data is the next intel inside" (3) are considered as common or general concepts that would deliver about the same values to all types of organizations. However, the "the web as platform" (1) concept scores slightly higher with respect to operational excellence organizations when compared to the other two types, while the "data is the next intel inside" (3) concept scores higher on customer intimacy. The same interpretation can also be seen in the result of the frequency analysis table above (see table 5.3).

This result should be able to give the direction of which web 2.0 concepts an organization should focus on when formulating an effective webstrategy by using the webstrategy framework.

Table 5.4 The mapping of the 7 web 2.0 concepts toward organization types based on their importance level in delivering business values.

Organization Type	Very Important	Important	Less Important
Customer Intimacy	Software above the level of a single device (6)	Rich user experiences (7)	End of the software release cycle (4)
	Harnessing collective intelligence (2)	The web as platform (1)	Lightweight programming models (5)
		Data is the next intel inside (3)	
Operational Excellence	The web as platform (1)	Lightweight programming models (5)	
	Software above the level of a single device (6)	Rich user experiences (7)	
		Harnessing collective intelligence (2)	
		End of the software release cycle (4)	
		Data is the next intel inside (3)	
Product Leadership	Harnessing collective intelligence (2)	Software above the level of a single device (6)	Data is the next intel inside (3)
	End of the software release cycle (4)	The web as platform (1)	
	Lightweight programming models (5)	Rich user experiences (7)	

5.2.2.2 Key Tool: The Analytical Framework

The analytical framework is developed to investigate the information gathered from the previous phases of the framework. This systematic tool gives the guideline on how the new webstrategy should be proposed, based on the information gathered in the previous phases. This analytical framework involves internal and external aspects of an organization. The internal aspects include *business strategy, business requirements, web requirements, value discipline, webstrategy direction & best practices, and assessment of current webstrategy*. The external aspects include *industry trends and technology breakthroughs*. The information about these aspects, in relation to the organization, were gathered by asking the questions in the previous phases of the webstrategy framework. Furthermore, this analytical framework is to be used in the *"webstrategy development"* phase of the webstrategy framework.

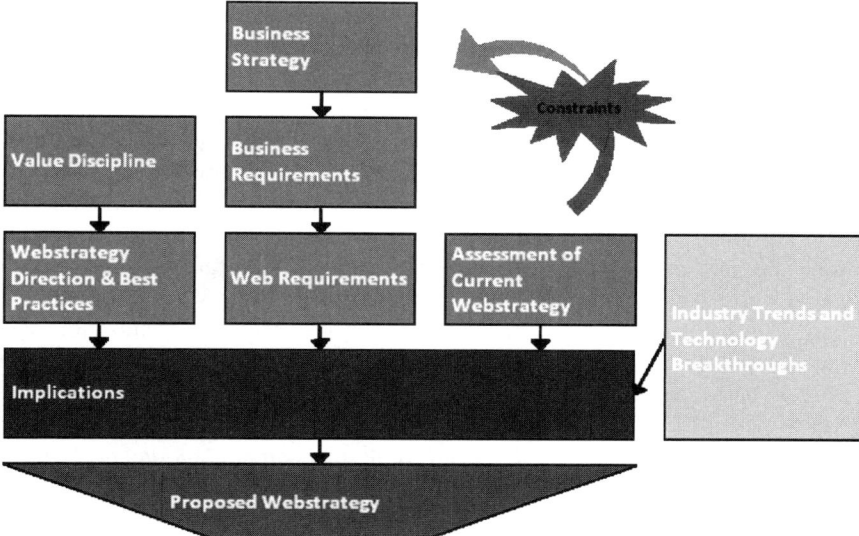

Fig. 5.6 The analytical framework

Some deliverables are expected to be created by utilizing this analytical framework. These deliverables are essential in formulating an effective webstrategy. The deliverables can be documented and should involve the following items:

- **Business Strategy**: The business strategy of the organization can be identified by analyzing the information gathered in the first phase of the webstrategy framework, namely *"awareness"*. In this phase, general questions about the organization are asked, including questions on its business strategy. This is usually the long term business plans of the organization to achieve its long term goals.
- **Business Requirements**: After the identification of the organization's business strategy, there is a need to list its business requirements. Business requirements are usually derived from the business strategy, however, these can also be derived with the combination with key stakeholders wishes and research outside the company. Business requirements constitute a specification of what the business wants and describe in business terms what must be delivered or accomplished to provide value. With the identified business strategy, along with the additional information obtained in the phase *"awareness"* of the webstrategy framework such as key stakeholders wishes, the business requirements of the organization can be formulated.
- **Web Requirements**: Web requirements are translated from the business requirements of the organization, and usually contain the necessities of web-

related technologies capabilities in order to support the business and achieve its objectives. Next to the business requirements, additional information can also be asked to aid the identification of web requirements.

- **Value Discipline**: The value discipline of the organization should be identified in the second phase of the webstrategy framework, which is "*anticipation and assessment*". In this phase, questions concerning the focus of how an organization, in its markets, has increased the value offered to customers over the long term are asked. The answers to these questions would give an adequate information of the organization's value discipline, thus, the organization type.

- **Webstrategy Direction & Best Practices**: The identification of organization type allows us to use the matrix key tool to give the webstrategy direction. With the help of this matrix, the webstrategy direction can be derived as to which web 2.0 concepts are essential in delivering business value to the organization. In this item, best practices available for this particular organization type can also be included. This deliverable refers to the "*formulation of direction (to-be)*" phase of the webstrategy framework.

- **Assessment of Current Webstrategy**: This deliverable can be produced from the information that is previously gathered in the "*anticipation and assessment (as-is)*" phase of the webstrategy framework. This should include not only the assessment of the current webstrategy, but also the impact on the business strategy. Any (potential) **constraints** from the current webstrategy that limit or do not support the effectiveness of the organization's business strategy are listed here.

- **Industry Trends and Technology Breakthroughs**: This deliverable concerns more of external influences, such as the trends in the industry (product and service trends, market trends, and movement trends of the competitors) and the technology breakthroughs (any emerging technologies) that currently penetrate and are able to deliver business values to the organization.

- **Implications**: Taking into consideration of the four deliverables, which are "*webstrategy direction & best practices*", "*web requirements*", "*assessment of current webstrategy*", and "*the industry trends and technology breakthroughs*", the implications are derived. These implications involve internal as well as external influences. Specific situations and conditions of the organization, such as the maturity of the organization compared to its competitors, the maturity of the products/services, the availability of resources, human capitals, skills and knowledge should also be taken into account. These implications must give clear ideas on which the formulation of the actual webstrategy to be proposed will be based.

- **Proposed Webstrategy**: This deliverable formulates the actual webstrategy to be proposed to the organization. The proposed webstrategy should be align with the organization's business strategy, capabilities, and goals. Note that the formulation process is based on the implications derived from the previous deliverable, in which internal (*webstrategy direction & best practices, web requirements,* and *assessment of the current webstrategy*) as well as external aspects (*industry trends and technology breakthroughs*) are intensively considered. Thus, the proposed webstrategy, with the current capabilities of the particular organization, is expected to effectively address the issues that the organization has, deliver the business values to the organization, and improve its business performance.

6 Conclusions

In this twenty-first century, where the knowledge-based economy has evolved from an industrial information economy into a networked information economy, IT technologies are crucial to the success of the organizations. Taking IT into an organization requires a good alignment between the capabilities of different business aspects and IT. Business models have also started to shift toward collaboration and community involvement. Organizations create pores to allow information and knowledge to flow in and out of the organization, which would stimulate creation of knowledge and innovation. This approach effectively gains through web 2.0 technologies and their underlying concepts, which suggests that collective intelligence, even from individuals, matters.

For an organization to successfully adopt web 2.0 concepts into its webstrategy, there are a number of aspects which need to be considered, including the value discipline which best describes its organization type and the unique value that is to be delivered in the long term. The webstrategy of the organization requires to be able to sustain and even improve this unique value to the next level in order to outperform its competitors. Therefore, the categorization of the web 2.0 concepts based on their effectiveness in addressing the issues and delivering business values to specific organization type was emphasized.

Next to the value discipline, webstrategy formulation involves other aspects as described in section 5. An effective webstrategy should consider its alignment with the organization's business strategy, objectives, resources and capabilities, as well as with the industry trends and technology breakthroughs. This research has sought to consider these elements and the alignment in formulating an effective webstrategy with the adoption of web 2.0 concepts for different types of organizations. The webstrategy framework and its key tools were introduced and the explanations of the fragments were provided. The differing needs of web 2.0 solutions for different organization types were also presented. The webstrategy framework as described in this chapter will assist in formulating an effective webstrategy by incorporating the appropriate web 2.0 concepts to effectively deliver business values for the organization.

References

Bächle M (2006) Social Software. Informatik Spektrum

Bachnik W, Kurylo L, Leszczynski PR, Rymszewicz E, Szymczyk S (2005) Quantitative Sociological Analysis of Blog Networks. arXiv:physics, vol. 1

Baoill AO (2004) Conceptualizing The Weblog: Understanding What It Is In Order To Imagine What It Can Be. Journal of Contemporary Media Studies

Barney J (1991) Firm Resources and Sustained Competitive Advantages. Journal of Management, (17), pp 99-120

Barua A, Kreibel CH, Mukhopadhyay T (1995) Information Technology and Business Value: an Analytic and Empirical Investigation. Information Systems Research, vol. 6, no. 1, pp 3-23

Batenburg R, Rutten R (2003) Managing Innovation in Regional Supply Networks: a Dutch Case of "Knowledge Industry Clustering". Supply Chain Management: An International Journal, Vol. 8, No. 3, pp 263-270

Batenburg R, Versendaal J (2004) Business alignment in the CRM Domain: Predicting CRM performance. In: T. Leino, T. Saarinen & S. Klein, Proceedings of the 12th European Conference on Information Sytems. Turku: Turku School of economics and business Administration (CD-ROM)

Batenburg R, Versendaal J (2006) Alignment matters – Improving business functions using the Procurement Alignment Framework. Institute of information and computing sciences, Utrecht University. To be discussed in the Workshop Inkoop Onderzoek Nederland (WION), January 2006, Lunteren, The Netherlands

Baumann M (2006) Caught in the Web 2.0. Information Today, vol. 23, issue 8, p 38

Benkler Y (2006) The Wealth of Networks: how social production transforms markets and freedom. Yale University Press

Beukers M, Brinkkemper S, Versendaal J (2005) Business Alignment in the Procurement Domain. Institute of information and computing sciences, Utrecht University technical report UU-CS-2005-001

Bharadwaj A, Bahradwaj SG, Konsynski BR (1999) Information Technology Effects on Firm Performance as Measured by Tobin's q. Management Science, vol. 45, no. 7, pp 1008-1024

Blau PM, Scott WR (1962) Formal Organizations. San Francisco: Chandler

Bontis N, Curado C (2006) The Knowledge-Based View of the Firm and its Theoretical Precursor. International Journal of Learning and Intellectual Capital, Vol. 3, No. 4, pp 367-381

Bordoloi B, Sircar S, Turnbow JL (1998) The Impact of Information Technology Investments on Firm Performance: a Review of the Literature. Engineering Valuation and Cost Analysis, vol.1, pp 171-181

Bordoloi B, Sircar S, Turnbow JL (2000) A Framework for Assessing the Relationship between Information Technology Investments and Firm Performance. Journal of Management Information Systems, vol. 16, No.4, pp 69-97

Breslin JG, Decker S, O'Marchu I (2004) Online Social and Business Networking Communities. DERI – Digital Enterprise Research Institute - Technical Report. Available online: http://www.deri.at/fileadmin/documents/DERI-TR-2004-08-11.pdf

Brown B, Harper R, O'Hara K, Perry M, Sellen A (2001) Dealing with Mobility: Understanding acces antime, anywhere. ACM Transactions on Computer-Human Interaction , 8 (4), 323-347

Brynjolfsson E (1993) The Productivity Paradox of Information Technology. Communication of the ACM, Vol. 35, No.12, pp 66-77

Brynjolfsson E, Hitt LM (2000) Beyond Computation: Information Technology, Organizational Transformation and Business Performance. The Journal of Economic Perspectives, Vol. 14, No. 4, pp 23-48

Chesbrough H (2003) Open Innovation: The New Imperative for Creating and Profiting from Technology. Harvard Business School Press

Chesbrough H (2006) Open Business Models: How to Thrive in the New Innovation Landscape. Harvard Business School Press; (1 edition)

Cook B (1999) Paradoxically Speaking: Increased IT Spending and the Lack of Productivity Improvements. Inform, Vol. 13, No. 5, p 40

Curry SR and Tetzeli R (1996) Getting Your Company's Internet Strategy Right. Fortune, Vol. 133, Issue 5, pp 72-78

Daft RL (2004) Organization Theory and Design. Mason: Thomson South Western

Dehning B, Stratopoulos T (2000) Does Successful Investment in Information Technology Solve the Productivity Paradox? Information & Management, vol. 38, no. 2, pp 103-117

Dennis AR, Kinney ST (1998) Testing Media Richness Theory in the New Media: The Effects of Cues, Feedback, and Task Equivocality. Information Systems Research , 9 (3), 256-274

Donaldson L (2001) Reflections on knowledge and knowledge-intensive firms. Human Relations, 54 (7), 955-963

Dos Santos B, Sussman L (2000) Improving the Return on IT Investment: The Productivity Paradox. International Journal of Information Management, vol. 20, no. 6, pp 429-440

Drucker P (1992) The new society of organizations. Harvard Business Review , 95-105

Etzioni A (1961) A Comparative Analysis of Complex Organizations. New York: Free Press

Gallois C, Gardner J, Jones E, Watson B (2004) Organizational Communication: Challenges for the New Century. Journal of Communication , 54 (4), 722-750

Garud R, Raghuram S, Wiesenfeld BM (1999) Communication Patterns as Determinants of Organizational Identification in a Virtual Organization. Organization Science , 10 (6), 777-790

Gilchrist A (2007) Can Web 2.0 be Used Effectively Inside Organisations? Bilgi Dünyası. Vol. 8, Issue 1, pp 123-139

Gill KE (2004) How can we measure the influence of the blogsphere?. In proceedings of the WWW2004 Conference, New York

Grant R (1996) Toward a knowledge-based theory of the firm. Strategic Management Journal, 17, 109-122

Haggie K, Kingston J (2003) Choosing Your Knowledge Management Strategy. Journal of Knowledge Management Practice, 4. Available online: http://www.tlainc.com/articl51.htm

Hara Y, Hino Y, Nakajima Sh, Tanaka K, Tatemura J (2005) Discovering Important Bloggers based on Analysing Blog Threads. In proceedings of the WWW2005 Conference, Chiba, Japan

Harris TE (2002) Applied Organizational Communication: Principles and Pragmatics for Future Practice. London: Erlbaum

Hoegg R, Martignoni R, Meckel M, Stanoevska-Slabeva K (2006) Overview of business models for Web 2.0 communities. In: Proceedings of GeNeMe 2006.- GeNeMe 2006.- Dresden, S. 23-37

InnoCentive (2008) http://www.innocentive.com. Accessed 12 May 2008

Internet World Stats: Usage and Population Statistics (2007) http://www.internetworldstats.com. Accessed 8 October 2007

Jashapara A (2004) Knowledge Management: An Integrated Approach. Essex: Pearson Education Limited

Jurkovich R (1974) A Core Typology of Organizational Environments. Administrative Science Quarterly, Vol. 19, No. 3, pp 380-394

Kakihara M, Sorenson C (2002) Mobility: an extended perspective. Proceedings of the 35th Annual Hawaii International Conference on System Sciences, pp 1756-1766. Hawaii

Kauffman RJ, Weill P (1989) An Evaluative Framework for Research on the Performance Effects of Information Technology Investments. Proceedings of the 10th Annual International Conference on Information Sciences pp 377-388

Kolbitsch J, Maurer H (2006) The Transformation of the Web: How Emerging Communities Shape the Information We Consume. Journal of Universal Computer Science, Vol. 12, No. 2, pp 187-213

Kumar R, Novak J, Raghavan P, Tomkins A (2004) Structure and Evolution of Blogspace. Communication of the ACM, vol. 47, no. 12

Manafy M (2006) The Collective Wisdom at Work. Econtent, vol. 29, issue 7, p 6

Mathes A (2004) Folksonomies – Cooperative Classification and Communication Through Shared Media. Available online: http://www.adammathes.com/academic/computer-mediated-communication/folksonomies.html

Mintzberg H (1980) Structure in 5's: A Synthesis of the Research on Organization Design. Management Science, Vol.26, No. 3, pp 322-341

Nurmi R (1998) Knowledge-Intensive Firms. Business Horizons, pp 26-32

Ohmae K (1982) The Mind of the Strategist: Business Planning for Competitive Advantage. Penguin

Oliver C (1997) Sustainable Competitive Advantage: Combining Institutional and Resource-Based Views. Strategic Management Journal, (18:9), pp 697-713

O'Reilly T (2005) What is Web 2.0: Design Patterns and Business Models for the Next Generation of Software. Available online: http://www.oreillynet.com/pub/a/oreilly/tim/news/2005/09/30/what-is-web-20.html

Patnayakuni N, Patnayakuni R, Rai A (1996) Refocusing Where and How IT Value is Realized: an Empirical Investigation. *Omega*, vol. 24, no.4, pp 399-412

Penz E, Sinkovics RR (2005) Empowerment of SME websites – Development of a web-empowerment scale and preliminary evidence. Journal of international entrepreneurship. Vol. 3, Issue 4, pp 303-315

Peppard J, Ward J (1999) 'Mind the Gap': diagnosing the relationship between the IT organisation and the rest of the business. Journal of Strategic Information Systems, 8(1), 29-60

Peppard J, Ward J (2003) Strategic planning for information systems, 3rd edition, Chichester, England, Wiley

Porter ME (1980) Competitive Strategy: Techniques for Analyzing Industries and Competitors. Free Press

Rappa M (2005) Managing the Digital Enterprise. Available online: http://digitalenterprise.org/index.html

Scheper WJ (2002) Business IT Alignment: solution for the productivity paradox (In Dutch). Deloitte & Touche, Netherlands

Schonfeld E (2006) The Economics of Peer Production

Spender JC (1996) Making Knowledge the Basis of a Dynamic Theory of the Firm. Strategic Management Journal. (17), pp 45-62

Tapscott D, Williams AD (2006) Wikinomics: How Mass Collaboration Changed Everything. Portfolio Hardcover

Thompson JD (1967) Organizations in Action. New York: McGraw-Hill

Timmers P (1998) Business Models for Electronic Markets. International Journal on Electronic Markets and Business Media. Vol. 8, no. 2, pp 3-8

Treacy M, Wiersema F (1993) Customer Intimacy and Other Value Disciplines, Harvard Business Review

Treacy M, Wiersema F (1995) How Market Leaders Keep Their Edge. Fortune, Vol. 131, Issue 2, pp 88-93

Wiig KM (1997) Knowledge Management: Where Did It Come From and Where Will It Go?, Expert Systems with Applications, Vol. 13, Issue 1, pp 1-14

Wikipedia (2008) Strategy. http://en.wikipedia.org/wiki/Strategy. Accessed 18 February 2008

Williamson OE (1979) Transaction-cost Economics: The governance of contractual relations. J Law Econ, October, pp 233-261

Chapter 8. Web 2.0: Issues for the Design of Social Networks

Sagar Bhatnagar

School of Management, State University of New York at Buffalo

Tejaswini Herath

School of Management, State University of New York at Buffalo

Raj Sharman

School of Management, State University of New York at Buffalo

H. Raghav Rao

School of Management, State University of New York at Buffalo

Shambhu J. Upadhyaya

Department of Computer Science and Engineering, State University of New York at Buffalo

Abstract

Social Networks have become part of our daily lives and recently there have been a deluge of social networking sites. People are using social networks to keep in touch with friends, family and community. Newer Web 2.0 technologies are encouraging social networking. With social networking sites surfacing every day, we believe it is worthwhile to draw the attention of the reader towards security and privacy related as well as other market and technological factors that should be considered while developing social networks. We discuss in detail the different elements of security and privacy of information that should to be addressed by the developers.

1   Introduction

In past few years interest in social networking has grown tremendously. There have been a deluge of social networking websites that have surfaced over the past few years and the user base for these is accruing at a phenomenal rate. Web 2.0, a platform that focuses on openness, read-write paradigms, participation from all, is shifting authority of content creation in hands of end-users and is encouraging social networking.

While there was a concern about the impact of internet on social life that the Internet would prompt people to withdraw from social engagement and become isolated, depressed, and alienated, PEW internet survey found that online world is a vibrant social universe where many Internet users enjoy serious and satisfying contact with online communities. These online groups are made up of those who share passions, beliefs, hobbies, or lifestyles, and involve communities that are local as well as virtual or global in nature. The findings support the occurrence of "glocalization" – a concept suggested by sociologist Barry Wellman suggesting the capacity of the Internet to expand users' social worlds to faraway people and simultaneously to bind them more deeply to the place where they live (Horrigan, 2001). In spite of the surge on on-line social networking, on-line communities face several important issues that need careful consideration. Although the features of social networking sites differ from one another, in general, they all allow you to provide information about yourself and offer some type of communication mechanism (forums, chat rooms, email, and instant messenger) that enables you to connect with other users. The nature of these sites due to on-line, interactive and relatively open environment introduces various security, privacy (Bausch & Han, 2006) and other risks. In addition, several other market and technology factors are essential for existence of these sites. In this article we evaluate the nature of on-line securities, issues they face and possible solutions to overcome some of these issues.

2   Nature of Social Networks

In general, a social network is a social structure made of nodes (which are generally individuals or organizations) that are tied by one or more specific types of relations. Online social networks, sometimes referred to as "friend-of-a-friend" sites, build upon the concept of traditional social networks. The Internet helps people find others who share their interests no matter how distant they are, and it also helps them increase their contact with groups and people they already know and it helps them feel more connected to them. The purpose of some networking sites may be purely social, allowing users to establish friendships or romantic relationships, while others may focus on establishing business connections. Classmates.com, one of the first social networking website created in 1995 by Randy Conrads helps members find, connect and keep in touch with friends and acquaintances from throughout their lives (Horrigan, 2001) while sites such as LinkedIn allow professionals to contact similar others. Sites such as Ancestry.com or Geni.com allow people to find about their family tree and get in touch with related others. By far the most popular social networking site "MySpace", with now over 168 million registered users ("Social network", 2007), has become the digital equivalent of hanging out at the mall for today's teens, who load the site with photos, news about music groups and detailed profiles of their likes and dislikes (Knowledge@Wharton, 2006). Other social network sites include Facebook, geared to college students; Orkut, geared towards teens and young; and LinkedIn, geared towards business professionals. ("Social network", 2007).

Table 1: Popular Social Networks Member details

Site	Members
MySpace	176,500,000
Windows Live Spaces	120,000,000
Orkut	46,423,762
Classmates.com	40,000,000
Xanga	40,000,000
Bebo	31,000,000
Friendster	29,100,000
Reunion.com	28,000,000
Broadcaster.com	26,000,000
Facebook	21,000,000

Top 10 Sites 2007 - Wikipedia ("Social network", 2007)

Site	Apr-05 (000)	Apr-06 (000)	YOY Growth
MySpace	8,210	38,359	367%
Blogger	10,301	18,508	80%
Classmates Online	11,672	12,865	10%
YouTube	N/A	12,505	N/A
MSN Groups	12,352	10,570	-14%
AOL Hometown	11,236	9,590	-15%
Yahoo! Groups	8,262	9,165	11%
MSN Spaces	1,857	7,165	286%
Six Apart TypePad	5,065	6,711	32%
Xanga.com	5,202	6,631	27%

Top 10 sites 2006 - Neilson Rating (Bausch & Han, 2006)

Social networks differ in the audience they serve, their network structures (which could be based on interests, geography or occupation) and type of features available. Table 2 compares some of the popular social networks and their characteristics (Wildbit.org, 2005).

Table 2: Comparison of Popular Social Networks

	Audience (Use)	Network Structure	End User Features	General Features
MySpace	Teens, young people (family, net-working)	22 forums with interest categories with 2 suble-vels	Blog, video, url photo, address book, bulletin calendar, email	Browse profiles, search, invite new people, film/ comedy/ music forum, fa-vorites, videos, classifieds, events
Orkut	Teens, young people (Personal connections)	None	Photo, video, book-marks, scrapbook, pro-file, testimonials	Friends (rank, best, good, ac-quaintances), search, Communi-ties, Orkut Media (gallery, lounge blog), Orkut News (an-nouncement, demographics)
LinkedIn	Business Pro-fessionals (Business networking)	None	Connections, network data, email list, recommendations	People search, Jobs & Hiring, Categorized service providers recommendations, Ask a ques-tion from professionals
Facebook	Students (College friendships)	None	Profile, friend finder, photos, myshares, notes, events, inbox	Browse profiles, search, invite new people

3   Privacy implications

Social networking sites rely on connections and communication, and thus they encourage users to provide a certain amount of personal information. Although online social networks are establishing novel forms of interaction among users, they raise many security and privacy concerns. Millions of people around the world, young and old, use these sites to communicate, find friends, family members, dates, and jobs. In doing so, they willingly reveal personal information to strangers as well as friends. The lack of face to face communication provides a false sense of security in these online communities. It is observed that on many social networking sites, members of community do not exercise the same amount of caution as they would when meeting someone in person (Acquisti & Gross, 2006; Stutzman, 2006). Accessibility to personal information available on these sites has made them venues for predators to search for victims. Online communities allow predators to form relationships online and then convince unsuspecting individuals to meet them in person leading to dangerous situation. The personal information revealed on these sites can also be used to conduct a social engineering attack such as phishing and identity theft.

While protecting personal information online is important cautionary measure, fair representation of oneself is also important in social networking. For example, in an on-line community where people meet friends or dates, it is important to have realistic picture of the other party. Similarly, for transactional on-line communities such as e-bay it is important to have valid and reliable information about the buyer, seller and the product. Misrepresentation of these can lead to variety of frauds. On-line identity presented correctly or misrepresented, and its implications, is an interesting and important research question in online social networks.

Most networks we know about encourage, but do not force users to reveal personal information such as their dates of birth, their cell phone numbers, or where they currently live; and yet, one cannot help but marvel at the amount, detail, and nature of the personal information some users provide (Acquisti & Gross, 2006). Would the privacy conscious members behave differently than relatively naive members of the community? Acquisti and Gross (Acquisti & Gross, 2006) found that an individual's privacy concerns are only a weak predictor of his membership to the network. Also privacy concerned individuals join the network and reveal great amounts of personal information. Some manage their privacy concerns by trusting their ability to control the information they provide and the external access to it. Authors found significant misconceptions among some members about the online community's reach and the visibility of their profiles.

Privacy issues are rampant in the new participative systems like blogs, online social networks where content is posted by the end user. Privacy may not be limited to self, but one's entire networks privacy is critical. For example, FOAF [Friend of a Friend] can expose private information for a chain of people connected to each other. This risks privacy for the entire network of people rather than a single individual. The current social networks have a number of privacy issues. For example, LinkedIn has some privacy issues related to leakage of professional information and resources of the people who set their profile on this site (Rand, 2007). MySpace poses a different case for privacy concerns. If a person knows the name of another person, the former can get access to demographic and other personal information of the latter just by searching the name of the latter. Therefore, it becomes important to incorporate effective countermeasures that ensure privacy of the user information on the social network.

There have been number of instances where blogs and online social networks have revealed classified information for a corporate or an individual to a third party just because that information was easily viewable and carelessly posted. These circumstances can result into lawsuits and heavy financial damages for the involved parties. The social network design elements should address these issues appropriately.

But how to ensure one's personal privacy and one's network privacy on an online community web site? Soft security measures over and above methods like cryptography and secure access can ensure confidentiality of information that floats on the network and exchanged among the users. Some considerations for privacy on a social network can be limiting access by means of limited audience, i.e. people who are viewing your posts to friends, acquaintances; and limited reach, i.e. the user have over all the other content on the social network? For example, can a person who has registered on a site like Facebook access all the other person's data or that can be controlled?

Privacy policies can mitigate several other issues related to the posted content and control the consequences associated with privacy breaches. The features of the web site's privacy policy should be designed comprehensively such that they address all scenarios of privacy breaches and spell out clearly written and specific guidelines for the user.

Security profiles determine the level and extent of privacy flexibility that end users can exploit. For example, in Orkut, one can check the property "disable profile visitors" which can prevent one from knowing who visited one's page and vice versa . But this is still incomplete. One can still view anyone's scrapbook and details of the scrap conversations. Future social networks should have security profiles with more exhaustive list of privacy settings for all permutations and combinations. There should be provision for the end user to categorize his content and security profile should include options to deal with each of these categories. This will enable privacy configuration much more comprehensively and minimize privacy breaches

Security profiles, privacy policies are some of the preventions mechanisms. Mechanisms that eliminate privacy issues in real time can also be used to strengthen the privacy practices. For example, a social network can build a "Privacy Warning Server" which generates warnings for end users and make them aware of any privacy loopholes in their settings. This will also help in mitigating cases of privacy breaches. These Privacy Warning Servers can compare a particular privacy setting with a benchmark and then generate respective warnings for the end user or even self-correct these loopholes by updating the security profiles.

4   Security Considerations for Online Communities

Online communities are used as platforms for extensive information exchange in today's internet space. These communities are places where people make friends, develop relationships and spend hours communicating. As a result the chances of frauds, attacks and security breaches are very high. How to ensure that people's privacy is not invaded and they feel safe and secured in interacting with each other on these online communities? For example, in Orkut, viewing a scrapbook (which is open to anyone who has registered with Orkut) can reveal private information of the relationships of that person. If one registers on MySpace and post something which one does not want others to view, there should be provisions to enable that. Currently, this provision is limited and using one's privacy settings one can configure these settings but there is room for improvement. Some of the main security threats on online social networks are discussed below:

4.1 Abuse, Inappropriate content, Identity Theft and other Threats

Child abuse, nudity, and harassment are some of the problems related to abuse. Underage children can be the target of abuse from unidentified people. Similarly, people who post their profile can post a nude profile – there is no way stopping them. On-line harassment or cyber-stalking where one individual harasses another individual on the Internet can range from simply annoying to deadly. Incidents of on-line harassment of classmates, or threatening messages to others are numerous.

Identify theft is one of the major problems on social networks. People can easily steal other's identity or create pseudo identity and carry out objectionable acts in that name without others knowing about the true identity of the perpetrator. For example, one can register on MySpace with the name of colleague and pass on inappropriate comments about another employee. When users have the flexibility to post, naturally there will be many instances of inappropriate content getting posted. For example, on YouTube.com lot of people posts inappropriate videos. Social network designers should ensure that there systems offer policing mechanisms that can prevent such incidents.

Setting limits, choosing audience and controlling your content are some of the other mechanisms that determine safety on online social networks. Choosing your audience on a social networking site is very critical for being safe. Similarly, setting limits or defining different levels of access to your personal space is an important element. Controlling the timing and extent of communications and defining relationships in the social network are some of the other aspects which can determine how robust the safety mechanism on an online community is.

4.2 Legal Issues

Service account legalities, material legalities, contract issues with the provider, copyright and trademark issues, third party issues, different liabilities on the social networks are some of the elements of legal aspects of the security that should be considered while designing your network. For people-to-people interactions, whether in real world or online through the online communities, there is bound to be legal and liability issues. For example, two criminals meet on MySpace and plan a robbery. Who is liable for such an act? In addition to the criminals is the service provider liable for providing a platform for framing a robbery. Such legal aspects have to be taken into account when charting out the website's terms of service. Similarly, there could be trademark and copyright issues on the content posted on these web sites.

4.3 Technological Issues:

New technologies like Web2.0, Web based VoIP can create new vulnerabilities for the online social networks. Web2.0 uses different mechanisms like RSS, Trackback, Pingback, Tagging etc –these create new vulnerabilities. For example, a syndicated page through RSS can create a backdoor. What if a malware instead of a genuine aggregator communicates to pull new information from that page into the aggregator software? Similarly, a malicious advertiser creates an inappropriate tag at a page to promote his business that can disguise under a name and when clicked leads to his site rather than what was apparent from the name of the tag. Similarly, VoIP framework built for online communication on a site can be used for launching attacks like SYN attack etc.

5   Network Considerations for Online Communities

In addition to the features provided for the member community, several other factors determine the effectiveness of social networks (Welman, 1997) in terms of ease and speed of information flow.

5.1 Boundedness

Boundedness refers to the proportion of network members ties that stay within boundaries of the social network. Networks can be "tightly bounded" or "unbounded". For example, health related social networks will benefit if there is a tight binding among nodes whereas marketing social networks will best operate when unbounded. IT designers should keep this point in mind and ensure that the design feature that defines how relationships between nodes will evolve should be in line with the boundedness desired.

5.2 Density

Density determines proportion of all possible ties (between two network members) that actually exist i.e. how many network members have contact or communication with all others. For example, social networks that are developed for organizations involving teams should be denser vis-à-vis those that involve lesser need for communication like one for old classmates. IT designers should create communication platforms for the desired density like online messaging for dense networks whereas offline messaging for sparse networks.

5.3 Exclusivity

Exclusivity is determined by whether people interact primarily one-on-one or are their individual contacts available to a wider set of persons. Social networks should be designed such that the type of interaction should address the level of exclusivity desired. For example, a network designed for supply chain partners will need to be less exclusive than the one designed for C2C ecommerce.

5.4 Social Control

Social control determines how do external sources create, constrain and manage a person's contacts and exchanges. For example, a social network for intra-organizational teams should be designed such that there is provision of more social control whereas a network like that for inter-organizational teams should have lesser provision of social control.

5.5 Network Externality

Network externality refers to the extent to which a network is useful as more and more people starting using it. For example, it's arguable that as more and more members register on MySpace, its usefulness increases more and more for everybody. IT designers should make sure the frameworks of their networks fully exploit this. i.e. when more and more people join the network, the frameworks enable more and more usefulness.

5.6 Range

The range of a network describes how large and diverse is the population within its boundaries. The designers should make sure network designs should address these ranges. For example, a network designed for a particular school will have limited range vis-à-vis one which is designed for many schools.

5.7 Strength of Ties

Granovetter defined the strength of ties (Granovetter, 1973) as "a probably linear combination of the amount of time, the emotional intensity, the intimacy (mutual confiding), and the reciprocal services which characterize the tie. Social networks that involve strong ties for example, a network for friends should ensure that there is provision of reciprocal services and emotional interaction whereas those involve weak ties for example a network like LinkedIn should be designed accordingly.

How nodes are distributed in the network also determine its effectiveness. There are some properties that are considered in the social network analysis which measure this effectiveness – some of these are described below: (Haythornthwaite, 1996) These factors determine how your network will look take the shape.

5.8 Network Centralization

A less centralized network has lesser chances of failure. Those networks that have evenly distributed nodes are better equipped for retaining their functionality in failure scenarios.

5.9 Degree Centrality

The degree of centrality suggests that what really matters is where the network connections lead to and how they connect the otherwise unconnected and not that more the number of connections better the network. i.e. what's important is the quality of connections and not their quantity.

5.10 Between Centrality

Theory suggests that a node with high betweeness has great influence over what flows and has more power. Minimizing nodes that are highly in between other nodes will ensure power is evenly balanced across the network. Networks should be designed such that there are a minimum number of the nodes occupying central positions and similarly minimum nodes sandwiched between others.

Network structures that optimize the network on these three dimensions will determine which social networks are effective and which are not in terms of their networking properties. Networks that are structured such that they have high local clustering exhibit the small world phenomenon. Small world phenomenon creates better social identity for people and shorter global path lengths. i.e. using local information of their immediate contacts only, people can find shorter global paths in the entire social network (Watts, 2004).

6   Market and Technological Considerations

Due to ever changing nature of social networking user base (see table 1), for the long term sustainability of the site several issues need to be considered from market, technology, as well as on-line security perspective. These can be considered by social network designers, programmers and managers who are involved in development and management of web based social networks.

6.1 Market Considerations

Many of the current social networking sites are targeted to young people only including teenagers, students and fresh graduates. While there are some sites such as Classmates.com and Ancestry.com that serve other age groups, many such age groups and purposes remain unexplored by social networks. We believe that social networks can be targeted to a wider set of people ranging from teenagers to middle-aged or senior citizens tapping into variety of needs and purposes. Market niches will also play a significant role in the applicability of social networks. These concepts and web 2.0 based technologies allowing for social networking have lot of potential to be applied to many contexts. For instance, these applications can also be used in emergency response such as campus emergency for allowing communication between various stakeholders. Custom-designed social networks that capture explicit requirements of these niche market segments can be beneficial to those niches as well as to the whole society. The key is to identify the right stakeholders and carry out the requirement analysis for these niches before developing social networks.

Vertical social networks are another consideration. Social networks for vertical industries will enable richer interactions. For example, a social network designed for pharmaceutical industry will facilitate richer collaboration and information exchange between members like druggists, sales agents and local shops

Porter et al in "Strategy and Internet" (Porter, 2001) argues that those web based systems will be successful that implement combinations of virtual and physical activities and make traditional activities better – the same applies to social networks also. For example, "LinkedIn" has been successful as it uses the concept of online professional connections making the traditional process of professional networking better over the World Wide Web.

6.2 Technology Considerations

Web2.0 is a platform that can be exploited for implementation of social networks. The key characteristics of Web2.0 that will be useful are self evolution, collaboration and participation. Social Networking site BigAdda.com by Reliance Corp. that was recently launched is based on Web2.0. Current online networks limit the flexibility for the end users in content creation. Web2.0 systems can create a platform where end users contribute content and collaborate further on the social networks.

AJAX (Asynchronous JavaScript and XML) has been a recent trend for designing rich user interfaces. We feel such technologies are an important consideration while designing social networks as they will facilitate faster transaction processing and help build rich user interfaces – some of the important technological elements for social networks

Fig. 1. Social networking service differentiation.

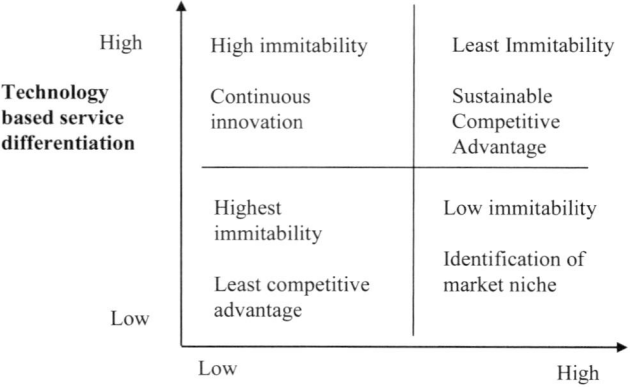

Market based service differentiation

Figure 1 compares the service differentiation of social networks on two dimensions: "Technology based" and "Market based". The above matrix highlights the significance of identifying market niches at the same time achieving high technology-based differentiation. Social networking services that utilize differentiation based on both dimensions create sustainable competitive advantage and are least imitable as compared to the services that lie in other sectors. Identification of market niches while designing your social network is critical. Social networks designed for special market domains that cater to the specific needs and also use high technology differentiation creates sustainable competitive advantage.

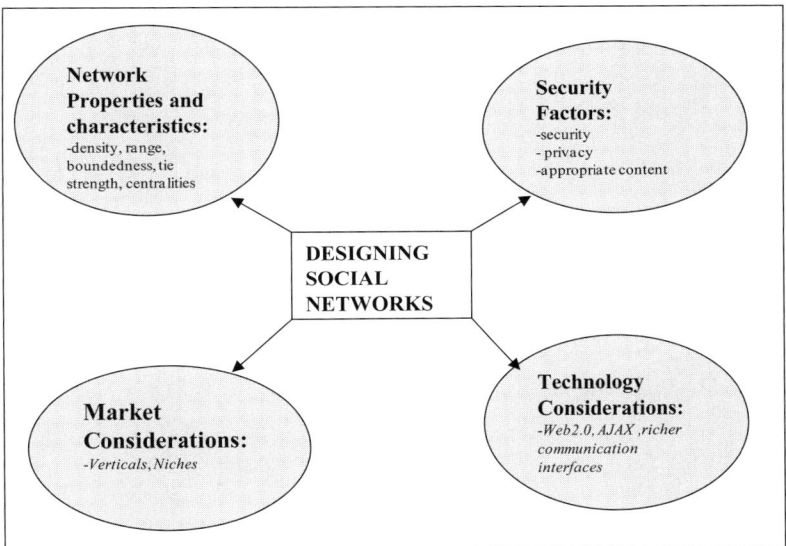

Fig 2. Design Factors for Social Networks.

7   Conclusion

Social networks are surfacing everyday so developers of these networks should consider the wide range of factors that determine the effectiveness of these networks. The extent to which considering the technological and market factors outlined in the above sections during developing the social networks can improve the effectiveness of these networks is a point to ponder? Perhaps, longitudinal studies that measure the performance of these networks can provide an accurate answer to these questions. Information technology professionals who develop social networks should constantly think of introducing new features in their networks that widen their scope in terms of applicability, usefulness and audience.

Social networking will continue to become popular and widely used in the coming years. Differentiating your social networks based only on technology will limit its life span and risk imitability by competition. However those services that use differentiations on both dimensions i.e. technology and market will create sustainable competitive advantage and value for the users. The network should be designed taking into consideration some of the dimensions that determine their effectiveness and efficiency like boundedness, range, audience, density, exclusivity and strength of ties. Security and privacy issues need to be addressed with innovative features.

Acknowledgments
This research is funded in part by NSF under grant # 0402388. The usual disclaimer applies.

References

Acquisti, A., & Gross, R. (2006, June 28-30). *Imagined communities awareness, information sharing, and privacy on the facebook.* Paper presented at the 6th Workshop on Privacy Enhancing Technologies, Cambridge, United Kingdom.

Bausch, S., & Han, L. (2006). *Social networking sites grow 47 percent, year over year*: Nielsen//NetRatings.

Granovetter, M. (1973). The strength of weak ties. *The American Journal of Sociology, 78*(6), 1360-1380.

Haythornthwaite, C. (1996). Social network analysis: An approach and technique for the study of information exchange. *Library and Information Science Research, 18*, 323-342.

Horrigan, J. (2001). *Online communities: Networks that nurture long-dostance relationships and local ties*: PEW Internet & American Life Project.

Knowledge@Wharton. (2006). *Myspace, facebook and other social networking sites: Hot today, gone tomorrow?*

Porter, M. E. (2001). Strategy and internet. *Harvard Business Review*, 63-78.

Rand, D. (2007). *Csis security research and intelligence.*

Social network. (2007).

Stutzman, F. (2006). An evaluation of identity-sharing behavior in social network communities. *International Digital and Media Arts Journal, 3*(1).

Watts, D. J. (2004). New science of networks. *Annual Review of Sociology, 30*, 243.

Welman, B. (1997). An electronic group is virtually a social network. In S. Kiesler (Ed.), *Culture of the internet* (pp. 179-205). Hillsdale, NJ: Lawrence Erlbaum.

Wildbit.org. (2005). Social networks research report. Retrieved April, 2008, from http://www.wildbit.com/wildbit-sn-report.pdf

Chapter 9: Wikis for Knowledge Management

Business Cases, Best Practices, Promises, & Pitfalls

Clif Kussmaul

Elegance Technologies, Inc., USA

Roger Jack

Elegance Technologies, Inc., USA

Abstract

This chapter describes how wikis and related tools can be used for knowledge management (KM), and describes processes and best practices for creating and deploying wiki-based KM systems. In particular, we consider the business cases from multiple perspectives, including: participating in KM systems; initiating KM projects; and developing wiki platforms. Thus, the chapter seeks to help readers understand what KM and wikis are, when and why they can provide value to individuals and organizations, who should be involved, and how to deploy them most effectively.

1   Introduction

This chapter describes how wikis and related tools can be used for knowledge management (KM), and describes processes and best practices for creating and deploying wiki-based KM systems. In particular, we consider the business cases from multiple perspectives, including: *participating* in KM systems; *initiating* KM projects; and *developing* wiki platforms. Thus, the chapter seeks to help readers understand *what* KM and wikis are, *when* and *why* they can provide value to individuals and organizations, *who* should be involved, and *how* to deploy them most effectively.

The chapter draws on our experiences using and contributing to multiple wiki platforms, and consulting for a variety of business, educational, and governmental organizations seeking to use wikis for KM, as well as our experiences working in global organizations and managing global virtual teams. We provide a multidisciplinary perspective, since effective knowledge management involves a variety of disciplines, including business, software development, psychology, and sociology.

1.1 Knowledge Management

Knowledge management (KM) can be defined as "the leveraging of collective wisdom to increase responsiveness and innovation" (Frappaolo 2006, p 8). However, von Krogh, Ichijo, and Nonaka (2000, p vii) prefer the phrase "knowledge enabling", arguing that knowledge cannot truly be managed. Regardless of terminology, making better use of what people in an organization already know can have enormous benefits (e.g. O'Dell and Grayson 1998, p 8-9). "In an economy where the only certainty is uncertainty, the one sure source of lasting competitive advantage is knowledge" (Nonaka 1991). This is particularly true for knowledge-intensive work, where professional often spend 20-25% of their time trying to find needed information (Koenig 2001). Frappaolo identifies four ways to use or apply knowledge:

1. Intermediation   connecting knowledge seekers with providers
2. Externalization   capturing knowledge in external repository
3. Internalization   extracting knowledge from external repository
4. Cognition   making decisions based on available knowledge

O'Dell and Grayson (1998) describe three main areas where KM can deliver value. The first focuses on customer relationships with the sales force and consultants. The second focuses on sharing best practices to improve internal operations. The third focuses on new product development and time to market.

Snowden (2006) identifies three ways in which KM differs from most other management trends. First, KM has multiple origins, in different domains, while many trends are inspired by a single source. Second, KM focuses more on helping people be more productive (despite problems with KM tools). Third, KM encourages distributed collaboration rather than centralized control and IT systems.

Views of KM have changed and evolved over time (e.g. Snowden 2002; Figallo and Rhine 2002). Initially, it focused on knowledge as objects that could be gathered and organized to support decision making and business process reengineering.

In the mid-1990s, the emphasis shifted to describing and sharing knowledge, recognizing an important distinction between *explicit knowledge*, which people can easily codify, from *tacit knowledge*, which is difficult for people to articulate, but often more valuable. The relationships between these two types of knowledge led to the SECI model (Nonaka 1991; Nonaka and Takeuchi 1995) (see table).

Table 1: SECI model of knowledge creation and transfer (Nonaka 1991)

Socialization	Tacit → Tacit
Externalization (or articulation)	Tacit → Explicit
Combination	Explicit → Explicit
Internalization	Explicit → Tacit

Szulanski (1994) reports that best practices can take over two years to propagate across an organization, and identifies four main barriers. First, people don't know that others in the organization have, or need, specific information. Second, people lack the time or resources to utilize available information. Third is the absence of existing relationships, since people prefer to use information from people they know and trust. Fourth, people don't appreciate the benefits of available information. Similarly, O'Dell and Grayson (1998, p 18ff) identify five barriers: organizational silos, reluctance to use ideas developed elsewhere, lack of common perspectives and terminology, focusing on explicit rather than tacit knowledge, and a lack of time or other resources.

Thus, to overcome these barriers, organizations invested in a variety of KM initiatives. However, these approaches tended to emphasize information that was easily quantifiable, the creation and use of KM platforms, and a knowledge officer or other executive sponsor (von Krogh, Ichijo, and Nonaka 2000, p 26). A survey of firms with KM systems (KPMG 2000, summarized in Koenig 2001) found that half to three-quarters failed to meet expectations, often due to problems with user training and education. Snowden (2006) argues that the SECI is not a good general model for KM, and that technology and other standards have been emphasized prematurely.

More recently, KM has shifted again to focus on knowledge as process, recognizing that it may be easier and more cost effective to find simple ways to help individuals and groups quickly locate others with relevant knowledge, rather than attempting to codify and catalog knowledge that may not be needed.

The history of KM parallels the history of software engineering in some interesting ways that will be relevant below. For many years, organizations emphasized tools to make individual developers more productive. In the 1980s, the need to coordinate large software projects (particularly for the military) led to development of the Capability Maturity Model (Paulk et al 1994) and other disciplined processes, which often emphasized detailed documentation as well as collection and analysis of performance measures. These processes often involved sequential phases (e.g. analysis, design, implementation, verification, and maintenance), known as the "waterfall model". Somewhat later, and partly as a reaction against such processes, "agile" development methods were developed (e.g. Highsmith 2002) and are increasingly popular. Most agile methods emphasize multiple short iterations, customer interactions, and working systems.

1.2 Wikis

A *wiki* is a web site with several distinctive features. (To distinguish the site from the supporting software, we refer to the latter as the *wiki platform*.) First, and most importantly, wiki pages (also called topics) can be created, edited, and linked together using a standard web browser, without specialized knowledge or experience. Initially, most wiki platforms used simplified markup conventions, but increasingly they include or support graphical text editors. Second, wikis store every previous version of every page, as well as who made the change and when. This enables users to see how the page has evolved, and to easily undo accidental or malicious changes. Third, wikis separate the visual appearance of the overall site from the specific content of a specific page. Thus, users focus on putting the right content in each page, and let graphic designers and the wiki platform determine consistent headers, footers, menus, color, fonts, and other details, so that the wiki looks like a coherent site, not a collection of random pages.

Most wiki platforms support keyword searching, and can attach images or other types of documents to wiki pages. Most platforms also provide some level of authentication and security to control which users can access which pages, and what actions they can perform. However, there is a strong tradition of minimizing restrictions, and using community norms and the page history to prevent or correct problems. Wikipedia, for example, allows anyone to view and edit any page (with some exceptions). Furthermore, most wiki platforms also make it easy to add new capabilities to the wiki without a detailed knowledge of the internal workings. "It's impossible for a software vendor to please everybody, and it's not a good business decision to do so, because the vendor should be focused on building an amazing, high-quality core product" (Mader 2008, p 54).

One clear benefit of wikis is the ease with which content can be created, edited, and linked. Unlike other web sites or documents which are often controlled by a few gatekeepers, wikis are easy to update continually, so they can be used for personnel directories, scheduling, and other dynamic applications. This freedom is balanced by the version history, so that people can see who made specific changes, and view or reinstate previous versions of a page. Wikis enable people to progress gradually from comments and minor changes to larger restructuring and more complex formatting. Wikis impose relatively little structure on content, so it is easy to adjust the site's navigational structure, or provide multiple parallel structures for different uses. This flexibility can also lead to confusion, particularly for newly created wikis; it is often helpful to have a designated facilitator, and adopt patterns, practices, and structures that have proven effective elsewhere (Mader 2008).

The first wiki was developed in 1994-1995 by Ward Cunningham (Leuf and Cunningham 2002); "wiki" is a Hawaiian word for "quick". Currently there are over 100 wiki platforms, with a wide variety of characteristics and features (CosmoCode 2008). Most wiki platforms are open source but there are also commercial platforms (see table).

Table 2: Popular wiki platforms

Wiki	URL	Open Source?	Notes
DokuWiki	docuwiki.org	Y	PHP
MediaWiki	mediawiki.org	Y	PHP (used by Wikipedia)
MoinMoin	moinmo.in	Y	Python
PmWiki	pmwiki.org	Y	PHP
TikiWiki	tikiwiki.org	Y	PHP
TWiki	twiki.org	Y	Perl
Confluence	atlassian.com	N	hosted or installed
PBwiki	pbwiki.com	N	hosted
SocialText	socialtext.com	N	hosted
WikiSpaces	wikispaces.com	N	hosted

Probably the best known wiki is Wikipedia "the free encyclopedia that anyone can edit" with over two million articles in English (Wikipedia 2008). People unfamiliar with wikis often assume incorrectly that Wikipedia is the model for all wikis (Mader 2008, p 25). For example, Wikipedia allows anonymous editing of most pages, while many wikis restrict access to members of a particular community, or are only available via an institutional intranet. Wikipedia is primarily an encyclopedia (although it also has areas for discussion, and to describe its internal processes), but wikis can support collaborative editing, discussion, and other uses, some of which are described in more detail below. Nevertheless, Wikipedia is a valuable example; Wikipedia entries have been proposed as conceptual identifiers for KM (Hepp, Siorpaes, and Bachlechner 2007), and their history provides rich data for models of collaborative editing (e.g. Viegas, Wattenberg, and Dave 2004; Viegas et al. 2007; Preidhorsky et al. 2007).

2 Wikis for Knowledge Management

Wikis can be used for a variety of KM applications, and their potential has been described in Business Week (Hof 2004) and The Wall Street Journal (Swisher 2004). "The chief difference between the wiki and more traditional content management (CM) or knowledge management (KM) systems is structure. ... the wiki starts off with the minimum possible structure and grows a custom structure based on how each person, team, or project uses it" (Mader 2008, p 41). Wikis can help to codify explicit knowledge and create maps or directories of tacit knowledge.

Content, pages, sections, and navigation schemes can be added as needed. Many wikis also provide way to define templates for particular types of pages. This makes it easier to create and update pages with consistent content and layout.

Chau and Maurer (2005) describe a case study of a software company using wiki-based experience repository to exchange ideas, document decisions and rationales, share social information, identify experts, and coordinate project tasks and collaboration. 58% of the content was in unstructured formats, demonstrating the roles of both tacit and explicit knowledge. 80% of read-accesses were to just over 20% of the pages, and 25% were to the top 10 pages. Similarly, 10 users made 75% of contributions, and 5 made 55%; most of the top contributors were developers, and none were managers, suggesting that the repository was mostly self-organized. Users reported that the largest motivating factors were 1) presence of needed information, 2) ease of contributing information, 3) desire to help others, and 4) encouragement from management. Wikis are also used for KM in university libraries (e.g. Blake 2005; Fichter 2006; Glogowski and Steiner, 2008), and university courses (e.g. Raman, Ryan, and Olfman 2005).

Majchrzak, Wagner, and Yates (2006) surveyed 168 corporate wiki users to understand why and how wikis are used in corporate settings. Most of wikis are used for KM in areas ranging from software development and project management to technical support, sales and marketing, and research and development. The median respondents use wikis that are 12-24 months old, with an average of 12 contributors and 25 other users. Older wikis tend to have more accesses and more participants, suggesting that wikis are sustainable beyond short-term projects. The survey examines three types of benefits from wiki use. In order of importance, participants report that contributing to the wiki: 1) makes their own work easier; 2) helps the organization to reuse knowledge, support collaboration, and improve processes; and 3) enhances the contributor's reputation. A factor analysis of wiki contributions suggests three main categories: 1) adding content to new or existing pages; 2) integrating, organizing, and rewriting existing content; and 3) adding comments and making minor corrections.

KM can benefit from other features and capabilities, which can be provided by a wiki or by separate tools (see Figallo and Rhine 2002, ch 7; and Wagner 2004). Threaded discussion forums are useful for archiving conversations; for example, every article in Wikipedia has a corresponding "talk" page for discussion about the article. Blogging can be very useful for unstructured KM (Cayzer 2000; Crudin 2006). More structured information can be stored in a traditional database or in appropriate wiki pages; for example, TWiki enables users to define specific fields in a form, which can then be associated with pages; this is useful for workflow applications such as document management and tracking defects and features. In some cases a wiki platform may provide enough functionality to obviate the need for other tools, simplifying the environment for users and IT staff. In other situations, a wiki can be the portal that accesses other tools which provide benefits that justify additional integration and learning. For example, a wiki can provide basic version control and task tracking capabilities, but software development teams may prefer a more specialized system that supports task tracking, source code version control, and wiki capabilities, such as Trac (from Edgewall Software), or a wiki integrated with other open source tools (Segetech 2007).

3 Best Practices

This section identifies a set of best practices for initiating wiki-based KM projects. Many of the practices are described in more detail elsewhere in this chapter.

Recognize whether the project is being initiated top-down or bottom-up. Particularly with wikis, both approaches are feasible. In the 1990s, KM often required significant resources for technology, integration, training, and other factors, so that a top-down mandate from leadership was often a necessary prerequisite for KM projects. However, the low cost, ease of use, and flexibility of a wiki mean that KM projects can start within a small group and gradually grow to include more people and a broader scope. Charman (2006) prefers a bottom-up approach because it becomes self-sustaining, while a top-down approach can stall when the mandate changes or priorities shift.

Assess your organizational culture. DeMarco and Lister (1999 p 4) remind software developers that "the major problems of our work are not so much *technological* as *sociological* in nature" (original emphasis). Sophisticated KM systems will be ineffective if your organizational culture values hording over sharing. People must believe that they will benefit from their contributions, and that their contributions will not be exploited, used against them, or attacked unfairly (Figallo and Rhine 2002, p 114). Address any cultural problems before worrying about IT. This is particularly true of wikis, since "a wiki cannot function without a community and should not be considered separately from it" (Blake 2006).

Test fast, fail fast, adjust fast. This statement is attributed to Tom Peters and is also central to most agile software development methodologies; it is probably the most important advice for any new project. Try to do the simplest thing that might work, then check to see how well it works, then decide what to do next. More structured "waterfall"-style processes may be necessary when deploying large enterprise systems, but wikis are so flexible that a more agile, iterative approach is generally more successful.

Decide whether the primary objective is to capture explicit knowledge, or map tacit knowledge. Hansen, Nohria, and Tierney (1999) examine how consulting companies approach KM, and conclude that organizations need to decide strategically whether to emphasize explicit or tacit knowledge, and that this decision has far-reaching implications. Those that emphasize explicit knowledge seek to develop materials that can easily be reused or customized for different purposes; this requires a larger investment for infrastructure, creating, and disseminating, but once materials are developed they can be reused very efficiently. On the other hand, organizations that emphasize tacit knowledge seek to make it easy to identify and connect with experts; this is easier to create, but there is less potential for reuse. Organizations can pursue either strategy successfully, but should avoid combining the two.

Identify an appropriate pilot project. The pilot project should be small enough to be manageable; it's better to do one thing well than many things poorly. The pilot should also be big enough to demonstrate the value of the KM system; if all of the participants work in the same office, a KM system might be unnecessary. The people involved in the pilot should be open to new approaches, focused enough to be successful, but diverse enough to be representative of the larger organization. "The pilot is important because it allows you to get wiki use started in a controlled environment, build examples that are extremely relevant to your organization, and develop the administrative and support structures that will keep things running smoothly" (Mader 2008, p 63).

Identify key roles and tasks for those roles. Mader (2008, p 12) provides a useful list of common patterns for user roles, and some "anti-patterns" to be avoided.

Keep the technology as simple as possible. O'Dell and Grayson (1998, pg 88-89) recommend spending less than 1/3 of project resources on IT, and using simple solutions for more valuable knowledge, including tacit knowledge.

Create a simple but representative structure. Remember that "all models are wrong, but some are useful" (Box and Draper 1987, p 424); keep the initial structure simple so that users can understand it and so that it can adapt as the KM system evolves. At the same time, make the structure complete enough to guide the way; "a structure that extends across the entire scope will indicate to users what the scope means in real terms" (Blake 2006).

Match part of the wiki structure to the organizational structure. Conway (1968) observed that system designs (particularly in software) mirror the structures of the organizations that produce them. Ensure that each team, department, or division using the wiki has its page, with links to parent, child, and sibling units. Fortunately, in a wiki it is easy to maintain multiple navigation structures, so knowledge can also be accessed in other ways.

Identify and develop structures to support key tasks. Create templates for commonly page types; most wikis can do this easily, and a template makes it easier to create new pages quickly and consistently. Some wikis (e.g. TWiki) support user-defined forms for more structured data. Some wikis also support (or have extensions for) tagging, where pages can be annotated with user-selected keywords, which can then be used to organize and visualize pages in ways not envisioned by the original navigational structure. Most open source wikis encourage the development of custom extensions; this requires more time and expertise, but may be appropriate for tasks with special requirements.

Develop bottom-up support. Identify key groups of users in the organization, and then identify and work to understand the key users in those groups. Help each group to adapt the wiki to its needs. Work to convert key users into evangelists for the KM project, so that they can help others in their group to get involved in the project, and then work to convert evangelists into trainers, since they have valuable insight into how others in their group work and how they could benefit from the KM project (Charman 2006). Look for emerging patterns or needs that can be leveraged to help the rest of the organization.

Develop top-down support. If there is a high-level champion for the KM project, he or she can help provide resources and support, and help to align personal incentives with business incentives (see below). Although a champion may be able to mandate participation, it is also important that he or she model participation and continually remind others to participate (Charman 2006).

4   Business Cases

To understand when and why wikis are used for KM, we need to consider distinct but interrelated business cases: 1) Why do software developers and software organizations develop and enhance wiki platforms to be used for KM? 2) Given that such platforms exist, why do organizational leaders initiate wiki-based KM projects? 3) Given that such projects are started, why do individuals in an organization participate in them?

It might appear that each business case is a necessary prerequisite for the next one – tools must be available for leaders to initiate a project in which individuals participate – and this may well have been the case in the first and second ages of KM (Snowden 2002) when KM systems required a large upfront investment. However, wikis can be deployed by small groups at little or no cost, and communities of practice (Wenger 1999) can develop without any technical infrastructure. Thus, the sequence should be reversed – we must understand why and how individuals will participate before we can initiate projects or develop tools to support them. Each business case is examined below, followed by a discussion of the relationships between them.

First, however, we briefly review some relevant background. Zipf's law (Zipf 1935) is an empirical description of the frequency distribution of rank data. If a set of N items is ranked in decreasing order of frequency, the frequency of the kth item is inversely proportional to its rank k. This relationship can be expressed as:

$$f(k;s,N) = \frac{1}{k^s H_{N,s}} = \frac{1}{k^s \sum_{i=1}^{N} \frac{1}{i^s}} \qquad (1)$$

where s is an exponent that characterizes the distribution. When s is 1, f(k) is proportional to 1/k; as s increases, the initial items account for a larger proportion of the observations. In the limit as N approaches infinity (∞), the harmonic number ($H_{N,s}$) becomes Riemann's zeta function (ζ):

$$f(k;s) = \frac{1}{k^s \zeta(s)} \qquad (2)$$

Zipf's law was originally described for the frequency of words in a text, but applies to the population of cities in a region, page hits on a web site (Huberman et al. 1998), the number of links in web surfing sessions (Levene, Borges, and Loizou 2001), Amazon.com book review (Nielsen 2006), and many other scenarios. Zipf's law is similar to the many popular "80-20" or "90-10" rules, such as 80% of the benefits (or the problems) coming from 20% of a system.

Figure 1 illustrates Zipf's law for two values of s (1.75 and 1.05). Dotted lines connect the frequency values in the probability mass function, while solid lines connect the corresponding cumulative density function. When s=1.75, the first item represents roughly 50% of the observations, and the second item represents roughly 15%, so that the first two items together represent roughly 65%, and the first five items represent roughly 80%. When s=1.05, the first item represents roughly 5%, and the first four represent roughly 10%.

Figure 1: Zipf's Law

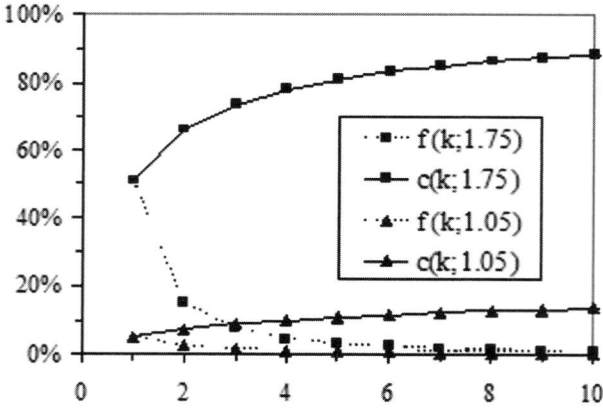

4.1 Participating in KM Projects

The success of a wiki KM system depends critically on participation, For example, people must be confident that the system will help them find needed knowledge, and they must be willing to contribute their own knowledge. Thus, creating and maintaining a KM system requires an understanding of roles and incentives.

It is useful to recognize that KM is a market (in the economic sense) with *sellers* (who offer or provide knowledge) and *buyers* (who use knowledge from sellers). However, "people rarely give away valuable possessions (including knowledge) without expecting something in return" (Davenport and Prusak 2000, p 26). Knowledge markets also have *brokers* who try to bring buyers and sellers together; the KM system is a broker, as are people in the organization who help to make such connections. A factor analysis of wiki contributions (Majchrzak, Wagner, and Yates 2006, see above) identifies a fourth role: editors who integrate and (re-)organize existing content. Mader (2008, p 12) identifies additional roles, including some detrimental roles.

People choose to participate in a KM system (in any of these roles) for a variety of reasons. For the project to succeed, it is critical to understand these motivations, particularly for people who contribute and maintain knowledge, "One of the challenges of knowledge management is to ensure that knowledge sharing is rewarded more than knowledge hoarding." (Davenport and Prusak 2000, p 29)

Davenport and Prusak (2000, p 31-34) identify three incentive categories. The most important is *reciprocity*; people give because they expect to receive. Next is *repute*; having a reputation for being knowledgeable has indirect benefits, such as greater reciprocity and job security. Third is *altruism*; some people make not care about immediate benefits, and some cultures encourage such behavior more than others. Similarly, Figallo and Rhine (2002, p 217) identify four categories. Some incentives are purely *personal*, such as a desire to help, learn, or achieve respect. Others are *cultural*, based on organizational norms. A third group of incentives are *goal-oriented*, such as a desire to get work done faster or to save money. The last set is *compensatory*; people can receive salary or bonuses for participating, or when their contributions benefit others. However, compensatory approaches can backfire; "if the process of sharing and transfer is not inherently rewarding, celebrated, and supported by the culture, then artificial rewards won't have much effect and can make people feel cynical" (O'Dell and Grayson 1998, p 82).

Different roles are likely to have different incentives. For example, content creators may seek to make their own work easier, while editors seek to improve the organization (Majchrzak, Wagner, and Yates 2006).

In addition to incentives, there are often simple but valuable ways to facilitate participation in a KM system. In general, wikis make it easy for anyone in the organization to update pages, rather than restricting such access to a group. Many wiki platforms allow users to define templates that make it easier to create new pages. In some cases, however, facilitating one role creates more work for another role. For example, a comment box may make it easier for occasional users to quickly add notes to a page; however, someone else may later need to incorporate or respond to the comment, creating more work.

4.2 Initiating KM Projects

In the 1990s, the need for significant up-front investments meant that most KM projects were initiated top-down, presumably on the basis of a return-on-investment (ROI) analysis involving some or all of the organizational benefits discussed above. The advantages of a top-down initiative include higher visibility, access to resources, and high-level champions. At the same time, it may be harder to convince people across the organization to invest the time and energy to help build a system when the individual benefits are not yet clear.

As KM priorities have shifted and the cost of supporting IT systems has decreased, it has become easier to initiate KM projects bottom-up, starting with small, self-selected pilot projects in which small groups address problems or opportunities that matter to them. Thus, a bottom-up approach generally requires fewer resources, and can start quietly. Once the initial projects have proven themselves, the system scope can gradually extend to other parts of the organization, or high-level support can be enlisted for a more rapid enterprise-wide deployment.

For both top-down and bottom-up initiatives, it is important to consider the relationships between the system scope (amount of knowledge, measured here in wiki pages), the number of people involved the project, their productivity (related to the effort they devote to the project, presumably), and the time over which they work. If system content changes very rarely (or slowly), then the relationship can be described as follows:

$$\left(\begin{array}{c} pages\ in \\ system \end{array} \right) = \left(\begin{array}{c} \#\ of \\ editors \end{array} \right) \left(\begin{array}{c} pages \\ edited \\ /\ week \end{array} \right) \left(\begin{array}{c} \#\ of \\ weeks \end{array} \right) \qquad (3)$$

Once the system is "complete", much less effort is needed to maintain it. However, if content changes, it is also important to consider the ongoing effort requires to keep the system current. This can be done by estimating the half-life of the system – the time it will take for half of the content to be outdated. The half-life can be used to estimate the number of pages that must be updated in a given time period, which interacts with the number of users, the fraction who contribute content in that time period, and their productivity.

$$\left(\begin{array}{c} pages\ in \\ system \end{array} \right) \left(1 - 0.5^{\left(\frac{1}{half\ life\ in\ weeks} \right)} \right) = \left(\begin{array}{c} \#\ of \\ users \end{array} \right) \left(\begin{array}{c} fraction \\ who\ edit \end{array} \right) \left(\begin{array}{c} pages \\ edited \\ /\ week \end{array} \right) \qquad (4)$$

To understand the effects of incentives and other actions on the various roles and the overall KM system, it may help to recall Zipf's law; a few people contribute the vast majority of the content, and many people rarely if ever contribute, although they may well use knowledge in the system; this is illustrated in figure 2.

Figure 2: Model of KM contributors

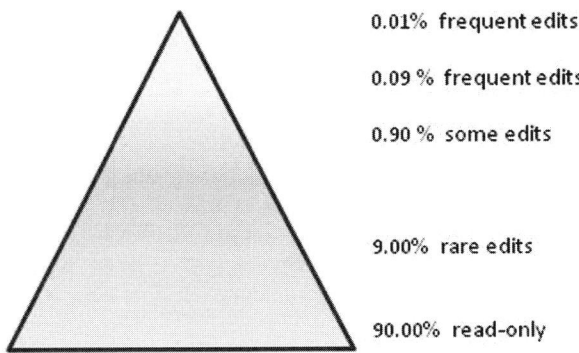

0.01% frequent edits

0.09 % frequent edits

0.90 % some edits

9.00% rare edits

90.00% read-only

According to Nielsen (2006), in most online communities 1% of participants contribute most of the content; 9% contribute occasionally, and 90% read but never contribute. Blogs are closer to 0.1%, 5%, and 95%, respectively, while Wikipedia is 0.003%, 0.2%, 99.8% - in other words, 1000 users contribute 2/3 of the content. Nielsen observes that it is impossible to overcome this inequality, but suggests some ways to encourage broader participation.

A particular KM system probably has an optimal distribution, even if that optimum cannot be computed. If only a few people contribute knowledge, then the system may not be useful, or those few people may become overwhelmed. On the other hand, a KM system run by a handful of knowledgeable or well-connected brokers might function quite well in some organizations. At the other extreme, if too many people contribute, it may be difficult to find the truly useful knowledge. Some online communities find that modest barriers result in higher quality content (e.g. Taylor 2007); the same idea may be true for KM projects within an organization.

4.3 Developing & Extending Wiki Platforms

Wiki KM systems are built on wiki platforms, which can be developed and supported via a variety of mechanisms. Watson, et al (2008) identify a spectrum of five software production models:

1. *Open Community*: Volunteers with little or no commercial stake work together on software that is freely available for others to use and modify, usually via one of several open source licenses (e.g. the GNU project).
2. *Sponsored*: For-profit or not-for-profit organizations sponsor open source software by providing funding, developers, or other resources (e.g. Apache).

3. *Professional Open Source*: For-profit organizations develop open source software, and generate revenue from complementary services such as training, support, and expert consulting (e.g. JBoss and MySQL). Expertise with the internal workings of the open source software is a key competitive advantage for these organizations.

4. *Corporate Distribution*: For-profit organizations identify best-of-breed open source projects and package them with improved distribution methods and complementary services (e.g. Red Hat).

5. *Proprietary*: An organization invests resources to create software, restricts access through legal and technical means, and generates revenue by licensing the software to customers, and through complementary services (e.g. Microsoft).

The boundaries between these models are often blurred, but wiki systems span the spectrum. Smaller wikis are often developed by open communities – often with just a handful of active developers. For many non-proprietary wikis, significant pieces of work are sponsored by companies that need specific enhancements. For example, we have developed TWiki extensions and enhancements on behalf of consulting clients. In most cases, sponsors are willing A few wiki platforms have formal consulting organizations (e.g. WikiRing.com and twiki.net), and provide significant revenue to key developers. Some wiki platforms (e.g. MoinMoin) are included in popular corporate distributions. Finally, there are also successful proprietary wikis.

Zipf's law also applies to open source projects (see figure 3). Typically there are a few very (often just one) key developers, assisted by a somewhat larger core team, who together do most of the actual development. Furthermore, there is often a larger supporting group of developers, particularly for wikis with architectures that make it easy to define extensions. However, non-developer users greatly outnumber developers (at least in successful wikis), and while the majority use the wiki platform only rarely, frequent or heavy users contribute to the platform by suggesting new features, identifying problems, developing or maintaining documentation, etc. Successful open source projects recognize the importance of engaging users at all levels and encouraging them to move up the pyramid.

Figure 3: Models of open and closed source contributors

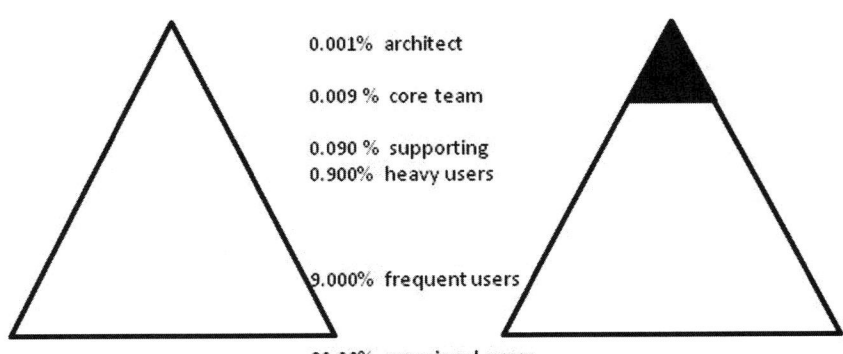

0.001% architect

0.009 % core team

0.090 % supporting
0.900% heavy users

9.000% frequent users

90.00% occasional users

Figure 3 also illustrates a key difference between open and closed source software. Both have user communities that exhibit Zipf distributions. The exact shape of the distribution (determined by the parameter s), depends on a variety of factors, including the complexity of the software and the size of the potential market. Anyone in the community can access open source software; while those at the bottom may choose to access it rarely, if ever, the cumulative effect of many small contributions can be considerable, as illustrated by the shading from bottom to top. However, in closed source software, only the very top of the pyramid can access the code and directly affect how the system works, as illustrated by the black triangle at the top of the right pyramid.

5   Conclusions

Table 3 summarizes the three business cases discussed above.

Table 3: Business cases, key roles, and major factors

Business Case	Key Roles	Major Factors
Participating	Buyers	individual ROI
	Sellers	reputation, organization benefit
	Brokers	reputation, organization benefit
	Editors	reputation, organization benefit
Initiating	Leaders	organization ROI, top-down
	Non-leaders	individual ROI, bottom-up
Developing & enhancing	Developers	organizational ROI
	Non-developers	individual reputation

However, there are also interactions between these business cases, as illustrated in figure 4. There is a market between developers and initiators; developers provide tools, training, support, and other materials in exchange for resources to support development, feedback on improving and enhancing the platform, and enhanced reputations for key developers and the platform itself. Similarly, initiators provide the wiki platform infrastructure, motivation, and various incentives (discussed above), in exchange for the KM system itself, which contains explicit knowledge and maps of tacit knowledge, as well for improved efficiency and profit.

Figure 4: Interactions between business cases

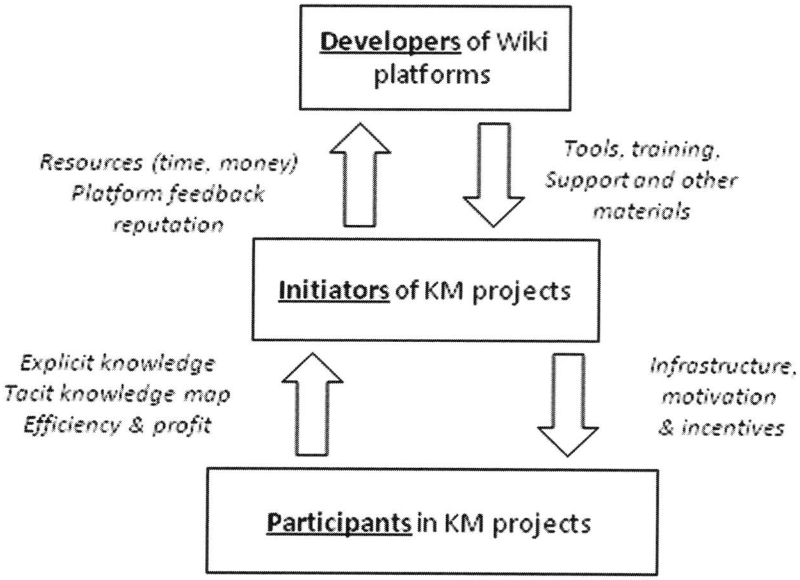

5.1 Implications & Future Directions

KM will continue to grow as a source of competitive advantage, and our understanding of how to manage (or enable) knowledge will continue to evolve. KM system will continue to become more distributed, in order to better match problems and opportunities across the organization, which may lead to the need for better "federated" tools to integrate and connect knowledge across larger enterprises.

Wikis will continue their rapid evolution. As wikis are increasingly used by non-technical users, ease of use will become an even more important factor. As wikis are used by larger and more traditional organizations, they will develop more sophisticated and user-friendly security and permission systems; the historically open wiki culture may lead to tension here. There will also be more ways to integrate wikis with other enterprise systems; in some cases a wiki may be the portal through which other systems are accessed, in other cases a wiki may be one of many tools accessed through another portal. Finally, there will almost certainly be consolidation in the wiki platform market; as users and organizations expect more capabilities and more specialization, individual wiki platforms will have to differentiate themselves, and many will fail to maintain a critical mass of developers. This should result in a smaller number of platforms with larger, more robust development communities.

Wikis will continue to be valuable for KM, particularly in areas and organizations with extensive tacit knowledge, or explicit knowledge which evolves quickly and is this not conducive to more structure KM systems. As wiki-based KM systems grow in scope and are used in larger organizations, they will need to strike a balance between consistency, for enhanced efficiency, and customization, to adapt to the ever changing knowledge landscape.

References

Alavi M, Leidner DE. (2001) Review: Knowledge management and knowledge management systems: Conceptual foundations and research issues. MIS Quarterly 25(1):107-136

Blake P (2006) Using a wiki for information services: Principles and practicalities. In Proceedings of New Librarians Symposium (NLS2006), Sydney, Australia

Box GEP, Draper NR (1987) Empirical Model-Building and Response Surfaces. Wiley

Cayzer S (2004) Semantic blogging and decentralized knowledge management. Communications of the ACM 47(12):47-52

Charman S (2006) An adoption strategy for social software in the enterprise. *Corante*. http://strange.corante.com/archives/2006/03/05/an_adoption_strategy_for_social_software_in _enterprise.php Accessed May 13, 2008

Chau T, Maurer F (2005) A case study of wiki-based experience repository at a medium-sized software company. Proceedings of the 3rd International Conference on Knowledge capture 185-186

Chauvel D, Despres C (2002) A review of survey research in knowledge management: 1997-2001. Journal of Knowledge Management 6(3):207-23

Conway ME (1968) How do committees invent? Datamation 14(4):28-31

CosmoCode (2008) WikiMatrix: Compare them all. http://www.wikimatrix.org. Accessed 10 May 2008

Davenport TH, Prusak L (2000) Working Knowledge. 2nd ed. Harvard Business School Press

DeMarco T, Lister T (1999) Peopleware: Productive Projects and Teams. Dorset House

Drucker PF, Garvin D, Leonard D, Straus S, Brown JS (1998) Harvard Business Review on Knowledge Management. 6th ed. Harvard Business School Press

Fenstermacher KD (2005) Revealed processes in knowledge management. Third Biennial Conference on Professional Knowledge Management, Kaiserslautern, Germany

Fichter D (2006) Using wikis to support online collaboration in libraries. Information Outlook, January

Figallo C, Rhine N (2002) Building the Knowledge Management Network: Best Practices, Tools, and Techniques for Putting Conversation to Work. Wiley

Frappaolo C (2006) Knowledge Management. 2nd ed. Capstone

Glogowski J, Steiner S (2008) The life of a wiki: How Georgia State University Library's wiki enhances content currency and employee collaboration. Internet Reference Services Quarterly 13(1)

Gonzolez-Reinhart J (2005). Wiki and the wiki way: Beyond a knowledge management system. http://www.uhisrc.com/FTB/Wiki/wiki_way_brief[1]-Jennifer%2005.pdf Accessed 10 May 2008

Grudin J (2006). Enterprise knowledge management and emerging technologies. In Proceedings of the 39th Annual Hawaii International Conference on System Sciences, Track 3, p57a

Hann IH, Roberts JA, Slaughter SA, Fielding R (2002) Why do developers contribute to open source projects? First evidence of economic incentives. In Proceedings of the 2nd Workshop on Open Source Software Engineering, The 24th International Conference on Software Engineering

Hansen MT, Nohria N, Tierney T (1999) What's your strategy for managing knowledge? Harvard Business Review 77(2):106-16

Hepp M, Siorpaes K, Bachlechner D (2007) Harvesting wiki consensus: Using Wikipedia entries as vocabulary for knowledge management. IEEE Internet Computing 11(5):54-65

Highsmith J (2002) Agile Software Development Ecosystems. Addison Wesley

Hof RD (2004) Something wiki this way comes. Business Week, June 7

Holsapple CW, Joshi, KD (2000) An investigation of factors that influence the management of knowledge in organizations. Journal of Strategic Information Systems 9(2-3):235-261

Huberman BA, Pirolli PLT, Pitkow JE, Lukose RM (1998) Strong regularities in world wide web surfing. Science 280(5360):95-97

King WR, Marks Jr PV, McCoy S (2002) The most important issues in knowledge management. Communications of the ACM 45(9):93-97

Koenig M (2001) User education for KM: The problem we won't recognize. KM World, December

KPMG Consulting (2000) Knowledge Management Research Report. London: KPMG Consulting

Leuf B, Cunningham W (2001) The Wiki Way: Quick Collaboration on the Web. Boston, MA: Addison-Wesley Professional

Levene M, Borges J, Loizou G (2001) Zipf's law for web surfers. Knowledge and Information Systems 3(1):120-129

Mader S (2008) Wikipatterns: A practical guide to improving productivity and collaboration in your organization. Wiley

Majchrzak A, Wagner C, Yates D (2006) Corporate wiki users: Results of a survey. In Proceedings of the 2006 International Symposium on Wikis, 99-104, Odense, Denmark: ACM Press

Mason D, Pauleen DJ (2003). Perceptions of knowledge management: A qualitative analysis. Journal of Knowledge Management 7(4):38-48

Nielsen J (2006) Participation Inequality: Lurkers vs. Contributors in Internet Communities.. Jakob Nielsen's Alertbox. http://www.useit.com/alertbox/participation_inequality.html Accessed May 14, 2008

Nonaka I (1991) The knowledge-creating company. Harvard Business Review 69(6):96-104

Nonaka I, Takeuchi H. (1995) The Knowledge-Creating Company: How Japanese Companies Create the Dynamics of Innovation. Oxford University Press

O'Dell C, Grayson CJ (1998) If Only We Knew What We Know: The Transfer of Internal Knowledge and Best Practice. 1st ed. Free Press

Paulk M, Weber C, Curtis B, Chrissis MB, et al. (1994) The Capability Maturity Model: Guidelines for Improving the Software Process. Addison Wesley

Priedhorsky R, et al (2007) Creating, destroying, and restoring value in Wikipedia. In Proceedings of the 2007 International ACM Conference on Supporting Group Work, Sanibel Island, FL

Raman M, Ryan T, Olfman L (2005) Designing knowledge management systems for teaching and learning with wiki technology. Journal of Information Systems Education 16(3):311-320

Segetech Ltd. (2007) Bugzilla/SVN/Wiki Integration. *Segetech Open Source Rendezvous*. http://oss.segetech.com/bugzilla-svn-wiki.html. Accessed May 22, 2008

Snowden D (2002) Complex acts of knowing: Paradox and descriptive self-awareness. Journal of Knowledge Management 6(2):100-111

Snowden D (2006) Whence goeth KM?. *Cognitive Edge*. http://www.cognitive-edge.com/2006/11/whence_goeth_km.php Accessed May 12, 2008

Swisher K (2004) 'Wiki' may alter how employees work together. The Wall Street Journal, July 29

Szulanski G (1994) Intra-Firm Transfer of Best Practices Project. Houston, TX: American Productivity and Quality Center

Taylor C (2007) Why commercial Wikis don't work. *CNN Money Business 2.0*. http://money.cnn.com/2007/02/21/magazines/business2/walledgardens.biz2/index.htm Accessed May 12, 2008

Viegas FB, Wattenberg M, Kriss J, van Ham F (2007) Talk before you type: Coordination in Wikipedia. In Proceedings of the 4th Annual Hawaii International Conference on System Sciences

Viégas FB, Wattenberg M, McKeon MM (2007) The hidden order of Wikipedia. In Proceedings of the 12th International Conference on Human-Computer Interaction, Beijing, P.R. China.

von Krogh G, Ichijo K, Nonaka I (2000) Enabling Knowledge Creation: How to Unlock the Mystery of Tacit Knowledge and Release the Power of Innovation. Oxford University Press

Wagner C (2004) Wiki: A technology for conversation knowledge management and group collaboration. Communications of the Association for Information Systems 13:265-289

Watson RT, Boudreau MC, York PT, Greiner ME, Wynn D (2008) The business of open source. Communications of the ACM 51(4):41-46

Wenger E (1999) Communities of Practice: Learning, Meaning, and Identity. 1st ed. Cambridge University Press.

Wikipedia (2008) Wikipedia: The free encyclopedia. http://en.wikipedia.org/wiki/Main_Page. Accessed 10 May 2008.

Wong KY, Aspinwall E (2005) An empirical study of the important factors for knowledge-management adoption in the SME sector. Journal of Knowledge Management 9(3):64-82

Zhu Z (2004) Knowledge management: Towards a universal concept or cross-cultural contexts? Knowledge Management Research & Practice 2(2):67-79

Zipf GK (1935) The Psychobiology of Language. Houghton-Mifflin

Chapter 10. Using a Semantic Forum as Learning Support

Marie-Hélène Abel

University of Technology of Compiègne, FRANCE

Abstract

We can qualify our society of information society or cognitive society. In such a context, learning became a mechanism of critical assistance not only from the point of view of training but also from the point of view of the new economy for which three keywords are: speed, just in time and relevance. This new economy and the advent of web 2.0 technologies imply new working forms and new learning forms. Within the approach MEMORAe we are interested in these new learning forms. We think that these ones are connected to the knowledge management practices and require web 2.0 applications. Thus learners are organized in communities and have to reach the good resources at the right moment; they must have the possibility to share their resources or knowledge with community members. To that end we developed a learning environment based on concepts of learning organizational memory and distributed semantic forum. In this chapter, we interest of the evolution of the concept of e-learning and define the role of web 2.0 applications in such a context. Then we present the links between knowledge management and e-learning. Finally, we describe the approach MEMORAe, the concept of semantic forum and the environment E-MEMORAe2.0 we developed before to conclude and present perspectives toward the use of a social web within our approach.

1 Introduction

We can qualify our society of information society or cognitive society. This is mainly due to the mobility. This one increases and becomes an essential factor for the new working forms. It is expressed by a geographical mobility that can be temporary (pendular movements, nomad work) or movements of workers in different countries. It can be also a professional mobility: more frequent changes of company, job during the professional life. These new working forms are the consequences of an evolution of the production towards the "service product" incorporating an increasingly large part "of immaterial". Information becomes a raw material of most of production, transformation or exchange operations. So, we are confronted, on one hand, with a generalization of the information and communication processing systems, and on the other hand with a demand either essentially of professional competences but also information processing competences and competences in more complex forms of cooperation.

In such a context, learning became a mechanism of critical assistance not only from the point of view of training but also from the point of view of the new economy for which three keywords are: speed, just in time and relevance (Drucker, 2003). The volatility of markets is such as it requires methods just in time to help employees, partners to learn. Becoming a learning organization is a way for an organization to stay competitive. The new learning forms are thus an integral part of the industrial challenges.

The term "Community of Practice", CoP, is relatively recent coinage, even though the phenomenon it refers to is age-old. The concept has turned out to provide a useful perspective on knowing and learning. A growing number of people and organizations in various sectors are now focusing on communities of practice as a key to improve their performance. CoPs are groups of people who share a concern or a passion for something they do and learn how to do it better as they interact regularly (Wenger 1998)

Communities of practice exist in any organization even if they are not bound by organizational affiliation. They are important to the organization functioning and become crucial to those that recognize knowledge as a key asset.

In some organizations, the communities themselves are becoming recognized as valuable assets. Thus, they serve both each member of the organization (specify his identity) and the organization itself. According to the study presented in (Lesser and Storck 2001), four areas of organizational performance are impacted by communities of practice: 1) Decreasing the learning curve of newcomers; 2) Responding more rapidly to needs and inquiries; 3) Reducing rework and preventing "reinvention of the wheel"; 4) Spawning new ideas for product and services.

Acting as a community of practice seems a prerequisite to an organization to enable its members to share experiences, knowledge and competencies i.e. to learn each other.

Within the approach MEMORAe (Leblanc and Abel, 2007) we are interested in these new learning forms. We think that these ones are connected to the knowledge management practices and require web 2.0 applications. Thus learners are organized in communities and have to reach the good resources at the right moment; they must have the possibility to share their resources or knowledge with community members. To that end, resources have to be easily created, stored, well described and indexed. That's why we focused on knowledge capitalization in the context of organizations and more precisely the capitalization of the resources related to these knowledge. We particularly worked on the way members of an organization could use this capitalization to get new knowledge and competencies.

We developed an environment based on the concept of learning organizational memory. In such an environment, resources are indexed by knowledge organized by means of ontologies, and different ways of exchange and communication are offered in order to facilitate the externalization of tacit knowledge. We defined the concept of semantic forum. Such a forum describes its content by way of ontology concepts. Each concept represents a forum domain; and each query with its answers is stored in a resource indexed by the concept concerned by the query. Thus a semantic forum is dedicated to a community which defines its own vocabulary by mean of ontology and by the way discussion topics.

In this chapter, we interest in the evolution of the concept of e-learning and define the role of web 2.0 applications in such a context. Then we present the links between knowledge management and e-learning. Finally, we describe the approach MEMORAe, the concept of semantic forum and the environment E-MEMORAe2.0[1] we developed before to conclude and present perspectives toward the use of a social web within our approach.

2   E-learning evolution

E-learning is a training context based on the diffusion of pedagogical contents by means of an electronic medium (diskettes, CD, Internet, Intranet, extranet, interactive television, etc). It can be composed of tools, pedagogical applications or pedagogical contents. It concerns different publics like pupils, students or adults. The first use these electronic media for academic training whereas the last want to improve their training or to update their knowledge.

The concept of online learning or Web Based Training appeared recently with the expansion of the Web. It forms one of the facets of the e-learning and is characterized by the use of Web technology. Teaching applications and pedagogical contents are diffused by way of an access to a computer network (Intranet, extranet or Internet): collaboration and interactivity are thus made possible. Thus online learning allows putting into practice theories of social and active learning by way of reflection, communication and collaboration (Tiffin & Rajasingham, 1995)

The online learning is finally a recent form of the e-learning. Concerning this form:

"eLearning is just-in-time education integrated with high velocity value chains. It is the delivery of individualized, comprehensive, dynamic learning content in real time, aiding the development of communities of knowledge, linking learners and practitioners with experts" (Drucker, 2000).

With this form of e-learning, teachers do not control totally anymore the delivery of the learning material to learners. Learners select, combine this material ac-

---

[1] http://www.hds.utc.fr/~ememorae/Site-MEMORAe2.0/

cording to their own needs. Learning contents must thus exist in their own right: we call them Learning Objects. Currently, we can find many definitions of Learning Objects. The most cited is the following:

"Learning Objects are defined here as any entity, digital or non-digital, which can be used, re-used or referenced during technology supported learning. Examples of technology supported learning include computer-based training systems, interactive learning environments, intelligent computer-aided instruction systems, distance learning systems, and collaborative learning environments. Examples of Learning Objects include multimedia content, instructional content, learning objectives, instructional software and software tools, and persons, organizations, or events referenced during technology supported learning." [LTSC, 2002]

This definition is so broad that different working groups have refined it but continue to use the term "learning object" or proposed their own terminology to define a concept generally very closed to the canonical definition. Among these definitions, we chose to reuse the one proposed by Wiley: "any digital resource that can be reused to support learning" (Wiley, 2000). First, this definition is based on the LTSC one, and second it includes web resources.

In order to facilitate their reuse, Learning Objects must be reached and indexed easily. To that end, the best way is to use metadata.

Metadata enable to describe web resources in order to make them usable by various online learning systems. They must ensure three essential functions to a better use of learning objects:

- Interoperability which is the ability of multiples systems with different hardware and software platforms to exchange and to use learning objects.
- Accessibility which is usually translated by a search greatly facilitated by an accurate description of the resource.
- Reusability which means that a learning object could be used as needed, in different learning contexts.

The most used metadata set is the LOM[2].

In the following, we use the term e-learning with the recent form meaning.

3   Role of web2.0 applications in e-Learning context

Most of the early web-based courses were designed to complement classical teaching methods for dissemination of courses materials. The online learning environments were used as tools for pedagogical material (learning object) delivery in which the students' role was passive: no exploitation of the web communication potential. We know that learning is an active process where learners build their knowledge and understanding (Wittrock, 1974) (Papert & al, 1991). However, ac-

---

[2] http://ltsc.ieee.org/wg12/

cording to (Ebner & al, 2007), we have not to forget learning is also a social process which proceeds through conversation (Motschnig-Pitrick & al, 2002) and interaction (Preece & al, 2002).

E-learning has the potential to put into practice this social process. However, to exploit this potential, e-learning requires facilitators to engage learners into interaction (Sargeant & al, 2006). We can distinguish several types of learner interaction (Moore, 1989):

- Interaction with content,
- Interaction with teacher,
- Interaction with other learners.

Bouhnik and Marcus propose to add a new type: interaction with new technologies (Bouhnik & al, 2006).

Web 2.0 technologies seem to be a good candidate to build e-learning environments taking into account a social process. Web 2.0 is a new generation coming from the classical Web which we call now Web 1.0. The main difference between the two generations is the control of contents. With Web 1.0, contents are controlled by the Web master and users can only read them. With Web 2.0, users are readers as well as contributors. Thus, when they contribute, users create contents that are aggregated automatically to form new contents. These ones are the result of the contribution of all participants, even the web master didn't expect that content will include in his pages.

Web 2.0 technologies offer to users distributed collaboration facilities (O-Reilly, 2005). They can be distinguished from web 1.0 technologies by various characteristic features:

- Community: Web 2.0 applications enable users to collaborate and share information easily.
- Mashups: An aggregation of various contents, data coming from different sites.
- Ajax[3] or LAMP[4]: These sets of technologies enable web masters to create responsive user interfaces.

Thus, Web 2.0 technologies seem to be a good way to produce facilitators in order to engage learners into the four types of interaction. These distributed collaboration facilities start to have a significant impact on e-learning. This one makes for a distributed control and coordinated actions between learners.

The most well-known web 2.0 applications are wikis and blogs. For few years wikis have been used in educational institutions as tools that promote sharing and collaborative creation of Web contents. A wiki is a collection of web pages designed to enable anyone who accesses it to contribute or modify content, using a

---

[3] Acronym for Asynchronous JavaScript and XML
[4] Acronym for Linux, Apache, MySQL and PHP

simplified markup language[5]. On a basic level wiki is a website comprising the collective work of many authors. Wikis are crucially different from blogs, which are also used in educational context, in that users can modify any entry, even material posted by others. Unlike to a wiki, a blog is a website maintained by only one individual, with regular entries of commentary, descriptions of events, or other material such as graphics or video[6].

Let's note that, although wikis are a tool for creating contents, they serve at the same time collaborative skills learning. Thus, wikis offer to students a collaborative environment where they learn how to work with others, how to create a community and how to operate in our society that we can qualify of cognitive society. In such a society the creation of knowledge and information is increasingly becoming a group effort (Richardson, 2006).

Achterman (Atcherman, 2007) retains five features that facilitate collaborative efforts:

- Ease of use: users can easily access to a wiki, add, modify, edit a content;
- Spaces for students to create contents individually, in small groups or large groups. Students can move from one space to another and easily transfer the content of one space to another;
- Ability to create a non linear document structure by way of hyperlinks;
- A built-in mechanism for reflection and metacognition. Many wikis propose a discussion or comment space where students can engage in conversation to justify their content addition;
- A means of tracking individual, small group and whole group in progress by way of an assignment.

Thus, the Web 2.0 key components are the facility of using creation tools and the collaboration/social interaction it offers. According to (Davis, 2005):

"Web 2.0 is an attitude not a technology. It's about enabling and encouraging participation through open applications and services. By open I mean *technically open* with appropriate APIs but also, more importantly, *socially open*, with rights granted to use the content in new and exciting contexts."

Following this way, Downes coined the term e-learning 2.0 which results from the combination of web 2.0 technologies and the collaboration/social interactions they offer in the context of learning application (Downes, 2008).

4   Links between web 2.0 and Semantic Web.

Web 2.0 applications and services enable non-specialist users to contribute to the Web. This leads to new requirements of Networked Information Retrieval

---

[5] http://en.wikipedia.org/wiki/Wiki/Wiki
[6] http://en.wikipedia.org/wiki/Wiki/Blog

(Zhang, 2007). Indeed, in the web 1.0 context, only the web masters created content and thus used professional data in order to enable any users to retrieve it by way of different methods such as subject catalogue-based retrieval, key words-based retrieval, metadata-based retrieval, etc. In the Web 2.0 context, due to the lack of semantic relation among contents, massive information produced by users can't be processed. This information generally consists in microcontents creation. Microcontents come from the various contributions of users such as images, collected bookmarks, queries and answers of forum and so on. The Web 2.0 applications should be able to reuse these microcontents freely in any place. To do this, microcontents need to be aggregated, managed, shared in order to be transferred and remixed in new contents dedicated to specific applications. Unfortunately, much of these forms of contribution are currently confined into private space or published in formats that hinder its reuse.

In the context of the Semantic Web, data on the web are published in machine-readable format using shared ontologies to give them a formal semantic, and interlinked on a massive scale (Shadbolt & al, 2006). Thus data can be retrieval easily. Publishing data using languages dedicated to the Semantic Web (RDF[7], OWL[8] or Topic Maps[9]), has different advantages: (a) Makes data retrieval by using a standard query language (SPARQL[10], TMQL[11]); (b) Facilitates the integration of data from different resources; (c) Allows the creation of machine-readable links between data resources. However, create Semantic Web applications necessitates specialist skills and it is a brake to their growth.

Web 2.0 and the Semantic Web have been previously considered as independent and even competing for the evolution of the Web. Each approach is supported by its own community. Due to their strengths and their weakness, we believe, like several colleagues, that these two visions are complementary:

"The Semantic Web can learn from Web 2.0's focus on community and interactivity, while Web 2.0 can draw from the Semantic Web's rich technical infrastructure for exchanging information across application boundaries." (Ankolekar & al, 2007, p 825).

According to the same authors, this is possible by providing simple, well-structured Web forms through which users can add comments, information to a web site without requiring any knowledge of the underlying technologies or principles. By following this approach, an environment should enable users to create content that is immediately usable on the Semantic Web. Users are guided and place their contribution in such a way that elicit semantic annotations are automatically associated.

---

[7] http://www.w3.org/RDF/

[8] http://www.w3.org/2004/OWL/

[9] http://www.topicmaps.org/

[10] http://www.w3.org/TR/rdf-sparql-query/

[11] http://www.isotopicmaps.org/tmql/

Semantic wikis are an illustration of this complementarity. They try to combine the strengths of Semantic Web and Wiki technologies. The wikipedia definition[12] specifies that a semantic wiki is a wiki that has an underlying model of the knowledge described in its pages. Regular wikis have structured text and untyped hyperlinks (such as the links in this article). Semantic wikis allow the ability to capture or identify further information about the pages (metadata) and their relations.

In the same way, we propose the concept of semantic forum. A semantic forum is an internet forum that has an underlying model of the knowledge described in its content. Such content is formed by users' questions and answers about specific topics concerning the forum theme. All the questions and their answers are micro-contents that we can described by the author, the date of posting but also by the theme and the topic it is about. In the case of a learning context, in order to not be disconnected with the learning activities, topics will be defined in advance by the training head. All this knowledge is defined semantically although users don't aware of this definition and language used to do it.

5   Links between e-Learning and Knowledge Management

Problems solving in collaboration becomes the main activity producing value in companies. The new working forms generate more and more informal situations of learning. The discussions around problems and\or projects, various meetings, etc. produce situations in which members learn and develop knowledge and particular competences. Thus companies try to take into account in their development policy the 'formal' training in the framework of e-learning projects but also the 'informal' training through the recognition of knowledge exchanges networks, and the formalization of knowledge capitalization procedures coming from the theory of the Knowledge Management (KM).

We can define KM as all the methods and the techniques allowing to collect, identify, analyze, organize, remember, and share knowledge between organizations members, in particular knowledge created by the company itself or acquired outside. Knowledge Management comprises a range of practices used by organizations to identify, create, represent, and distribute knowledge for reuse, awareness and learning[13].

So, KM systems and e-learning systems serve the same objectives: facilitate the development of competences and learning in organizations (Schmidt, 2005). They are moreover complementary. E-learning systems are used as support by learners so that they can develop their knowledge. They offer to them structured educational contents and opportunities of intercommunication about specific subjects.

---

[12] http://en.wikipedia.org/wiki/Semantic_wiki
[13] http://en.wikipedia.org/wiki/ Knowledge_management

The KM systems offer possibilities of access to knowledge by means of contents management systems. These kinds of systems aim at managing all the contents of a company. They concern at the same moment not structured electronic information (digital documents) and structured information (databases).

This complementarity between e-learning and KM is strengthened by the use of tools and specific platforms integrating human resources management, training management and information sharing.

In spite of this context, several studies showed that the connections between e-learning and KM are not operationnalized (Efimova & al, 2002). According to Ras (Ras & al, 2005), this is due to various barriers on conceptual or technical level. We can mention:

- Problems on conceptual level: for example (Ley & al, 2005) propose an environment of workplace composed of three spaces: a working space, a knowledge space and a learning space. The main problem concerns the connections between these spaces. Each space has its own structure which reflects the mental model of its users.
- Problems on a technical level: the spaces of work, knowledge or learning are implemented on different systems. Each system possesses its own structure of contents.
- Problem of Neglecting Learning Processes: though they facilitate purpose-oriented learning, KM systems don't explicitly address learning processes.

Associating Web 2.0 and Semantic Web approaches, as we see in the previous section, could offer a platform that overcomes these barriers. Indeed, Web 2.0 technologies facilitate the creation of social networks. A social network is in a way a community of practice. According to Wenger: "Communities of practice are groups of people who share a concern or a passion for something they do and learn how to do it better as they interact regularly." (Wenger, 2008)

Members can interact in face-to-face or online meetings. With the advent of web 2.0 technologies, creation of online communities is facilitated but a community is not defined by the use of such technologies. A community of practice is identified by means of three crucial characteristics (Wenger, 2008):

- The domain: Members have to share the same domain of interest, this one identifying the community.
- The community: Members interact, share information, discuss about the domain of interest to learn from each other.
- The practice: Members are practitioners and develop a shared directory of resources concerning their practices (experiences, documents, tools…).

Wenger specifies that communities develop their practice through activities and gives some typical examples: documentation projects, discussions, requests for information, seeking experience, etc. Finally, communities of practice are formed by people who engage in a process of collective learning. This learning can be the objective of the community members or is the results of their interactions. They provided a new approach, which focused on people and on the social structures that enable them to learn with and from each other. Because they offer informal training situations, organizations have interested in this approach for few years. Wenger explains this interest by different reasons:

- Communities of practice enable members to take collective responsibility for managing the knowledge they need.
- Communities among members create a direct link between learning and performance.
- Members can address the tacit and dynamic aspects of knowledge creation and sharing, as well as the more explicit aspects.
- Communities are not limited by formal structures: they create connections among people across organizational and geographic boundaries.

6   The MEMORAe approach

The acts to teach, to learn and to work are never socially isolated. They are the cultural resultant, articulated and developed through a defined practice gathering in a virtual or real space actors questioning themselves and wondering about the need of knowledge, abilities and attitudes to acquire competences specific to a given academic or professional domain[14].

Our aim, within the approach MEMORAe, is to operationalize connections between e-learning and knowledge management in the context of learning organization. To that end, our objective is to model and build a learning environment taking into account at the same time these two aspects (Abel & al, 2008).

In order to assess our approach, we chose to build organizational memory for academics organization: a course on applied mathematics at the University of Picardy (France). This choice of applications is justified by two observations:

- A course is made of actors (learners, instructors, trainers, course designers, administrators, etc.), resources of different types (definitions, exercises, etc.), written in various forms (books, reports, etc.) and on various supports (paper, video, audio, etc.) thus knowledge and competences which it must bring. In this sense, a course is an organization.
- Learner which participate in a course must get ready to their professional life and thus with an organizational learning.

Let us specify that in the context of an organization of academic type:

- Organizational knowledge is knowledge teachers want to transmit and learners must assimilate. The actors of such an organization must thus be able to exchange about this knowledge.

---

[14] http://www.tact.fse.ulaval.ca/ang/html/cp/intro.htm

- The objective is to get ready students for their professional life, i.e. to learn to learn.

In the following, we first present bases of our approach. Then, we specify how we put into practice our learning organizational memory and explain its use in an organizational learning context by way of the memories modelling and a semantic forum. We finish by presenting the evaluations carried out.

6.1 Approach base: the concept of Learning Organizational Memory

Bases of the approach MEMORAe coming from work studies in e-learning and knowledge management domains.

On the e-learning side, these last years, the learning environments' modelling was studied in educational engineering according to two principal approaches:

- Approach by the resources, based on the paradigm of the learning objects;
- Approach by the activities, based on the concepts of learning units, activity and teaching scenario.

On the knowledge management side, knowledge engineering proposes concepts, methods and techniques making it possible to model, formalize, acquire knowledge in organizations to operationalize, structure or manage in the broad sense. These methods and tools are intended to support the dynamics of knowledge in the organization.

Within the framework of the approach MEMORAe, we propose to associate knowledge engineering and educational engineering in order to model and build a learning environment according to the approach by the resources. In the knowledge engineering area, extending the definition proposed by (Van Heijst & al, 1996), (Dieng & al, 1998) consider an organizational memory as an "explicite, disembodied, persistent representation of knowledge and information in an organization, in order to facilitate its access and reuse by members of the organization, for their tasks." So, we made the choice to test and evaluate the contribution of the organizational memories based on ontologies in a context of training within a learning organization. Thus, extending the definition given by (Dieng & al, 1998), we propose the concept of Learning Organizational Memory for which users' task is learning.

6.2 Learning Organizational Memory into practice

Within the approach MEMORAe, first we were interested in the knowledge capitalization in the context of organizations and more precisely the capitalization of the resources related to this knowledge by means of an organizational memory. This work was realized in the framework of the project MEMORAe (Abel & al, 2006). We particularly focused on the way organization actors could use this capitalization to get new knowledge.

Let's remind that the design of an e-learning application implies to focus on the learner, giving him the means to be active, to make him understand the resources that are at his disposal and to teach him how to search and to use them. Articulating a training starting from knowledge grains offers more individualization possibilities. Generally, it consists in dividing the training content into small parts, using a semantic mark-up.

On the contrary, within our approach, we propose to organize the training content around concepts to learn. These concepts don't refer to a course unit part, but to knowledge or competences to acquire. Consequently, there is no need to cut off existing documents or to produce new documents corresponding to these concepts. Concepts to learn are used as indexes to access resources related to them. A concept to learn can refer to several resources (giving several means to acquire it) and a resource can be referred to by several notions (giving several means to retrieve it).

To that end, we developed the environment E-MEMORAe as support for learning organizational memory. In such a system resources are indexed to knowledge organized by means of ontologies: domain and application. The domain ontology, defines concepts shared by any organization; the application ontology defines concepts dedicated to a specific organization. Using these ontologies, actors can acquire knowledge by doing different tasks (solving problems or exercises, reading examples, definitions, reports, etc.). We used Topic Maps[15] as a representation formalism facilitating navigation and access to the resources. Such formalism has a XTM[16] specification that consists in an XML syntax allowing its expression and its interchange. It also has its own query language TMQL[17].

The ontology structure is also used to navigate among the concepts as in a roadmap. The user has to access to the resources which are appropriate for him.

Thus our environment is dedicated to be used by members of a "Semantic Learning Organization" (SLO). In the Information Systems context, a SLO is a concept that extends the notion of learning organization in a semantic dimension. A SLO must be considered as a learning organization in which learning activities

---

[15] http://www.topicmaps.org/
[16] http://www.topicmaps.org/xtm/
[17] http://www.isotopicmaps.org/tmql/spec.html

are mediated and enhanced through a shared knowledge representation of the domain and context of the organization (Sicilia & al, 2005).

E-MEMORAe aims at helping the users of the memory to acquire organization knowledge. To this end, users have to navigate through the application ontology that is related to the training, and to access to the indexed resources thanks to this ontology.

The general principle is to propose to the learner, at each step, either precise information on what he is searching for, or graphically displayed links that allow him to continue its navigation through the memory. He has no need to use the keyboard in order to formulate a request, even if the environment allows doing it.

To be more precise, the user interface (Figure 1) proposes:

- Entry points (left of the screen): they enable users to start their navigation with a given concept. An entry point provides a direct access to a concept of the memory and consequently to the part of the memory dedicated to it. They were chosen by the head of the course who considers them as essential.
- Resources (bottom of the screen) related to the current concept: they are ordered by type (books, course notes, sites, examples, comments[18], etc.). Starting from a map concept or an entry point, the user can directly access to associated resources. Descriptions of these resources help him to choose among them.
- A short definition of the current concept: it enables users to get a preview of the concept and enables them to decide if they have to work it or not.
- A history of the navigation: it enables the learner to remind and to be aware of the path he followed before. Of course, he can get back to a previously studied notion if he wants to.
- Least but not last, the part of the ontology describing the current resource is displayed at the centre of the screen.

---

[18] The comments are the only elements of the memory that the user can modify as (s)he wants. An a posteriori control is made by the editorial committee in order to keep them or not.

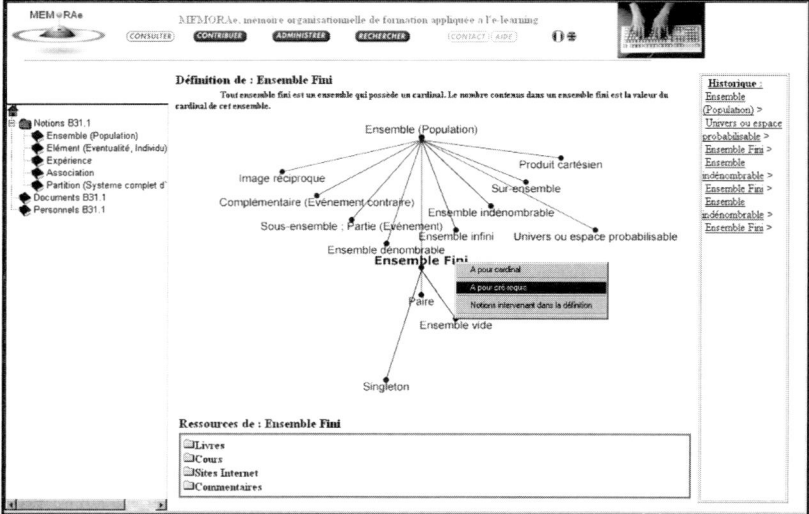

Figure 1: Navigation interface of E-MEMORAe

Within such an environment learning can occurs through the navigation among the concepts map or in making an exercise, in reading a book or an annotation and so on.

6.3 Organizational Learning context

According to Dogson (Dogson, 1993), a learning organization is a company which builds structures and strategies in order to increase and to maximize the organizational learning.

Organizational learning is an emergent property of the interaction between the organization members. Thus organizations form a place of synergies allowing the creation of knowledge higher than the one of their members. It is a question of collective intelligence. This one can be defined in terms of circulation of ideas, of diffusion of practices. It is thus a question of being interested on the way in which organization members develop capacities of acquisition, storage, processing and use of information. Thus, the organizational learning does not relate to private knowledge of the individuals but collectivized knowledge which they mobilize in the organization. This type of knowledge is at the interface of a private knowledge and a public knowledge.

Within project MEMORAe we interested in online learning environment taking into account an active process where learners build their knowledge and understanding. The project MEMORAe2.0 is an extension of the project MEMORAe. Within the framework of this second project we are interested in using the

MEMORAe approach in an organizational learning context (Leblanc & al, 2007). We wanted to facilitate social process which proceeds through conversation and interaction. To that end, we decided to exploit Girod works about organizational memory model (Girod, 1995) and web 2.0 technologies.

Memories modelling

Following the Girod works (Girod, 1995), we distinguish three levels of organizational memory and we propose to consider them by way of two memory types:

- Group memory: this kind of memory enables all the group members to access knowledge and resources shared by them. The group is at least made of two members. We distinguish three types of group memory corresponding to different communities of practice:
  - o Team memory: The team memory capitalizes knowledge, resources, communication concerning any object of interest of the group members.
  - o Project memory: The project memory capitalizes knowledge, resources, communication concerning a project. All the information stored is shared by the members who work on the project.
  - o Organization memory: this memory enables all the members of the organization to access knowledge and resources without access right. These resources and knowledge are shared by all the organization members.
- Individual memory: this kind of memory is private. Each member of the organization has his own memory in which he can organize, and capitalize his knowledge, resources.

Thus we base our approach on an organizational memory that makes a difference between knowledge and resources of: a) the whole organization; b) a community of practice in the organization – the organization is constituted of different communities of practice even if it can be seen as a community of practice itself; and c) an individual.

In order to put into practice this modelling we developed a new environment called E-MEMORAe2.0 (Figure 2). This one re-uses general principles of E-MEMORAe and gives the possibility of learners to have a private space and to participate to share spaces according to their rights. Let's notes that all the memories share the same ontologies.

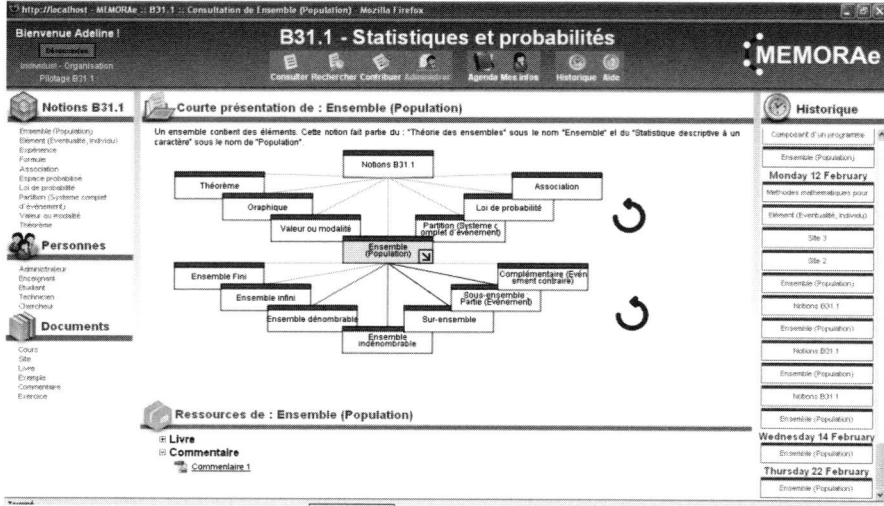

Figure 2: E-MEMORAe2.0 Navigation Interface.

When a user logs on he directly accesses to his individual memory. He can then navigate through the application ontology and access to resources which he himself added. He also can access to another memory by a click on the name of the memory in the high left part of the general menu.

This change of memory makes possible:

- Addition of entry points (Figure 3) shared by all the group members.
- Visualization of resources capitalized by the group members (cf Figure 4).

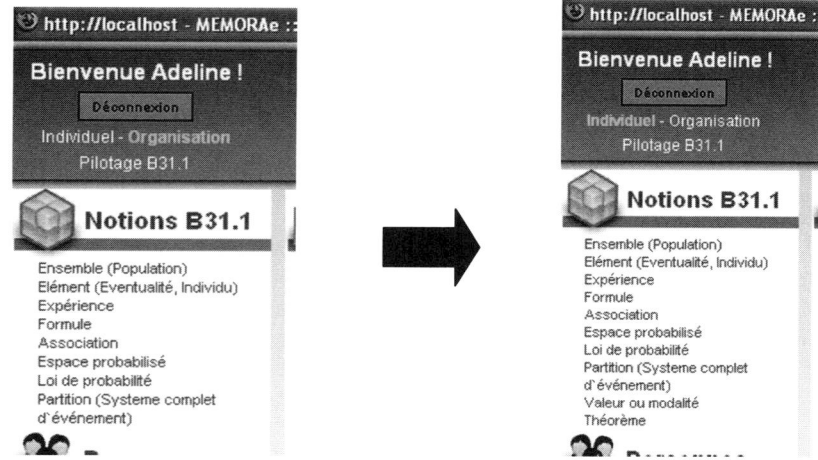

Figure 3 : Visualization of the individual and organizational memory entry points (in French)

Thus figure 4 shows different resources from different memories concerning the same concept. The user indexed two types of resources in his individual memory (books and comment) and can access to other resources such as training supports or exercises in the organizational memory.

Figure 4. Visualization of the individual and organizational resources (in French).

Ontologies enable to organize and capitalize exchanges. In order to facilitate the externalization of tacit knowledge, we chose to associate exchange resources to each concept of the application ontology. Exchange resources concern a concept and can be asynchronous (forum, blog, e-mail) or synchronous (chat). They give the opportunity to group members to exchange and share information on a subject; this subject/concept indexes the exchange resource.

MEMORAe forum

Within the approach MEMORAe, we consider a forum as a set of microcontents or micro-resources. We decided to manage these micro-resources like any resources in the memory. Thus we defined the concept of MEMORAe-Forum which is an exchange resource and is linked to one micro-resource of question type and 0 or n resources of answer type. Each micro-resource is indexed by a concept of the application ontology and has an author, a date of contribution.

In such a way, each group memory has its own forum organized around the shared ontology. All the forum contributions are distributed in the resource space among the other resources. Users don't access to the forum itself but to the memory resource space and then select resources of MEMORAe-Forum type to contribute to the forum. So there is not explicit forum where users can visualize all contributions of members but it will possible to build this presentation form with the functionality export we plan to develop.

In the following we present an example of the forum use in E-MEMORAe2.0. Figure 5 shows how users can access to a forum associated to an ontology concept in a group memory. They just have to select the right memory then the concept concerned by the question and the resources indexed part. At this step, they have to click on the type 'Forum': the list of question subjects that were already posted is printed. If users want to post their own question, they have to click on the bubble icon (placed at the right of the term Forum) and then specify their subject and their question. If they want to read answers to this question subject, they have to click on the subject itself. A window opens (Figure 6) and presents: (1) the subject and the question (top part), (2) the different answers with their author. At each time, the date of the contribution is registered.

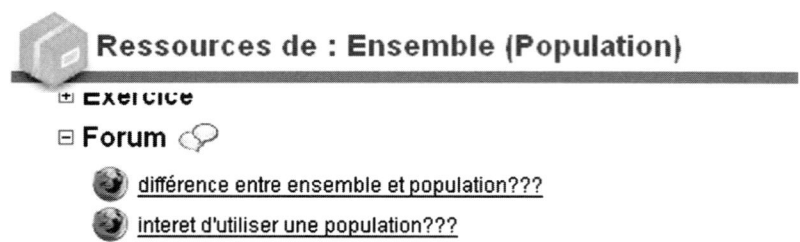

Figure 5. Forum Access (in French)

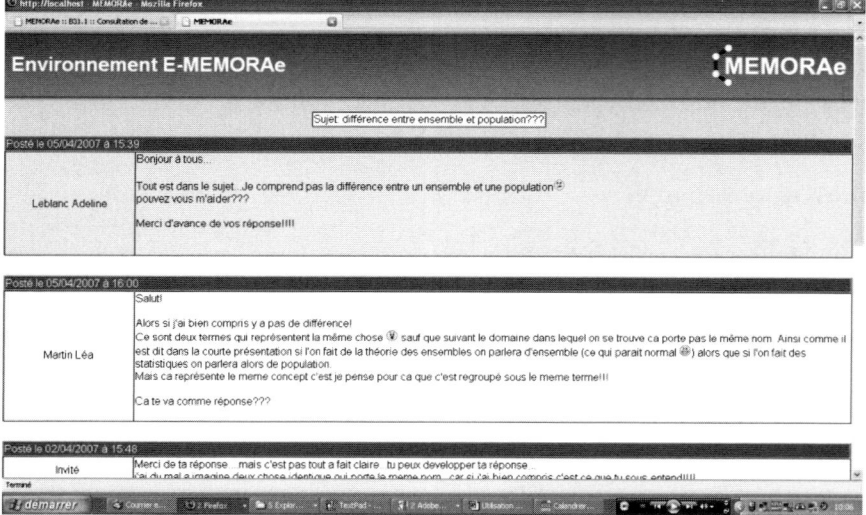

Figure 6. Forum Resource (in French)

Within the approach MEMORAe we linked semantic web and web 2.0 approaches: we implemented a semantic forum in such a way that users contribute to produce resources semantically described without specialist skills. Seeing queries and answers as resources should offer facilitators to engage learners into interaction: they see these resources when they access to the resources part and then can be questioned.

Evaluations

All the evaluations were realized with students of University of Picardy attending the course of applied mathematics.

The E-MEMORAe evaluation gave us encouraging results. It concerned organization level. Students appreciated to have access to documents by the way of the training concepts (Benayache & al, 2006).

The E-MEMORAe2.0 evaluation has begun and aims to experiment the two other levels through project-based activities. To do this we organized two evaluations. For these two evaluations, students are grouped in pairs and each pair has to solve a problem. Each student can access to his individual memory, to the memory of his pair and to the training memory. He can add resources in his memory or in his group memory and thus exchange resource and knowledge. Students have three weeks to solve a problem.

The first evaluation concerned students in mathematics. These ones hadn't computers and see each others everyday. They had a computers room at disposal and the problem to solve was given a mark. The second evaluation concerned students in computer science, they had a computer, saw each other everyday and the problem to solve wasn't given a mark.

With these two evaluations, our main objective was to see how E-MEMORAe2.0 could facilitate organizational learning within communities of learners. More precisely we wanted to be sure learners:

- Use their different memories: During the evaluation students have a login and a password.
- Add new resources in their individual memory or in their group memory or entry points.
- Use forum.

  Here and now, we noted:

- Students navigated through the environment and access to different resources.
- Students used their different memory.
- Students tested the forum.

The first evaluation was disturbed by strikes; however students appreciated the environment and said they would like to continue to use it. All of them accessed to right resources helping them to solve the problem and most of them added resources (essentially web sites and, of course, their problem solving). They tested the forum but not really used it. They explained that by the fact they see each other everyday

The second evaluation is not so good. Students said they appreciated the environment; they tried it but didn't use it. The reason is: the training was optional and the problem to solve was not given a mark.

To conclude, we think that to initiate the use of such an environment, learners must have an interest: distance learning, solve a problem marked, review, etc.

In order to better evaluate the forum, we plan to make some new evaluations with distance students. We also plan to examine to what extent industrial organizations, and companies could benefit of this approach. However it should be noted that software environments are not sufficient to promote organizational learning. It is also a question of culture, as well at university as in any other organization.

7   Conclusion

Due to the new working forms, information takes a more and more important place in our society. This one can be qualified of information society. This context implies new learning forms. Learning is an active process but also a social process. The advent of web 2.0 technologies play a bigger and bigger role in e-learning: the term e-learning 2.0 was introduced by Downes (Downes, 2008). New learning forms are a part integral of the industrial challenges. Becoming a learning organization is a way for an organization to stay competitive. Such an organization is an organization in which work is anchored in an organizational culture which allows and encourages the training at various levels: individual, group and organization. Each organization actor is a kind of continuous learner. He has to reach the good resource at the right moment. That necessitates this resource is stored and well described, indexed.

Within the approach MEMORAe we are interested in these new forms of learning. We consider that these ones are connected to the knowledge management practices and require web 2.0 applications.

In this paper we presented links between e-learning and knowledge management in the context of the new economy. We described the approach MEMORAe and we showed how we used semantic web approach and web 2.0 technologies to develop it in the E-MEMORAe2.0 environment. This one is based on the concepts of learning organizational memory. Due to the modelling of the different memories (individual, group, organization), the global memory can be considered as a support for a constellation of communities of practice. In order to offer facilitators to engage learners into interaction we introduced into group memories a distributed semantic forum.

Our perspectives are to better develop the social aspects offered by our environment. To that end, we plan to add more web 2.0 technologies in E-MEMORAe2.0 such as blogs, facilitators to create shared resources, social networks. We also plan to test social aspects of our environment with students from different universities attending the same training.

References

Abel M.-H., Benayache A., Lenne D., Moulin C (2006) "E-MEMORAe: a content-oriented environment for e-learning." In E-learning networked environments and Architectures: A Knowledge processing perspective. by Samuel Pierre (ed.) Springer Book Series: Advanced Information and Knowledge Processing (AI & KP), pp 186-205.

Abel, M.-H. Abel and Leblanc, A. (2008) " An Operationnalization of the Connections between e-Learning and Knowledge Management: the MEMORAe Approach" Proceedings of the 6th IEEE International Conferences on Human System Learning, Toulouse, France, 14-16 May 2008, pp. 93-99.

Ankolekar, A., Krötzsch, M., Thanh Tran, Vrandecic, D. (2007) The two cultures: mashing up Web 2.0 and the Semantic Web. Proceedings of the 16th International Conference on the World Wide Web, WWW2007, Banff, Alberta, Canada, May 8-12, 2007, pp. 825-834.

Atchcerman, D. (2007) Beyond Wikipedia: Using Wikis to Connect Students and Teachers to the Research Process and to One Another http://advancingtechnology2007.blogspot.com/2007/06/beyond-wikipedia-using-wikis-to-connect.html

Benayache, A., Leblanc, A., Abel M.-H. (2006) "Learning memory, evaluation and return on experience" Workshop of Knowledge Management and Organizational Memories, ECAI2006, Italy, pp.14-18, 2006.

Davis, I. (2005) Talis, Web 2.0 and All That. http://iandavis.com/blog/2005/07/talis-web-20-and-all-that?year=2005&monthnum=07&name=talis-web-20-and-all-that

Dieng, R., Corby, O., Giboin, A. et Ribière, M. (1998) "Methods and tools for corporate knowledge management." In Proceedings of the 11th workshop on Knowledge Acquisition, Modeling and Management (KAW'98), Banff, Canada, pp. 17-23.

Dodgson, M. (1993) "Organizational Learning: A Review of Some Literatures". Organizational Studies 14 3, pp. 375-394.

Downes, S. (2008) E-learning 2.0 http://www.elearnmag.org/subpage.cfm?section=articles&article=29-1

Drucker, P. (2000) "Need to Know: Integrating e-Learning with 17-20 September, Crete, Greece, 2007, pp. 408-413. High Velocity Value Chains." A Delphi Group White Paper.

Ebner, M.., Holzinger, A. and Maurer H. (2007) Web 2.0 Technology: Future Interfaces for Technology Enhanced Learning? C. Stephanis (Ed.): Universal Access in HCI, Part III, HCII 2007, LNSC 4556, pp. 559-568, Springer-Verlag Berlin Heilderberg 2007.

Efimova, L. et Swaak, J. (2002) "KM and E-learning : toward an integral approach ?" In Proceedings of KMSS02, EKMF, pp. 63-69.

Girod, M.S. (1995) "La mémoire organisationnelle". Revue Française de Gestion. Vol. 105, septembre-octobre, pp. 30-42, 1995.

Leblanc, A., Abel, M.-H. (2007) "Using Organizational Memory and Forum in an Organizational Learning Context." Proceedings of IEEE/ACM ICDIM'07, The Second International Conference on Digital Information Management, 2007, pp. 266-271.

Lesser, E. L. and Storck, J. (2001) "Communities of practice and organizational performance." In IBM Systems Journal Knowledge Management, Vol. 40, No. 4, 2001, PP. 831-840.

Ley, T., Lindstaedt, S. N. et Albert, D. (2005) "Supporting Competency Development in Informal Workplace Learning." Lecture Notes in Computer Science, Springer-Verlag, Berlin Heidelberg, vol 3782, pp. 189-202.

LTSC (2002) http://ltsc.ieee.org/wg12/

Motschnig-Pitrick, R. and Holzinger, A. Student-Centered Teaching Meets New Media: Concepts and Case Study. IEEE Journal of Educational Technology & Society 5(4), pp. 160-172, 2002.

O'Reilly, T. (2005) What is Web 2.0 – design patterns and business models for the next generation of software. http : //www.oreillynet.com/lpt/a/6228

Papert, S. and Harel, I. (1991) Constructionism. Ablex Publishing, Norwood (NJ).

Preece, J., Sharp, H. and Rogers, Y. (2002) Interaction Design: Beyond Human-Computer Interaction. Wiley, New-York.

Ras, E., Memmel, M. et Weibelzahl, S. (2005) "Integration of E-Learning and Knowledge Management – Barriers, Solutions and Future Issues." In: K.-D. Althoff, A. Dengel, R. Bergmann,

M. Nick, T. Roth-Berghofer (Eds). 3rd Conference Professional Knowledge Management – Experiences and Visions, Berlin: Springer. http://www.easy-hub.org/stephan/raspostlokmol05.pdf

Richardson, W. (2006) Blogs, wikis, podcasts, and other powerful web tools for classrooms. Thousand Oaks, CA: Corwin Press.

Sargeant, J., Curran, V., Allen, M., Jarvis-Selinger, S. and HO, K. (2006) Facilitating interpersonal interaction and learning online: Linking theory and practice. Journal of Continuing Education in the Health Professions 26(2), pp. 128-136.

Schmidt, A. (2005) "Bridging the Gap between Knowledge Mabagement and E-Learning with Context-Aware Corporate Learning". Lecture Notes in Computer Science. Springer-Verlag, Berlin Heidelberg, pp. 203-213. http://herakles.fzi.de/ aschmidt/Schmidt_LOKMOL05_Extended.pdf

Shadbolt, N.R., Hall, W. Berners-Lee, T. (2006) The semantic Web revisited, IEEE Intelligent System 21 (2006) pp. 96-101.

Sicilia, MA and Lytras, M., "The semantic learning organization", The Learning Organization: An International Journal, Volume 12, Number 5, 2005.

Tiffin, J., Rajasingham, L. (1995) In Search of the Virtual Class: Education in an Information Society. London: Routledge.

Van Heijst, G., Van der Spek, R. And Kruizinga, E. (1996) "Organizing Corporate Memories. " In B. Gaines, M. Musen eds, Proceedings of KAW'96 Banff, Canada, November, pp. 42-1 42-17, 2006.

Wenger, E. (1998) „Communities of Practice: Learning as a Social System." In Systems Thinker, Vol. 9, No. 5, june/july 1998, http://www.co-i-l.com/coil/knowledge-garden/cop/lss.shtml

Wenger, E. (2008) http://www.ewenger.com/

Willey, D. A. (2000) http://reusability.org/read/chapters/wiley.doc

Wittrock, M.C. (1974) Learning as a generative process. Educational Psychologist11, pp.87-95.

Zhang, Z. and Tang, J. (2007) Information Retrieval in Web 2.0. In IFIP International Federation for Information Processing, Volume 251, Integration and Innovation Orient to E-Society Volume 1, Wang, W. (Eds), (Boston:Springer), pp. 663-670.

Chapter 11. Towards OpenTagging Platform using Semantic Web Technologies

Hak Lae Kim

DERI, National University of Ireland, Galway, Ireland

John G. Breslin

DERI, National University of Ireland, Galway, Ireland

Abstract

Many social media sites such as Del.icio.us, Flickr, or weblogs have recently become popular. This has led to adoption of tagging functions on traditional web sites at a steady pace. However, producing tagging data from these sites without supporting the social exchange involved can be regarded as an incomplete set of metadata. Although tagging captures our individual conceptual associations, the tagging system itself does not promote a social transmission that units both creators and consumers. To achieve social transmission environments for tagging, we need a formal conceptual model to represent the tagging activity and a service platform to encourage its exchange and interoperation.

1   Introduction

The label *tagging* has been applied to a fast-growing number of web sites where content has a tag that is primarily created by users themselves. Tagging is used in many social media applications such as weblogs, social bookmarking, and social networking applications. While the primary purpose of tagging is to help users organize and manage their resources, collective tagging data is used to organize and retrieve information via folksonomies, which are types of distributed classification (Gruber, 2008). A tag, or a labeled keyword, is a type of metadata for items such as resource links, web pages, pictures, blog posts, etc. and is primarily created not by machine agents, but by human users. A tagger, who the entity is creating tags, does not necessarily have to be an expert but may simply be the creator of an annotation or the consumer of an item. It is important to remember that resources can be tagged with as many or as few words as desired; there is no restriction to placing objects in one category (Shirky, 2005). Tagging is a way of representing concepts, with a free-form list of keywords, by using the cognitive association techniques of a tagger without enforcing categorization (Kim et al., 2008). Both creators and consumers of tagged items can share their collection of tagging data. Since a large number of users participate in creating, adding, and sharing metadata in the form of keywords, this is regarded as a highly social and democratic process.

The term *folksonomy* means the practice and method of collaboratively creating and managing tags for the purpose of annotating and categorizing content (Mathes, 2004). The term, first coined by Tomas Vander Wal[19], is a fusion of the two words '*folk*' and '*taxonomy*' and it became popular on the Web around 2004 with social software applications such as social bookmarking or photograph annotation. For instance, some well-known implementations of folksonomies are del.icio.us (a social bookmarking system) and Flickr (a photo-sharing web site). CiteULike, using a similar approach to del.icio.us, focuses on academic articles, and there are a number of multimedia sites that support tagging such as Last.fm for music and YouTube for video. The power of folksonomies is obtained through an aggregate summary of the information that we are interested in, and this improves social reinforcement by enabling social connections and by providing social search mechanisms. Quintarelli (2005) points out that "*without a social distributed environment that suggests aggregation, tags are just flat keywords.*"

2   What are the Problems of Current Social Tagging and Systems?

Although social tagging and folksonomies have a lot of advantages (visualization, navigation, etc.) to offer the different users who tag content items in social media sites, critical drawbacks with current tagging systems are that 1) there is no formal conceptualization in order to represent tagging data in a consistent way (Kim et al., 2008), and 2) there is no interoperability support for exchanging tagging data among different applications or people (Gruber, 2008). The simplicity and ease-of-use of tagging leads to a lack of precision with keyword ambiguity caused by misspelling certain words, singular vs. plural, synonyms, morphologies, or too-personalized tags (Golder and Herbermann, 2006; Halpin et al., 2006; Marlow, 2006). Since there are many different manners of using tags, one may not be able to understand what a given tag is about. These limitations come from a lack of standards for tag structures and little semantics for specifying the exact meaning. Aside from these problems, social tagging systems do not provide a uniform way to share and reuse tagging data amongst users or communities (Kim et al., 2007). There is no consistent method for reusing one's personal set of tags among

---

[19] http://www.vanderwal.net/random/entrysel.php?blog=1750

people or communities. Although some folksonomy systems support export functionality using their open APIs and share their data via a closed agreement among sites, these systems do not offer a uniform and consistent way to share, exchange, and reuse tagging data for leveraging social interoperability. Therefore, it is not easy to meaningfully search, compare, or merge "*similar collective tagging data*" from different applications (TagCommons, 2007).

With the usage of tagging systems increasing daily, these limitations will become critical. To overcome the limitations of current tagging systems, we need to look at an open platform for tagging similar to OpenSocial[20] that provides a common set of APIs for social networking applications across multiple web sites.

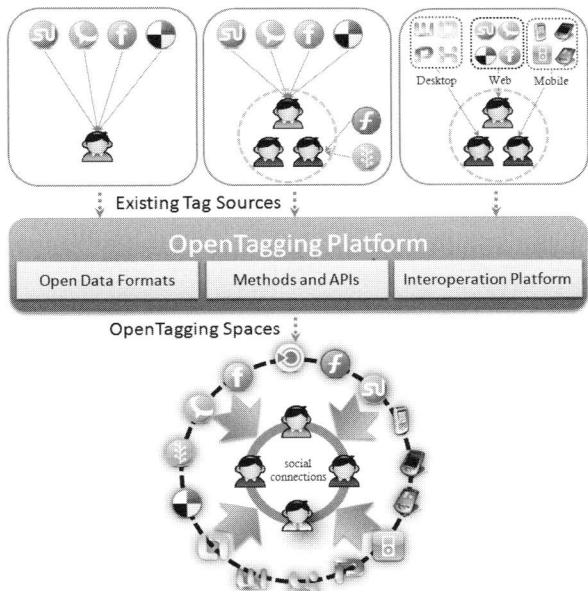

Figure 1. The OpenTagging Platform

We can see three different scenarios of using tagging data from existing tag sources in Figure 1.

- Individual perspective: Users participate in diverse social media sites by contributing to tagging activities. Although they are able to collect the tagging data resulted from these activities, the real challenge is to integrate and combine this data into a comprehensive personal view.

---

[20] http://code.google.com/apis/opensocial

- Community perspective: On the side, users are part of different communities and projects, and interact with the members of these communities by sharing or exchanging tagging data between them. In this setting, a new issue arises, i.e. the reuse of the data across multiple communities.
- Heterogeneous environments: Regardless of the individual or community perspectives, tagging data can be produced in several environments, like on the Desktop, on the Web, or even on the Mobile Web. Even so, we want be able to reuse our set of tags indifferently of the environment. However, there is no consistent method for interoperation of tagging data amongst different environments.

3 Components of the OpenTagging Platform

The goal of OpenTagging aims to make tagging data open, more universal, and apply it across any number of social tagging sites. Through continuously user participations on the platform, users can make their customized folksonomies to organize their data by their needs and interests. The interaction of diverse objects such as users, tags, and resources on the platform brings emergent semantics of tagging data and leverages social connections among participants. In order to allow users and developers to implement the social capabilities underlying tagging data, the platform consists of the open data models, the export and sharing methods, a consistent platform for interoperating one's personal set of tags between either web-based systems, desktop, and mobile applications, or for transferring tags among the desktop, the web, or the mobile.

3.1 Open data formats

These aim for specifying tagging data in a formal way. The data formats for common conceptualization of tagging data can be represented by an ontology to make a minimal commitment. A conceptualization of tagging data and activities is called 'Tag ontology' and there are some implementations using OWL (Kim et al., 2008). It is also important to note that some classes and properties from well-known RDF vocabularies (SIOC, FOAF, and SKOS etc) can be used to represent tagging activities. This approach can be considered as a method to enhance semantically links of tagging data.

3.2 Methods

In order to collect, share, or exchange tagging data, or create a bridge among heterogeneous social tagging sites, methods should implement by types of mashups. In general, most social media sites offer open APIs to expose their data and we can gather the data using them. It, however, is hard to integrate and interoperate data through diverse applications on syntactic and structural means; we need semantic techniques such as SA-REST (Semantically Interoperable and Easier-to-Use Services and Mashups) (Sheth et al., 2007).

3.3 Platform

The Semantic Web is a useful platform for linking, exchanging, and interoperating supports on tagging data collected from heterogeneous social tagging sites (Breslin & Decker, 2007). The platform supports a social ecosystem that interlinks among objects such as individual and individual, individual and communities, or individual and the tags themselves and leverages social connections based on tags. In addition, the platform allows users to reuse and exchange tag data between people across different sources (systems) in existing social networks, which could be used to connect people who may have a common interest, or set of interests.

4   Open Data Format for Describing Tags: Social Semantic Tags

The SCOT ontology aims to describe the structure and the semantics of tagging data and to offer social interoperability of the data among different sources. Tagging is an activity or a process in which a tagger 'assigns' some tags he or she 'creates' or 'uses' on some resources. In order to represent this activity, the model represents tags clouds, the tags themselves, the resources that are being tagged, and the users that create these tags. The model also describes the properties of the tags, including their occurrence frequencies, and other tags that are used in conjunction with them. In addition to representing the structure and the semantics of tags, the model allows the exchange of semantic tag metadata for reuse in social applications and enables interoperation amongst data sources, services, or agents in a tag space. These features are a cornerstone to being able to identify, formalize, and interoperate a common conceptualization of tagging activity at a semantic level. Figure 2 gives a detailed example of a tagging activity describing by SCOT instance. The Tagcloud class consists of metadata related to tagging activity such as taggers, sites, and creators and of statistical information to describe overall tag usage such as total posts, total tags, or total frequency of tags in a site. The Tag class describes a concept of an individual tag. This class includes many properties to represent the semantics (scot:acronym, scot:synonym, scot:spellingVariants, etc) and numerical features (scot:ownAFrequency and scot:ownRFrequency, etc) of a tag. The Cooccurrence class describes co-occurring tags and the co-occurring frequencies among tags.

SCOT aims to incorporate and reuse existing vocabularies as much as possible in order to avoid redundancies and to enable the use of richer metadata descriptions for specific domains.

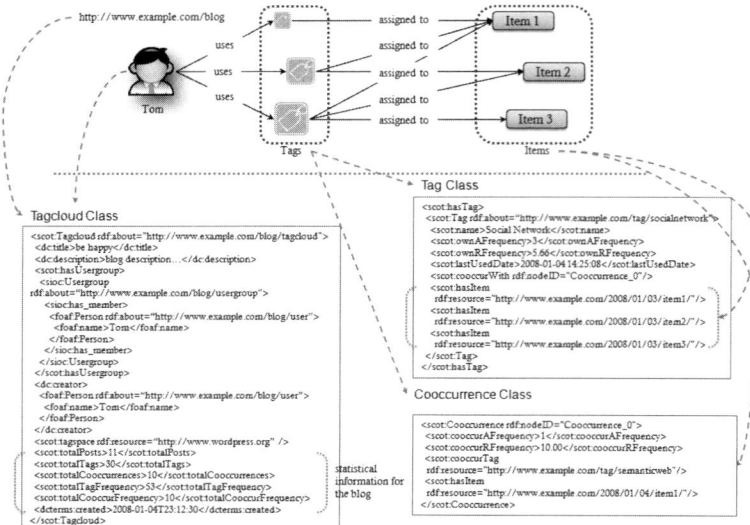

Figure 2. An example of SCOT instance. The SCOT models tagging activity for typical online communities including taggers, tags, items, and these relationships.

This ontology model has been made with a number of vocabularies including DC (Dublin Core Metadata)[21], FOAF (Friend-of-a-Friend)[22], SIOC (Semantically Interlinked Online Communities)[23], and SKOS (Simple Knowledge Organisation Systems)[24]. Figure 3 illustrates the relationships among these vocabularies.

4.1 How can users create SCOT instance?

We do not force any burden on users in relation to creating the semantic data and do not expect users to understand 'what the Semantic Web is' or 'what an ontology is'. We have provided SCOT Exporter[25] which automatically create semantic metadata from a set of tagging data. For instance, the SCOT Exporter for WordPress, which is a plug-in, allows the production of SCOT instance data from a certain blog. This Exporter is activated in the plug-in menu on the WordPress administration panel and it requires no user configuration in order to work. The instance created by the Exporter is located in '*http://yourhost/scot/scot.rdf*', when

---

[21] http:// dublincore.org

[22] http://foaf-project.org

[23] http://sioc-project.org

[24] http://www.w3.org/2004/02/skos

[25] http://scot-project.org/applications/wp-exporter/

tags are changed in the blog, the instance is dynamically updated. The initial version for the export has developed based on the assumption that categories in WordPress are used as tags. We also offer the exporter for the Ultimate Tag Warrior[26], a popular and powerful WordPress plugin, which allows a user to add tags either through the Write Post page in WordPress in a tag box.

4.2 How can we provide interoperation amongst different sources?

To realize the OpenTagging platform, we make it possible to exchange, compare, and integrate tagging data across different applications or sources and to offer interoperation in the tag spaces. Although a user can create a SCOT instance data set using a SCOT Exporter from a single online community such as a weblog, the Exporter provides a simple method for exposing a SCOT instance without interoperation mechanisms. Thus we need a method for sharing and interoperating this semantic metadata.

5   The int.ere.st Web site and its Methods

int.ere.st[27] is a web site where people can manage their tagging data from various sources, search resources based on their tags which were created and used by themselves, and leverage a sharing and exchanging of tagging data among people or various online communities (Kim et al., 2007). The site (see Figure 4) is a platform for providing structure and semantics to previously unstructured tagging data via various mashups. The tagging data from distributed environments such as blogs, social web sites can be stored in a repository as SCOT instances via the Mashup Wrapper, which extracts tagging data using open APIs from host sites. For instance, the site allows users to dump tagging data from del.icio.us, Flickr, and YouTube and these tagging data sets are transformed into SCOT instances on a semantic level. Thus, all instances within int.ere.st include different tagging contexts and connect various people and sources with the same tags. In addition, users can search people, tags, or resources and can bookmark some resources or integrate different instances. Through this iterative process, the tags reflect distributed human intelligence into the site. The following are some of the main methods implemented in the site.

The screenshot (fig. 2) shows the search results for the tag 'ontology.' In this example, the left-hand side shows SCOT instances with associated detailed information such as top tags, the creator, number of members and items, total tags, total

---

[26] http://www.neato.co.nz/ultimate-tag-warrior/

[27] http://int.ere.st

co-occurrence tags, and tag spaces. If a user clicks on a title in the search results, the right-hand side visualizes a tag cloud for the selected SCOT instance with related items.

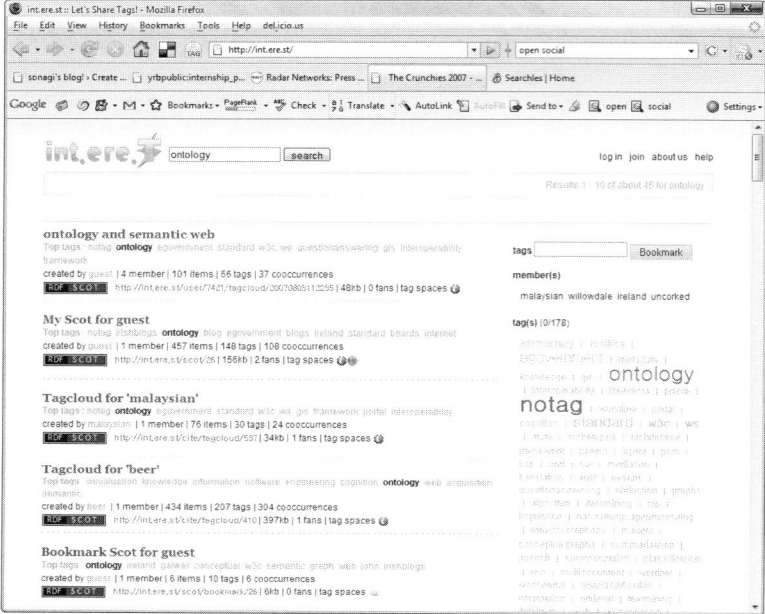

Figure 3. int.ere.st web site

5.1 Aggregate

A user can gather a collection of tagging data that he or she has assigned to resources in distributed applications. For instance, the site can aggregate bookmarks, images, and videos with tags from del.icio.us, Flickr, YouTube, or other online applications using their open APIs. The collected data is automatically transformed into semantically structured data that includes the relationships among users, tags, and resources. If tagging data is already created by the SCOT exporter in a certain blog, a user can directly import the instances from their site. We also provide an importing method in which users can import their SCOT instances from a file or URL. Then, the aggregator for the collected or imported instances runs periodically and automatically. This is a first step for sharing tags from different resources in different tag spaces.

5.2 Search & Browse

There are several ways to search tag information on the site. Firstly, a tag search allows users to look for similar patterns of tagging or persons with related interests based on tags. Secondly, a user can search for tags or resources using SPARQL-based semantic search methods with these search operators: "and", "or", co-occurring tags, and broader or narrower relationships. These operators enable users to restrict their search conditions. Thirdly, when the '*created by*' field from the search results is clicked for a specific SCOT instance, all SCOT instances created by the creator are listed. This will help users find interesting new people in the system, much as a user refers to instances to find interesting new ones.

5.3 Bookmark

We also provide a bookmarking and tagging method for each SCOT instance so that a user can participate in the tagging activity and share experiences with other people. If a user is interested in tagging data from a certain instance, he or she can create a bookmark, with tags, for the instance. We provide '*fans*' as a concept for a list of such people; when someone has added a certain SCOT as a bookmark, a fan connection is created. Social connections can be made with other individuals interested in just about any topic. In addition, a user can take advantage of all the work other people have done. A list of bookmarked instances is located in the "my interest" menu.

5.4 Share

The site exposes various and structured types of user contributions in the system and also connects to other sources of data using Semantic Web technologies. For instance, personal information can be exposed as FOAF and SCOT instances in the system can be mapped into SIOC. The SCOT ontology can be classified with several types such as "imported", "bookmarked", and "integrated" one in the system. The bookmarked type is created by other users; the integrated type (that is a merging of at least two instances) is created by the logged in user; the imported ontology can be either of the two. The bookmarked type is described using the property from FOAF and the integrated type is mapped to the FOAF maker property. In addition, all types of SCOT instances for a certain user are mapped to the Item class from SIOC. This process can be done automatically. The mapping among SIOC, FOAF and SCOT together provides a way to enhance social connections that are distributed and shared among people.

6   int.ere.st as a Platform

int.ere.st is the first OpenTagging platform for the Semantic Web, since users can manage a collection of tagging data in a smarter and more effective way as well as search, bookmark, and share their own as well as other's tagging data via the underlying SCOT ontology. Those functionalities help users exchange and share their tagging data based on Semantic Web standards. The site is compatible with other Semantic Web applications, and its information can be shared across applications. This means that the site enables users to create Semantic Web data, such as FOAF, SKOS, and SIOC automatically. The RDF vocabularies can be interlinked with the URIs of SCOT instances that are generated in the site and shared in online communities.

7   Conclusions

We discuss the OpenTagging platform for interoperation of social tagging data. The platform allows users to reuse and exchange tagging data between people across different sources (systems) in existing social network, which could be used to connect people who may have a common interest, or set of interests. Although it's still in an early stage, we hope additional effort will make the OpenTagging platform more practical and useful. We expect that the SCOT project (http://scot-project.org) provides open discussions for community and the int.ere.st as a test-bed continues to bring novel approaches and solutions to problems in social tagging and interoperation processing.

References

Breslin, J.G. and Decker, S., (2007). The Future of Social Networks on the Internet: The Need for Semantics, IEEE Internet Computing, vol. 11, no. 6, pp. 86-90, Nov/Dec.

Golder, S. and Huberman, B. A. (2006). The Structure of Collaborative Tagging Systems. Journal of Information Sciences. 32(2). 198--208.

Gruber, T. (2007). Ontology of Folksonomy: A Mash-up of Apples and Oranges. Intl Journal on Semantic Web and Information Systems. 3(2).

Gruber, T. (2008). Collective knowledge systems: Where the Social Web meets the Semantic Web. Journal of Web Semantics 6(1). 4-13.

Halpin, H., Robu, V. and Shepard, H. (2006). The Dynamics and Semantics of Collaborative Tagging. In Proceedings of the 1st Semantic Authoring and Annotation Workshop (SAAW06).

Kim, H. L., Yang, S. K., Breslin, J. G. and Kim, H. G. (2007). Simple Algorithms for Representing Tag Frequencies in the SCOT Exporter. in IAT. IEEE Computer Society. pp. 536-539.

Kim, H.L., Passant, A., Breslin, J., Scerri, S., Decker, S. (2008). Review and Alignmnet of Tag Ontologies for Semantically-Linked Data in Collaborative Tagging Spaces, In Proceedings of the 2nd International Conference on Semantic Computing, San Francisco, USA.

Marlow, C., Naaman, M., Boyd, D. and Davis, M. (2006). HT06. tagging paper. taxonomy. Flickr. academic article. to read. in HYPERTEXT 06: Proceedings of the seventeenth conference on Hypertext and hypermedia. ACM Press. New York. NY. USA. pp. 31--40.

Mathes, A. (2004). Folksonomies - Cooperative Classification and Communication Through Shared Metadata. Retrieved June 25. 2008. from http://www.adammathes.com/academic/computer-mediated-communication/folksonomies.html.

Quintarelli, E. (2005). Folksonomies: power to the people. Retrieved June 25. 2008. from http://www.iskoi.org/doc/folksonomies.htm.

Sheth, P.A., Gomadam, J., Lathem, J. (2007). SA-REST: Semantically Interoperable and Easier-to-Use Services and Mashups, IEEE Internet Computing, vol. 11, no. 6, pp. 91-94, Nov/Dec.

Shirky, C. (2005). Ontology is Overrated: Categories. Links. and Tags. Retrieved 25 June. 2008. from http://www.shirky.com/writings/ontology-overrated.html.

TagCommons, (2007). Functional Requirements for Sharing Tag Data, Retrieved 25 June, 2008, from http://tagcommons.org/2007/02/28/functional-requirements-for-sharing-tag-data/.

Chapter 12. Evolving from 1.0 to enterprise 2.0: an interpretative review-Empirical stages and approaches towards the new (virtual) working environment

Mariano Corso

School of Management, Polytechnic of Milano, ITALY

Antonella Martini

Faculty of Engineering, University of Pisa, ITALY

Andrea Pesoli

School of Management, Polythecnic of Milano, ITALY

Abstract

An Intranet initiative shouldn't be interpreted as an una tantum project, but within a longer evolution process which makes it assumes a more and more relevant role in facilitating and sustaining organisational change. Evidence demonstrated that Intranet has radically changed its role: from a predominantly unidirectional top-down channel for communication & information (the 1ˢᵗ era) to a what we defined "Virtual Workspace", an integrated working environment where employees can find what they need to work, to learn, to know and to interact with others (the 2ⁿᵈ era). 2006 empirical results provide evidence that a new stage of the abovementioned process emerged, pushed by further emergent worker needs and enabled by social computing tools, Service-Oriented Architecture, BPM, mash up and new supply model (i.e. software-as-a-service): the enterprise 2.0. The chapter analyses that evolution, basing on a 5-year empirical research which involved a panel of 110 firms, and provides a framework of analysis and an evolution model.

1   Introduction

The intensification of competition forces companies to compete more and more on their ability to manage and enhance the value of intellectual capital, but this ability has to be rethought in order to deal with globalization and new organizational challenges (continuous innovation of products and business models, increasing workforce dispersion, growing importance of inter-organizational relationships, orientation to processes more than to functions) on one side, and new technological opportunities (the availability of new ICT-enabled services and the evolution of IS in terms of interoperability and integration) on the other.

As a consequence, the traditional ways to share and manage knowledge become inadequate and workplace has to change accordingly to give workers complete support for their real needs: to reconnect them to the professional and social network of the company, preventing loss of knowledge and to provide them with opportunities for interaction and learning, thus supporting their job and their professional growth, long term employability, ultimately improving job satisfaction and attractiveness. In this scenario, the availability of new, ICT-enabled services and particularly of web and mobile communication services makes it possible to overcome geographical (the work-place is everywhere the worker is), time (the worker creates value whenever it is required) and organizational barriers (the concepts of colleague, competitor and supplier have to be rethought and become more worker- and relationship-focused).

The most recent innovation is the Web 2.0. This phenomenon has led to the diffusion among users of functionality and interaction metaphors that initiate in the Web environment and then spread within the company, are bringing with them greater usability of the user interface and a human-machine interaction paradigm more centred on user needs. Also termed as the 'consumerisation' of IT, the in-company developments focus on the construction of environments in which the worker can choose which collaboration and social computing tools to use and in which context. These tools can range from web-mail to more advanced integration, messaging and mobility support solutions, real-time multi-media and distributed contributions (blog, wiki, social network, folksonomy and RSS, and functionality such as video sharing, podcasting, page-rank and instant messaging).

In addition, the Information System (IS) evolution in terms of interoperability and integration is speeding up the convergence towards the web application usage, while making the borders of the different IS more and more fuzzy. Intranet, ERP and CRM, which were once distinct ICT application systems, are merging and overlapping, while developing increasingly into communication and collaboration tools. There is an important point of contact between the Web 2.0 (i.e. Internet as an application platform) and Information Systems in the use of *mash-up* technologies as integration solutions and in *Software as a Service* as a model for web application delivery.

As a result of this continuous evolution, the emerging IS is not just a sum of its components, but it can be a (virtual) working 'space' which gives complete support to workers' multidimensional needs. All this means that (new) ICT is conceived as an enabler and a facilitator of the social mechanisms through which workers create, transfer, share and reuse knowledge; in other terms, ICT can become a key factor to design the near future organization. However, as one of the most frequent causes of partial or total failure of an Intranet project is certainly the undervaluation of the importance of the organizational aspects (most of the companies manage the implementation project in a purely technical perspective without systematically facing the organizational and the change management aspects to exploit the potential of the technology), to exploit the potential of the technology, we need to look at people and the 'way' they construct the environment in which they work and interact. The role – and the challenge – of ICT is, therefore, to reproduce a social reality made up of interpersonal relationships, collaboration and communication flows, and possibly enhance this reality by emphasizing openness and collaboration.

In this way, the role – and the challenge – of ICT is to reproduce a social reality made up of interpersonal relationships, collaboration and communication flows, and possibly enhance this reality by emphasizing openness and collaboration.

Empirical evidence (for details see Corso et al. 2008) demonstrated that Intranet radically changed its role: from a predominantly unidirectional top-down channel for communication & information - the 1st era - to a new (virtual and dynamic) working environment, a creative, open working space focused on workers, their needs, specific working conditions and interaction with others - the 2nd era. Literature points out that an Intranet initiative evolves in scope, both in spatial and time dimensions. From the first point of view (space), it encompasses all the value chain processes and extends beyond the immediate organization's internal work to include relationships with business partners and external agencies. From the second point of view (time), it evolves through different maturity phases, in which it changes its characteristics and organisational role. In this sense, an Intranet initiative shouldn't be interpreted as an *una tantum* project, but within a longer evolution process which makes it assumes a more and more relevant role in facilitating and sustaining organisational change. It's a process of innovation and change management, whose effectiveness depends on a fine combination of strategic, organizational and technological choices which require to be carefully planned. For this reason, it would be extremely useful and urgent to develop guidelines to manage the evolution (avoiding barriers) of such projects.

The challenge for management theory is clear: to provide empirically grounded and actionable knowledge for companies to design and implement new ICT-enabled (virtual) working environments able to extend the boundaries of their knowledge creation to their mobile workers, customers and suppliers.

In order to contribute to fill in the empirical gap, in 2003 a permanent Observatory has been established with the aim of:

- analyzing the state of the art of Intranet projects from a strategic, organizational and technological point of view and monitoring their evolution;
- identifying the levers/barriers to Intranet project evolution;
- creating and exploit the Intranet culture in Italy;
- acting as a landmark for a community of people interested in developing the strategic role of Intranet

Basing on a 5-year empirical research conducted by the Observatory, this chapter gives evidence on the evolution of Intranet projects and on different approaches the companies have followed, providing an interpretative model of it.

The article is organized as follows: § 2 provides a concise literature review; § 3 illustrates the methodology, while §§ 4, 5 and 6 report the research evidence.

2 ICT and the working environment: a brief literature review

After a brief review of the literature on ICT approaches, which provide justification for the key role of ICT in organizational design, we focus on Intranet as of its prominent role in the market of web applications.

2.1 Approaches to ICT

From the 1970-1980s on, ICT has developed from simple processing to relational and organizational technologies, progressively increasing their organizational impact on the company and making the integrated planning of ICT and the organizational framework crucial.

In the literature, various perspectives have been developed ranging from the tech-determinism view and the organizational determinism one to a 'dual' perspective (for details see Corso et al. in 9th CINet Conference proceedings). This latter view seeks to develop a synthesis between the first two perspectives, which conceive ICT as an independent and a dependent variable respectively.

Technology can be considered simultaneously as dependent and independent variables, because the technology/organization relation cannot be seen statically, but is rather a dynamic relation, in which technology is molded by organizational characteristics, while, in turn, becoming the premise and limitation of subsequent organizational decisions. In this way, technology takes on a meaning tied not only to its intrinsic characteristics, but also to the institutional, organizational and symbolic context in which it is introduced.

According to this approach, on the one hand, organizational design cannot neglect the opportunities offered by ICT, while on the other, the effective and efficient development of ICT in a company environment must pay due regard to organizational variables, both from the point of view of systemic coherence and from that of managing the associated process of organizational change.

New ICT provide new opportunities and challenges for the development of the new knowledge workplace, but in itself it is not the solution: culture, people and behaviours play the greatest role. Therefore, the challenge is at the organizational and managerial level.

Accordingly to this logic, ICT is interpreted and then used as a set of tools to recreate a social reality of interpersonal relationships and communication flows, possibly enhanced by emphasizing openness and collaboration.

2.2 ICT as a key factor to design the future organization

In the knowledge society, ICT can play a key role as organization design lever for three reasons, which are also the priorities for the development of the new generation Information Systems (IS):

- it can make the decision-making processes more agile and effective;
- it can enables more sustainable and new forms of organizing work
- it can foster innovation and change

Regarding reason a), today's IS generates enormous quantities of data and information that are often difficult to consult and interpret making people to be less and less capable of making quick and effective decisions. This is the phenomenon of so-called information overflow, i.e. as the availability of information increases, decision-makers do not necessarily become more effective in their choices.

In response, management (in particular top level) is often little convinced of the real value of ICT as a decision-making tool, and privileges 'other' means, such as the hierarchy, direct interpersonal relations and experience, to make quick decisions. In contrast, through advanced document management systems, for example, the overview and accessibility of documents can be improved, and information linked through workflow systems to the activities and process phases in which it is most frequently used. Moreover, the integrated exploitation of collaboration systems makes the use of content more animated by flanking explicit and implicit knowledge. Finally, advanced ISs provide top management with environments highly focused on the information selected, dashboards to control and monitor major indicators, as well as competitive/business intelligence tools able to extract from the enormous quantity of available data the few important pieces of information for the decisions. The need for new organisational models (reason b) emerges from the following trends (Corso et al. 2006):

- increasing workforce dispersion which creates barriers to the sharing of knowledge and expertise among individuals. Dispersion is both at geographical level - how people are integrated to the rest of the organisation - and at contractual one – how they relate to it.

- geographical dispersion: nowadays the concept itself of the workplace is changing. People spend an increasing a mount o f their working time outside the physical boundaries of their company, often in mobility and interacting with customers or people from partner organizations. Also when working inside the company, people often change positions and work in multi-disciplinary virtual teams. As a consequence, individuals have fewer and fewer opportunities for face to face interaction with their colleagues and can hardly rely on their own experience.
- contractual dispersion: provisional nature of employment, loose forms of contractual links to the company and high level of turnover, while in many cases considered competitive needs, make people's stay with organizations temporary and partial, thus creating barriers to the sharing of knowledge and expertise among individuals.
- growing importance of inter-organisational relationships: since competition occurs not so much among companies as among networks, the network, more than the single company, becomes the context in which individuals have to assimilate and transmit knowledge;
- orientation to processes more than to functions: people working in multi-disciplinary teams are less and less in touch with colleagues with the same "functional" competencies.

ICT tools have to recreate a social reality, with its interpersonal relationships and communication flows, and possibly augment it by emphasising openness and collaboration. In this sense, ICT becomes the organization layout as well as the social fabric of knowledge and relations. A quite important role in this perspective is played by the so called Knowledge Workplace technologies: a set of web-based applications that a worker can access to through the Intranet of the firm he works for.Finally, reason c). In order to survive firms are required to continuously innovate their products, services and business models (Magnusson and Martini, 2008). All this calls for capturing and managing knowledge from customers, competitors and technologies as well as fostering change and competence reconfiguration.

A new IS generation that integrates work environment, personal relations and collaboration, can play a key role in innovation as it can:

- promote process change and reconfiguration, shifting barriers to innovation;
- spreading vision to give workers the sense of direction and innovation stimuli;
- supporting access to knowledge and new idea generation;
- enabling collaboration between different units;
- opening organization to capture stimuli from partners.

In this sense, ICT can be an enabler of innovation and change.

2.3 Perspectives on Intranet

There are many definitions of Intranet, ranging from a purely technological interpretation (in this case, the Intranet is conceived as an organizational network pro-
tected by firewalls which exploits Internet working technologies) to a functional
view, in which an Intranet is seen as an infrastructure that supports business applications. In our analysis, Intranet will be interpreted as *all the web technologies-
based ICT applications/services that support business processes and which an organization can present to employees* (Corso *et al.* 2008). In other words, an Intranet is a way of thinking and organizing people, work and interaction.

Intranet can be used as information repositories to help employees gain knowledge about the business and its competitive environment, as well as tools to update company knowledge when employees leave. Intranet helps organizations
access knowledge resources and act as a link between geographically-dispersed
employees. It allows the development of a naturally expanding, flexible and easy-
to-use Knowledge Management System, that encourages employees to take advantage of the system. Intranet overcomes organizational hierarchies, formal communication policies, physical barriers and social groupings to make knowledge available to everyone.

Since its infancy around 1995, Intranet has evolved from an internal method of
document organization and dissemination developed from groupware to a more
sophisticated and complex organizational tool. In particular, Intranet has evolved
in scope, both in spatial and time terms. In the first case (space), it encompasses
all the value chain processes and extend beyond the immediate internal work of
the organization to include relationships with business partners and external agencies. Secondly (time), Intranet must develop from being conceived as a project to
being conceived as a process for innovation and change management. In this
sense, an Intranet initiative should not be interpreted as a *una tantum* project, but
as a longer evolutionary process in which the system assumes an increasingly important position in facilitating and sustaining organizational change. A diverging
interpretation brings firms to operate myopically, without setting the organizational and technological premises for an effective development of the Intranet in the
longer term. The use of the Intranet as an information repository helps employees
to know better the business in which they operate and their competitive environment, while capturing knowledge. Intranet helps firms to access their knowledge
resources and connect workers operating in different geographical locations. Indeed, new, integrated collaboration tools turn an Intranet itself into a tool capable
of '*dissociating workers from their desks*'. Thanks to these collaboration tools,
Intranet is becoming simple and flexible Knowledge Management Systems, as
well as resources that employees can use to build a virtual environment able to
overcome organizational hierarchies, as well as physical, geographical and social
barriers. Furthermore, the diffusion of an ever-increasing number of ICT applications requires Intranet to solve the difficult problem of information overflow, whe-

reby employees are overloaded by often useless information which hinders an effective decision-making process. With the definition of access profiles and to the construction of employee working spaces, Intranet puts employees at the centre of their work, so boosting and giving value to their competencies, while returning the use of ICT to a human level.

Many studies have been carried out to define the "state of the art" of Intranet applications (business models, strategies, governance structures, impacts and performance, etc.) and specify roadmaps to support management in choosing and implementing applications (Greer 1998; Harris and Berg 2002; Murgolo-Poore et al. 2001; Tyndale 2002). In Italy, Intranet applications has so far not been studied in depth. Moreover, peculiarities in the Italian/European market (e.g. prevalence of small and medium enterprises, limited number of enterprises operating in high technological markets, limited role of financial markets, etc.) restrict the application of the results of empirical analyses carried out in international contexts (in particular, from the US where most research is conducted).In particular, there are some questions which require a strong empirical evidence:

1. at explicative level:

   - how has the role of Intranet in the company changed?
   - what are the stages of this evolution process?
   - what are the approaches adopted by the companies towards those stages?
   - what barriers and levers exist in the evolution process?

2. at normative level:

   - what are the tools and the steps (i.e. the guidelines) for managing that process?

Obviously, to answer to the explicative questions is a pre-requisite for the normative level. This contribution provide evidence from a 5-year research to answer to level 1 questions.

3   Methodology

We adopted a multiple case studies methodology, as it allows us to understand the complexity of the organizational phenomenon and answer the questions 'how and why'.The number of companies in the Observatory panel has grown progressively during the research period, from 29 in 2002-03, to 50 in 2004, 70 in 2005, arriving at 110 in 2006 and 70 in 2007. Each year, a number of new participating companies has been added, while the majority of the firms analyzed in a particular year reiterated the intention to take part in the following year's study. As a result of this availability, many case studies have been examined longitudinally.

The approach adopted is both interpretative and normative: the goal is (a) to understand the current situation as well as the past developments and future prospects of intranets, and (b) to compare the Intranet development and different characteristics so as to define a model to explain the evolutionary dynamics and the possible benefits obtained with these environments. The case studies have been analyzed also retrospectively.

The choice of cases is based on the pre-requisites that the companies operate in Italy and have undertaken at least one major ICT project in the previous 5 years. The people contacted were mainly the heads of information systems, intranet managers or the immediate subordinates of top management.

Data were collected with a view to obtaining the greatest amount of information possible on the intranet and its external context. Various sources were used and both qualitative and quantitative data were included in order to obtain triangulation of the information collected. Specifically, data were obtained from the following sources:

-   documentation on the company analyzed;
-   a questionnaire of 71 closed questions and a 'comments' field in which interviewees could complete their replies with extra information;
-   semi-structured interviews with various company figures (e.g. head of information systems, head of intranet, managers from the Human Resources and Internal Communication departments, line staff);
-   on-line analysis of the intranet, the available tools and the relative level of use, as well as of any interactions between individuals visible via the web.

The comprehensibility and completeness of the questionnaire were tested in advance in pilot interviews. The interviews of approximately one and a half hours were carried out (after return of the questionnaire) either by telephone or face-to-face. The use of a semi-structured form leaves ample freedom both to the interviewer and the interviewee, while ensuring that all the important arguments are addressed and all the necessary information collected. A check-list was devised with the arguments to be addressed, while the order of the questions, the level of detail regarding specific questions, and the words used, etc. could be decided by the interviewer during the meeting. The check-list maintained the replicability of the request for information in various situations.

All the interviews were recorded and transcribed. Subsequently, a report giving the important data in objective terms was prepared. Following and initial screening of the companies based on the defined criteria, 130 firms were contacted, of which 110 agreed to take part in the research.

4   An interpretative view of the evolution process: the 1st era

The Intranets analysed (29 in 2002-03, 50 in 2004 and 70 in 2005) can be mapped on the basis of six macro-functionalities and the value chain macro processes they support. Although an Intranet can envisage all, or most, of these functionalities, three models have been identified on the basis of their focus on some functionalities rather than others:

- Institutional Intranets are essentially aimed to value chain supporting activities (internal communication, management of human resources, administration and control, facility management, etc.). They are mainly based on Publishing and Self-Service functions, with a certain tendency to incorporate Document Management applications as well;
- Knowledge Management Intranets seek to facilitate the accumulation, archiving and sharing of knowledge; they are based, in the main, on Document Management and Community functions, even if in some cases, Publishing and Collaborative Work tools are also present;
- Operations Intranets are created to support the value chain primary activities (operations, sales, marketing, etc.); they are generally built on the Legacy Integration and Collaborative Work functions, address a specific group of workers (those involved in the process supported) and therefore have a more limited area of application; in some cases Document Management and Community functions also play an important role.

Fig.1. 1st era Intranet model

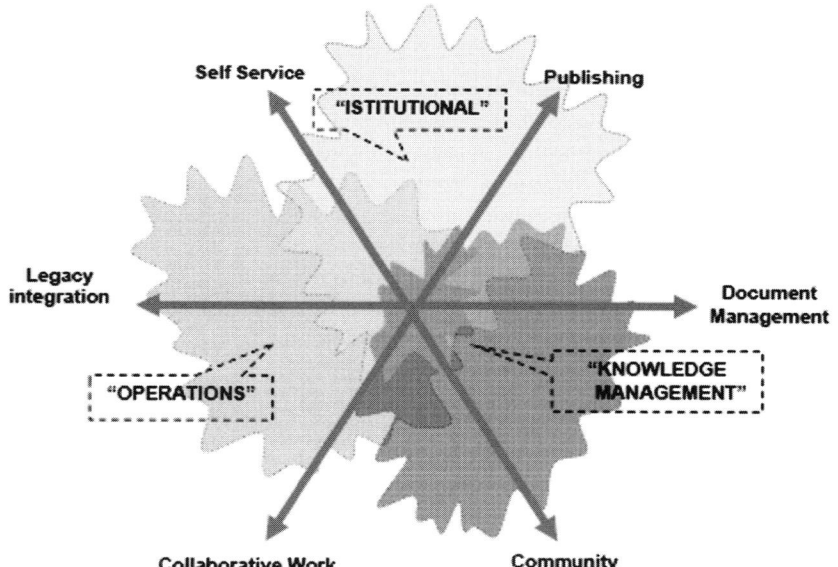

Fig.2. Evolution in the 1st era

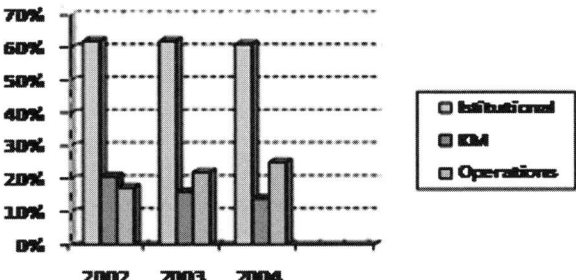

Most of the Intranets fit into the Institutional model, while Knowledge Management and Operations Intranets are less common.The absence of a strategic intent in the technology choices (*ad hoc* solutions developed with a limited budget) also results in a low level of integration between the Intranet applications and other IS, in particular legacy and ERP systems. Consequently, the Intranet becomes *de facto* a separate system compared to the daily functioning of processes.

There is little integration between the various Web-based applications devoted to employees, so that configurations are mainly of the application island type, in which individual components are replicated and are not placed in common. Such a configuration, which makes the dividing lines of the Intranet itself unclear, presents various critical factors: low effectiveness, as a result of different means of browsing; lack of efficiency, as a result of the duplication of some components and badly engineered integration ('spaghetti integration'), a lack of flexibility in new application development, as all components have to be re-thought and re-constructed each time.

The main barrier emerging from the analysis is precisely the lack of strategic planning in the Intranet infrastructural elements. Such planning requires the creation of a common infrastructure based on agreed standards and including the logic for the user interface presentation, the common services (e.g. user identification and authentication, security, search tools, etc.) and the logic for the integration with the other corporate information systems.With few exceptions, the impacts on the organisation are limited. The Institutional Intranets, which are the simplest and most common, have the smallest impacts. There are, however, some noteworthy cases, in which together with particular company changes (e.g. turnarounds or M&A), the Intranet has made a significant contribution to enhanced information transparency and a greater sense of belonging among company staff.The impact of Knowledge Management Intranets is also relatively limited and often no more than the greater availability of information. Generally speaking, these Intranets are felt to be insufficiently rooted in organisational processes, also because there is not sufficient integration with other corporate information systems.

In contrast, the Operations Intranets appear to have a more concrete impact on organisations and, consequently, on company performance. Albeit strictly within the domain of the specific processes supported, the Operations Intranets are a good example of how Intranet, if they manage to become part of the process operations, can create a new organisational dimension and gradually modify the tasks of individual employees and their relations.

From the evolution point of view, there have been minimal developments in the three years analysed, and these changes have mainly concerned slight improvements in existing functionalities. Most Intranets remain essentially confined to support processes, typically 'Human Resources Management and Internal Communication' and continue to offer mainly informational services. This suggests that there is still a reductive view of Intranets, which are primarily considered as service tools for employees, but detached from core company processes.

Few Intranets are considered and managed as strategic initiatives. Indeed, over and above public declarations, budgets are still short-term and small, there is no real commitment from top management, and the interest of line managers is still low, or at best, inconstant.However, looking at the performance of the 'best' cases (which account for no more than 20% of the panel), the picture changes. In this group, there are Intranets which are taking major steps in the direction of the support of core processes and the development of 'interactive' services. In the progress towards a more in-depth support of core processes, Intranets are going to converge increasingly with IS and ERP systems.

A first point of contact between Intranets and ERP is in the user interface. An increasing number of ERP modules provides a web interface, if only as a natural evolution of technology compared to the previous client/server mode. This offers the opportunity for integration with the Intranet environment, with not only technological, but, above all, management consequences. Furthermore, if on the one hand, more developed Intranets are tending to support core processes in increasing depth, even taking on part of the operations traditionally assigned to ERP systems, the latter are developing towards complete coverage of information needs. Therefore, the marriage of Intranets and ERPs, two systems with complementary characteristics and limitations, would appear inevitable. ERP focuses on processes, Intranet on people and relations. If ERP is the way in which processes work, Intranet is the way to interface these processes with the people who work with them. There are also some differences from a technological point of view. ERP offers stable and consolidated technologies, structured and well-defined (if rigid) schemes, while web technologies can reach everybody quickly with information and innovative services following the needs of individuals and organisations flexibly. The arrival of new demands leads to the coming together of two initially separate worlds: the new ERP systems need greater flexibility to move closer to people and keep up with constantly changing companies. To develop towards more strategic roles, the Intranet needs to enter into primary process operations, i.e. no longer merely information or support processes, but a single and complete access point for employees to company processes.

4.1 Lessons learned

The analysis of the cases reveals a substantial difference between the best ones, in which changes towards strategically significant processes and functionality are underway, and the majority of the initiatives that have developed little.

The difference regarding convergence with other Information Systems is even stronger. While in most cases, the Intranet is kept clearly separate from the managerial IS and ERP systems, the examples of good practices present a gradual process of convergence which brings the traditional dividing lines between these two different worlds into question.

The real reason for this state of inertia is rarely technological. The principal factor that discriminates the successes from the partial failures seems to be the company's attention in managing and accompanying the initiative as a process of organisational change.

In the unsuccessful cases, the company merely introduces tools and technologies without any substantial organisational or managerial measures. This can produce a gap between perceived needs and proposed solutions that leads to user dissatisfaction. In Institutional and Knowledge Management Intranets, which impact on processes that are not central to the users' task, this dissatisfaction simply results in little use of the system. In Operations Intranets, which are often indispensable tools for users' activities, the dissatisfaction can become annoyance and organisational conflict.

In best cases, on the other hand, the introduction of technology was accompanied by an agreed communication and change management strategy aimed at modifying the behaviour of individuals and company units.

The problem of governance

One of the most frequent causes for the partial or complete failure of an Intranet project is, therefore, the significant underestimation of the importance of organisational aspects. Most companies manage implementation projects from a purely technical point of view, without addressing organisational and change management questions in a systematic way. Both in the development and in the management phases, for example, companies still show little awareness in defining governance solutions, which in most cases appear to be emerging decisions, rather than the fruit of an agreed organisational plan. A lack of vision, an absence of commitment, conflicts of responsibility, jealousies and misunderstandings between roles and organisational units are among the most frequently cited barriers to the development of Intranets.

However, within this situation, there is an important point: although the Intranet rarely attracts the attention of top management, it is an intrinsically 'interfunctional' question.

Any attempt to constrain the Intranet governance within a functional 'box' (IT, Internal Communication, Human Resources, specific lines, etc.) always causes problems. Everything falls on environments that are not integrated, with disparate logic, duplicated resources and negligible or hidden development budgets.

These problems, which already existed with traditional Intranets, become particularly critical when the Intranet seeks to widen its borders:

- first, in addition to the technological problems already mentioned, the integration of legacy and ERP systems also comes up against problems of responsibility and authority, as well as the prejudices of those that feel that the Intranet can be a tool for communication and the management of services for people, but it not sufficiently efficient or reliable to support company core processes. It is not infrequent for this to slow down development and keep the two separate apart: i.e. the 'operations' Information Systems administered by line managers, and the Intranet dedicated to communication and services for employees administered by staff managers. In this case, the IT function is often stuck in the middle, aware of the potential benefits of integration, but unable to manage the strategic and organisational implications to the full;
- the expansion towards other organisations meets the problems of co-ordination between staff from different companies;
- the inclusion of 'other' web applications often faces difficulties tied to prejudices and jealousies between different functions. Lines are often opposed to the excessive integration of systems that they have promoted and financed within what is seen as a staff environment. It is particularly significant, for example, that Field Force Automation, Sales Force Automation and CRM are not integrated into the Intranet (which would considerably strengthen this environment), but are often kept deliberately separate.

The solution to these problems requires the re-design of the governance system, i.e. 'the set of roles, decision-making processes and organisational mechanisms which guide and regulate the functioning and development of the Intranet'.

The problem of evolution

The retrospective analysis and monitoring of the panel reveal that Intranets evolve through various stages of maturity: in each of them they change their characteristics and their role in the organisation.

Three fundamental phases in the Intranet evolution have been identified:

- The emergent stage: in this phase the birth of the Intranet is boosted by the local bottom-up initiatives, as a sort of collection of local applications implemented in order to answer to contingent stimuli and requests.
- The rationalization stage: it is characterised by a wider awareness of the Intranet presence and of its potential role. Its development happens through a top-

down process aimed at rationalising what was implemented in the past and to pursue strategic objectives.

- The strategic stage: it is the phase of greater maturity, characterised by the reassessment of the role of the Intranet that becomes a strategic tool to bring the processes on the web and to create new relational and collaborative spaces between people.

Except for few cases, the analysed Intranets are still in the "emergent development" or "rationalisation" phases, in which Intranet is still interpreted as "a strongly circumscribed" project both in space and in time:

- in *space*, as in most cases, the Intranet involves only a 'reduced' portion of the company processes: support processes in the case of Institutional Intranets; primary processes in the case of Operations Intranets; tied to the management of knowledge in the case of Knowledge Management Intranets;
- in *time*, as the Intranet projects are often managed as *one-off* projects with a beginning and an end.

In this view, there is a lack of the necessary vision to conceive and plan the Intranet evolution as a lever of organisational and strategic change. To arrive at the strategic stage, it is necessary to move to 'planned development', in which, once the spatial and temporal limitations of the vision have been overcome, management can re-think the Intranet evolution plan as a kind of *roadmap* of change.

To overcome the space borders means to think to the Intranet as a puzzle that, piece after piece, has to cover the entire organisational value chain, supporting all the processes – from the support to the primary processes, from the knowledge intensive to the operating processes: potentially, there is not any process belonging to the value chain that cannot be improved by means of a wise use of the Intranet technologies properly integrated with the "traditional" information systems.

To overcome the temporal borders means to think to the Intranet as a process that, step after step and according to an incremental approach, has to identify, define and put the single piece of the puzzle, up to arriving to the completion of the puzzle itself.Both of these developments require a strong and real management commitment who, fully realising the potential of the Intranet, provide the technical and organisational conditions to allow the Intranet to evolve with corporate strategy. The move to planned development thus requires the establishment of the conditions for change through the definition of:

- a *technology strategy* that lays the infrastructure foundations for the effective development of each applications and, above all, for their efficient integration;
- an *organisational strategy* that creates the conditions for the effective management of change through the introduction of the Intranet and the respective re-design of processes, competences and organisational relations. This strategy includes a governance of development that defines responsibility, mechanisms and rules for the planning of the Intranet, a day-to-day governance that defines operational roles, content and service

management policy, user involvement measures and change management, and a widespread network culture among workers with respect to the skills and habits regarding collaboration and the use of network tools.

5 An interpretative view of the evolution process: the 2nd era

For years, Intranet was seen merely as an information channel of use in managing unidirectional communication towards employees or providing them with some service. In most of the cases, first era objectives were related to:

- improving timeliness, transparency and reliability of internal communication through a unique and integrated information platform;
- simplifying the process of distribution and management of information;
- improving he sense of belonging and corporate identity;
- eliminating paper documentation and reducing hard costs.

However, from 2004 a new vision of Intranet emerges: a tool centered and focused on people and their needs, but with a strategic objective to create a complete workspace to support employees' day-by-day operations, knowledge management, collaboration and communication processes.

It is no longer a question of using the Intranet to improve internal communication, spread company culture or eliminate paper documents. The objectives concern operations and, in many cases, the creation of a profiled and customised environment involving users not only in work, but also in company life, creating and initiating a new system of relations. This also occurs via the integration in the Intranet of new communication tools and different company Information Systems, so providing a working environment that offers employees full operational support (Fig. 3). On the basis of the research results, the more advanced Intranets are extending their border to the support of core processes and are becoming increasingly integrated in management and legacy systems.

The more advanced Intranets tend to open up (as do companies as a whole) to the contribution of external players (customers, suppliers, partners, etc.). Secondly, the boundary with other web-based systems (e.g. CRM applications) is often just an excuse and tends to fade in the more developed Intranets. Finally, but even more importantly, advanced Intranets tend to integrate to an ever-greater extent with legacy systems. In some cases, it is the latter which take on a web interface and are progressively integrated into the Intranet environment; in others, the Intranets are extended to include functionality typical of legacy and ERP systems. These are signs of the emergence of a new generation of Information Systems that is profoundly integrated with the communication system, i.e. full-blown virtual work environments, and able to sustain a company's internal and external processes dynamically and flexibly. The Intranet of the future will constitute the social texture of organisational relations: systems designed around people, in which the latter find processes and relations.

Fig. 3. Initial vs current objectives

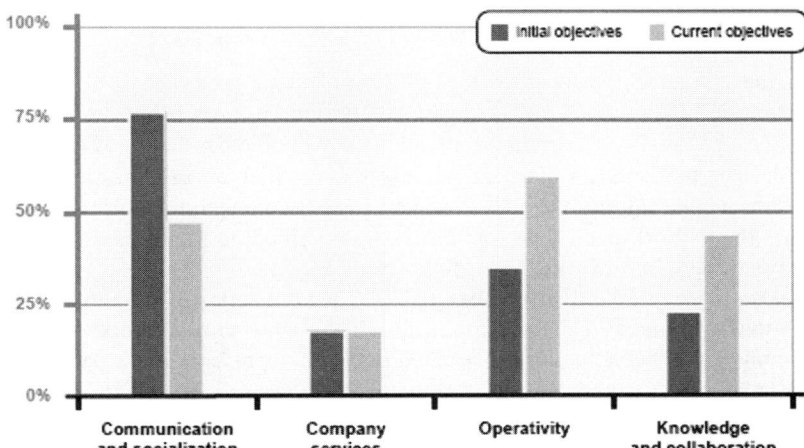

It seems to us that the Intranet has radically changed its role from a technological view in '90s to a predominantly unidirectional, top-down channel for communication & information (the 1st era) and to a what we have defined as a "Virtual Workspace", an integrated working space where employees can find what they need to work, to learn, to know and to interact with others (the 2nd era).

This new vision finds further confirmation in the strategic relevance that in now attributed to the Intranet. In most cases, it is considered comparable with other ICT projects or higher, and in 30% of the cases its importance has increased with respect to previous year. This increase in strategic relevance and budget is accompanied by strong attention from top management, which in most of the cases, is one of the sponsors of the project, and a growing involvement of staff and line functions.

5.1 Framework for the virtual workspace

From the literature review and the empirical analysis it emerged the following points:

- the Intranet concept is monolithic only at a theoretical level: for firms, the term "Intranet" groups very different ICT applications with respect to the objectives, supported processes, technologies and links with existing IS. Hence, whatever attempt to generalize is methodologically difficult and requires - as a *conditio sine qua non* - a clear definition of the boundaries and the typologies of the analyzed applications;

- the boundaries between Intranet and other IS are changing, because of their mutual convergence process; hence it is no longer useful to refer to functionalities and supported processes to distinguish an Intranet from other IS;
- unlike other ICT applications, such as ERP and CRM, Intranets always have a stronger focus on the employee than on business processes

For these reasons, we decided to look first at employees and *how to support* their work and interactions, rather than at supported business processes and functionalities. The v-W is composed of all web technologies-based ICT applications/services that support business processes and which an organisation can put forward to its employees. We take 'Intranet' to mean the web infrastructure which supports the v-Workspace. The framework was defined on the basis of the literature review and of a previous 4-year field study (Fig. 4).

In order to work effectively, each employee needs a series of supports and conditions that a company can design and provide via the virtual Workspace. Four dimensions have been identified; each dimension represents a virtual personal 'space' where the worker can find what he needs to do his job, to learn, to interact with others:

- *company services*: as workers and citizens of their company, employees need those services (e.g. work time management, refund of expenses, job posting) and those resources (booking facilities, purchase requests, IT help desk, library system) which allow them an effective and comfortable working life. At a rapidly decreasing cost (using self-service systems) below that of traditional services, the v-W provides better quality services;
- *communication & socialization tools*: employees live in their working environment and try to find the answer to their socialization, sharing and membership needs there; with a v-W, a firm can satisfy those needs by creating opportunities for socializing (usually through interactive IT services on after-work topics, leisure-time forums, bulletin boards, championships, etc.) even in situations characterized by physical dispersion of the workforce and high staff turnover and company restructuring that mean that people work for only limited and temporary periods for a company, so creating barriers to the sharing of knowledge and expertise. Institutional communication is both unidirectional to update employees on news related to the organization and its activities, bulletins, regulations and procedures, and bi-directional to collect suggestions and information from employees;
- *knowledge management & collaboration tools*: in order to be effective, employees need access to the codified knowledge, to be connected to the professional and social network and to be able to share experience and information; with a v-W, a firm can connect staff and provide them with opportunities for interaction and learning. These tools can be collaboration-oriented, i.e. tools to manage projects and teams, share agendas and documents, send SMS, instant

messaging and videoconference. Such solutions overcome geographical and temporal barriers in extended organizations and are particularly utilized to help interfunctional/international teams to collaborate at limited cost and with little time effort. Alternatively, they may be KM tools (more oriented to develop and share knowledge rather than support a team, i.e. forum, mailing list, tools to look for experts of specific topics, blog, wiki, document management systems, e-learning platforms). They can support both explicit knowledge sharing (as document management and business intelligence tools) and tacit collaboration (forums, surveys, expert search, blog, wiki, etc.)

- **Fig. 4. The v-Workspace dimensions**

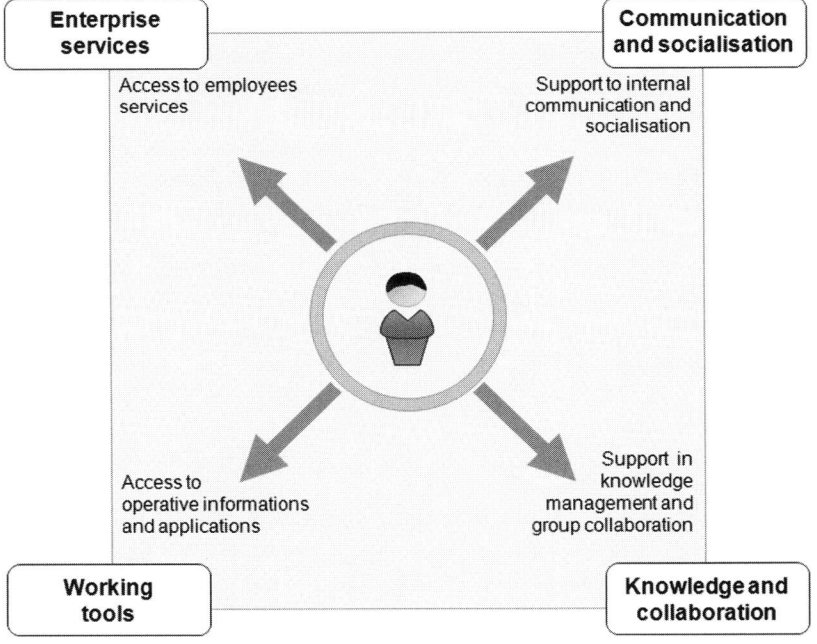

- _operation tools_: to provide personal and integrated access to operative tools (i.e. the web desk for banks, electronic patient data management) and information (product and service catalogues, operational manuals and procedures, customer and supplier information, competitive and market analysis, reporting).

The virtual Workspace is not a mere technological evolution but it is above all a great opportunity to re-design the organization using ICT as an enabler, supporting business strategy and process reconfiguration, stimulating innovation and collaboration between workers and units. The Intranet should develop its role from a tool for recovering local efficiency, to a tool developed to re-think processes, create new working spaces and collaboration spaces, prepare and anticipate the organisational change and accelerate the evolution of firms toward new strategies.

5.2 Lessons learned

Clear signs of development emerge from the 2006 data, in which the beginning of a transformation of the Intranet into what is termed the integrated Virtual Workspace is evident.Even if each of the dimensions in Fig. 4 can provide concrete benefits to a company, the empirical analysis of the most advanced cases reveals that the organizational impact is more effective, the more the v-W manages to integrate several dimensions. However, evolution towards an integrated environment comes up against considerable barriers both in technical and, in particular, in organizational and cultural terms.

From the analyses of the cases it has been identified (1) the stages of development, which correspond to the different levels of progressive integration of the v-W dimensions into a single, worker-oriented environment and (2) the approaches followed by the companies.

The problem of evolution

From the 110 cases analysis, four evolution stages have been identified. They correspond to the different levels of progressive integration of the v-W dimensions into a single, worker-oriented environment (Fig. 5):

1. *Embryonic stage* (13% of the cases)
   At this level, the intranet provides very little support in all of the v-W dimensions: sponsorship is very limited or completely absent; management and development depend on the initiative and goodwill of the intranet manager who is often only part-time and without a clear mandate; functionality and content are implemented as contingencies and outside any clear and recognized plan.
2. *Focused stage* (39% of the cases)
   Depending of which of the v-W dimensions is emphasized, we have the 4 spaces - *Employee Service (ES)*, *Internal Communication (IC)*, *Business Community (BC)* and *Operative Work (OW)* – previously reported. In the majority of the cases, the change from stage 1 to stage 2 occurs as a response to specific pressure from a company function or staff position that collaborates with IS in the control of the intranet. Depending on whether this function is Human Re-

sources, Internal Communication or a line, development tends to focus respectively on ES space (4% of the cases), IC space (20% of the cases), or OW space (11% of the cases). Sponsorship of just the few models focused on the BC space (4% of the cases) is less clear-cut and predictable.

3. *Composite stage* (39% of the cases).

Governance is extended and the Intranet develops by combining different dimensions. The benefits of integration make it possible to overcome the technological, organizational and cultural barriers and difficulties resulting from the creation and management of a more complex environment. The organizational and business impact becomes significant and justifies broader sponsorship which also includes top management.

4. *Advanced stage* (9% of the cases).

The Intranet loses a specific focus and reaches a very high level of support of all dimensions, becoming an integrated v-W. Sponsorship is elevated and the development objectives aligned with the company's organizational strategies.

Fig. 5. The evolution stages

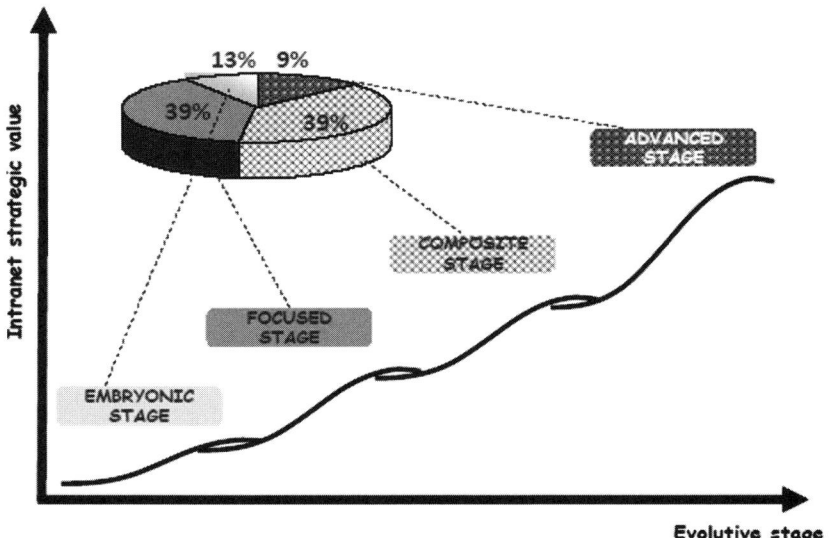

The approaches followed by the companies

We tried to understand the approaches followed by companies from stage 2 to stage 4.

First of all, the analysis of the cases revealed the presence of different orientations reflecting the different ways in which the role of the v-W in supporting individuals is interpreted.

A first axis relates to the nature of the priority support to be provided to employees, i.e. regarding specific work ('tasks') or company life as a 'citizen' within the organization. A second dimension regards the context to be supported, i.e. the individual or the social and relational sphere. We can, therefore, talk respectively of an orientation towards tasks or company life, towards the individual or the relation. These orientations can be related to the dimensions of the v-W.

Given these orientations, we can classify four composite models representing different integration approaches (Fig. 6):

- *company-life-oriented spaces* (21% of the cases) are models that integrate internal communication and socialization with access to company services. This is the most common of the composite models, as it faces relatively minor organizational barriers. Sponsorship comes from Internal Communications and HR staff who together with Information Systems see the intranet as a means to free themselves for low value-added activities to concentrate on more strategic work, guaranteeing at the same time better levels of use and an internal service. The benefit of integration resides in the creation of a more attractive user environment able to manage relations between employees and the organization fully;

- *employee-oriented spaces* (10% of the cases), in which the operational dimension combines with services. These models are developments of focused Operative Work space and Employee Service models that are progressively enriched by providing access to new services and applications. From the employees' point of view, this is a natural evolution as it provides an integrated environment of support services and tools for individual tasks, i.e. a kind of virtual desktop accessible from any location. Consequently, the benefit of integration is a greater level of use and a more central role for the intranet. From an organizational point of view, the difficulty is in combining tools that are traditionally managed by staff units with others usually organized by lines. Another problem limiting integration is the need to combine onto a single platform applications that were often developed on legacy systems whose replacement is difficult to justify from an economic point of view.

- *task-oriented spaces* (4% of the cases) combine the operational dimension with that of collaboration and knowledge. These are evolutions of operative spaces that enhance the possibility of interaction or, more rarely, of collaborative spaces in which access to particular employee tools is integrated. This creates a complete environment supporting a specific team or professional family, a sort of virtual 'open space' in which individuals can express and improve their professional expertise and interact with colleagues. The benefit of integration is enhanced individual and group effectiveness and the opportunity to create common practices and develop greater professional identity. In many cases, the difficulties concern resistance to integrating into a single environment operative, collaboration and knowledge management tools that are traditionally kept separate.

- *relation-oriented spaces* (4% of the cases) are models that combine the dimensions of communication and socialization with those of collaboration and knowledge. This leads to an environment in which both vertical (top-down or bottom-up) and horizontal (formal or informal) organizational relations between colleagues are more richly supported, so combining institutional communication, socialization and knowledge exchange. The benefits of the integration can be traced back to fuller and more effective internal communication overcoming traditional limitations of excessive formality and one-sidedness, as well as broader access to the knowledge base.

Fig. 6. The approaches to evolve from stage 2 to stage 4

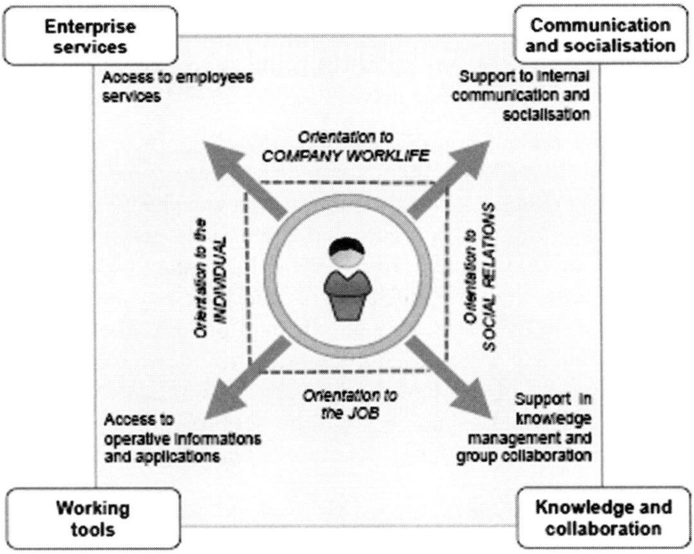

The problem of governance

The change from a composite model to an integrated v-W is a significant evolution and requires a further extension of governance. The main barrier derives from the fact that the creation of such a workspace is more than a simple juxtaposition of focused or composite environments. Different perspectives and points of view need to be combined to construct an environment providing an overall view of people and their needs.

The benefits that derive from the creation of an integrated v-W are not easily turned into monetary returns and their development therefore requires considerable vision on the part of management.

The major barriers to this process of integration do not appear to be technological, but rather political and organizational. Control of development and of communications and operative environment management, in particular, is often entrusted to different units and managers that find it difficult to pursue integration that would reduce their independence and require the unification of management and development approaches that have traditionally been separate.

Nevertheless, there are forces that may eventually overcome this resistance, enabling convergence towards single, integrated environments:

- the need to re-engineer the organization and its processes in the face of mergers and internationalization;
- the need to develop and manage new skills and professional families distributed across the country;
- the need to control and improve the processes within ever more complex and geographically dispersed competence networks.

Given these needs, the availability of integrated v-Ws is a powerful tool in re-engineering organizations, making them more flexible, dynamic and reconfigurable, so becoming a factor stimulating innovation and change.

However, this objective requires a significant increase in awareness among those controlling the Intranet. They must stop viewing the Intranet with the eyes of those who design 'desktops, drawers and blinkers' and look beyond the narrow space of the screen to provide 'spaces for relations and opportunities', in which people are free to move and find stimuli and opportunities, develop professional expertise, and set up networks of relations. In this way, the intranet will become a virtual workspace, through which companies will be able to stimulate and direct effective behavior among workers with regards innovation, collaboration and sharing.

In overcoming the limitations of traditional systems, the advanced v-W contributes to the development of a creative and open environment, breaking down barriers and re-assessing stereotypes and prejudices:

- space barriers: the workplace is everywhere that individuals need (and want) to use their capacities;
- time barriers: the myth of fixed working hours is overcome; people can and must be asked to create value when it is needed, and must be given frequent opportunities to find a new balance between their working and private lives;
- organizational barriers: 'my colleague can help to create value for my company (and for me as a professional)', the concept of competitor, supplier and collaborator needs to be re-considered in terms more closely centered on the individual and the relation.

One of the fundamental determinants at the basis of the success/failure of intra-net is the capacity to manage the organisational change process which is embed-ded in intranet introduction, development and management. This stresses the im-portance of the 'intranet governance': the set of roles, decisional processes and organisational mechanisms that regulate and address intranets functioning and evolution, with the aim of creating an alignment with the strategic and organiza-tional priorities.

6   From v-Workspace to Enterprise 2.0

The term "Enterprise 2.0" derives from Web 2.0 and is often used to indicate the introduction and implementation of social software inside a company, and the so-cial and organizational changes associated with it. The term was coined by And-rew McAfee, professor at Harvard Business School to refer to *"simple, free plat-forms for self-expression"* (McAfee's blog, March, 24 2006). He soon followed up with a refined definition: *"Enterprise 2.0 is the use of emergent social software platforms within companies, or between companies and their partners or custom-ers."* (McAfee's blog, May 27, 2006).

Since then it has been given different definitions by scholars and practitioners: Enterprise Web 2.0 (Hinchcliffe[28]) and Social Computing (Forrester). We think that E2.0 calls for a broader vision of either organizational and technological model evolution, which includes the design of an adaptive architecture (SOA and BMP), Web 2.0 collaboration tools and the virtual Workspace as enabling plat-form for connections and processes.

> *E2.0 is a set of organizational and technological approaches steered to enable new organization models, based on open in-volvement, emergent collaboration, knowledge sharing, inter-nal/external social network development and exploitation.*

Enterprise 2.0 is not in itself a technological phenomenon, but rather the result of a progressive, social and organisational development that finds an important ac-celerating factor in ICT.

The Enterprise 2.0 vision of the central role of the user is also not in itself some-thing new, but was already part of the 2nd generation of Intranets. Virtual Work-spaces seek to support users who, as 'company citizens', need to exploit corporate services and make use of socialisation, collaboration and operations areas.

The change form a traditional Intranet to a Virtual Workspace is an evolution process in which there is a progressive change of objectives and a growing strategic

---

[28] "… which is the application of Web 2.0 technologies to workers using network software with-in an organization or business." In Hinchcliffe's blog. Web 2.0 definition updated and Enterprise 2.0 emerges, November 5, 2006.

centrality. The change from the Virtual Workspace to the Enterprise 2.0 can be seen as part of the same development process, within which, however, it constitutes an evident point of discontinuity, a sort of '*genetic mutation*' that results in attention being paid to the broader dimension where people live their professional lives; this dimension presents 'new needs' that cannot be satisfied within a 'closed' organisational space.

From an organisational point of view, Enterprise 2.0 is a point of discontinuity that breaks the boundaries of the Virtual Workspace both in terms of opening up the organisation to 'external' players (customers, suppliers, partners) and of rethinking the traditional schemes of collaboration, knowledge sharing, and management of functional and hierarchical relations, so questioning the rigid stereotypes regarding the workspace and working hours.

6.1 Framework for Enterprise 2.0

The emerging needs (Davenport 2005; Tapscott and Williams 2006; AAVV 2007) that E2.0 tries to respond to can be divided into six key dimensions (Fig. 7):

- *open belonging*: people increasingly feel, and actually are, as "members" of extended dynamic networks rather than single organisations: through E2.0 technologies (content management systems shared by the Intranet, Extranet and Internet, KM tools and collaboration tools open to external players, Intranet integrated operating applications such as the supply chain management systems) it is possible to supply secure and selective access to information, tools and connections that go beyond the company's boundaries, interacting in an increasingly rich and effective manner with suppliers, consultants, partners, customers and other networked players;
- *social networking*: people increasingly need to develop and maintain that network of relations that is becoming a more and more important asset for their professional efficiency (Cross et al. 2005; Surowiecki 2004). E2.0 tools and approaches that track down people from basic information (such as the traditional telephone book or online presence) or by associating advanced profiles (such as competence mapping, expert search, social networks) support the development and management of relations to track and contact co-workers and experts inside and outside the organisation, keeping their interest, skill and role profiles updated at all times;
- *knowledge networks*: to prevent their knowledge and skills being "surpassed" soon, workers must be able to build their own network to have access to knowledge and information from different sources, both explicit (document management systems, Business Intelligence, video-sharing, pod-casting, RSS) and implicit (systems that ease interaction between experts, such as forums, mailing lists, surveys, blogs, folksonomies, wiki) – Dearstyne 2007;

- *emergent collaboration*: in an increasingly fast and unpredictable competitive scenario, people need to create cooperative settings in a fast, flexible way, even outside the formal organisational patterns. E2.0 technology enables people to do this, through faster and richer opportunities for interaction, both synchronous (chat, instant messaging, video-conference) and asynchronous (diary sharing, project management, exchange and co-editing of work documents, texting) which enable them to overcome geographical and time barriers in extended organisations;
- *adaptive reconfigurability*: in response to the endless changes taking place in corporate policies and strategies, people need to quickly reconfigure their own processes and activities. Such technologies as SOA, BPM, mash-up, SaaS, RIA can give the companies, and sometimes the users themselves, the tools they need to redefine and adapt their processes in a dynamic, flexible and personal way that can hardly be given by any traditional technology;
- *global mobility*: people spend an increasingly large share of their time far from the workplace and often in a state of mobility. New ICT enables them to be connected in any place and at any time of day through their own network of tools, thus making the workspace and working time more flexible, using systems for supplying staff services (authorisation workflows), internal communication, mobile office services (from simple emails to mobile access to the Intranet) and operational services, such as sales force automation and field force automation.

Fig. 7. From v-Workspace to Enterprise 2.0 framework

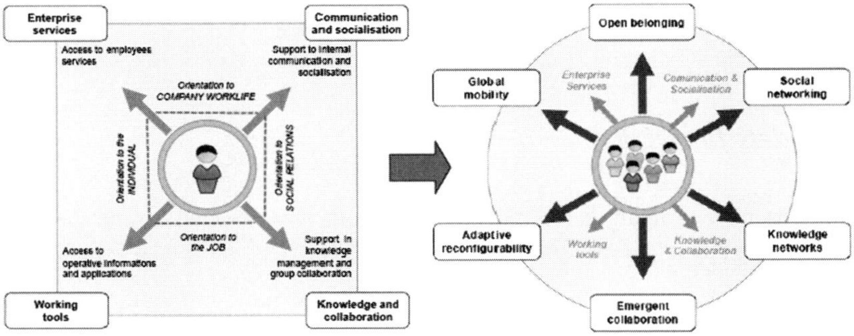

6.2 Methodology

Considering the emergent nature of the phenomenon and a substantial lack of empirical researches, the proposed research methodology combines compared case studies, surveys and a sort of co-laboratory. Specifically:

- 70 case studies were carried out through a questionnaire and direct interviews to the management of medium/large-sized Italian companies (manufacturing, banking, PA, assurance, pharmaceutical, services);
- a survey was administered to 65 Chief Information Officers in order to understand their view of the E2.0 phenomenon;
- an online community – Enterprise20.it (see http://www.enterprise20.it) – was developed in order to promptly receive cues and suggestions to refine the research from the participating firms, vendors and experts. It acts as a laboratory and a landmark for the E2.0 phenomenon.

In addition, direct interviews to main ICT players were performed in order to understand trends and scenarios on the vendor side. Preliminary results have been discussed and validated through the Enterprise20.it online community.

The comprehensibility and completeness of the questionnaires were tested in advance in pilot interviews. The interviews, of approximately one and a half hours, were carried out (after returning the questionnaires) either by telephone or face-to-face. The use of a semi-structured form leaves ample freedom both to the interviewer and the interviewee, while ensuring that all the important arguments are addressed and all the necessary information collected. A checklist was devised with the subjects to be addressed, while the order of the questions, the level of detail regarding specific questions, and the words used, etc. could be decided by the interviewer during the meeting. The checklist maintained the reproducibility of the request for information in various situations.

All the interviews were recorded and transcribed; subsequently, a report was prepared.

Preliminary results have been discussed and validated through the Enterprise20.it, with the participating firms, vendors and experts.

6.3 Models for E2.0

In function of a company's position on six parameters, we can define three different models or paths towards Enterprise 2.0 (Fig. 8):

- *Social Enterprises* that emphasise the creation of new collaborative schemes, knowledge sharing and relationship management. This model represents a major opportunity, but also a fundamental challenge for companies. With today's new tools, it is possible to connect people and share large quantities of information ever more quickly and cheaply, so overcoming temporal and geographic limitations and the organisational barriers to communication and knowledge transfer, and creating new organisational and strategic effectiveness and flexibility;
- *Open Enterprises* that move towards a broadening and opening-up of the Virtual Workspace in terms of means of access and external players; in this sense, Information Systems are seen as open to contributions from different people

and sources, and offer services and information selectively to external players and organisations, creating new means of interaction with customers, suppliers, partners and consultants which often become full-blown process, product or service innovations. These models often also supply an effective response to the mobility and territorial dispersion of people and activities; reconnecting people to their networks guarantees the flexibility, speed and robustness of operational and decision-making processes;

- *Adaptive Enterprises* that focus on flexibility and re-configurability of company processes; in this case, an environment is created which can support processes and respond more easily to the changing needs of the company and the user. Realising an adaptive enterprise means creating a space that can support corporate processes in an increasingly flexible way, orchestrating the flows of information by means of an agile integration infrastructure, and subsequently helping them to evolve in order to maintain a constant alignment over time with the changing needs of the company and specific employees by means of advanced tools to manage processes and integrate content from different sources.

Fig. 8. The models for E2.0[29]

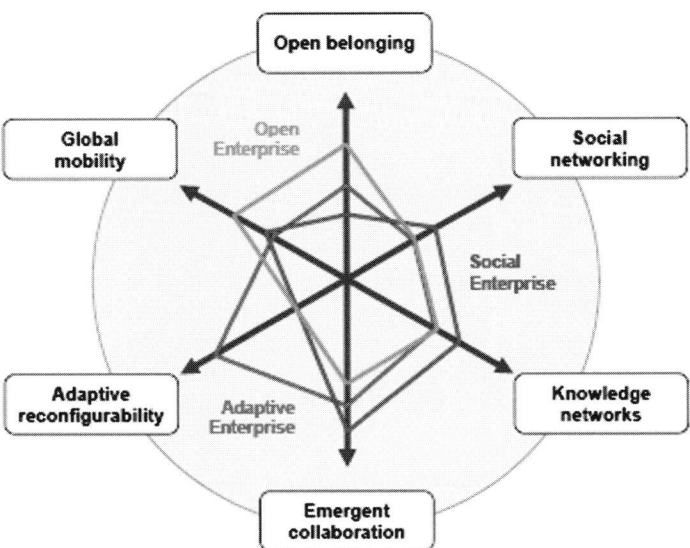

All the paths analysed offer significant opportunities for innovation, but these opportunities also imply growing needs for organisational change that currently stop many companies from taking the Enterprise 2.0. Indeed, numerous initiatives (48%) are still in an embryonic stage, with limited support for all the dimensions.

---

[29] The three models stand for the average support to the six dimensions in the organisations that adopted it (not the average in the overall sample).

The social enterprise

Social Enterprise seems to be the most popular (24% of cases). As shown in red in Figure 8, it is the need for emergent collaboration, shared knowledge and development of internal and external social networks which drives the evolution of the organisational model. Although unable to start from technology, this is a process which can be enabled by it. The technology used includes both tools that have been available for some time in the ISs – such as document management, instant messaging, diary sharing, etc. – and innovative social computing tools borrowed from Web 2.0.

To understand the real impact of these tools on the organisation, a detailed analysis of the *Social Enterprises* approaches adopted in the cases have been performed. It emerged a high level of maturity in terms of:

- *commitment* the organisation gives to the community in terms of allocated resources (tools, people, etc) and level of legitimisation;
- *level of users' involvement and participation*.

These Social Enterprises often create environments that are not targeted to the corporate population at large but to specific groups or communities. The level of users' participation and proactive involvement is high when they see the community as an important element to increase their wealth of knowledge, create new relations and increase their "organisational" effectiveness and visibility. In addition, a number of users, as well as using them, proactively participate in the creation of contents, take part in discussions and create interpersonal relations of trust and *mutual engagement*. At the same time, the top management's commitment is also high, and the organisation recognises the community as an important means to achieve its business purposes, by proactively supporting it and allocating it substantial resources.

Basing on the specific groups or community characteristics they are targeted to - the focus level (specificity of the involved members and therefore of the subjects addressed), cohesion (intensity of bonds between members), stability of involvement (time the community members remain in the community) and interactivity (frequency of relations between members) - four types of SE virtual environment con be selected (Fig. 9):

- *Professional Families.* Environments targeted to communities of "cohesive" people which the members permanently belong to, with the members sharing the same interests and problems, usually relating to the same job (for instance, Information System, Research & Development communities, etc). Their purpose is to ease the exchange of knowledge, share *best practices* and network the "experts" to tackle common problems. In professional families, interaction is key, value is given by the creation of contents by the members, and participation is boosted by the quality of the resources and the availability of experts. In such cases, the "interactive" means are of primary importance but they must be combined so as to promote relations (expert search, skill mapping, etc.), exchanges (forums, instant messaging, etc.), and let the members create and dis-seminate contents (wiki, document management, blogs, etc.).

- *Teams.* Environments targeted to focussed communities, which are often short lived because they are "instrumental" to achieving a shared but "transient" goal. A typical example are the communities that are created to manage pro-jects the purpose of which is to support the operational process and encode im-plicit knowledge and documents that have not been formalised yet so that they can be reused in other projects. The means used in these cases usually boost synchronous and asynchronous cooperation between people (such as chats, in-stant messaging, video-conference, project management, diary sharing, docu-ment sharing and co-editing).
- *Clubs.* Communities of people who have shared interests but are poorly cohe-sive (for instance, sales networks, promoters, etc.). They often stand out for a limited interaction between the members for whom contents are much more important than relations. The key ingredient to make it a community is there-fore the involvement of the members in the creation of valuable contents (in-formation on resources, blogs, wiki, document management systems, etc.). If the members do not participate in the creation of such contents, the benefits of a participatory system are thwarted, with the risk the community may disappear once the members have seen all they were interested in ("low stability"). Since at first the members are not prone to interacting with each other, "discussion" systems (forums, chats, etc.) need not be used from the very start. However, with time, the most loyal members wish to be more involved in the contents and with other people with whom they share the same interests, so interactive tools need be introduced for such communities to turn into "stable families".
- *Agorae.* "Open" communities with limited members' focus and cohesion, which often result in transient involvement and variable levels of interactivity. The subjects addressed may vary, and the members do not establish permanent relations. It is a temporary condition that risks disappearing unless it is ruled by the organisation (by setting up a focus, by pushing the members to be involved, etc.).

A classification of the aforesaid communities helps recognise how the members interact (with the others and with the content) and determine organisational and individual impacts. To do this, each SE case has been mapped in terms of impacts on three major dimensions (Fig. 10):

- *Impact on processes:* we checked whether the community led to a change in the processes in terms of improving performance (efficiency and effectiveness) and in terms of innovation and change (redesign of the process);
- *Impact on knowledge:* it has been valuated the impact of the community on the creation and dissemination of implicit and explicit knowledge through systems that enhance people's skills and turn them into the organisation's shared assets;

- *Impact on connections:* we considered the effects in terms of support to the creation of vertical and horizontal relations, overcoming the barriers of traditional organisational structures and promoting cross-cooperation.

As to the impact on processes, it results that *families* and sometimes *clubs* usually have an impact in terms of improvement of performance and innovation. *Teams* help improve efficiency and effectiveness in the achievement of a specific goal, but because of their short life they hardly ever result in process innovation. Finally, *agorae* usually have limited impact on processes because of their members' poor focus and short-lived involvement.

Looking at the impact on knowledge, *families* support both the creation of new knowledge and the dissemination of encoded knowledge to all the members involved. Because they have few relational tools, *clubs* have more impact on the dissemination of encoded knowledge but hardly result in the members' creating new knowledge. *Agorae* usually help the members collect some information, which however is not often encoded and disseminated. Finally, *teams* help disseminate and create knowledge between few members.

Fig. 9. Distinctive features of Social Enterprise virtual environment

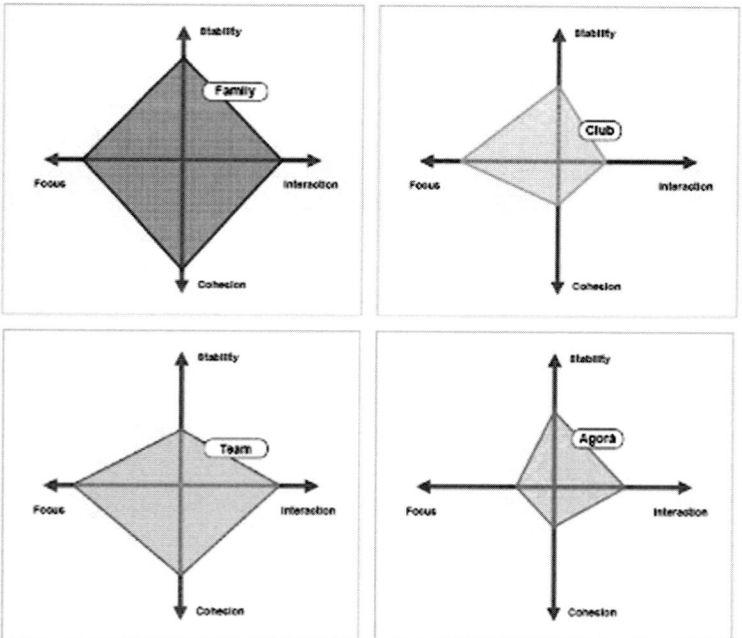

Finally, looking at the impact on relations, *families* support both the creation of new connections, especially when the members are geographically distant and therefore could hardly come into contact with each other, and the management and enrichment of such relations by providing several tools for mutual help and exchange, *Teams* are very effective in managing connections through several interactive systems but, since they are closed and temporary, they hardly ever result in the creation of new, permanent relations. Usually, *agorae* are very open and help create new connections, which however are then managed in different spheres. At first, *clubs* do not support horizontal connections as much as they support instead vertical ones and interactions with contents, and therefore these communities have the lowest impact on horizontal connections.

The analysis of the cases shows that, regardless of the implemented model, the SE is a great opportunity and at the same time a fundamental challenge for the organisations: as times and costs decrease all the time, tools become newer and newer and more and more effective, people can be connected with each other and large amounts of information can be shared, overcoming geographical and time barriers and organisational barriers that hinder communication and knowledge transfer, creating new spaces of effectiveness and strategic and organisational flexibility.

Fig. 10. Impacts of Social Enterprise on processes, connections and knowledge

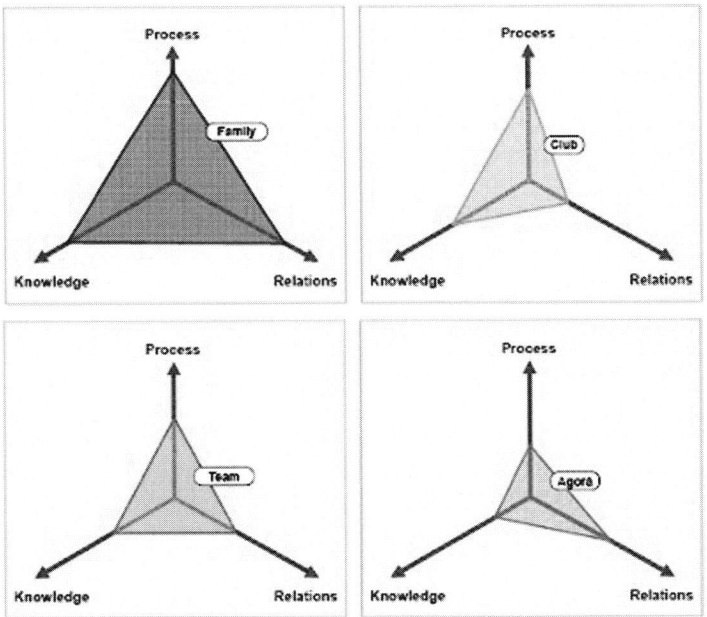

The other two E2.0 models

We briefly report a short profile of the other two E2.0 models.

- *Open Enterprises* that move towards a broadening and opening-up of the Virtual Workspace in terms of means of access and external players; in this sense, Information Systems are seen as open to contributions from different people and sources, and offer services and information selectively to external players and organisations, creating new means of interaction with customers, suppliers, partners and consultants which often become full-blown process, product or service innovations. These models often also supply an effective response to the mobility and territorial dispersion of people and activities; reconnecting people to their networks guarantees the flexibility, speed and robustness of operational and decision-making processes;
- *Adaptive Enterprises* that focus on flexibility and re-configurability of company processes; in this case, an environment is created which can support corporate processes and respond more easily to the changing needs of the company and the user. Realising an adaptive enterprise means creating a space that can support corporate processes in an increasingly flexible way, orchestrating the flows of information by means of an agile integration infrastructure, and subsequently helping them to evolve in order to maintain a constant alignment over time with the changing needs of the company and specific employees by means of advanced tools to manage processes and integrate content from different sources.

7 Future developments

Face of the increasingly power and accessibility of ICT technologies and of users ever more inclined to ask the change, what are the obstacles which prevent organizations to shift to E2.0, grasping its benefits?

Main difficulties in E2.0 implementations are not from tech side but from a knowledge lack of opportunities, a difficulty in economic benefit identification and valuation, together with the need of organizational change. In other terms, the barriers are not technological but cultural ones: most of the companies manage the implementation project in a purely technical perspective without systematically facing the organizational and the change management aspects.Particularly critical is the definition of governance - the organizational choices that determine the division of the responsibilities and the key criteria to be followed in the planning and management of an initiative. Inadequate decisions regarding governance are often difficult to be modified and can jeopardize the development possibilities and the project effectiveness.

E2.0 governance will be emergent, open and collaborative. The traditional governance systems are put in crisis: all the roles tend to move, at least in part, to final user, who will decide what to do, achieve it and then handle it by himself. Without an appropriate governance the risk is the proliferation of different and not integrated IS. The CIO will be faced with a dilemma: on the one side, the opportunity to animate and stimulate the initiative of line through new ICT tools introduction, on the other the need to introduce standards and rules in order to not lose control and the role in front of a IS increasingly governed by the user.

Tomorrow main challenges that management has to deal with can be summarized in the following ones:

- How to stimulate, understand and anticipate demand from internal users?
- How to leverage on suppliers of external services without becoming too dependent?
- How to drive and channel energies associated with spontaneous contributions of users?
- How much and how to open to external users and contributors without compromising security and intellectual property?

The objective for management theory is therefore to provide empirically grounded and actionable knowledge (guidelines) for companies to design and implement new ICT-enabled (virtual) working environments able to extend the boundaries of their knowledge creation to their mobile workers, customers and suppliers.

References

AAVV (2007) The future of the web. MIT Sloan Management Review 48:49-49

Anderson C (2006) The long tail: why the future of business is selling less of more. Hyperion, New York

Benkler Y (2006) The wealth of networks: how social production transforms markets and freedom. Yale University Press

Chesbrough H (2003) Open innovation: the new imperative for creating and profiting from technology. Harvard Business School Press, Boston

Corso M, Giacobbe A, Martini A (2008) Rethinking knowledge management: the role of ICT and the rise of the virtual workspace. International Journal of Learning & Intellectual Capital, 4

Corso M, Giacobbe A, Martini A, Pellegrini L (2006) What knowledge management for mobile workers?. Knowledge and Process Management Journal, special issue on continuous innovation and knowledge management 13:206-217

Corso M, Martini A, Pellegrini L, Pesoli A (2008) From 1.0 to 2.0: a continuous innovation matter. Results of a 5-year field research. 9th International CINet Conference "Radical challenges in innovation management", Valencia, Spain, September 8-9

Corso M, Martini A, Massa S, Pellegrini L, Testa S (2006) Managing dispersed workers: the new challenge in knowledge management. Technovation 26:583-594

Cross R, Liedtka J, Weiss L (2005) A practical guide to social networks. Harvard Business Review 83:124-132

Davenport TH (2005) Thinking for a living: how to get better performances and results from knowledge workers. Harvard Business School Press, Boston

Dearstyne BW (2007) Blogs, mashups, & wikis. Oh, my!. Information Management Journal 41:24-33

Greer T (1998) Understanding Intranets. Microsoft Press

Harris K, Berg T (2002) Business-to-Employee: the roadmap to strategy. Gartner Group

Hinchcliffe D (2006) Web 2.0 for the enterprise?. Enterprise web 2.0 blog entry. http://blogs.zdnet.com/Hinchcliffe/?p=3. Accessed 27March 2007

Magnusson M, Martini A (2008) Dual organizational capabilities: from theory to practice. the next challenge for continuous innovation. International Journal of Technology Management 42:1-19

McAfee AP (2006) Enterprise 2.0: The dawn of emergent collaboration. MIT Sloan Management Review 47:21-28

McKinsey (2007) How business are using Web 2.0: a McKinsey global survey. McKinsey Quarterly. http://www.mckinseyquarterly.com/How_businesses_are_using_Web_20_A_McKinsey_Global_Survey_1913_abstract. Accessed 29 April 2008

Murgolo-Poore ME, Pitt LF, Ewing MT (2001) Intranet effectiveness: a public relations paper–and-pencil checklist. Public Relations Review 28:113-123

Surowiecki J (2004) The wisdom of crowds: why the many are smarter than the few and how collective wisdom shapes business, economics, societies and nations

Tapscott D, Williams AD (2006) Wikinomics: how mass collaboration changes everything. Portfolio Penguin Group, New York

Tyndale P (2002) A taxonomy of knowledge management software tools: origins and applications. Evaluation and Programm Planning, 25:183-190

Chapter 13. Embedding Web 2.0 Strategies in Learning and Teaching

Vladlena Benson

Department of Informatics and Operations Management, Kingston University, UK

Barry Avery

Department of Informatics and Operations Management, Kingston University, UK

Abstract

Many researchers see Web 2.0 technologies as having the potential to transform e-learning and traditional teaching methods. Significant attention has been paid to the evaluation of some of the Web 2.0 tools in education, however an accepted pedagogical model has yet to emerge. Web 2.0 technologies have become an essential part of student lives, now educators are turning to them in search of more effective teaching strategies. This paper describes some of the popular Web 2.0 technologies in use in education and highlights their pedagogical value. We draw attention to the implications of the use of these tools applied in learning and teaching, and the factors and barriers that influence their successful adoption.

1   Introduction

The advent of Web 2.0 has caused a significant change in the way that the internet is used in all sectors of the knowledge economy, including education. The deep penetration of Web technologies into the lives of students over the last five years has been suggested by a number of researchers (Green and Hannon 2007; Kohut et al. 2007; Boulos and Wheeler 2007). Immersion in digital technology is argued to have influenced aptitudes and interests of students in ways significant for education. Multiple studies (Frund 2000; Oblinger and Oblinger 2005; Tapscott 1999) suggest that the digital generation, encompassing current students and those about to enter HE, learn differently compared with preceding generations of students. They are claimed to be active communicators dependent on Web technologies for accessing information and for interacting with others.

With the emergence of Web 2.0, learners have developed a social world that is parallel to their everyday work and study activities. Looking at a group of students in the learning cafe at a university library, we see them using laptops as they appear deeply consumed by something, studying perhaps? They exchange words pointing to their screens and appear thrilled. Perhaps they find their assignment electrifying or are studying something exciting on the LMS? Looking closer we see that they are actually in a different world – logged in to Facebook, looking at pictures, checking out videos, chatting away. They are socialising, just not in what educators call a 'face-to-face mode'. They are comfortable and intuitive users of technology, adapting easily to new arrivals in the digital world, hardly needing any external guidance on how to learn to use a new application or gizmo.

Extensive research (Bennet et al. 2008; Prensky 2001) into the digital generation phenomena has concluded that current students and those coming into HE are different to the students from even five years ago. Digital learners use technologies as an intrinsic part of their lives (Green and Hannon 2007). They cannot imagine student life without the Web, mobile phone, an iPod, a computer, plus a networked social life. The digital generations are intuitive users of technology and research studies (Alonzo et al. 2005) have kneaded the possibilities offered by the first four of the essentials in the list above.

Current research shows a growing interest towards harnessing the opportunities offered by Web 2.0 in educational settings (Naeve et al. 2006; Boulos and Wheeler 2007; Andersen 2007). However, the phenomenon of Web 2.0 has not broken into HE for pedagogical use as it has into the lives of the students. Many researchers see Web 2.0 as having the potential to transform e-learning and traditional teaching methods (Lytras and Naeve 2006; Owen et al. 2006; Kohut et al. 2007).

This article attempts to outline the Web 2.0 applications fit for purpose in higher education and summarises their pedagogical value as compared to traditional Web 1.0 tools. Successful realisation of Web 2.0 based learning requires a thorough understanding of the potential barriers influencing acceptance of these technologies by educators and learners alike. The capabilities of Web 2.0 and their application in higher education raise a range of questions connected to copyright, content ownership, content reuse and the place of the educator in these democratic peer based networks. In this article we explore the implications of Web 2.0 that may affect established educational values and standards. Finally we suggest some possible directions for further research and discussion.

2   Background

The first generation of the World Wide Web (now redesignated as Web 1.0), has had a significant impact on the educational sector (Alexander 2002; Williams et al. 2005; Picciano and Dziuban 2007). We have seen a considerable change in the delivery methods, classroom dynamics, development of new pedagogies and emergence of a new approach to education, coined e-learning. Web 1.0 technologies are playing an increasingly important role in HE (Bennet et al. 2008) despite some significant limitations on interactivity and static read-only capabilities. Web 2.0 introduces the writable Web, where Web-based applications exploit peer-to-peer user-generated content and offer complex dynamic graphical user interfaces (previously only seen in desktop applications. In this section we explore the possibilities offered by the advent of Web 2.0 and discuss its application to education.

2.1 Exploring Web Usage Patterns among Learners

Current research shows that learners are skilful in using a wide variety of educational technologies ranging from unsophisticated information search to customisable technologies for interpersonal communication and social networking (Prensky 2001; Green and Hannon 2007). Recent data on the use of the Internet in the UK proves that students are more inclined than other occupational groups to undertake communication activities online (Dutton and Helsper 2007).

Some interesting findings about the web activity of over six hundred undergraduate students from a non-IT focused fields of study (Benson 2008), show that irrespective of gender or field of study, students deem themselves confident and intuitive users of technology. Gaining an insight into learners' aptitude towards the web and computer technology is important as it may serve as a potential indicator of Web 2.0 readiness.

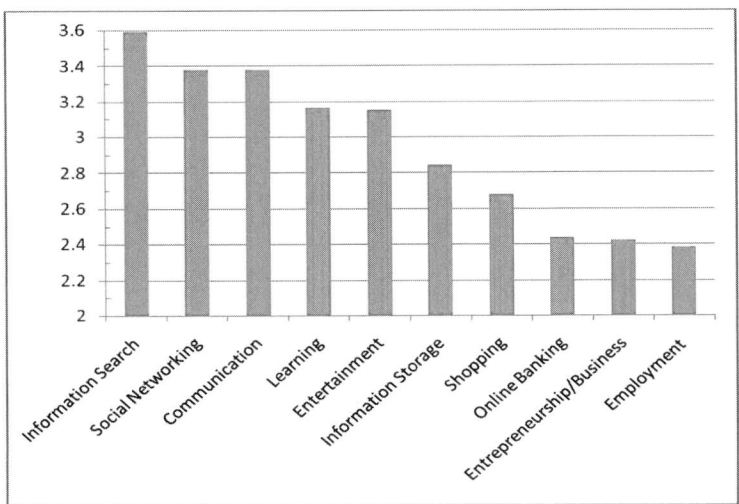

Fig. 1. Patterns in Learners' Use of the Web (Benson 2008).

Recent studies show that young people have developed a hierarchy of digital activities, especially when it comes to assessing their potential for learning (Green and Hannon 2007). Unlike the preceding generation, current learners are very conscious about their time and deem some activities as more worthwhile than others.

The World Wide Web occupies an important place in their daily lives with significant proportions of learners spending over three hours a day online. Also, it was revealed that female learners are more likely to spend more than eight hours a day on the Web compared to males (Benson 2008). The study indicated that students use the Web primarily as the source of information, being ranked as the number one activity task in their daily Web practices (see fig. 1). Social networking and communication came as second and third most popular activities respectively. These were followed by learning and entertainment activities. It appeared that on-line shopping, online banking and entrepreneurship are among the least popular web activities among younger students. The author raises a further question of whether this is caused by a limited inclusion of business and entrepreneurial on-line ventures in HE curriculum.

Overall, the research presents a general picture of current learners as active users of Web capabilities for communication and social networking. Being so adapt in the Web 2.0 social space, students are already establishing new learning practices which incorporate their interpersonal communication and social networking habits.

2.2 Building on the Web 1.0 -Based Learning Frameworks

A number of conceptual models of online learning have been developed in recent research (Alexander, 2001; Moule, 2007; Salmon, 2005, etc.). However, Alexander's framework for implementation of e-learning initiatives in Higher Education deserves particular attention. It addresses stakeholder issues in the educational process, as well as support and development mechanisms. Table 1 attempts to summarise some crucial aspects to the design and implementation of e-learning initiatives in HE.

Table 1: Alexander's Framework for the Design, Development and Implementation of E-learning.

University Context	Instructor Perception	Instruction Planning	Teaching Strategies
Institutional vision for e-learning	Encouragement to faculty to undertake staff development	Develop an increased understanding of the students	Faculty encouraged to provide informative and timely feedback to students
Technology Development Plan	Encourage reflection of Faculty view regarding e-learning in-	Design assessment to complement learning objectives	Provide understanding of the learning process prior to learning activities

itiatives			
Faculty workload policy incorporating e-learning	Reflect on planning and use of technology	Mechanisms to provide useful and timely feedback	Include activities to develop group work skills.
Reliability of Technology	Increase understanding of how students learn	Preparation of students for different learning activities and learning modes	
Support facility for staff and students	Increase understanding that high quality e-learning opportunities are available	Embedding management skills in learning activities	
Staff development opportunities including pedagogy, management, technology and design		Planning for context of implementation	
Provision of time release for faculty engaged in e-learning developments		Obtaining copyright clearance for materials used.	

3   An Overview of the Emerging Web 2.0 Technologies and their Applications in Education

Developing a Web 2.0-enabled teaching strategy is more complex than setting up a blog or wiki. It requires a profound understanding of teaching and learning processes, the stakeholders involved and, additionally the enabling technology. In this section we will attempt to summarise popular Web 2.0 tools and highlight their applications in education, including:

- Audio and Video 2.0
- Blogs
- Bookmarking 2.0
- Community 2.0
- Wikis.

3.1 Audio and Video 2.0

A podcast is "a digital recording of a radio broadcast or similar program, made available on the Internet for downloading to a personal audio player", (as defined in the New Oxford American Dictionary). Recently in addition to audio, the definition has expanded to include video. The term podcast was initially formed from a combination of "broadcasting" and iPod. More generally podcasting refers to the method of distributing multimedia files over the Internet using syndication feeds, for playback on iPods, MP3/MP4 players, other mobile devices and personal computers. The major difference to the previous use of such audio formats is the automatic syndication feature of podcasts. Having subscribed to a podcast (via audio/video feeds) the listener receives automatic updates each time new content become available. The software can then automatically download the new content and place it on the appropriate audio device. In education, podcasts are applied as a content source for teaching. However the 2.0 nature of podcasting also supports peer-to-peer sharing of information, promoting reflection, integration and collaboration.YouTube(http://www.youtube.com/), a Web 2.0 video sharing service has been a popular source of educational material. Mashups, a new trend in remixing or overlaying, two or more original sources of content - especially video and audio, have become popular in the recent years. Resources of video and audio material are now widely accessible online, along with Podcast search engines (Yahoo!) and Podcast directories (GetaPodcast). These search engines rely on indexing/tagging to facilitate search through the vast amount of materials.

3.2 Bookmarking 2.0

Social bookmarking sites allow maintaining of a personal collection of links online. Wikipedia defines social bookmarking as the capability to "classify resources by the use of informally assigned, user-defined keywords or tags".It is similar to using bookmarking in a Web 1.0 browser to organise favorite links. The social bookmarking aspect stems from the way that personal collections of online links can be made accessible to others. Bookmarking 2.0 facilitates the search of links through tags, which are typically one word keywords associated with the page. There are social bookmarking services of particular use to education, especially del.icio.us (http://del.icio.us/) which stores the tag words and URLs, whereas FURL (http://www.FURL.net) offers the capability to save a complete copy of the page for offline access. CiteULike (http://www.citeulike.org/) is a social bookmaking service facilitating interface with research databases and journal publications. As an educational process, bookmarking can be used in a variety of ways, such as automatically updating a sharable reading list, or finding the most recently writ-ten articles or pages. Group work can be facilitated through shared access to a list of research articles or sources of data. Social bookmarking is an excellent resource discovery tool which can simplify sharing of web links in a group of learners or researchers of similar interests.

3.3 Blogs 2.0

Blogs are straightforward content management tools primarily used to build diaries, or web sites around some theme or subject area. At times a blog may be similar to a journal with chronological entries incorporating commentary, photos, podcasts, video and other multimedia on specific topics. It is possible to share or network blogs to other blogs on the same issue or topic.

Table 2: Teaching with Blogs

Feature	Benefits
Distribute Resources	Ubiquitous access to teaching materials and resources
Host online discussions	Forum functionality is very straightforward; Streamlined communication and discussion moderation
Collaborative online publications	Engaging and straightforward way for students to contribute, edit, design and publish collaborative work
Share news, updates, class information	Streamline communication with students
Create spaces for student and instructor blogging	One hub for student blogging moderated by instructors
Integrate multimedia, slideshows, videos, etc. into the blogs	Incorporate multimedia and more into text blog to illustrate, engage and improve teaching.
Organize teaching process	Keep your resources, schedule, etc. in one place
Use it for feedback	Create a blog as a place for students and colleagues leave feedback and discuss issues.
Share teaching plans	Keep students informed of the course events and deadlines.

Educational blogging sites, such as edublogs (http://edublogger.org), allow educators to create, manage and moderate student blogs with minimal administrative effort or specialised knowledge. As summarised on the edublogs site, blogs can be used in teaching in a wide variety of ways (see table 2).

3.4 Community 2.0

Social networking has redefined the way in which the digital generation communicate and share information, replacing face-to-face interaction with digital communications. Social network services enable searching, sharing information, communication of interests and shared activity amongst community members.

The educational value of a social networking service is that it enables users to share information within a dynamic network of colleagues and fellow students linked through user profiles. The data in these profiles serve as links, which display other network members who incorporated that element in their profile. Users can navigate through profiles based on a certain criteria and communicate with others via messaging, blogs, etc. Members can register as friends and gain access to various sorts of restricted information such as pictures, personal details and private blog entries. Although some concerns about the educational use of social networking sites have been expressed (Anderson 2007), learning is a social activity and social networking services have the capability to connect and engage learners. The application of social networking services for peer-support in higher education has been received positively. Social networking sites can be useful tools in setting up groups and discussion environments for group project, modules or even university-wide. Some investigations into developing virtual communities in higher learning have been analysed in (Lupicci 2007; Hotrum 2008). Continuous learning and pedagogical multiplicity are being linked to the use of social networks in education, where a continuity of the learning process and the community continue past the course end, as described by (Hotrum 2008) as follows:

1. Creating an informal network space for students and instructors with personal profiles, blogs and resource repository. This is especially relevant on courses highly reliant on peer-support, such as MBA's and part time studies.
2. Enabling group work in a controlled temporary space acting as a VLE but with more advanced communication and content generation tools, including reflecting journals, groupware tools, e-portfolio management and knowledge construction active beyond the term of study.
3. Evolving this pace into a continuous learning community and knowledge sharing network space, promoting further sharing, connecting and the use of the knowledge base.

3.5 Wikis

A simple way to add and edit content on a website, sometimes without registration, coined as wiki has become a popular approach to web content authoring. The advantage of a straightforward user interface and no requirements for specialised knowledge make wikis a compelling choice for educators and learners when it comes to collaborative authoring of web content. Wikis are gaining popularity in education as a useful tool to increase collaboration and engagement among students. Learners may use wikis to collaborate on a group project, share information or compile research results. The world's largest multilingual encyclopedia – Wikipedia (http://www.wikipedia.org) is built as a wiki and allows adding content by virtually anyone.

4   Discussion

Significant attention has been paid to the evaluation of some of Web 2.0 tools in education (Green and Hannon, 2007); however an accepted pedagogical model has yet to be developed. What will it take for this to happen? Will a shift in pedagogical paradigm be necessary? The capabilities of Web 2.0 make it an enabling technology - a vehicle which has the potential to improve, enable, and make learning more interesting, exciting and straightforward. Having made significant investments into traditional Learning Management Systems many HE institutions found them lacking the expected level of interest from learners. On the contrary, students actively populate Facebook with information about their courses, discuss assignments, argue the pros and cons of particular subject areas and interact with each other virtually. The obvious user enthusiasm for social networking sites, which emphasise the inherent content sharing and production characteristics of Web 2.0 technologies, is apparent.Is this because LMS is viewed as centralised, controlled, regulated environment and represents an old style of learning (even in its most blended form)? Has LMS design failed to take into account the variety of learning processes that can occur, or even the dynamic variety of teaching styles that experienced tutors use. Digital learning communities succeed where there is emotional investment in the learning which is occurring – typically where the learner has control over the production process. The nature of sites such as Delicious, Youtube or Facebook encourages the participatory nature of peers - the technology allows content to be seen, shared and built on.

Personal Learning Environments, which (so far) are a loose, may take the students forward with more control over the process. Sites such as Facebook or MySpace thrive or fail on the ease of the user interface – the majority of users on these sites don't read a manual, watch an on-line tutorial, or seek technical assistance – it simply isn't required. This is radically different to the complex manual and terminology required which lecturers face when first encountering a commercial Learning Management System - most of them have extremely complicated interface arrangements, attempting to cover every single possible type of event and customisation option that may or may not be used. Finally, building on the experience and popular application of e-learning, it is imperative to establish proven web 2.0-base pedagogical frameworks. Following on from the crucial aspects deemed instrumental to the success of e-learning (Alexander, 2001) web 2.0 – based educational frameworks must be based on similar pillars of:

- University context – is a HE institution ready for Web 2.0 technologies; institutions need to respond by resolving traditional organisational issues surrounding technology, staff and student support.
- Instructor's perception and kills of Web 2.0 technology;
- Instructional planning - careful pedagogical planning oriented towards learning outcomes, not technology development of appropriate assessment strategies;
- Teaching Strategies – focusing on providing learners with a clear understanding of the learning process prior to learning activities.

Technology and education are sometimes seen as areas which challenge each other. Some researchers indicate that educators are less technology-inquisitive and regard learning new technology as an administrative burden (Laurillard, 2002). It is imperative for these technologies to be simple and transparent if they are to be embraced with equal effectiveness by both educators and learners.

The provision of support for both staff and students, gaining an in-depth understanding of the university context and thorough planning are the aspects which may determine the success of harnessing Web 2.0 technologies will drive wider acceptance by HE instructors.

5 Conclusions

As Web 2.0 technology deepens its impact on the day-to-day life and is increasingly used by the successive generation of learners, the educational sector will be put under pressure to embrace it. This may have a significant effect on the delivery, assessment and learning strategies.

We are witnessing the emergence of a life-long learning community lasting far beyond the traditional term of study. In the years to come Web 2.0 will transform the traditional learning life cycle and make it last after a student leaves University walls. Current learning systems are attempting to integrate social features to compete with online social networks. However, the fact that learning management systems traditionally expire at the end of a study term loses the embedded knowledge and communal learning bond, which may lead to diminished participation, engagement and lessen the quality of student work. On the other hand, the integration of online social networking into educational process will facilitate life-long learning and promote the formation of specialised knowledge communities.

In this article we have discussed the implications of the Web 2.0 tools applied in learning and teaching, factors influencing their successful adoption, and possible barriers. Some possible directions suggested for further research included developing a proven Web 2.0 pedagogical framework integrating design, development, implementation of Web 2.0–based learning systems in HE. Also, issues surrounding content creation, remixing and repurposing surrounding copyright issues and content ownership were left open for further discussion.

References

Adams, A.M. (2004). 'Pedagogical underpinnings of computer-based learning', *Journal of Advanced Nursing,* 46 (1), pp. 5-12

Alani, H., Hall, W., O'Hara, K., Shadbolt, N., Chandler, P. and Szomszor, M. (2008) Building a Pragmatic Semantic Web. *IEEE Intelligent Systems*, 23 (3). pp. 61-68

Alexander, S. (2001). 'E-learning developments and experiences', *Education & Training*, 43, pp. 240-248

Alonso, F., López, G., Manrique, D. and Viñes, J.M. (2005). 'An instructional model for web-based e-learning education with a blended learning process approach', *British Journal of Educational Technology*, 36 (2), pp. 217-235

Anderson, P. (2007) *What is Web 2.0? Ideas, technologies and implications for education*, JISC Technology and Standards Watch report Accessed on July 8, 2008 available at www.jisc.ac.uk/media/documents/techwatch/tsw0701b.pdf

Armitage, S. and O'Leary, R. (2003). 'e-Learning Series No 4: A Guide for Learning Technologists'. LTSN Generic Centre

Aroyo, L. and Dicheva, D. (2004) 'The new challenges for e-learning: the educational semantic web', *Educational Technology and Society*, 7(4), pp.59–69

Aspden, L. Helm, P. (2004). 'Making the Connection in a Blended Learning Environment', *Education Media International,* 41 (3), pp. 245-252.

Bennet S., Maton K., Kervin L. (2008) 'The 'digital natives' debate: A critical review of the evidence', *British Journal of Educational Technology*, Published online February 2008 http://www3.interscience.wiley.com/journal/120173667/abstract

Benson V., (2008*) Perceptions of Trust and Security: Is the digital generation ready for web 2.0-based learning*? To appear in the Proceeding of 1st World Summit on the Knowledge Society, September, 2008.

Berners-Lee T., (2006). "The Fractal Nature of the Web," World Wide Web Consortium, 1998–2006, www.w3.org/DesignIssues/Fractal.html

Belawati, T. (2005). 'The impact of online tutorials on course completion rates and student achievement', Learning, Media and Technology, 30 (1), pp. 15-25

Biggs, J. (1999). Teaching for quality learning at university. Oxford: Society for Research into Higher Education and Open University Press

Boulos, M.N.K and Wheeler, S. (2007). 'The emerging Web 2.0 social software: an enabling suite of sociable technologies in health and health care education', *Health Information and Libraries Journal,* 24, pp. 2-23

Conole, G., De Laat, M., Dillon, T. and Darby, J. (2006). JISC LXP: Student Experiences of Technologies Final Report. Retrieved 15 September, 2007, from: http://www.jisc.ac.uk/media/documents/programmes/elearning_pedagogy/lxp%20project%20final%20report%20dec%2006.pdf

Cooper J.(2006) The digital divide: the special case of gender. *Journal of Computer Assisted Learning*, 22 (5), pp 320-334

Devedzic, V. (2003) Key issues in next-generation web-based education, *IEEE Transactions on Systems*, Man, and Cybernetics, Part C – Applications and Reviews, 33(3), pp.339–349

Dutton. W.H. and Helsper, E.J. (2007). The Internet in Britain 2007. Oxford Internet Institute, the University of Oxford.

Edublogs, Accessed on July 8, 2008 at http://edublogs.org/10-ways-to-use-your-edublog-to-teach/

Facebook http: // faceFrand, J. (2000). The information-age mindset: changes in students and implications for higher education. EDUCAUSE Review, 35, September-October, 14–24.

Ginns, P. and Ellis, R. (2007). Quality in Blended Learning: Exploring the Relationships between On-Line and Face-to-Face Teaching and Learning. *Internet and Higher Education*, 10, pp.53-64.

Green, H. and Hannon, C. (2007) Their Space: Education for a digital generation. London: DEMOS.

Johnson S. (2005) Everything Bad is Good for You: How today's popular culture is actually making us smarter. London: Penguin Books.

Hotrum, M. (2008) Personal Learning Environments and Evolutionary Pedagogy. Accessed on July 8, 2008 available at http://choicelearning.blogspot.com/2008/06/personal-learning-environment-and.html

Kohut, A., Parker, K., Keeter, S., Doherty, C. and Dimock, M. (2007), A Portrait of "Generation Next". Washington DC: Pew Research Center

Luppicini R (2007) Online Learning Communities: Communities in Distance Education, ed. by Lupiccini R., Computer-Assisted Instruction.

Laurillard, D. (2002). Rethinking university teaching: A conversation framework For the effective use of learning technology (2nd ed.). London & New York: RoutledgeFalmer

Lytras M., Naeve A.,(2006) "Semantic E-learning: Synthesizing Fantasies", *British Journal of Educational Technology*, 37(3), pp. 479-491

Lytras, M.D., Rafaeli, S., Downes, S., Naeve, A. and de Pablos, P.O. (2007) 'Editorial', Int. J. *Knowledge and Learning*, 3 (4), pp.367–371

Moule, P. (2007). 'Challenging the five-stage model for e-learning: a new approach', *Research in Learning Technology*, 15 (1), pp. 37-50

Naeve A., Lytras M., Nejdl W, Harding J., Balacheff N., (2006) 'Advances of Semantic Web for E-learning: Expanding learning frontiers', *British Journal of Educational Technology*, 37(3), pp. 321-330

Oblinger, D. & Oblinger, J. (2005). Is it age or IT: first steps towards understanding the net generation. In D. Oblinger & J. Oblinger (Eds), Educating the Net generation pp. 2.1–2.20

O'Hara K. & Shadbolt N.(2008) The Spy in the Coffee Machine: The End of Privacy as We Know It, Oneworld, 2008.

Picciano, A., & Dziuban, C. (2007), Blended learning: Research perspectives. Needham, MA: Sloan

Prensky M., (2001) Digital Natives, Digital Immigrants, *On the Horizon, NCB University Press*, 9(5)

Salmon, G. (2005). 'Flying not flapping: a strategic framework for e-learning and pedagogical innovation in higher education institutions', *Research in Learning Technology*, 13 (3), p. 210-218

Shadbolt N., Berners-Lee T., and Hall W.(2006)The Semantic Web Revisited. *IEEE Intelligent Systems*, 21(3), pp. 96–101

Tapscott, D. (1999). Educating the Net generation. *Educational Leadership,* 56, 5, 6–11

Weitzner D. et al. (2005), 'Creating a Policy-Aware Web: Discretionary, Rule-Based Access for the World Wide Web',Web and Information Security, Idea Group, 2005, pp. 1–31

White, D. (2007). Results and analysis of web 2.0 services survey. UK: JISC. Retrieved from http://www.jisc.ac.uk/media/documents/programmes/digitalrepositories/spiresurvey.pdf

Chapter 14. Teaching-Material Crystallization: Wiki-based Rapid Prototyping for Teaching-Material Design

Wen-Chung Shih

Department of Information Science and Applications, Asia University, Taiwan (R.O.C.)

Shian-Shyong Tseng[30]

Department of Computer Science, National Chiao Tung University, Taiwan (R.O.C.)

Department of Information Science and Applications, Asia University, Taiwan (R.O.C.)

Jui-Feng Weng

Department of Computer Science, National Chiao Tung University, Taiwan (R.O.C.)

Abstract

To support individualized and adaptive learning, teachers are encouraged to develop various teaching materials according to different requirements. However, traditional methodologies for designing teaching materials are time-consuming. To speed up the development process of teaching materials, our idea is to use a rapid prototyping approach which is based on automatic draft generation and Wiki-based revision. Since the Wiki-based authoring is a collaborative activity, "how to collaboratively revise the teaching material without conflict and with higher social agreement via community members" becomes a challenging and interesting issue and we define it as the Teaching Material Crystallization problem. A Delphi-like questionnaire-based crystallizer has been proposed to support both the social agreement process and the resolution of conflicting opinions. The evaluation was conducted using a two-group t-test design. Experimental results indicate that teaching materials can be rapidly generated with the proposed approach.

---

[30] Corresponding author

1   Introduction

During the past decade, e-Learning applications have advanced at an amazing pace. With the trend of individualized and adaptive learning, there will be a great demand to various teaching-materials. A typical approach to content design is ADDIE (ADDIE, 2004), which consists of five stages: Analysis, Design, Develop, Implement, and Evaluate. The primary disadvantage is its time-consuming development process. In addition, it requires expensive human resources. Furthermore, redundant efforts could happen when different sites develop teaching materials for the same course units simultaneously. To solve the problem, a new method is needed for teachers to rapidly develop their own course materials.

Our idea is to design teaching materials by a rapid prototyping approach based on automatic draft generation and Wiki-based revision. Rapid prototyping is the process of quickly building and evaluating a series of prototypes of a system, which has been widely applied to manufacturing, software engineering, etc (Luqi, 1989). First, a draft is automatically generated by combining relevant teaching materials retrieved from learning object repositories (Shih et al., 2008a). Next, we adopt a Wiki-based authoring environment to revise the automatically generated draft. Wiki is an accessible markup language for people to edit a site together (Louridas, 2006). Wikipedia is the most successful Wiki-based project (Wikipedia, 2004). Our method is to utilize the collaborative intelligence and labor to accelerate the revision process.

To collaboratively construct the teaching material which may be accepted for most of authors, a social agreement teaching material is defined as a teaching material with the degree of social agreement larger than a given threshold, where the social agreement degree value falls in the range of 0 to 1 and the larger value means the higher social agreement degree. Our concern is "how to collaboratively construct the teaching material without conflict and with higher social agreement via community members to express the targeted educational topic", and this problem is defined as the Teaching Material Crystallization Problem.

Based on the aforementioned ideas, we have proposed a rapid prototyping approach, which is composed of three phases: 1) automatic draft generation, 2) Wiki-based revision, 3) teaching material crystallization. The goal is to reduce the development time of teaching materials. Firstly, the system attempts to clarify users' intention by interactive ways, such as asking questions, requesting more query terms, etc. Then, users' queries are expanded by using domain expertise to retrieve more relevant documents. Next, the system searches for existing teaching-materials related to the expanded query in the repository. Then, the retrieved documents are combined into a draft automatically. In the second phase, the draft is placed in a Wiki-based authoring environment for collaborative revision.

In the teaching material crystallization phase, the iterative, group decision support methodology called Modified Delphi Method is applied to converge and resolve the conflicts of the assertions. In the modified Delphi method, the discussion group is formed firstly with several discussion members and one communication leader. Next, the discussion and conflict resolution processes are performed with several rounds until the social agreement is achieved. There are three stages in each round which are the brainstorming stage to allow the users contribute their opinions in the initial round, the response compiling stage to let the communication leader classify the opinions and list the conflict points, and the conflict resolution stage to allow the group members evaluate the opinions by questionnaire or revise their opinions to achieve the agreement.

The advantages of the proposed approach are twofold: time-saving and low-cost, which result from effective sharing and reusing of resources. Meanwhile, our primary contribution is the idea of a rapid prototyping approach to teaching-material design. In particular, a teaching material crystallization mechanism has been designed to achieve social agreement in the Wiki-based revision process. Also, we have implemented this approach. Twenty four randomly selected teachers from elementary schools participated in an experiment based on a two-group t-test design. Experimental results show that teachers in the experiment group can generate high-quality teaching materials more rapidly than those in the control group.

The rest of this chapter is organized as follows. In Section 2, we review background knowledge and related work on this research. Then, the problem and the proposed approach are presented in Section 3. Next, implementation and experimental results are discussed in Section 4. Finally, the concluding remarks are given in Section 5.

2   Preliminaries and Related Work

This section briefly introduces the preliminaries of Wiki and rapid prototyping, which are essential to this work. Next, previous researches related to this chapter are also described.

2.1 Wiki Technology

Web 2.0, characterized by the techniques of blog, Wiki, RSS, mashup, etc., has been widely discussed and referred to as the second generation of web-based services (O'Reilly, 2005). The term "Wiki" originates from the Hawaiian "wee kee wee kee," which means "quickly." In the domain of computer science, a Wiki is a web-based hypertext system which supports community-oriented authoring, in order to rapidly and collaboratively build the content. The concept of Wiki was proposed by Ward Cunningham in 1995 as the Portland Pattern Repository, to create an environment for co-workers to share specifications and documents for software design.

Wiki is not the first technology for collaboration. Other collaborative technologies, such as discussion boards, have also been widely used for years. Nevertheless, the primary reason why Wiki is so attractive can be attributed to the successful application, Wikipedia (Wikipedia, 2004). Traditionally, an encyclopedia is built by a number of experts with a tremendous amount of time and money. However, Wikipedia is an innovative project which endeavors to build an online open-source encyclopedia based on Wiki and GNU Free Document License (http://www.gnu.org/licenses/#FDL). This system began in 2001, and the number of English items exceeds 500,000 in 2005. The rapid growth of the Wikipedia system shows that the concept of the Wiki is both viable and feasible. In addition, there are many related projects based on Wiki, such as Meta-Wiki, Wiktionary, Wikibooks, Wikiquotes, to name a few (http://meta.wikimedia.org/wiki/-Complete_list_of_Wikimedia_projects).

The attractive characteristics of Wiki, which favor its use, can be summarized as follows.

- Rapidness. The Wiki pages can be rapidly constructed, accessed and modified, in hypertext form.
- Simpleness. A simple markup scheme (usually a simplified version of HTML) is used to format the Wiki pages, instead of the complicated HTML.
- Convenience. Links to other pages, external sites, and images can be conveniently established by keywords. Moreover, the targets of the keywords, links, need not exist when the links are built. They can be appended later.
- Open Source. Each member can create, modify and delete the Wiki pages at will. Wiki content is not reviewed by anyone before publication, and is updated upon being saved.
- Maintainability. Wiki maintains a version database, which records its historical revision and content, thus enabling version management.

To run a Wiki-based site, it is necessary to deploy a Wiki platform. The requirements of a Wiki platform include editing, links, version management, sandboxes (test-bed), and search functions. Many Wiki platforms have been developed and used in various fields. For example, MediaWiki (http://www.mediawiki.org/wiki/MediaWik), which is used by Wikipedia, is a widely used tool. PBwiki (http://pbwiki.com/), which is developed by PHP languages, is adopted by many libraries.

2.2 Rapid Prototyping

Brainstorming involves redefining the problem, generating ideas, and seeking new solutions. The general idea is to create a climate of free association through trading ideas and perceptions of the problem at hand. Better ideas are expected from brainstorming than from individual thought because the minds of more people are tapped. The productive thought process works best in an environment where criticism is avoided, or at least dampened.

System development is a continuous and fundamental task in many domains, so effective and efficient approaches to system development are demanded by developers. Traditional system development life cycle paradigms, such as the waterfall model, focus on verifying the system requirements during the early stages, and then go through the whole process to generate the perfect product. However, this approach is not suitable when the requirement can not be clearly defined at the beginning. Therefore, evolutionary approaches, such as rapid prototyping, are proposed to alleviate the limitations.

There have not been a clear definition of rapid prototyping (RP) though this technology has been successfully used in many fields, including commercial, military and academic applications (Gordon & Bieman, 1995). Generally speaking, RP is recognized as technologies which rapidly realize the conceptual model of a final product of system without incurring too much cost. The purpose of RP is to incrementally clarify the requirement and refine the prototype. The techniques for rapid prototyping could date back to the late 1980s and were mainly used in manufacturing. Nowadays, RP is applied for many other domains, even in educational applications. For example, RP has been used to create the lecture contents of the IT SoC certificate program (Kim & Park, 2007).

Many RP methods have been proposed in the literature. Although these procedures are not exactly the same, they conform to the following workflow:

1. initial definition of requirements
2. rapid implementation of a prototype
3. user evaluation and requirement refinement
4. implementation of refined requirements
5. repeat step 3 and step 4 until completion

An early model simply relates traditional design steps to prototypes, consisting of need assessment and analysis, prototype building, prototype utilization, system installation and maintenance (Tripp & Bichelmeyer, 1990). Another example, used to design computer-based courseware, is a three-stage model: analysis, development and evaluation (Yang, Moore, & Burton, 1995).

RP has also been applied to instructional design for both generating high quality product and reducing development time. Jones and Richey reported eight RP applications in instructional design (Jones & Richey, 2000), including educational software design, instructional videos, etc. The aforementioned researches illustrate that RP is an effective approach to system development in educational applications. In the case of adaptive e-learning, educators are usually encouraged to rapidly develop various personalized teaching materials. The challenges result from varied requirements and timely pressure, which are similar to the motivation of RP. In this work, we adopt the concept of RP to design teaching materials, facilitating the rapid authoring process.

2.3 Related Work

Due to the advances in information technologies and the requirements of courseware, more and more teachers are able and willing to design their own teaching materials and make them accessible on the Web (Iorio, Feliziani, Mirri, Salomoni, & Vitali, 2006; Lanzilotti, Ardito, Costabile, & Angeli, 2006; Sierra, Fernández-Valmayor, Guinea, & Hernanz, 2006). In addition, a growing number of large-scale projects aim to construct learning content repositories (Kassahun, Beulens, & Hartog, 2006; Kiu & Lee, 2006). For example, in 2002, the National Science Council of Taiwan approved a resolution on the "National Science and Technology Program for e-Learning," planning to spend $120 million within a 5-year period (ELNP, 2002). These educational contents are mainly based on Sharable Content Object Reference Model (SCORM) (SCORM, 2004), which has become a popular standard for creating sharable and reusable teaching materials for e-Learning. With the popularization of e-Learning, how to find and reuse these existing materials becomes an important issue.

Teaching materials are one of the important elements in instruction and learning activities. A large amount of work has been devoted to the methodology of teaching-material design. Some scholars (Nkambou, Frasson, & Gauthier, 1998) presented an authoring environment for the development of course materials. However, this approach depends on educational experts to participate in the development process. In order to facilitate the reuse of SCORM learning objects and customization of course materials, a system named Teaching-Material Design Center (Wang & Hsu, 2006) was proposed, reusing e-material from different providers and integrating them for a particular course. Nevertheless, this system still relies on human experts to design a satisfactory teaching material. The recent works of Coffey (Coffey, 2007) and Wang (Wang, 2007) addressed the issues of courseware maintenance and enhancement. The former designed a meta-cognitive tool for courseware development and reuse, and the latter presented a course material enhancement process. Briefly speaking, aforementioned approaches to designing teaching materials are time-consuming. Also, expensive human-resource costs are involved.

To help teachers rapidly develop course materials, the WARP (Wiki-based Authoring by Rapid Prototyping) method has been proposed in (Shih et al., 2008b). The key aspects of WARP include: reuse, automation and collaborative authoring. Domain expertise was used to search for useful teaching materials in learning object repositories. By means of knowledge acquisition tools and automated merging algorithm developed by ourselves, the process can be automated and sped up. A Wiki-based authoring environment was used to exploit collaborative intelligence for revision. The five phases of the WARP approach are shown in Figure 1.

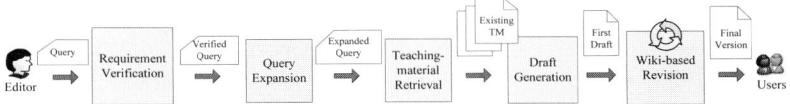

Fig. 1. The process of WARP

- **Phase 1: requirement verification**

The purpose of this phase is to clarify users' information need specified by query terms. The system verifies the scope of the query in the domain ontology by asking questions to the user interactively.

- **Phase 2: query expansion**

This phase aims to increase the searching performance by expanding the query. A rule-based method is utilized to represent the searching heuristics and to infer appropriate searching strategies.

- **Phase 3: teaching-material retrieval**

Relevant teaching materials stored in the e-Learning grid are retrieved in this phase. A global index, built in a bottom-up way, is used to speed up the access process.

- **Phase 4: draft generation**

The first version of the draft is automatically generated by merging the teaching materials found in the previous phase.

- **Phase 5: Wiki-based revision**

A Wiki-based authoring tool is used to facilitate collaborative revision for the draft.

The WARP approach is extended in this work to address the teaching material crystallization problem.

3   Teaching Material Crystallization

To speed up the development process of teaching materials, our idea is to use a rapid prototyping approach which is based on automatic draft generation and Wiki-based revision. In this section, the teaching material crystallization problem is presented first. Then, the proposed approach and its components are described.

3.1 Problem Description

In the SCORM (Sharable Content Object Reference Model) standard, a Content Package (CP) is defined as a package of learning materials, and a Learning Object Repository (LOR) is a database where the Content Packages are stored. A Content Package is modeled as a k-ary tree with three levels: root, chapter, and section, where the section nodes contain the content and the internal nodes represent the structural information, as shown in Figure 2. The content is represented by a vector. In addition, a CP is associated with a set of Metadata. To enable content-based retrieval, the well-known Vector Space Model is applied to represent the text content. Also, the LOM metadata is included in this model of CP. Hereafter, teaching materials, SCORM-compliant documents, and Content Packages are used interchangeably.

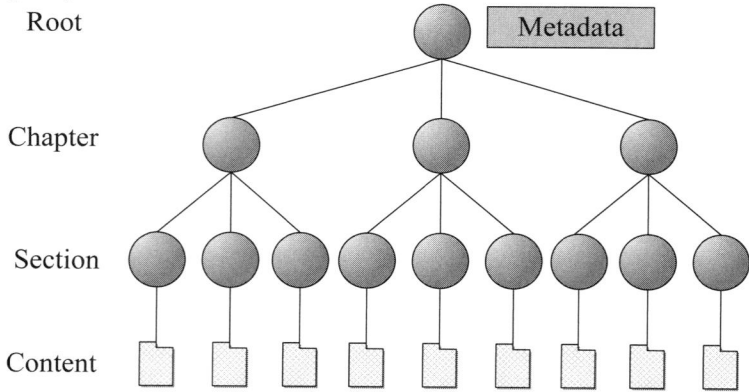

Fig. 2. The tree model of a content package

The feature vector of a CP is represented by a term-weighting vector, v_{CP}.
where V means the set of vocabulary and $|V|$ is its size. The term-weighting w_i is evaluated using the extended Vector Space Model proposed by Trotman (Trotman, 2005). The idea of this weighting scheme is to emphasize the importance of some structure. For example, the same word appearing in Abstract and the last Chapter of a book has different significance.

A query Q is modeled as a set of keywords. The feature vector of a query Q is

$$v_{CP} = <w_1, w_2, ..., w_{|V|}>$$

denoted by v_Q,

$$v_Q = <q_1, q_2, ..., q_{|V|}>$$

where V means the set of vocabulary and $|V|$ is its size. The term-weighting q_i is 1 if the i-th keyword in the vocabulary, V, is a term in the query. Otherwise, q_i is 0.

We will now define the notion of similarity between a query and a content package, which means the relevance of the content package to the query. Let Q be a query with feature vector v_Q, and CP be a content package with feature vector v_{CP}. The Similarity $sim(Q, CP)$ is defined by:

$$sim(Q, CP) = v_Q \cdot v_{CP}$$

where the operation is inner product of vectors.

The editor, who submits the query to develop a teaching material, is usually a teacher who is not necessarily an expert in courseware design. Domain taxonomy and a thesaurus are assumed to be available for the material development process. Also, the designer can reuse any existing teaching materials in LORs.

We assume that the course ontology, built by educational experts, is available, as shown in Figure 3. The subject matter is mathematics for nine-year coherence curriculum at low-grade elementary-school level, according to Ministry of Education in Taiwan. The course ontology is modeled as a rooted tree $O = <N_O, E_O, root>$ that consists of a finite set of node N_O, a finite set of edges E_O, and a *root* node in N_O. N_O represents the set of nodes in the tree. Each node in N_O represents a concept in this ontology and is associated with a set of keywords, which describe the concept. For example, the set of keywords of the node "Arithmetic Operations" is {"addition", "subtraction", "multiplication", "division"}. An edge in E_O connects a node and its child node, which expresses the hierarchical relation of the two nodes. For instance, the edge connecting "Geometry" and "Shapes" means the former is a more general concept than the latter. Finally, the *root* node in this example is the "Mathematics" node.

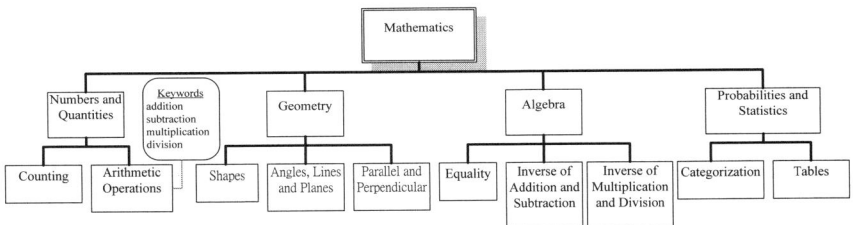

Fig. 3. The ontology of mathematics at elementary-school level

Based on the definitions above, the Teaching-Material Crystallization Problem (TMCP) can be described as follows. Since the content of teaching material is revised collaboratively, the different opinions of authors may cause the inconsistency of the teaching material. Thus, in this work, "how to collaboratively construct the teaching material without conflict and with higher social agreement via community members to represent the targeted learning domain" is defined as the Teaching-Material Crystallization Problem (TMCP). Accordingly, two technical issues emerge in order to solve the OCP.

1. How to collect the contributed opinions, and conclude the agreements or conflicts of the community members.
2. How to converge the teaching material to achieve the social agreement.

3.2 Overview

To help teachers rapidly develop course materials, we propose the WARP (Wi-ki-based Authoring by Rapid Prototyping) method, based on the idea of a rapid prototyping approach. The key aspects of WARP include: reuse, automation and collaborative authoring. We use domain expertise to search for useful teaching materials in learning object repositories and reuse them. By means of knowledge acquisition tools and automated merging algorithm developed by ourselves, the process can be automated and sped up. Finally, we use a Wiki-based authoring environment to exploit collaborative intelligence for revision.

As shown in Figure 4, the WARP approach is composed of three phases.

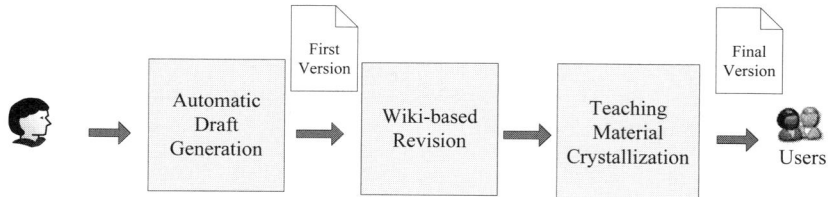

Fig. 4. Overview of the Wiki-based rapid prototyping process

- Phase 1: automatic draft generation

The purpose of this phase is to automatically generate the first version of the teaching material by merging existing teaching materials found in the previous phase. The reason is based on the observation that it is easier to revise a document than to construct one from scratch.

The algorithm is based on level-wise clustering, and its main concept is union of different learning objects from relevant teaching materials. In addition, it re-tains the most similar learning object as the cluster center. Also, the clustering process is guaranteed to converge. The algorithm is shown as follows.

Algorithm: Draft Generation Algorithm (DGAlg)
Symbols Definition:
  T_1, T_2: Content Package trees; the two teaching materials to be merged
  L: the depth of a Content Package tree
  T: a Content Package tree; the merged teaching material
Input: T_1 and T_2
Output: T
Step 1: For $i := L$ to 1
    1.1: cluster nodes at the same layer
    1.2: If there exists a cluster with more than one node
        Then retain the node with the larger similarity value
Step 2: modify the links between layers

Step 3: Return the merged teaching material.

Example 1. Teaching-Material Merging
We assume that there are two teaching materials to be merged: A and B, as shown in Figure 5. After merging, the node with the highest similarity is retained, say, A_0 and B_{10}.

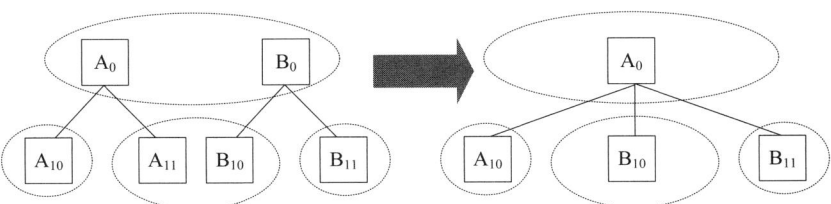

Fig. 5. An example to merge two teaching materials

- Phase 2: Wiki-based revision

In the previous phase, the draft is rapidly generated by computers, but it still needs to be revised by human editors to guarantee its readability. In order to increase the efficiency of the consequent revision process, we adopt a Wiki-based approach. By means of collaborative efforts, the draft is expected to be rapidly revised. Our belief in this approach comes from the successful example of the Wikipedia project, which aims to compile an encyclopedia by web users.

- Phase 3: teaching material crystallization

A questionnaire is used to efficiently gather information from respondents and is effective to acquire users' opinions of specific issue. To achieve the social agreement, a Questionnaire-based Crystallizer is proposed to make the group decision for the conflict resolution by the community members.

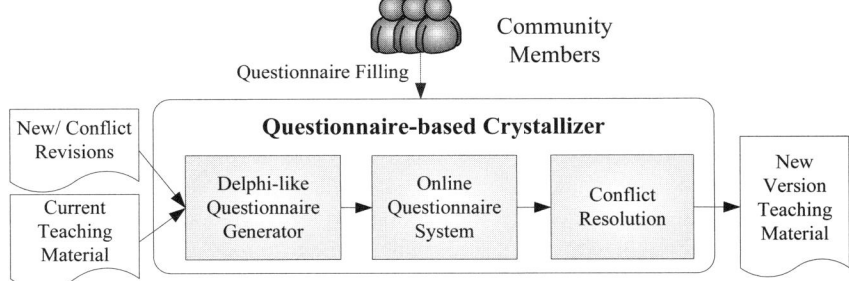

Fig. 6. Questionnaire-based Crystallizer

As Shown in Figure 6, from the folksonomies contributed by community members, the Delphi-like Questionnaire Generator process is proposed to automatically detect these conflicting assertions. Accordingly, in this process, an appropriate questionnaire will be generated by means of selecting the suitable questionnaire item templates to resolve the conflicts. In the Online Questionnaire System, the community members are asked to evaluate the new assertions or resolve the conflict assertions based on the concept of the modified Delphi-like method. Whenever the amount of receiving questionnaires for new assertions exceed the predefined threshold, the Conflict Resolution process will be triggered to make these questionnaires results converge and generate the new version of teaching material.

3.3 An Illustrative Example

An example is presented to illustrate how teachers of an elementary school use the WARP method to collaboratively design a teaching material for the "Area" unit in the third-grade Mathematics course. The ontology of the "Shape" unit is shown in Figure 7. The keyword "Area" is associated with the "Shape" node. The overall process is summarized as follows.

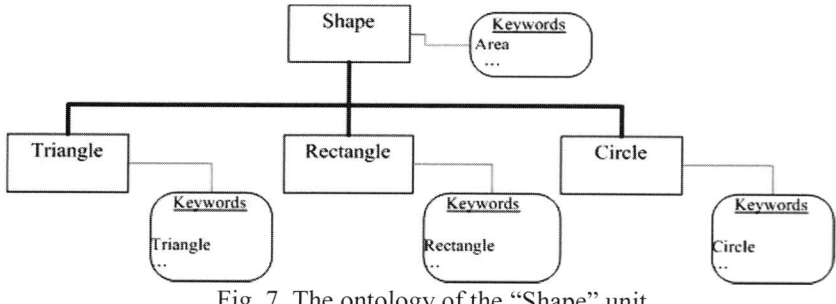

Fig. 7. The ontology of the "Shape" unit

- Phase 1: automatic draft generation

The teachers express their requirement by specifying the keyword "area" and metadata "grade" (its value = 3). In order to increase the precision of searching, the teachers define the strategy of query expansion as "Specialization." After inference, the system recommends another three keywords to refine the original query: "Triangle," "Rectangle," and "Circle." The teachers adopt the "Triangle" as an expanded keyword. Consequently, the expanded query, "area and triangle," is sent to the search engine for searching. According to the expanded query and the specified metadata, three teaching materials are found in the repositories, as shown in Figure 8.

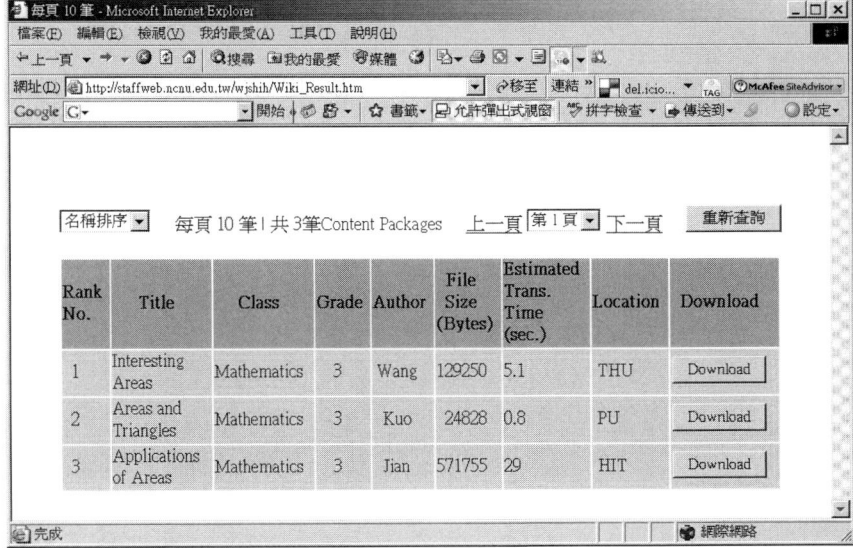

Fig. 8. Screenshot of search results

The top two relevant teaching materials are retrieved for draft generation in the next phase. The outlines of the two teaching materials are shown in Figure 9. The first teaching material, with the name "Interesting Areas," consists of five lessons. The second one, with the name "Areas and Triangles," has six lessons.

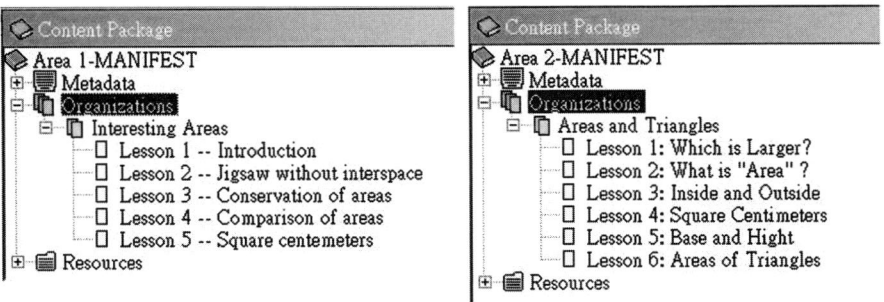

Fig. 9. The outlines of the two teaching materials

The first version of the draft is automatically generated by merging the teaching materials found in the previous phase. In this phase, redundant modules are removed. For example, both teaching materials have a lesson about "square centimeters." The two lessons are clustered into one group, and one of them is removed from the draft. Similarly, lesson 2 of the second teaching material is removed after the clustering process. The resultant draft consists of nine lessons. The outline of the draft is shown in Figure 10.

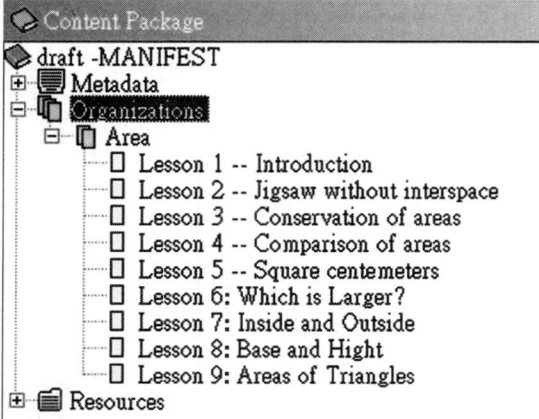

Fig. 10. The outline of the draft

- Phase 2: Wiki-based revision

The teachers use a Wiki-based authoring tool to facilitate collaborative revision for the draft. Through the Talk page, the revision work is coordinated. In this phase, inappropriate content is modified, and the presentation of content is adjusted. Finally, the teaching material is composed of six lessons, organized into two modules, as shown in Figure 11.

| article | discussion | **edit** | history | report a problem |

Area:WARP

The topic about area in the Mathematics for the third-grade students.

Contents [hide]
1 Basic
  1.1 Lesson 1 Introduction
  1.2 Lesson 2 Jigsaw without interspace
  1.3 Lesson 3 Which is Larger?
2 Advanced
  2.1 Lesson 4 Comparison of Areas
  2.2 Lesson 5 Conservation of Areas
  2.3 Lesson 6 Square Centimeters
  2.4 Lesson 7 Inside and Outside

Basic

Lesson 1 Introduction

An Overview of Area

Area is one of the most concepts in everyday use of our life. You can find

Fig. 11. The final version (a) outline; (b) Wiki page

4   Experimental Results

In this section, the implementation and evaluation design are described. Then, experimental results are presented and discussed.

4.1 Implementation and Design of Evaluation

In order to evaluate the proposed approach, we implemented the aforementioned algorithms, and built a prototype for Wiki-based authoring. The Wiki-based authoring interface is shown in Figure 12.

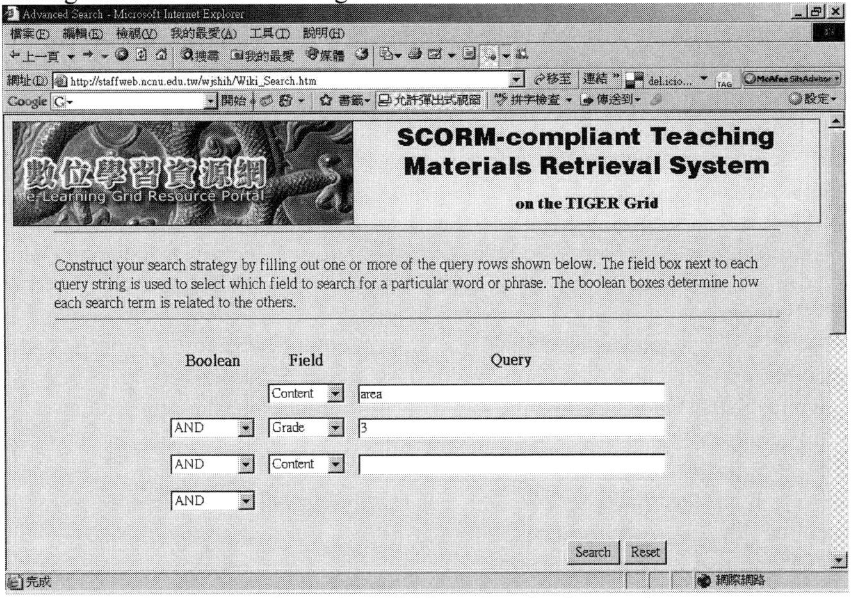

Fig. 12. Interface of a Wiki-based authoring environment

The prototype is built on a grid test-bed, which is composed of four domains. The middleware is Globus Toolkit 4.0. To elicit the expertise of searching experts, we use the DRAMA tool (Lin, Tseng, & Tsai, 2003), which is a suite of toolkits for knowledge engineering developed by KDE Lab. of NCTU. We use this tool for rapid acquisition of searching rules.

We apply the WARP approach to an elementary school mathematics Course. Participants are 24 teachers from three elementary schools in Nantou, Taiwan. The course is mathematics for the third grade. The existing teaching materials are retrieved from repositories built by Ministry of Education, Taiwan.

The existing teaching materials are mainly retrieved from two learning content repositories built by Ministry of Education, Taiwan. One is named "A Service Station for Learning" (http://content.edu.tw), built in 2000. The other is named "The Six Great Learning Networks," (http://learning.edu.tw), built in 2004. This site consists of six subjects: life education, health medicine, nature ecology, history and culture, humanities and arts, science and education. The content is featured by colorful and interesting presentation.

4.2 Experiment 1: Evaluation of WARP

The objective of this evaluation is to answer the question: is the teaching-material development time using WARP significantly shorter than one using a traditional approach?

(1) Experimental Design

A two-group t-test was employed. It is a widely used method to test whether the difference between two means is significant. It can measure the difference of two groups.

(2) Tools

The participants are provided with an internet-enabled environment. That is, they can access information and content available on the web.

(3) Sample

Twenty-four teachers from three primary schools in Nantou, Taiwan, are selected as participants. They are randomly divided into two groups, each with twelve teachers. One is named the experimental group, and the other is named the control group.

(4) Hypothesis

A null hypothesis was set up, which is that no significant difference exists between the development times of the two groups.

(5) Treatment

The experimental group was provided with the WARP environment while the control one was not. That is, teachers of the control group can only search for existing teaching materials and revise them manually. Furthermore, teachers of the experimental group formed a Wiki community, and participated in Wiki-based revision.

(6) Results

The development times of the control group and the experimental group are illustrated in Figure 13. "WARP-v1" means the development time of the first version by the WARP approach. Similarly, "WARP-v2" and "WARP-v3" represent the second and the third version respectively. The t-test gives the probability that the difference between the two means is caused by chance. The difference between sample means of the control group and "WARP-v3" is 42.3. Since the t-ratio is significant at 0.05 and above, the null hypothesis can be rejected. This evaluation showed that the development time of the experimental group is significantly shorter than the control group.

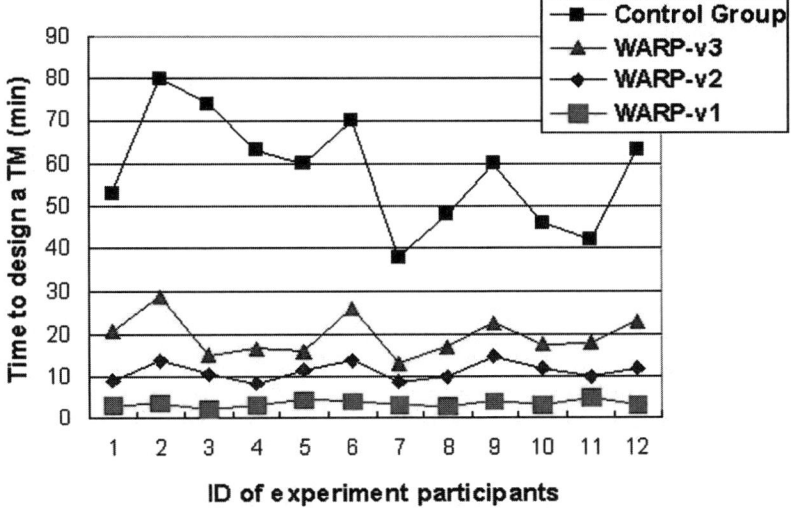

Fig. 13. Comparison of development time

A total of 45 items about feedback from teachers were collected during the Wiki-based authoring process by examining postings on Talk pages, and were classified along the following four dimensions:

Postings for comments. 26 postings are related to coordination of editing activities. For example, "I would like to suggest pruning lesson 9. The content of evaluating areas seems too difficult for the third-grade students." (Talk page for lesson 9, as shown in Figure 14)

Replies to comments. 14 postings are responses to comments of others. For example, "I agree with that the calculation of area for a triangle is too hard for this stage." (Talk page for the article on lesson 9, as shown in Figure 14).

Polls. 2 voting sessions were organized by users to decide on controversial editing actions. For example, "The vote is this: Should the above paragraph be included in the lesson? The three possible answers are: Yes, No and Abstain" (Talk page for lesson 3).

Off-topic remarks. 3 postings are unrelated to the content. For example, "I will suggest my colleagues to try this interesting tool" (Talk page for Area:WARP).

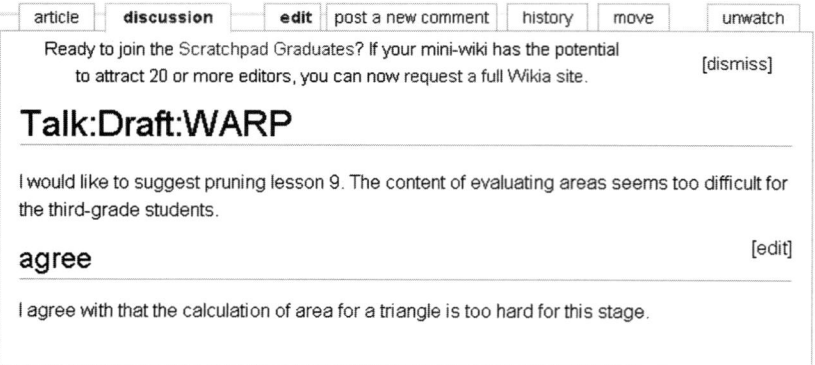

Fig. 14. Screenshot of Wiki's Talk pages

4.3 Experiment 2: Evaluation of Query Expansion

This experiment investigated whether the proposed intelligent query expansion could enhance the performance of the original query. Figure 15 shows the precision value from the twelve teachers of the experimental group who used the WARP tool to search for relevant teaching materials. The precision values ranged from 0.7 to 1.0 with the WARP and from 0.2 to 0.7 with the original query. The next experiment measured the recall value, as shown in Figure 16. Similarly, the WARP approach could improve the performance of the original query.

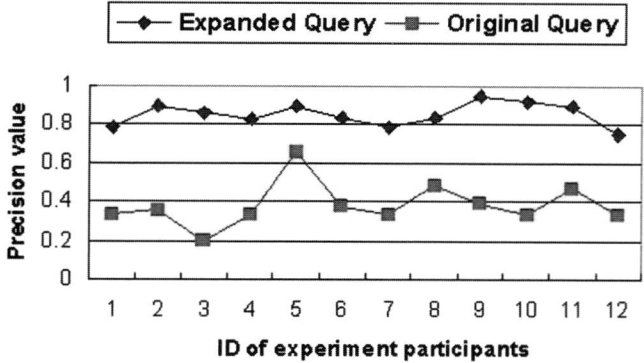

Fig. 15. Comparison of precision

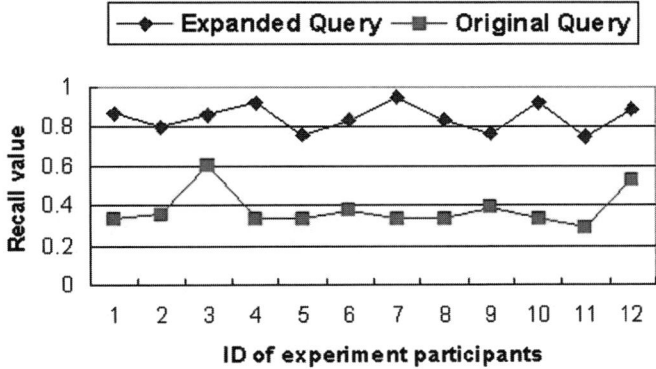

Fig. 16. Comparison of recall

4.4 Discussion

The Wiki-based revision for teaching material produces both individual and collective benefits. The individual who makes a knowledge contribution can see it immediately published, thus observing the contribution outcome without delay and with pride of authorship. This immediacy between action and positive outcome may very well create a positive reinforcement effect for the author. Immediacy of results has social impacts as well. First, any published result is visible and therefore potentially beneficial to others right away. As others see useful contributions being made, they can use these contributions, as well as build upon them and add their own associated knowledge.

The teaching material produced by the proposed approach has two advantages: variety and innovation. On the one hand, the draft is generated from several relevant teaching materials, which results in its variety of content. On the other hand, the draft is revised by many authors. In this process, different ideas are added in the draft, thus resulting in its innovation.

Wikis enable instant publication of content. As soon as an author saves the new content, it becomes immediately visible to all readers viewing the page. No coordinator is involved in the publication process. Nevertheless, there are safeguards. For instance, Wikis maintain a temporal database of earlier page versions, and roll-back to an earlier version requires only a few clicks. However, from the viewpoint of Wiki designers and administrators, the storage and management for temporal revision are challenges when the Wiki system scales up. Grid platform is a suitable solution to these problems, which can provide resource for the storage and operation of temporal revision.

We discuss the quality of teaching materials produced by WARP in two aspects: content and presentation. First, the quality of the final version heavily depends on the effort of involved authors. The proposed merge algorithm can help to automatically collect relevant learning objects. However, it depends on human authors to refine the draft, such as course sequence, content selection, etc. For example the draft has evolved from a flat course structure to a two-level hierarchy, which is more organized and understandable for students. Second, currently available Wiki platforms are mostly text-based, and allow users to upload image files. However, multimedia learning objects can not be easily edited on current Wiki platforms. Therefore, in this work, most of the multimedia learning objects in original teaching materials are skipped because of the limitation of Wiki platforms. Consequently, the final version is mainly composed of texts and figures, as shown in Figure 17.

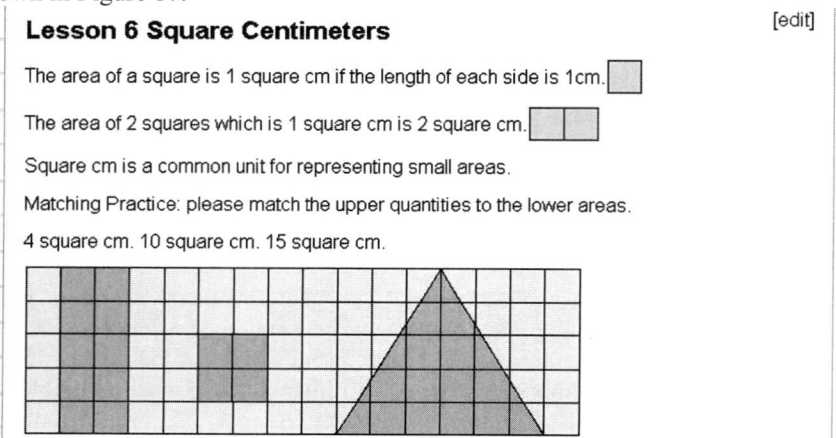

Fig. 17. Screenshot of Wiki pages

5   Conclusion and Future Work

This chapter describes a Wiki-based rapid prototyping approach to designing teaching materials for e-Learning applications. It is characterized by a time-saving development process, minimal human involvement, reducing redundant effort and high-quality teaching materials. The evaluation was carried out using a two-group t-test design. Experimental results indicate that teaching materials can be rapidly generated with the proposed approach. In the near future, we will conduct experiments to evaluate the quality of teaching materials developed by the proposed approach. Also, more participants with different background knowledge and teaching experiences will be invited to evaluate the proposed system. We expect that the proposed approach can assist novice as well as experienced teachers to develop useful course materials rapidly and easily. Furthermore, elicitation of users' requirements and content management for e-Learning grids will be investigated.

Acknowledgements

This research was partially supported by National Science Council of Republic of China under the number of NSC95-2520-S009-007-MY3 and NSC95-2520-S009-008-MY3.

References

ADDIE. (2004). ADDIE design [On-line]. Retrieved Mar. 7, 2007, from http://ed.isu.edu/addie/design/design.html

Coffey, J. W. (2007). A meta-cognitive tool for courseware development, maintenance, and reuse. *Computers & Education, 48*, 548-566.

Condor. (2004). Condor Project. 2006, from http://www.cs.wisc.edu/condor/

ELNP. (2002). National Science and Technology Program for e-Learning. Retrieved Mar. 12, 2007, from http://elnp.ncu.edu.tw/

Foster, I. (2002). The Grid: A New Infrastructure for 21st Century Science. *Physics Today, 55*(2), 42-47.

Foster, I., & Kesselman, C. (1997). Globus: A Metacomputing Infrastructure Toolkit. *International Journal of Supercomputer Applications and High Performance Computing, 11*(2), 115-128.

Gaeta, M., Ritrovato, P., & Salerno, S. (2003). *ELeGI: The European Learning Grid Infrastructure.* Paper presented at the Proceedings of 3rd International LeGE-WG Workshop: GRID Infrastructure to Support Future Technology Enhanced Learning.

Gordon, V. S., & Bieman, J. M. (1995). Rapid prototyping: lessons learned. *IEEE Software, 12*(1), 85-95.

Iorio, A. D., Feliziani, A. A., Mirri, S., Salomoni, P., & Vitali, F. (2006). Automatically Producing Accessible Learning Objects. *Journal of Educational Technology & Society, 9*(4), 3-16.

Jones, T. S., & Richey, R. C. (2000). Rapid prototyping methodology in action: a development study. *Educational Technology Research and Development, 48*(2), 63-80.

Kassahun, A., Beulens, A., & Hartog, R. (2006). Providing Author-Defined State Data Storage to Learning Objects. *Journal of Educational Technology & Society, 9*(2), 19-32.

Kelly, G. A. (1955). *The Psychology of Personal Constructs* (Vol. 1). New York: W. W. Norton.

Kim, E. O., & Park, J. H. (2007). *Study on the rapid prototyping methodology of the lecture contents for the IT SoC certificate program.* Paper presented at the IEEE Int. Conf. Microelectronic Systems Education (MSE'07).

Kiu, C.-C., & Lee, C.-S. (2006). Ontology Mapping and Merging through OntoDNA for Learning Object Reusability. *Journal of Educational Technology and Society, 9*(3), 27-42.

Lanzilotti, R., Ardito, C., Costabile, M. F., & Angeli, A. D. (2006). eLSE Methodology: a Systematic Approach to the e-Learning Systems Evaluation. *Journal of Educational Technology & Society, 9*(4), 42-53.

Lee, C.-H. L., & Liu, A. (2005). *Modeling the query intention with goals.*

Lin, Y. T., Tseng, S. S., & Tsai, C.-F. (2003). Design and implementation of new object-oriented rule base management system. *Expert Systems with Applications, 25*(3), 369-385.

Louridas, P. (2006). Using wikis in software development. *Software, IEEE, 23*(2), 88-91.

Luqi. (1989). Software evolution through rapid prototyping. *Computer*, 13-25.

Nkambou, R., Frasson, C., & Gauthier, G. (1998). A new approach to ITS-curriculum and course authoring: the authoring environment. *Computers & Education, 31*(1), 105-130.

O'Reilly, T. (2005). What Is Web 2.0. Retrieved Mar. 7, 2007, from http://www.oreillynet.com/pub/a/oreilly/tim/news/2005/09/30/what-is-web-20.html

Salton, G., & McGill, M. J. (1983). *Introduction to Modern Information Retrieval*. New York: McGraw & Hill.

SCORM. (2004). Sharable Content Object Reference Model (SCORM). 2006, from http://www.adlnet.org/

Shih, W.-C., Tseng, S.-S., & Yang, C.-T. (2008a). Using Taxonomic Indexing Trees to Efficiently Retrieve SCORM-compliant Documents in e-Learning Grids. *Journal of Educational Technology & Society, 11*(2), 206-226.

Shih, W.-C., Tseng, S.-S. & Yang, C.-T. (2008b). Wiki-based Rapid Prototyping for Teaching-Material Design in e-Learning Grids. *Computers & Education, 51*(3), 1037-1057.

Sierra, J. L., Fernández-Valmayor, A., Guinea, M., & Hernanz, H. (2006). From Research Resources to Learning Objects: Process Model and Virtualization Experiences. *Journal of Educational Technology & Society, 9*(3), 56-68.

Tripp, S., & Bichelmeyer, B. (1990). Rapid prototyping: an alternative instructional design strategy. *Educational Technology Research and Development, 38*(1), 31-44.

Trotman, A. (2005). Choosing Document Structure Weights. *Information Processing and Management, 41*, 243-264.

Wang, H.-C. (2007). Performing a course material enhancement process with asynchronous interactive online system. *Computers & Education, 48*(4), 567-581.

Wang, H.-C., & Hsu, C.-W. (2006). Teaching-Material Design Center: An ontology-based system for customizing reusable e-materials. *Computers & Education, 46*(4), 458-470.

Wikipedia. (2004). Wikipedia. Retrieved Mar. 7, 2007, from http://www.wikipedia.org/

Yang, C., Moore, D. M., & Burton, J. K. (1995). Managing courseware production: an instructional design model with a software engineering approach. *Educational Technology Research and Development, 43*(4), 60-70.

Chapter 15. Prediction Markets, an Emerging Web 2.0 Business Model: Towards the Competitive Intelligent Enterprise

Georgios Tziralis

School of Mechanical Engineering, National Technical University of Athens, Greece

George Vagenas

School of Mechanical Engineering, National Technical University of Athens, Greece

Stavros Ponis

School of Mechanical Engineering, National Technical University of Athens, Greece

Abstract

The Web evolves rapidly. Day by day, it hosts more of both personal and business activities, while people constantly spend more of their time online. However, the shaping of well-structured business models able to monetize most of Web 2.0 services is rather lagging beyond their users and usage, if it exists at all yet. While Web 2.0 services tend to be mainstream, their business models and exploitation are definitely not. This rather harsh reality is further amplified in enterprise settings, where the adaptation of such practices to empower the 'Enterprise 2.0' is still at its infancy and the potential of transforming collective to competitive intelligence remains latent.This chapter presents and analyzes a core and emerging Web 2.0 concept, prediction markets, a mechanism nearly synonym to the notion of 'wisdom of crowds'. We focus on its relevant business models and highlight the ones that are capable of reaching the latter and great potential. In this effort, a review and critique of relevant literature is provided, proving the late emergence of such models and the rather unexplored nature of the subject, particularly in the business world. Attempting to address this gap we prescribe such applications, by giving shape to the empowered by prediction markets competitive intelligent enterprise. The ground is definitely fertile for such an enterprise; however, relevant techniques remain at an early adopter level of penetration and yet absent from their potential perfect match, the 'long tail' of enterprises, namely SMEs. Driven by such considerations, we introduce and document the concept of competitive intelligence as a promising and fitting application area of Web 2.0 business models and, among them, prediction markets. Finally, building on these potentials, we document and provide specifications on a prediction market Web 2.0 business tool and model that will ultimately give boost to a truly competitive intelligent enterprise.

Keywords: Prediction Markets, Competitive Intelligence, SME, Enterprise 2.0

1 Introduction

The Web evolves rapidly, hosting more of both personal and business activities. As people constantly spend more of their time online, the cyber world can be harshly separated from the real one and our social and professional life gets increasingly attached to WWW's offerings. This great evolution that mainly took place in the second half of the current decade has lead to a fundamental reassessment of the Internet scene, giving birth to 'Web 2.0', a term often accredited to O'Reilly (2005). Still, 'Web 2.0' seems to be a dubious concept that is hard to define. Despite the wide discussion among academicians and field scientists a consensus on a solid definition is far from being achieved.

According to Tim O'Reilly (2006) "Web 2.0 is the business revolution in the computer industry caused by the move to the Internet as platform, and an attempt to understand the rules for success on that new platform". However, not everyone agrees on the revolutionary character of Web 2.0 since for some it stands far from a radically new version of the Web perceived only as another marketing trick to absorb fluctuations created after the dot.com bust. Notably, Tim Berners-Lee argues about the 'nonsense of such a term' (Laningham 2006), since most of its technical specifications and components have existed since the early days of the Web (Anderson, 2006). From a technical perspective this view can be hardly refuted since, even AJAX, which is considered as a major technical update of Web 2.0, is a mere additional layer building on top of a pre-existing web architecture. Accordingly, it seems that Web 2.0 cannot be confined to "hard boundaries" since it is more like a "gravitational core" (O'Reilly, 2005) that holds together a diverse set of applications including among others blogs, wikis, multimedia sharing services, content syndication, podcasting and content tagging services - folksonomies. These are not really new technologies, but services that are transforming user experience, changing the face of the Web.

Going back to its beginnings, the Web was largely about navigating static web sites and solid lines between active content providers and passive content consumers used to exist. Nowadays, things have dramatically changed and fundamental reassessments of the way both businesses and individuals as well as developers and users experience the Worldwide Web have occurred. Among them, the consideration of the web as a platform focused on services instead of software, the emergence and value of network effects, and the significance of user-generated data are all properties that definitely characterize Web 2.0 (O'Reilly 2005, Anderson 2007). Towards a taxonomy of all these features, it is argued that the most fundamental of Web 2.0 components essentially lies in empowering the actions of collecting, organizing, making accessible and finally building on the top of the content submitted by users; in other words, providing a platform to breed and accommodate their collective intelligence (Högg et al. 2006).

As evident, these changes are not limited to technology, showing a recursive, cause and effect relationship with the global socio-economic evolutions. In this sense, the Web is becoming an unprecedented global and democratic cyber space, opening up new and largely unexplored opportunities for individuals and businesses alike. In this new Web, ideas, experiences, goods and services can be freely exchanged and the process of knowing is a community-based and collaborative endeavor (Alexander, 2006). Based on the above, it might not be farfetched to claim that Web 2.0 is rather "an idea in people's heads rather than a reality. It's actually an idea that the reciprocity between the user and the provider is what's emphasized. In other words, genuine interactivity, if you like, simply because people can upload as well as download" (Fry, 2007).

The concept of participation, on which Web 2.0 is based has also great economic implications and opens up significant new potentials for enterprises. In the Web 2.0 era, "companies can design and assemble products with their customers, and in some cases customers can do the majority of the value creation" (Tapscott and Williams, 2007). In such a case, Web 2.0 can lead to a co-operative economy in which value creation is based on networking and peering, while some authors even talk about "free labor"(Terranova, 2000). This trend has even triggered the enhancement of classical economics with terms and notions like the 'Wikinomics' (Tapscott and Williams, 2007) and the 'economics of attention' or 'reputation' (Davenport & Berk, 2001). The common ground of these novel approaches seems to lie in the efforts towards shaping well-structured business models capable to monetize most of Web 2.0 services. Unfortunately, a closer look to current literature and business press proves that these attempts present a significant lag when compared with Web 2.0 unstructured use and wide application. Among the few existing efforts one can discern that of Tapscott and Williams (2007) who identify seven Web 2.0 business models including peer pioneers, ideagoras, prosumers, new Alexandrians, platforms for participation, global plantfloor and Wiki workplace. However, in practice, with the exception of advertising, the vast majority of Web 2.0 services have proven viable only under external funding, in exchange of prospects for future profitability, which often never comes.

Although most efforts are still too early in evolution to support final judgment, one could argue that this rather harsh reality is further amplified in the enterprise setting. While the latest evolutions would typically suggest enabling companies to outperform the competition by harnessing and integrating services provided by others (Musser and O'Reilly, 2006), the adoption of such practices by the business world, popularized by the term 'Enterprise 2.0' (McAffee 2006), is still at its infancy. In the same context, the potential of transforming collective to competitive intelligence remains latent.

This chapter's intent is to present and analyze a core Web 2.0 concept, as well as its relevant business models, and particularly the ones that are capable of reaching the aforementioned objectives. We focus on prediction markets, a mechanism nearly synonym to the notion of 'wisdom of crowds', which is located in the heart of the collective intelligence's and Web 2.0's cloud of topics. Prediction markets emerged fairly recently as a promising forecasting mechanism able to effectively handle the dynamic aggregation of dispersed information among various agents. The interest that this mechanism attracts has recently met significant expansion in terms of both conducted research and applications (Tziralis and Tatsiopoulos 2007), while prediction markets are up to now accepted as a widely used forecasting mechanism (Armstrong 2006).

In order to lay the foundations of our proposal, we initially provide a concrete description of the prediction markets' mechanism under the prism of Web 2.0. We then proceed to present a comprehensive literature review on the subject, updated and extended on the top of our previous one (Tziralis and Tatsiopoulos 2007) which will provide a unique point of reference for the research field. The review covers both theoretical research and applications of the topic, while the exposition of the totality of case studies so far will shape a holistic understanding of the current state-of-the-art on the field.

We further move on to categorize, describe and critique existing business models that have utilized prediction markets so far, either as their core or secondary component. In addition, the late emergence of such models and the yet rather unexplored nature of the subject is documented, followed by evidence on the very low penetration of these new concepts in enterprise settings. Moving on to the heart of this chapter we attempt to highlight the great potential impact of adopting and applying prediction markets' in a business context, especially that of SMEs (small and medium enterprises). In this way we aspire to give shape to the potential of the empowered by prediction markets competitive intelligent enterprise.

Competitive intelligence is defined as the process by which enterprises are able to gather, analyze and manage their own information, as well as the information about their external competitive environment, in order to enable optimal decision making, at least in terms of their competition. While the ground is definitely fertile for the competitive intelligent enterprise, such techniques remain at a premature level of penetration, mostly implemented by large organizational entities and yet absent in their potential perfect match, the 'long tail' of enterprises, namely SMEs. Under the Web 2.0 prism, competitive intelligence can be seen as a mechanism for capturing the 'wisdom of crowds' in a systematic and goal oriented way and transforming it into a strategic asset, with great value creation possibilities, towards Enterprise 2.0. Driven by such considerations, we introduce and document the concept of competitive intelligence and its tight linkage to Web 2.0, while we also attempt to monitor its applicability, methods and uses so far. Finally, we conclude this paper with an insightful discussion of possible Web 2.0 applications that are in the position to support CI processes by utilizing the power of prediction markets.

In summary, this chapter contributes to the Web 2.0 literature with a complete reference point to both prediction markets and competitive intelligence, while it also provides an extended catalogue of relevant business models, either proposed or already in use. In that way we aim to provide a solid theoretical basis and a source of additional value for both academics and practitioners that aspire to utilize the power of Web 2.0 in their current or future research and/or business activities.

2   Prediction Markets

According to O'Reilly (2005), Web 2.0 has clearly emerged as the "gravitational core" of principles and practices that happened to tie together and gave shape to its platform. In this context and by closely examining its core components, Web 2.0 can be ultimately perceived as a platform for harnessing collective intelligence. The virtues of collective intelligence were yet known since the era of Aristotle (Sunstein 2008), who suggested that (in Barker, 1972) (ca 334-323 BC) *"when diverse groups all come together [...] they may surpass-collectively and as a body, although not individually-the quality of the few best. [...] When there are many who contribute to the process of deliberation, each can bring his share of goodness and moral prudence... some appreciate one part, some another, and all together appreciate all. [...] Provided the mass of the people is not too slave-like, each individual will indeed be a worse judge than the experts, but collectively they will be better, or at any rate no worse."*

One could argue that Aristotle had already sketched the properties of diversity of opinion, independence, decentralization and aggregation, which were nominated several centuries later by Surowiecki (2004) as the core elements of the 'wisdom of crowds', a concept naturally tight to Web 2.0 itself. In this context, the tasks of deliberation and aggregation of diverse and independent opinions seem perfectly fitted to Web 2.0 tools, while, among the various ones available, prediction markets aroused as the most suitable to fulfill the promises of the wisdom of crowds. In the following we attempt a deductive description of this mechanism.

Markets, in general, are social structures to enable the exchange of rights or services and goods. More specifically, financial markets can be defined as institutions that bring together buyers and sellers to trade financial products, namely securities, commodities or other fungible items. Such institutions incorporate by their very nature and facilitate, in one way or another, the four fundamental functions of investment, hedging, speculation and information aggregation. Several institutions have been deployed during the years to efficiently support these functions, mostly by focusing on just one of them. To name a few, stock markets are created and operating with the primary purpose of capital allocation, futures markets scope in hedging risks and betting markets serve as a physical destination for wagering.

However, each one of these institutions facilitates also and in parallel the entirety of all core market functions. For example, stock markets serve as a hospitable environment for speculation as well, while hedging could be accomplished by holding a wide portfolio of the traded assets and stock prices are unbiased estimators of firm fundamentals (Mandelbrot 1966). In this context, there exists significant evidence supporting the general presence of the fourth native function of markets' operation, namely their aggregative and predictive nature. This presence is strong even in institutions that were designed with different objectives in mind, in both investing (Admati and Pfleiderer 1987, Chen et al. 2007, Grossman and Stiglitz 1980, Hellwig 1980, Holmstrom and Tirole 1993, Lo 1997), hedging (Jackwerth and Rubinstein 1996, Krueger and Kuttner 1996, Roll 1984) and wagering cases (Boulier and Stekler 2003, Debnath et al. 2003, Figlewski 1979, Gandar et al. 1998, Schmidt and Werwatz 2002, Thaler and Ziemba 1988, Winkler 1971).

Still, while well established and widely used market institutions to fully exploit each of the first three essential features of markets' operation exist, the fourth fundamental function was not a raison d'être of a market till the comparatively recent emergence and development of prediction markets. Prediction markets are defined as markets for contracts that yield payments based on the outcome of an uncertain future event (Arrow et al. 2007). Such institutions are intentionally designed and run for the primary purpose of mining and aggregating information scattered among traders, while, by subsequently transforming this information into market values, they produce directly interpretable predictions about specific future events (Tziralis and Tatsiopoulos 2007).

The term "prediction markets" does not appear to be the single or definitive way to refer to the aforementioned concept. On the contrary, the relevant terminology is rather extended, including the essentially equivalent or more specific terms of 'information markets', 'decision markets', 'electronic markets', 'virtual markets', 'political stock markets', 'election stock markets', 'artificial markets' and 'idea futures'. Moreover, Tziralis and Tatsiopoulos (2007) document that the term 'information markets' is even more popular, in terms of literature references, than the 'prediction markets' one. However, no matter what kind of applications they are referring to or if there is a consensus on the definition details or not, we shall continue using the latter term, as its usage seems lately to be verified in most citations and business cases.

Prediction markets are typically considered as a rather novel and promising research area. However, the first implementation of the concept goes one and a half centuries back. Rhode and Strumpf (2004, 2007) document that markets for predicting the outcome of US elections have operated in Wall Street between 1880 and 1940. Relevant trading activities had grown enormously in size during the early nineties, in such a way that they occasionally outperformed the New York stock exchange, by openly trading securities on city, state and national races, which then were usually receiving substantial media coverage on a daily basis. Rhode and Strumpf (2007) report that the average bet volume in presidential historical markets was about 22 million (in 2000 US dollars), while the 1916 election has accumulated 158 million (2000 US) dollars alone. However, during the Second World War critiques on issues like moral hazard, election tampering, information withholding and strategic manipulation raised, which, in accordance with the emergence of scientific polls, drove political betting markets to extinction (Rhode and Strumpf 2004).

The concept's reincarnation took place only half a century later, when in 1988 a few researchers of the University of Iowa created experimental virtual markets on political contracts, with a clear initial focus on studying market dynamics. Results appeared from the very beginning to be more than encouraging, as documented in the early works of the nineties (Forsythe et al. 1992, Berg et al. 1996, Berg et al. 1997, Forsythe et al. 1994, Forsythe et al. 1992 and Forsythe et al. 1999). Yet today, the so-called Iowa Electronic Markets stand as the longest running case of contemporary prediction markets, while their track record indicate a significant superiority in terms of forecasting accuracy versus the polls, even if the maximum amount wagered in any election was more than 200 times less the average betting volume of historical markets (Berg et al. 2003).

The suggestion that markets might be created specifically to aggregate information has matured from serial research attempts, the latter of them in the field of experimental economics (Plott and Sunder 1982, 1988, Plott 2001), which returned a Nobel prize in Economics to its pioneer, Vernon Smith (Nobel E-Museum 2003, Morris 2004). Other fundamental keystones include the contributions of Hayek on open markets and their efficient and effective facilitation of information aggregation through prices (Hayek 1945), the efficient market hypothesis which states that an efficient market continuously reflects the sum of all available information about future events into security prices (Fama 1965), as well as the theory of rational expectations, which acknowledges the ability of markets to convey information through the prices and volumes of traded assets (Muth 1961, Lucas 1987). However, the concept of prediction markets in its previously defined form was firstly introduced and illustrated by Robin Hanson, in a series of articles published between 1990 and 1992 (Hanson 1990a, Hanson 1990b, Hanson 1991 and Hanson 1992) that could be perceived as the very first texts on the topic which was later labeled as prediction markets.

Early works of the previous decade on the subject were mostly focused on political market applications that aroused, next to IEM, in Germany (Beckmann and Werding 1996, Kuon 1991), Canada (Antweiler and Ross 1998, Forsythe et al. 1995 and Forsythe et al. 1998), Austria (Murauer 1997 and Ortner et al. 1995) and Sweden (Bohm and Sonnegard 1999). Together with the contributions of Ortner's

PhD Thesis and inaugural experimental applications in Siemens Austria (Ortner 1996, Ortner 1997, Ortner 1998), these articles more or less constitute the totality of documented references on the concept of prediction markets till late nineties.

Nevertheless, the basis for further development had already been laid and the evolution came to follow in an almost exponential pattern, as Tziralis & Tatsiopoulos (2007) analytically document. This pattern, which today seems to be equally valid, was applied both in theory and experiments, as well as in various applications. We cover the milestones of the first ones in this paragraph, while we next move on to a detailed analysis of implemented applications and their business models.

Among the most significant contributions to the subject was the introduction of two proper market mechanisms, namely market scoring rules (Hanson 2003) and dynamic pari-mutuel market (Pennock 2004), which are especially fitting to the needs and virtues of prediction markets. Other works of special value include the descriptive and popular texts of Wolfers and Zitzewitz (2004), Spann and Skiera (2003) and Berg and Rietz (2003).

Experimental applications in other than enterprise settings that have been reported in the academic literature involve, except from the aforementioned cases of IEM and other political markets, markets on various sport events (Debnath et al. 2003, Schmidt & Werwatz 2002), trading on product ideas (Chan et al. 2001, 2002), opinion surveys (Dahan et al. 2007), box office movies prediction (Spann & Skiera 2004), estimations on technologies' buzz (Mangold et al. 2005) or even influenza activities (Polgreen et al. 2007). Moreover, there exists some work on analyzing the behavior and accuracy of well-established non-experimental prediction marketplaces, like the ones of Chen et al. (2005) and Servan-Schreiber et al. (2004) regarding sport events on Tradesports and Newsfutures, or the contributions of Gruca (2000), Gruca et al. (2003, 2005) and Pennock et al. (2000, 2001, 2001) regarding box office predictions on Hollywood Stock Exchange.

Moving into the enterprise space, academic references and analyses on the use of prediction markets as internal decision support tools for various organizational functions seem to be rather few. The inaugural attempts by Ortner (1997, 1998) on forecasting projects' delivery time in Siemens Austria and, in parallel, by Chen et al. (2001, 2003, 2004) in HP sales forecasting were only lately followed by others. More recent attempts include demand forecasting in Intel (Hopman 2007), idea markets in Siemens (Soukhoroukova 2007) and GE (LaComb et al. 2007), predicting selected balanced scorecard indicators in Nokia (Glienke et al. 2007), while the concept's application in Google (Cowgill et al. 2008) clearly marks another milestone for the concept's diffusion.

Therefore, we argue that the integration of the prediction markets concept in real life enterprise settings in terms of documented cases in the literature is significant but rather limited. Furthermore, we came across a phenomenon elegantly described as information on prediction markets' cases not being preferably published, mainly on academic sources but also on popular media. Potential reasons may vary, ranging from business tactics of not disclosing information about the enterprise tools in use up to the need of a significant volume of potentially confidential data and publication cycle time. In the following, we attempt a comprehensive list of enterprises that are reported in the public domain to anyhow use internal prediction markets. Table 1 presents references from academic resources or popular media, while the –by no means exhaustive– list of enterprises reported to use such tools also includes Motorola, Qualcomm, InfoWorld, MGM, Chiron, Frito Lay, TNT, Yahoo, Corning, Masterfoods, Pfizer, Abbott, Chrysler, General Mills, O'Reilly and TNT.

Enterprise	Target	Reference
Siemens Austria	Project delivery time	Ortner 1997, 1998
HP	Printer sales	Chen et al. 2001, 2003, 2004
Intel	Corporate allocation, planning, forecasting	Hopman 2007
Siemens	Ideas	Soukhoroukova 2007
General Electric	Ideas	LaComb et al. 2007
Google	Various	Cowgill et al. 2008
Eli Lilly	Drug efficacy	Kiviat 2004
Microsoft	Product shipment dates	Kiviat 2004, King 2006
Archelor	Sales volume, prices	King 2006
Nokia	Balance scorecard indicators	Glienke et al. 2007
Intercontinental	Ideas	Lohr 2008
Best Buy	Sales	Dye 2008
Electronic Arts	Financial planning	Lohr 2008
Swisscom	New services demand	Lohr 2008
Cisco	Chip defects prediction	Lohr 2008

Table 1: A non-exhaustive list of enterprises using prediction markets, as reported in academic resources or popular media

The variation of running cases and their range of application clearly indicates the wide applicability of the mechanism and to some extent its great potential. Moreover, the concentration of references in the last couple of years suggests a substantial growth of the concept's diffusion in the enterprise world, in close analogy to the growth documented previously in research conducted on the subject. This concentration may also indicate a further relationship between prediction markets and Web 2.0, at least at the extent of their correlated recent evolution.

Despite the evidence of prediction markets' stable evolution in the enterprise arena, during recent years, one can not overlook the fact of few existing prediction markets services providers. This fact on the one hand proves the concept's usefulness but on the other it can be a severe alert of its inability to be translated into a viable business model. A successful business model even for the most bright ideas is never a trivial task since it requires a win-win long lasting business situation for all business entities participating in both the provision and the consume side of the service offering.

Therefore, taking into consideration the significant increase in the number of reported prediction markets applications, one can argue without much hesitation or justified doubt that there is a substantial expected value for the enterprise consumer side. What remains to be discussed is the potential value from a prediction market web service provider's perspective. This is attempted in the remainder of this section.

In general, it is argued that there are three major approaches to monetize a prediction markets web service from a provider's perspective. The first one seems rather intrinsic to the nature of a virtual market, as it regards trading commissions, while it is only applicable to real money markets. In a permutation of the classic e-commerce model, the market facilitator could add a price on the offered market service, by earning a specified commission, either per transaction basis or on the profits gained by each trader. Such a model may provide a significant flow of income, directly analogous to the size and participation across the available user base, but at the same time constitutes a potential barrier for gaining new traders. The model is successfully implemented by high traffic marketplaces like Betfair and InTrade/TradeSports, however its use is still problematic in countries like the United States, where a clear legal distinction between event contracts and gambling has not yet been determined (Arrow et al. 2007, CFTC 2008). Another significant barrier to the commission-based business model applies to enterprise prediction markets. In such cases, the use of real money is typically non-acceptable, for a variety of both ethical and practical reasons. As a result the first major business model is nearly not applicable to the under focus intra-enterprise marketplaces.

The next logic option for value creation and revenue build-up is the well known and successfully applied in other web 2.0 business models solution of advertisements. The success of the advertising business model could be mainly attributed to its indirect nature. Adopting the advertising model, the provider does not monetize the service itself -which is typically given for free- but the attention that users pay to the service. Typically through textual ads or banners, this attention is partially redirected to the message and website of the advertiser, who finally returns a fee to the service owner. Clearly, the viability and profit of a prediction marketplace using a sole advertising model definitely requires an extensive user base. So far, for example, the only prediction marketplace that has demonstrated such a volume of users is Hollywood Stock Exchange, which naturally adopted the advertising model. However, even if the essential requirement of a strong user base typically diminishes the applicability of a revenue model based solely on ads, this requirement can be severely relaxed when advertisements are applied in a complementary fashion. Indeed, the majority of available prediction markets services currently use or offer the option of serving advertisements, the income of which may end up to the service provider or the marketplace host, namely the enterprise. However, same to the commissions' model considerations arise for internal enterprise uses, as the monetization of employees' attention is typically illogical or even non-acceptable.

The shortcomings of previous revenue models and the inherent prohibitions that their own nature creates seem to be significantly relaxed in the case of a third option that seems to gain ground into becoming the dominant revenue model attempting to monetize enterprise prediction markets application and their related business models. This option regards user or enterprise-paid services, where the enterprise compensates the third party service provider to create an internal marketplace for its organizational needs. One may argue that, as long as the complexity and cost for developing a home brewed software solution remains high or, at least, significantly higher than utilizing an off-the-shelf and highly customizable web service, this option will be popular enough to stand as a viable business model for both enterprise customers and service providers. Indeed, with the exception of a few software corporate giants, like Google and Microsoft, which have deployed their own solutions, the vast majority of enterprises that utilize prediction markets for decision support have adopted the paid services solution. As a result, this business model has aroused as the most fitting one for a prediction markets web service provider and is today adopted by nearly all current market players.

In this section so far we attempted a detailed literature review of prediction markets followed by a tight integration of the PM concept within the Web 2.0 armory of emerging applications. Furthermore, the usefulness of the PM business model for contemporary enterprises has been presented followed by a relatively long discussion on the available revenue models from a service provider's perspective. In other words, so far we have managed to describe the Web 2.0 application that can be transformed into a viable business model, offering solutions to problems that contemporary enterprises are confronting. What is still missing is the application playground, or the problematic area that our proposed business model is aspiring to heal. Therefore, in the next section, we attempt a brief literature review of the Competitive Intelligence (CI) management practice followed by a short discussion about the appropriateness of Web 2.0 applications in Enterprise CI support.

3 Competitive Intelligence

Gathering information about competition for the formulation of an effective business strategy is most of the times a very time consuming, complicated and far from trivial process. Acquiring a concise and clear knowledge of the competition, including identities and its projected images, pricing information, strengths and weaknesses, supplier schemes and customer base structure, is of critical importance for the contemporary enterprise struggling to survive in the new unstable and hyper-competitive business environment of the 21th Century. In this demanding enterprise playground, being competitive intelligent in the sense of learning from the mistakes of others and avoiding them or by adopting their strong points and trying to incorporate them in your business function can be the discriminating difference between painful failure and soothing success. A competitive intelligent enterprise knows when to enter a market, what entry strategies to use, when to raise or drop prices, improve customer service, repackage its offer, protect from various risks, undertake more attractive product adaptation, break up its competitors' alliances and supply chain, and so on (Gikandi, 2007).

Competitive Intelligence is neither a new term nor a soon to be forgotten research hype. It's been around for decades and was mostly perceived as a branch of traditional Knowledge Management emphasizing on external knowledge sources in order to enhance knowledge based competitive advantages (Nonaka, 1991; Prusak, 1996). The emergence of the Internet paradigm, enabling almost anyone with a browser to gain access to an ocean of data and information turned the searchlight beam directly on to Competitive Intelligence and its potential, attracting large numbers of practitioners, business analysts and academic researchers. Since then, numerous are the efforts for a definitive interpretation of CI attempting to determine a commonly accepted scope and set its context (Herring, 2002; Giese, 2002; Miller, 2001).

In this Chapter we adopt the definitions of Fleisher and the Society of Competitive Intelligence Professionals (SCIP) which in combination, we believe, they provide the essence of this emerging scientific area. Fleisher (2007) defines CI as "the process by which organizations gather actionable information about competitors and the competitive environment and, ideally, apply it to their planning processes and decision-making in order to improve their enterprise's performance". In the same frequency, the definition of SCIP (2007) views CI as "the legal and ethical collection and analysis of information regarding the capabilities, vulnerabilities, and intentions of business competitors". The combination of these two definitions in our opinion provides an adequate description of the CI process and relaxes the concerns raised by many researchers of the field related to the often misuse of the term when referring to illegal and unethical actions for acquiring competitive information and industrial espionage.

As already mentioned, enterprises used to practice competitive intelligence long ago before Internet's brave new world came to existence. Back then, enterprises made significant investments to a rather slow, tedious, expensive and cumbersome process supported by traditional tools such as the telephone, fax machine and face to face interviews. Not rarely depending on the investments and therefore the size and wealth of the organization, internal efforts to assemble CI information were unsuccessful or ill resulted. In that case, enterprises had to turn to external consulting institutions and buy the so much desired reports for a high price and most of the times in a paper format. Under these circumstances, it is easily deduced that only large and wealthy enterprises were able to practice effectively CI processes and thus CI as a topic remained rather secluded and bounded to a "circle of privilege" defined by company size, culture, wealth and sometimes industry.

Things started to change with the advent of the Internet and nowadays almost anyone with a personal computer and an Internet access can practice competitive intelligence and have a fair amount of adequately filtered results within hours. Even a non internet proficient user can gain access to available Web Sources ranging from personal home pages to corporate Web sites and professional statistical and information services for prices starting from as low as 8$ a month for online access to a range of databases (Gikandi, 2007). This evolution does not change the fact that large enterprises still have greater potential for conducting CI studies but for sure it smoothes the differences in both magnitude and method of approach enabling small and medium sized companies (SMEs) and in some cases micro enterprises as well, to get their hands on the intelligence they need to conduct successful world trade at an affordable price.

Based on the above description, one could easily assume that Competitive Intelligence has already gained a significant place in everyday business practice of both large and smaller enterprises. Unfortunately, this is hardly the case. Our literature study proves that currently CI is used in a structured manner (a well defined and documented process) by large companies and is considered as a strategic tool that supports competition (Madden, 2001; Toit, 2003) but the situation changes when company size or wealth is reduced. In the later case CI approaches become rather anarchistic and ill structured if not completely absent. Case studies of well organized CI applications in SMEs can be found in France (Didier, 2006) and Canada (Calof & Breakspar, 1999) but they seem to be bright exceptions, when compared to the American literature from which CI in the SME context is almost absent (Brandau & Young, 2000). And this happens despite the wide recognition of the importance of SMEs in employment and economic development (Observatory of European SMEs, 2003).

Undoubtedly, SMEs are in great need of the benefits CI can provide them since globalization is putting immense pressure on them and the only means they have to fight back is innovation (Whitfield and Szeto, 1997), making their need for competitive intelligence an imperative. Furthermore, we claim that SMEs constitute a fertile ground for applying CI, since not only do they need it, but they also have a flair for exploiting foreign sources of knowledge (Robinson, 1982), in contrast to larger organizations (Prahalad & Ramaswamy, 2004). A core requirement of SMEs in order to engage in KM and CI specific initiatives is the provision of pragmatic and immediate benefits in competitive advantages (Kerste & Muizer, 2002), which is the exact target of the proposed research.

In doing so, we support the argument that the emergence of Web 2.0 business models can play a significant role towards the empowerment of CI support in SMEs. We base this argument on the basic characteristics of Web 2.0 these being democracy, servicing the long tail (SMEs though large in numbers seem to constitute the long tail of subserviced entities when it comes to CI), exploitation of the network effect and the new perspective on software viewed as a service and not a package. To further support our perspective, in the next section we present an insightful discussion on a Prediction Markets enabled CI approach. In our opinion, this discussion will set the necessary conceptual basis for the elaboration of an innovative Web 2.0 platform capable of utilizing the power of the opinion makers and the now emerging prediction markets paradigm in an attempt to resolve main issues and overcoming core impediments of CI application in SMEs.

4   Prediction Markets Enabled CI – A Discussion

Web 2.0 has ultimately enabled the creation, contribution and sharing of information, in ways never thought possible a few decades before. This reality described by some authors as an ocean of available information serves simultaneously as both a unique opportunity and a protective barrier to the promise of a truly competitive intelligent SME. Blogs, wikis, social networks, business and scientific portals or other components of the deep web present a potential, as well as an extra resource-intensive task for information extraction. In this context, each business model and the potential of its application is finally assessed on the basis of effectively handling the information explosion that enterprises are nowadays experiencing.

Hopefully, recent developments contributed CI mechanisms and technologies that are considered to be able to handle this information overload. The respective software market is steadily growing, providing solutions for the data collection and organization activities. Such solutions are based on intelligence agents (Bui & Lee, 1999; Fuld, 1999; Boureston, 2000), which ensure that the system is sensitive to the evolving marketplace needs (Martin, 1992), as well as push technologies or analytical services, including data warehousing and mining, OLAP and information sharing applications (Shaker & Gembicki, 1999).

The above CI technologies and tools attempt to transform the unstructured information that largely exists in Web 2.0 into a structured and goal oriented set of meaningful information based on specific business needs. However, the result of this filtering process is far from being complete or providing ready-to-use information for the purposes of decision support. For one thing, the development of a CI tool that provides extensive tracking of relevant information on the web is nearly a utopia, at least considering the resources of an SME. Moreover, data collected still need to be validated and triangulated, checked for omissions, and looked for inconsistencies and anomalies (White, 1998). The latter is of extreme importance since information derived from the Web is not always valid, not to mention the fact that competitors may be trying to prevent others from getting at key inputs, through the practice of diffusing false information with the intent of deception (Dishman & Nitse, 1999). It occurs that strict CI procedures, purely utilizing artificial agents or algorithms, have some limitations, both on their efficiency and potential as business models. The age-old struggle of man versus machine seems not to yield optimal solution near its edges, in our case.

To address these considerations, a new and promising approach is necessary that can enrich and evolve the practice of competitive intelligence, giving it the necessary thrust to proceed in the Web 2.0 era. Such a service, designed to collect, merge and filter relevant information from the experts and provide dynamic, accurate, and fully quantified consensus views presents –to our opinion- a fairly appropriate tool for aggregating expert's information and early capturing market trends. Building on this potential we put forward and prescribe a novel prediction market Web 2.0 business model that will ultimately give boost to a truly competitive intelligent enterprise.

In essence, what we propose is the possibility of an integrated and innovative approach utilizing the power of Web 2.0 applications and business models, such as prediction markets in order to achieve the ultimate goal which is the Competitive Intelligent Enterprise. In that sense, a Web 2.0 platform is created that can act as a global corporate radar (Pollard, 1999), thus supporting effectively business decision making. In the core of our business model lie emerging collective knowledge-based Web 2.0 applications such as the blogs, wikis and social networks to name a few. These applications constitute the unstructured sources of information, necessary for the operations of overlying CI and prediction markets tools that process the information and create tangible reports for the system's users. It should be noted here, that according to our approach, prediction markets come to serve as a separate layer of a human-powered meta-filter of information, which finally moves the mix of man versus machine usage into a more optimal balance for decision support.

Human agents possess a unique capacity of adopting and processing new information. In our case, for example, managers could quickly filter and learn from various kinds of information on the competition that an SME faces. At the same time, they typically suffer from biases and shortcomings (Armstrong and Brodie 1999). These properties stand to make artificial agents able to perform complementary to the faults and virtues of human ones. The latter however involves a robust mechanism able to combine the opinions of the many, while also cutting down the imperfections and maximizing the advantages of human nature. An abstract representation of the proposed approach is depicted in Figure 1.

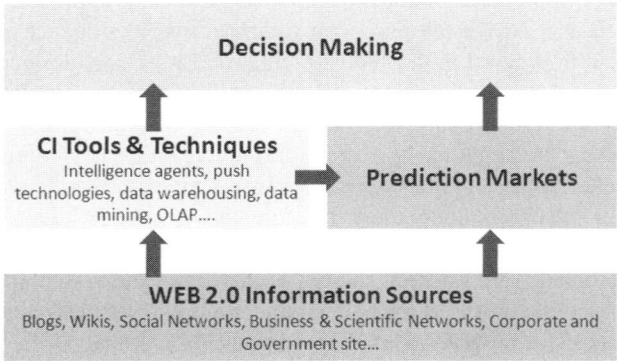

Fig. 1. The Proposed Approach

In conclusion, we do believe that prediction markets seem to offer an ideal match. In the settings of an SME, employees possess and are able to contribute information of significant value on CI topics of interest. The Web, undoubtedly, constitutes a deep and rich resource of information, fundamentally essential for providing input in existing analytical tools and techniques. Moreover, managers and employees shall be able to take advantage of both pure web sources, as well as the outputs of the CI tools under use. At this stage, prediction markets come to perform the aggregation of various opinions and estimations of all employees that –by building on both Web 2.0 and CI inputs, as well as on their experience and information– seamlessly provide clear inputs to the decision making processes. The latter, however continue to be served also by CI tools, ultimately enabling the enterprise that builds on inputs and processes of both tacit and implicit nature and receives aggregated signals from both the web, artificial and human agents.

References

Admati AR, Pfleiderer P (1987) Viable allocations of information in financial markets. Journal of Economic Theory 43:76–115

Anderson N (2006) Tim Berners-Lee on Web 2.0: "nobody even knows what it means". http://arstechnica.com/news.ars/post/20060901-7650.html. Accessed November 10, 2006

Anderson P (2007) What is Web 2.0? ideas, technologies and implications for education. JISC Technology and Standards Watch, February 2007. http://www.jisc.ac.uk/media/documents/techwatch/tsw0701b.pdf Accessed 15 September 2007

Antweiler W, Ross TW (1998) The 1997 ubc election stock market. Canadian Business Economics, 6:15–22

Armstrong SJ (2006) Findings from evidence-based forecasting: Methods for reducing forecasting error. International Journal of Forecasting 22:583-598

Armstrong S, Brodie R (1999) Forecasting for Marketing. In Hooley GJ, Hussey MK (eds) Quantitative Methods in Marketing, 92-119, International Thompson Business Press

Arrow KJ, Forsythe R, Litan RE, Gorham M, Hahn RW, Hanson R, Kahneman D, Ledyard JO, Levmore S, Milgrom PR, Nelson FD, Neumann GR, Ottaviani M, Plott CR, Schelling TC, Shiller RJ, Smith V, Snowberg EC, Sunder S, Sunstein CR, Tetlock PC, Tetlock PE, Varian HR, Wolfers J, Zitzewitz E (2007) Statement on prediction markets. AEI-Brookings Joint Center Related Publication 07-11

Barker E (1972) Aristotle, Politics. Oxford University Press, London

Beckmann K, Werding M (1996) 'Passauer wahlborse': Information processing in a political market experiment. Kyklos, 49:171–205

Berg JE, Forsythe R, Rietz TA (1997) The iowa electronic market. In Dean Paxson and Douglas Wood (eds) Blackwell Encyclopedic Dictionary of Finance, 111–113. Blackwell, Oxford UK

Bohm P, Sonnegard J (1999) Political stock markets and unreliable polls. Scandinavian Journal of Economics, 101(2):205–222

Boulier BL, Stekler HO (2003) Predicting the outcomes of national football league games. International Journal of Forecasting, 19(2):257–270

Boureston J (2000). Using intelligent search agents for CI. Competitive Intelligence Magazine. 3(1): 32-36.

Bui T, Lee J (1999) An agent-based framework for building decision support systems. Decision Support Systems. 25: 225-237.

Chan NT, Dahan E, Kim A, Lo A, Poggio T (2002) Securities trading of concepts. MIT, Working Paper No. 172

Chan NT, Dahan E, Lo A, Poggio T (2001) Experimental markets for product concepts. MIT, Working Paper No. 149

Chen KY (2005) Markets as an information aggregation mechanism for decision support. Doctor of Philosophy Thesis, School of Information Sciences and Technology, The Pennsylvania State University, Pennsylvania

Chen KY, Chu CH, Mullen T, Pennock DM (2005) Information markets vs. opinion pools: an empirical comparison. Proceedings of 6th ACM conference on Electronic commerce, ACM Press, Vancouver BC

Chen KY, Fine LR, Huberman BA (2001) Forecasting uncertain events with small groups. Proceedings of 3rd ACM conference on Electronic Commerce, Tampa, Florida, 58–64

Chen KY, Fine LR, Huberman BA (2003) Predicting the future, Information Systems Frontiers 5:47–61

Chen KY, Fine LR, Huberman BA (2004) Eliminating public knowledge biases in information aggregation mechanisms. Management Science, 50-983–994

Chen Q, Goldstein I, Jiang W (2007) Price informativeness and investment sensitivity to stock price. Review of Financial Studies, 20:619–650

Commodity Futures Trading Commission (2008) Concept release on the Appropriate regulatory treatment of Event Contracts, Request for Public Comment

Cowgill B, Wolfers, J, Zitzewitz E (2008) Using Prediction Markets to Track Information Flows: Evidence from Google. Working Paper. http://bocowgill.com/GooglePredictionMarketPaper.pdf. Accessed 11 February 2008

Dahan E, Soukhoroukova A, Spann M (2007) Preference Markets: Organizing Securities Markets for Opinion Surveys with Infinite Scalability. Working paper

Davenport TH, Beck JC (2001) The Attention Economy: Understanding the New Currency of Business. Harvard Business School Press, Boston

Debnath S, Pennock DM, Giles CL, Lawrence S (2003) Information incorporation in online in-game sports betting markets. In Proceedings of the 4th ACM conference on Electronic commerce, ACM Press, San Diego

Debnath S, Pennock DM, Giles CL, Lawrence S (2003) Information incorporation in online in-game sports betting markets. Proceedings of 4th ACM conference on Electronic Commerce 258-259, ACM Press, San Diego

Dishman P, Nitse P (1999) Disinformation usage in corporate communications: CI'ers beware. Competitive Intelligence Review. 10(4): 20-29.

Dye R (2008) The promise of prediction markets: a roundtable. The McKinsey Quarterly, 2:83-93

Fama EF (1970) Efficient Capital Market: A Review and Empirical Work. Journal of Finance, 25:383-417

Figlewski S (1979) Subjective information and market efficiency in a betting market. The Journal of Political Economy, 87(1):75–88

Forsythe R, Frank M, Krishnamurthy V, Ross TW (1995) Using market prices to predict election results: the 1993 ubc election stock market. Canadian Journal of Economics, 28(4a):770–794

Forsythe R, Frank M, Krishnamurthy V, Ross TW (1998) Markets as predictors of election outcomes: Campaign events and judgement bias in the 1993 ubc election stock market. Canadian Public Policy, 24(3):329–351

Forsythe R, Nelson F, Neumann G, Wright J (1994) The 1992 iowa political stock market: September forecasts. The Political Methodologist, 5:15–19

Forsythe R, Nelson F, Neumann GR, Wright J (1992) Anatomy of an experimental political stock market. American Economic Review, 82(5):1142–1161

Forsythe R, Nelson F, Neumann GR, Wright J. Anatomy of an experimental political stock market. American Economic Review, 82(5):1142–1161

Forsythe R, Rietz TA, Ross TW (1999) Wishes, expectations and actions: a survey on price formation in election stock markets. Journal of Economic Behavior Organization, 39:83–110

Fry S (2007) Web 2.0 (Video interview). http://www.videojug.com/interview/stephen-fry-web-20. Accessed 10 October 2007

Fuld L (1999) Competitive intelligence on the Web: Finding true net worth. EContent, 22(4): 16-24.

Gandar JM, Dare WH, Brown CR, Zuber RA (1998) Informed traders and price variations in the betting market for professional basketball games. The Journal of Finance, 53(1):385–401

Glienke D, Ankenbrand B, Gebauer M (2007) Communicating strategy with information markets. EC'07, June 12, San Diego

Grossman SJ, Stiglitz JE (1980) On the impossibility of informationally efficient markets. The American Economic Review, 70(3):393–408

Gruca TS (2000) The iem movie box office market: integrating marketing and finance using electronic markets. Journal of Marketing Education 22:5–14

Gruca TS, Bergand J, Cipriano M (2003) The effect of electronic markets on forecasts of new product success. Information Systems Frontiers 5:95–105

Gruca TS, Bergand JE, Cipriano M (2005) Consensus and differences of opinion in electronic prediction markets. Electronic Markets 15:13–22

Hanson R (1990a) Could gambling save science? encouraging an honest consensus. In 8th

Hanson R (1990b) Market-based foresight: a proposal. Foresight Update, 10:1–4

Hanson R (1991) More market-based foresight. Foresight Update, 11:11

Hanson R (1992) Idea futures: Encouraging an honest consensus. Extropy 3(2)

Hanson R (1992) Idea futures: Encouraging an honest consensus. Extropy, 3(2)

Hayek F (1945) The use of knowledge in society. American Economic Review, 35:519-530

Hellwig MF (1980) On the aggregation of information in competitive markets. Journal of Economic Theory, 22(3):477–498

Högg R, Meckel M, Stanoevska-Slabeva K, Martignoni R (2006) Overview of business models for Web 2.0. GeNeMe 2006, Dresden

Holmstrom B, Tirole J (1993) Market liquidity and performance monitoring. The Journal of Political Economy, 101(4):678–709

Hopman J W (2007) Using Forecasting Markets to Manage Demand Risk, Intel Technology Journal, 11(2)127-136

International Conference on Risk and Gambling, London

Jackwerth JC, Rubinstein M (1996) Recovering probability distributions from option prices. The Journal of Finance, 51(5):1611–1631

Kagel JH, Roth AE (1995) Handbook of Experimental Economics. Princeton University Press

King R (2006) Workers, Place Your Bets. BusinessWeek, August 3, http://www.businessweek.com/technology/content/aug2006/tc20060803_012437.htm. Accessed 1 March 2008

Kiviat B (2004) The End of Management? Time, July 6, http://www.time.com/time/insidebiz/printout/0,8816,1101040712-660965-1,00.html. Acessed 1 March 2008

Krueger JT, Kuttner, KN (1996) The fed funds futures rate as a predictor of federal reserve policy. Journal of Futures Markets, 16(8):865–879

Kuon B (1991) Typical trading behavior in the german election markets 1990. University of Bonn Department of Economics, working paper

LaComb CA, Barnett JA, Qimei P (2007) The Imagination Market. Information Systems Frontiers, 9:245-256

Laningham S (2006) DeveloperWorks Interviews: Tim Berners-Lee. http://www-128.ibm.com/developerworks/podcast. Accessed 14 March 2008

Lo A (1997) Market efficiency: stock market behaviour in theory and practice. Edward Elgar, London

Lohr S. (2008) Betting to Improve the Odds. New York Times, April 9, http://www.nytimes.com/2008/04/09/technology/techspecial/09predict.html

Lucas RE (1972) Expectations and the neutrality of money. Journal of Economic Theory, 4(2)103-124

Mandelbrot B (1966) Forecasts of future prices, unbiased markets, and 'martingale' models. The Journal of Business 39(1):242–255

Mangold B, Dooley M, Dornfest R, Flake GW, Hoffman H, Kasturi T, Pennock DM (2005) The tech buzz game. IEEE Computer 38:94–97

Martin JS (1992) Building an information resource center for competitive intelligence. Online review. 16(6): 379–389.

McAfee AP (2006) Enterprise 2.0: The Dawn of Emergent Collaboration. MIT Sloan Management Review, 47(3):21–28

Morris A (2004) The Nobel Prize in Behavioral and Experimental Economics: a Contextual and Critical Appraisal of the Contributions of Daniel Kahneman and Vernon Smith. Review of Political Economy 16(1)3-41

Murauer G (1997) Vergleich von Wahlprognosen durch Meinungsumfragen und Bewertung durch Boersen anhand der Oberoesterreichischen Landtagswahl 1997. Diplomarbeit, Technische Universitaet

Musser J, O'Reilly T (2006) Web 2.0 Principles and Best Practices. O'Reilly Radar Report, Nov. 2006

Muth J (1961) Rational expectations and the theory of price movements. Econometrica, 29(6):315–335

Nobel E-Museum (2003) The Bank of Sweden Prize in Economic Sciences in Memory of Alfred Nobel 2002, http://www.nobel.se/economics/laureates/. Accessed 1 March 2008

O'Reilly T (2006) Web 2.0 Compact Definition: Trying Again. http://radar.oreilly.com/archives/2006/12/web-20-compact-definition-tryi.html. Accessed 15 June 2007

O'Reilly T (2005) What is Web 2.0? Design patterns and business models for the next generation of software. http://www.oreillynet.com/pub/a/oreilly/tim/news/2005/09/30/what-is-web-20.html. Accessed 1 February 2007

Ortner G (1996) Experimentelle Aktienmaerkte als Prognoseinstrument: Qualitaetskriterien der Informationsverarbeitung in Boersen am Beispiel Political Stock Markets. PhD thesis, Universitaet Wien

Ortner G (1997) Forecasting markets - an industrial application, part i. Technical University of Vienna, Department of Managerial Economics and Industrial Organization, working paper

Ortner G (1998) Forecasting markets - an industrial application, part ii. Technical University of Vienna, Department of Managerial Economics and Industrial Organization, working paper

Ortner G, Stepan A, Zechner J (1995) Political stock markets. the austrian experiences. Zeitschrift fuer Betriebswirtschaft, (4/95):123–135

Pennock DM, Lawrence S, Giles CL, Nielsen FA (2000) The power of play: efficiency and forecast accuracy in Web market games. NEC Research Institute, working paper No.168

Pennock DM, Lawrence S, Giles CL, Nielsen FA (2001) The real power of artificial markets. Science 291:987–988

Pennock DM, Lawrence S, Nielsen FA, Giles CL (2001) Extracting collective probabilistic forecasts from web games. Proceedings of 7th ACM SIGKDD international conference on Knowledge discovery and Data Mining, San Francisco, California 174–183

Polgreen PM, Nelson FD, Neumann GR (2007) Use of Prediction Markets to Forecast Infectious Disease Activity. Healthcare Epidemiology, 44:272–279

Pollard, A. (1999). Competitor intelligence: Strategy, tools and techniques for competitive advantage. New York, Pitman

Rhode PW, Strumpf KS (2004) Historical Presidential Betting Markets. Journal of Economic Perspectives, 18(2):127-142

Rhode PW, Strumpf KS (2007) Manipulating Political Stock Markets: A Field Experiment and a Century of Observational Data. University of North Carolina, working paper

Roll R (1984) Orange juice and weather. The American Economic Review, 74(5):861–880

Schmidt C, Werwatz A (2002) How accurate do markets predict the outcome of an event? The Euro 2000 soccer championships experiment. Max Planck Institute for Research into Economic Systems, Technical Report No. 09–2002

Schmidt C, Werwatz A (2002) How accurate do markets predict the outcome of an event? The euro 2000 soccer championships experiment. Max Planck Institute of Economics, Strategic Interaction Group, Discussion Paper

Servan-Schreiber E, Wolfers J, Pennock DM, Galebach B (2004) Prediction markets: does money matter? Electronic Markets 1(4)243–251

Shaker SM, Gembicki MP (1999). The warroom guide to competitive intelligence. New York, McGraw-Hill.

Skiera B, Span M (2004) Opportunities of virtual stock markets to support new product development. In Albers S (ed) Cross-Functional Innovation Management, Verlag Gabler, Wiesbaden, 227–242

Soukhoroukova A, Spann M and Skiera B (2007) Creating and Evaluating New Product Ideas with Idea Markets. Working paper

Sunstein CR (2008) Neither hayek nor habermas. Public Choice 134:87–95

Tapscott D and Anthony DW (2007) Wikinomics: How Mass Collaboration Changes Everything. Penguin, New York

Terranova T (2000) Free Labor: Producing Culture for the Digital Economy. Social Text 18(2): 33-57

Thaler RH, Ziemba WT (1988) Anomalies: Parimutuel betting markets: Racetracks and lotteries. The Journal of Economic Perspectives, 2(2):161–174

Tziralis G, Tatsiopoulos I (2007) Prediction Markets: An Extended Literature Review. The Journal of Prediction Markets 1:75-91

Winkler RL (1971) Probabilistic prediction: Some experimental results. Journal of the American Statistical Association, 66(336):675–685

Brandau, J. and A. Young (2000). "Competitive Intelligence in Entrepreneurial and Start-Up Businesses", Competitive Intelligence Review, Vol. 11 (1): 74 - 84.

Calof J. and Breakspar, A. (1999). Survey of Canadian R&D Companies: Awareness and Use of Competitive Technical Intelligence in Canadian Technology-Intensive Industry. CI Survey for NRC/CISTI. Available at: http://www.nrc.ca/cisti/ref/nrcci_e.html.

Danet, Didier (2006). "Competitive Intelligence and SMEs: Small Firms are They Less Intelligent Than the Large Ones?" Available at SSRN: http://ssrn.com/abstract=875405.

Fleisher, C.S. & Bensoussan, B.E. (2007). Business and Competitive Analysis: Effective Application of New and Classic Methods. Upper Saddle River, New Jersey: FT Press.

Geise, D. (2002). Counterpoint: The word intelligence carries too much baggage. Competitive Intelligence Magazine. 5:2.

Gikandi D., (2007). Gathering International Competitive Intelligence on the Web, www.4hb.com, last accessed 20/04/2008.

Herring, J.P. (2002). Point: the word is intelligence Competitive Intelligence Magazine. 5:2.

Kerste, R., & Muizer, A. (2002). "Effective knowledge transfer to SMEs: lessons from marketing and knowledge management', retrieved June 18, 2004, from EIM Business and Research Policy: www.eim.net/pdf-ez/B200202.pdf.

Madden, J. (2001). Overview of best practices in CI, in Managing frontiers in Competitive Intelligence, Westport, Quorum Books.

Miller, S. (2001). Competitive intelligence: An overview. Alexandria, VA: Society of Competitive Intelligence Professionals.

Nonaka, I. (1991). The Knowledge Creating Company. Harvard Business Review, November-December, 96.

Observatory of European SMEs. (2003). SMEs and Cooperation. Enterprise Publication.

Prahalad, C., & Ramaswamy, V. (2004). "The Future of Competition: Co-Creating Unique Value with Customers", Boston, MA: Harvard Business School Press.Prusak, L. (1996). The Knowledge Advantage. Strategy and Leadership, 24 (2).

Prusak L (1996) The knowledge advantage. Strategy and Leadership 24(2), 6–8.

Robinson, R. (1982). "The importance of "outsiders" in small firm strategic planning", Academy of Management Journal, 25, 80-93.

Society of Competitive Intelligence Professionals. (2007). About SCIP. http://www.scip.org/2_overview.php, last accessed 20/4/08.

Toit (du), A.S.A., (2003), "Competitive intelligence in the knowledge economy: what is in it for South African manufacturing enterprises?, International Journal of Information Management, Volume 23, Issue 2, April 2003, pp. 111-120.

White D (1998) Competitive Intelligence. Work Study. 47(7): 248–250.

Whitfield, R, Szeto, I. (1997). "Business process reengineering for small building products manufacturers", Journal of Management in Engineering, Vol. 13 No.6, pp.84.

Chapter 16. Innovation Culture for Knowledge Management in new e-Ra

Irene Samanta Rounti

Technological Education Institute in Piraeus

Abstract

In the current global business world, knowledge management is the most significant factor for the improvement of business procedures that leads to innovation. Organizations will have to include innovation as an indispensable operational function in their medium-term or long-term plans. The key findings of this study were that successful learning organizations had adopted a culture based on innovation, had management support for innovation, were aware of the relationship between innovation and strategic planning and where employees' contribution to innovation was recognized and rewarded.

1   Introduction

In a rapidly change economic environment firms in order to succeed in a global base take into account the acquisition of appropriate knowledge as a consequence the management of organizational leaning is fundamental (Drucker 1968; Toffler 1990). Therefore there is a necessity for organizations to adopt systematic approaches to sharing and managing knowledge. Also, it is crucial that companies think about how their employees acquire new knowledge (Guglielmino and Guglielmino, 2001).Organizations have to implement and manage human resource development programs taking into account to different learning styles and attitudes. Although there has been a huge amount of theoretical and practical research studying the nature of knowledge management, there is a need for synthesizing its contributions in a more manageable and pragmatic way. Managers are aware of the new dynamics playing in the new economy and the consequent greater importance of knowledge within their organizations. However, due to the complexity and abstraction of this concept, managers might become confused about how to act in order to improve their knowledge management related activities. Furthermore, the increasing development of new information and communication technologies and the emphasis of consultants and technology developers on the use of technology might have distorted the concept of knowledge management per se and the important potential of information and communication technologies to support knowledge management processes.

To deal with a theoretical approach to organizational learning is identified to better understand how firms acquire new knowledge to disseminate successfully for both business and technology. A firm's actual capacity to innovate depends upon various factors, such as the internal structure of an organization to assist and facilitate innovation, but also the accumulation of innovation knowledge continuously supplying innovations with resources and capabilities. The interaction of those factors helps firms to create a mechanism of improving innovation capacity (MIIC). MIIC benefits the research and development (R&D) process for new products in order to meet customer needs and create new markets (Szeto, 2000). Innovation capacities can be developed and maximized as part of a continuous improvement of the firm's competitiveness, through knowledge creation, knowledge management, total customer satisfaction, benchmarking, information technology, strategic alliances and empowered employees.

Through an exploratory research study conducted by Neely et al. (2001), was investigated the relationship between business performance, innovation and the internal and external factors which can facilitate innovation within a company. Research findings about the effect of IT technology on employees sharing information behavior are mixed but it is not clear if support knowledge sharing as replacing face-to-face communication (Mirand and Saunders, 2003).Some studies found the use of such technology enhances knowledge sharing (Dennis 1996) while others could not find any effects (Warkentine et al 1997) or even come to the conclusion that it inhibits knowledge sharing (McLead,1997).

Denning (2000) recognized that innovation culture is necessary for the development of e-commerce with knowledge being shared not only between staff but also with networks and the partners.

2 Knowledge Management as a result of Innovation Culture

According to previous researches (Harari, 1994; Nonaka, 1994; West, 1992), the organizations that are able to stimulate and to improve the knowledge of their human capital are much more prepared to face today's rapid changes and to innovate in the domain where they decide to invest and to compete. All competitive efforts, which come from competitors' knowledge and innovations, affect the success of firms' strategies (Curren et al., 1992). (Cited in Carneiro A., 2000, pp. 87-98).Therefore the knowledge development in the area of innovation technology, the specialization on business processes, and innovative products is the strongest source of competencies.

Probst et al. (2000) suggest that knowledge management is the management of a company's corporate knowledge and information assets as well as its business processes to encourage a better and more consistent decision making. Knowledge management is recognized as the fundamental activity for obtaining, growing and sustaining innovation in organizations in a rapidly change environment (Malhotra, 2000; Marr and Schiuma, 2001). Davenport and Grover (2001) and Liebowitz (2000) support that the successful use of firm's corporate knowledge across its business processes increase a long-term success and growth. Nonaka and Takeuchi (1995) conceptualize knowledge management as the management of those processes that manage the generation, dissemination, and utilization of knowledge. Bose and Sugumaran (2003) and Cegarra and Rodrigo (2005) identify a knowledge management process structured into three continually interacting phases: knowledge acquisition (KA), knowledge distribution (KD) and knowledge utilization (KU).Although there are many attempts to define knowledge, it is an ambiguous and rich concept which points many directions simultaneously. Here we will describe the main dimensions of knowledge and the nature of knowledge management.

Drawing on the definition made by Polanyi (1966), we distinguish tacit knowledge, which is personal and unconscious, from explicit knowledge, which can be articulated. Despite being simple to be understood, this epistemological distinction is extremely important when managing knowledge. Explicit knowledge may be articulated, and therefore, copied or transferred easily. Therefore, explicit knowledge might result a required but not distinctive resource in organizations. On the contrary, due to the unconsciousness characteristic of tacit knowledge, this kind of knowledge is difficult to be captured or imitated, so it might be a potential strategic source of competitive advantage. However, this fact also impedes the measurement of tacit knowledge. Hence, we opt for operationalising tacit knowledge indirectly by assessing the objects and processes where it resides or is created.

Another important dimension of knowledge depends on the location of knowledge. Individual knowledge is the knowledge possessed by individuals. Knowledge is intrinsically linked to people, since they know and have the skills to act. On the other hand, organizational knowledge refers to the knowledge commonly shared within the organization, that is, a collective understanding. Organizational knowledge is shaped by the organizational routines, symbols, behavioural norms and values, etc., that is, the organizational culture, which has been developed over time and, thus, is distinctive of the firm. Thus, Barney (1986) states that the organizational culture is a valuable, rare and imperfectly imitable. The strategic importance of organizational knowledge has aroused in the new economy, since due to the globalisation of the markets individuals easily move from firms taking their experiences with them. Therefore, is based on the knowledge management life cycle: knowledge creation, knowledge storage and retrieval, knowledge transfer and knowledge application (Alavi and Leidner, the analysis of the factors influencing the development of organizational knowledge is of critical importance.

Knowledge management cycle might happen at different levels within the organization, from the individual level to the external level. The adoption of this perspective is also very interesting since it might allow us to identify what levels in the organizations are stronger or weaker, whether some of them are more significant than others, etc.

The focus on the dynamic nature of knowledge is consistent with the concept of capabilities, introduced by Amit and Schoemaker (1993), who claim that the value of the resources does not reside in them, but in the way in which they are used. Thus, capabilities are embedded in the organization and its processes (Makadok, 2001).

Organizations are social entities, where culture acts as the invisible glue that unites individuals into social structures (Smircich, 1983) and holds part of the collective knowledge, the organizational and tacit knowledge, and shapes the routines and ways of acting within organizations. Therefore, it is important to include culture as a potential complementary capability of knowledge management. Based on the existing literature, we propose mission, vision and values of the firm, internal communication through team working, empowerment and reward systems leadership coaching to form the culture construct.

At the same time, several studies have researched the influence of culture on organizational performance and even their interaction with other factors such as leadership or high-performance human practices. Most of the studies have found positive relationships between culture and organizational performance (Chan et al, 2004; Ghobadian et al, 2002; Denison and Mishra, 1995). Although most authors notifying the role of culture on knowledge management. In this study we analyse the impact of organizational culture on knowledge management and organizational performance simultaneously.

2.1 Knowledge Sharing

Knowledge sharing has been recognized as being strategic and as a means of leveraging firm and industry competitiveness (Kogut et al. 1992; Nonaka et al. 1995). Many studies have looked at the factors that inhibit or encourage knowledge sharing within and between organisations. Most of the barriers seem to address people, organisations and/or technology features (Huysman et al. 2002; Lindsey 2003), or to cross these three categories like culture, lack of rewards (Barson et al. 2000; Hall et al. 2004) and information culture (Jarvenpaa et al. 2000).It can be argued that knowledge sharing involves a conscious desire, willingness, and therefore, the concept of trust plays a preponderant role in it. Other authors have also referred to the importance of leadership, common purpose and trust (Brazelton et al. 2003), and social resources (Brown et al. 2000), were said to enhance the willingness to share knowledge. Regarding the consequences of knowledge sharing, scholars have asserted implicitly its correlation with the improvement of firm's effectiveness.

2.2 Linking new e-Ra economy with business performance through knowledge management

E-business differs fundamentally from traditional business because of the key role that IT takes in acting as a conduit, enabler and facilitator for different business functions. Some e-businesses operate on a physical market, others on a virtual one and others on both. The aim of this research is to explore how knowledge management can enable e-business implementation in Greek firms. Is there a knowledge management process to implement e-business systems and, if there is, which strategies are more likely to ensure a successful implementation of the systems in new e-Ra? This paper attempts to address these questions through an empirical study of e-business medium firms in different sectors of activities in Greece. The majority of such firms faces an intense competition and therefore are highly induced to enter processes for knowledge management and systematizing the 'learning' process (Osland and Yaprak, 1995).

According to Bhatt (2000), organizations adapt themselves to their external environments by designing responsive structures and systems. A key mechanism in the design of such systems is knowledge codification (KC), which involves converting knowledge into machine-readable forms and storing them for a future use (Bose and Sugumaran, 2003). Malhotra (2000) asserts that knowledge codification delivers a JiT information.

Hagel and Armstrong (1997) suggest that implementing new and flexible technologies and systems facilitates communication constructing, bridge networks among people and on-the-job training and learning. This is the traditional view often adopted by larger organizations, Gold et al (2001) and Malhotra (2000).

Gold et al. (2001) has recognised two strategies of knowledge management and their effects on 'e-business'. In order to implement technological systems in new e-Ra, companies need to assure and sustain the acquisition and distribution of knowledge as prior steps. Through the acquisition and distribution of knowledge, firms raise a dynamic process where teams groups are continuously able to increase their capacity to codify knowledge. Therefore companies need to insert and sustain knowledge management capabilities through the development and integration of currently available technologies. Consequently, firms that seek for better and more effective adaptation to the new economy follow some steps before implementing and introducing their product or service to the market that intends to create an environment in which innovation is built in and developed within every employee. These steps are identified by Johannessen et al, 2001:

- 1st Step: Managerial Orientation
- 2nd Step: Organizing Innovation

- 3rd Step: Cooperation Development
- 4th Step: Leadership Practice
- 5th Step: Performance Growth

In addition as knowledge acquisition and distribution contributes to fostering knowledge utilization and Malhotra (2000) refers as the basic tools of knowledge management we can propose that in order to implement e-business systems, companies need to provide and support these strategies as the prerequisite step to e-business performance.

3   Developing the Conceptual Model

Drawing on the theory, the model (Figure 1) aims to research knowledge management, as the main capability, and its interaction with other concepts (e-business, organizational context and organizational culture). The integration of these factors will allow us to have a better understanding due to a greater and more holistic theoretical coherence.

3.1 Innovation culture construct to share knowledge

In the current global business world, innovation management is the most significant factor for the improvement of business procedures. If corporations intend to be competitive in a constantly changing environment, they will have to transform technological and scientific achievements into better and more effective products, in order to dominate at the domestic or international level. There are studies which have investigated the impact of e-Ra as a capability and their impact on innovation culture. However, all the constructs agree with the human and technical aspects involved in the adoption of new technology. According to Melville et al (2004), most empirical studies support a positive relationship between information and communication technologies and organizational performance (Bharadwaj, 2000; also Melville et al (2004) cite: Lehr and Lichtenberg, 1997; Lichtenberg, 1995; Siegel, 1997).

H1: New e-Ra global environment positively influence innovation culture

H2:New e-Ra global environment positively influence organizational performance

According to the results of Powell and Dent-Michallef (1997), "information technology alone does not produce sustainable performance advantages but advantages can be gained by using information technology to leverage intangible, complementary human and business resources". Thus, new e-Ra economy has an indirect effect by leveraging knowledge management capabilities

3.2 Tasks of knowledge management process

Organizations are entities, (Smircich, 1983) and culture holds part of the collective knowledge, the organizational and tacit knowledge, and shapes the routines and ways of acting within organizations. Therefore, it is important to include culture as a potential complementary capability of knowledge management previous academic research into innovation culture has focused on various aspects of this topic, including different innovation culture perspectives (Christensen and Rosenbloom, 1995). From a network perspective, innovation culture emerges from collaborations or alliances for new developments. From a marketing perspective, innovation relies on the need and expectation changes of markets, which are then incorporated into the process of product development and emerge as marketable new products. From a management perspective, innovation is the management of all resources (from within and outside) of a firm to foster new ideas for new development. From a technological perspective, innovation tends to be a technological change or breakthrough applied to new product development (Szeto, 2000). *H2: Innovation culture positively influences on firm's Knowledge management*

3.3 Organizational Context

Regarding knowledge management, Lee et al (2003) argue that context is a key issue when dealing with organizational knowledge. Knowledge management activities might vary depending on the stability of the environment, the technological turbulence, etc. Internal structure, organizational dispersed ness, and composition of the stakeholders, among others. Consequently, it can be proposed that:

H3: knowledge management capabilities are mediated by the organizational context

Figure 1: Conceptual Model

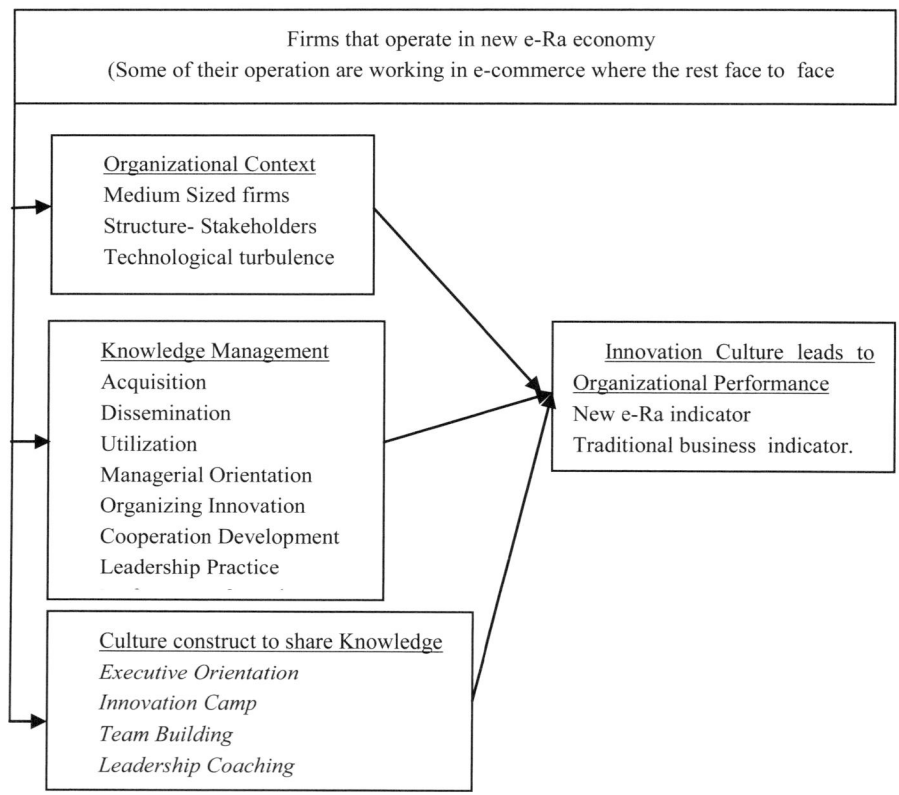

4 Research results

Knowledge management establishes discipline and is examined in medium-sized firms along with its status and role and what their policy implications are. The criteria used for the selection of the participating firms were the sector categorization with a satisfactory representation of different kinds of commercial and industrial companies together with the private sector of services. The population of the MSFs comprises of 1525 business firms according to the ICAP (2004) research study. The firms chosen for the sample should have an R & D department or invest to that direction. The number of firms that composed the sample was 10%, 99 of which responded to the questionnaire with rate of respond 65, 1%.

4.1 Defining the firms' behavior towards new e-Ra economy

From the research analysis, two groups of firms emerged which include different characteristics towards innovation culture. In the first group knowledge management is developed in internal environment, which influences the companies directly. In the present research, it is noticed that top management has a tendency to develop an innovation culture, which has as a result a reference to a specific innovation strategy with specific procedures towards innovation with fast ways of innovation transmission to new e-Ra, so that networks that promote innovation are developed. In the second group, the companies are placed in a human-centric system with a future prospect to move from the traditional business to new e-Ra economy. There is a conjugation and a balance between the human-centric and the technocratic systems. The company's development for creating scale economies is accomplished through an occasional partnership or stable long-term partnership. This shows the psychological tendency of managers to maintain their independence, given that a great percentage of medium – sized businesses, in Greece, they are referred to as family businesses.

4.2 Knowledge Management Cycle in medium–sized firms in Greece

The results were verified that the dissemination and utilization of the knowledge management is in a satisfactory level. The high level of management has focused on the importance of an innovation culture and has inspired innovation values, to a certain extent, in the business environment.

The most important factor that assists a firm to be the leader is the extent to which the innovation culture has been transmitted in the firm's internal environment. The majority of Greek firms have developed knowledge management processes to contribute effectively creating an innovative cycle, where new ideas are generated from different perspectives. The diffusion of the knowledge is transmitted through the products which are distributed in the marketplace or processes are implemented throughout the organization. Their application then generates ideas for improvements, and so the cycle is repeated. Organizations that belong to the first group spend most of their innovation effort envisioning the change to new e-Ra and shape their strategies to that direction.

4.3 Knowledge Management benefits

Firms consistently track the benefits obtained from innovative activity by measuring some important factors. As far as innovation benefits are concerned, managers of Cluster 1 pay more attention to the satisfaction of their customer's needs. These shows the orientation corporations innovate, wishing to top their customer's preferences.

Improvement of the product value is of equal importance as loyalty to the firm's brand. Measuring the benefits pays less attention to their employees' performance as managers don't consider it as a semantic indicator. This is due to the fact that medium-sized firms are customer-oriented in order to acquire profit in the short-term and don't aim at invest long-term benefits from their employees.

4.4 Knowledge management Sources

The majority of the respondents in Cluster 1, in order to create a product or to improve their processes, prefer mainly to research the procedures their competitors/customers apply in the market. The basic characteristic of the innovative first group of firms is the attempt to introduce new processes for the adaptation in the new e-Ra, while the second group of firms aims at improving the processes. Therefore the Cluster 1 (C1) of firms has adopted radical business processes and changes to face the dynamic business environment. Firms of C1 continuously re-define and adopt organizational goals, purposes, and manage the knowledge as a "way of doing things". Collaboration with external organizations is considered to be an important innovation source. The sample indicates that most of the companies examined follow an occasional cooperation with an external organization, such as a university or research institute aiming at gaining useful information for potential market and technological changes.

An important finding is that a significant percentage does not accept the concept of partnerships. Regarding technology acquisition, firms prefer to develop technology in their Research and Development (R&D) department, considering research as the most reliable way of achieving technological and competitive advantage. Access to innovation is created by the vast majority through the development of an R&D department, which is also verified by the previous result concerning independence maintenance, while a small percentage develops innovative technology through a partnership. The managers' leadership skills are also sufficiently developed, providing the personnel with the right directions for innovative results. The leading activities of managers provide the personnel with the right directions so as for the firm to prove more productive by making use of the knowledge offered.

4.5 Leadership Competencies manage knowledge driving to Innovation Culture

A set of variables identifies the leadership's competencies in the area of knowledge management and innovation culture. On a scale from one to five ("not at all" to "consistently and effectively") the two groups of firms demonstrate the following behaviours. Managers' skills in C1 develop the knowledge management sufficiently, providing the personnel with the right directions for innovative results. Consequently the benefits derived from these leadership competencies are innovation culture, and encourage the active communication between co-workers and among other divisions. Cooperation, team spirit and lastly emphasis on idea-generation are the main priorities for managers to create an innovative model that ties business strategy into the day-to-day innovative process.

Form	Cluster 1	Cluster 2
Our organization has moved beyond hit-and-miss innovation to a more strategic e-commerce approach that is aligned with our growth strategies.	4,24	3,41
Our organization has fostered a culture that expects everyone, at every level, to contribute to the innovation e- process.	4,27	2,91
Our organization has built networks, pathways and platforms that promote the flow of innovation both internally and externally through alliances and partnerships	3,99	2,78
Our organization has adopted/adapted a step-by step funnel process that facilitates idea generation/collection right through the development of a business case and deployment of the new product/service/process.	4,04	2,53
Our organization has created opportunities to learn by building e-commerce systems that capture key leanings from the innovation process and communicate these leanings across the entire enterprise.	3,97	2,63
(Visionary Leadership) I take the mystery out of innovation by defining it. As a leader, I have lead our team through a process to define what innovation really means inside our organization/business unit. We've developed a clear, concise definition of innovation based on our organizational culture and internal/external parameters.	3,96	2,66
(Aligning for Success) I link innovation to our business goals. As a leader, I've positioned innovation within my business unit/department, as an integrated aspect of our organization's overall success--not as a gimmick. We have created an Innovation Model that ties our business strategies into the day to day innovative process.	4,01	2,88
(Strategic Decision Making) I define challenges specifically. As a leader, I have targeted important challenges that require innovative solutions. I have prioritized these areas and I've allocated resources to ensure implementation.	3,82	2,97

(Communication) I encourage actives communications. As a leader, I've created an environment of mutual support among co-workers. I've facilitated discussion across the organization by helping to set up effective lines of communications no only in our own team, but also among other departments/divisions.	4,40	3,50

4.6 Resource Allocation and its Impact on Innovation Success

The results below recognize how the Greek firms are allocating resources in relation to their innovation strategies. They have mandated a certain percent of an individual's work time to be dedicated to informal idea generation, exploratory thinking, and experimentation. Specifying the time they allocate it is among 6-10% and 11-15% of staff's time. In addition firms, in order to better improve the capabilities of leaders, teams and individuals they allocated funds for performance improvement programs and tools to utilize their innovative potential and perform to their fullest (58 firms). Besides, funds have been allocated by the C1 of firms to create a dynamic, knowledge-based e-learning system for communicating across the organization. Finally organization rewards and recognizes innovative outcomes on the part of individuals and teams

5 Conclusions

The globalization of product and service markets is accelerating. Greek firms face increasing competition, not only for sales, but also for technical know-how and skills. In this environment, competitiveness at the company level depends crucially on the speed with which new products can be brought to the marketplace at lower cost. Similarly, the creation of wealth depends to a very large extent on the speed with which knowledge management through scientific and technological breakthroughs is converted into practical and attractive solutions. Innovation – the ability to reap the rewards of scientific achievement – due to KM requires much more than the ability to turn a new idea into a working product .Efficient flows of technology are not enough; ready supplies of finance and of business skills are also needed (Ahanotu, 1998). In short, what is needed is a dynamic, self-sustaining culture of innovation. Specifically, the companies that demonstrate innovative leadership are characterized by a relatively high contribution of machinery and equipment costs to their operations; devote relatively more company resources to R & D; consider innovative ideas promptly; and have a strategic plan in operation that leads their team through a process to define what innovation really means inside their organization/business unit. They've developed a clear, concise definition of innovation based on their organizational culture and internal/external parameters and cooperate with research institutions and universities. Innovative firms spend more on R & D than the less innovative firms, a fact which confirmed by Danskin et al. (2005). Also, firms possessing internal technical expertise are more innovative than firms without such expertise as Carneiro (2000) substantiated. Innovative firms cooperate with outside scientific and technical establishments and make deliberate efforts to survey externally generated ideas. The development of innovative business capacity needs a long lasting effort, and that is the reason why management should welcome any type of alteration. In every organization, there are unlimited qualifications for the implementation of innovation and improvement. Firms that belong to C2 have set a low or moderate value (medians between 2.5 and 3 for the corresponding variables) for the culture of the innovation process that they have adopted, while they have set a low value (medians between 2 and 2.5 for the corresponding variables) for the leading capabilities of their leader.

Firms that belong to C1 seem to have adopted a certain policy for innovation while their leader has certain managing skills leading the team to this direction (medians 4 and 5 for the corresponding variables), diffusing the innovation into the internal environment of the firm, which means there is effective communication. Firms of C1 link the goals through communication and include tactics referring to internal effective communication. The successful linking between the aims of the company and the challenges of the new e-Ra of economy will be carried out effectively with the positive handling of knowledge management (KM). In this way will be able to correlate KM and innovation culture for the outcomes of strategic decisions.

This means that firms implement a specific innovative strategy which results from the procedures that facilitate the production/collection of innovative ideas among the employees at any level. This research investigates if there is some kind of benefit when a manager managing the knowledge receiving from innovative environment orders the employees to spend as much time as they can so as to adopt the innovation culture. The deduction is that corporations which make this kind of order bring the following benefits: connection of innovation with the goals of corporation, purifying defiance, and communication, all parameters of the qualifications that guide to the innovation and to the organizational performance..

References

Ahanotu, N.D. (1998) "Empowerment and production workers: a knowledge-based perspective", Empowerment in Organizations, Volume 6 Number 7, pp. 177–186.
Ambastha, A. and Momaya, K. (2004) "Competitiveness of firms: Review of theory, frameworks, and models", Singapore Management Review, 2004 Volume 26 Issue 1, p. 45.
Amit, R. & Zott, C. (2001) Value Creation in e-business. Strategic Management Journal, 22 (6/7), 493-520.
Amor, D. (2002) The E-Business (R)Evolution. 2nd Edition, Prentice Hall, New York.

Barney, J. (1991) "Firm resources and sustained competitive advantage", *Journal of Management*, Volume 17 Number 1, pp. 99–120.

Boone, Christophe & Woody Van Olffen. 2000. Psychological team diversity and strategy implication: theoretical considerations and an empirical study. Maastricht University.

Brown, M. (2002) The use of banner advertisement with pull-down menus: a copy testing approach. Journal of Interactive Advertising, 2 (2), 12-37.

Barson, R.J., Foster, G., Struck, T., Ratchev, S., Pawar, S., Weber, F., and Wunram, M. (2000). Inter- and intra-organisational barriers to sharing knowledge in the extended supply chain, in B. Stanford-Smith and P.T. Kidd (eds.). E-business: Key Issues, Applications and Technologies, IOS Press, Amsterdam, pp. 367-373.

Carneiro, A. (2000) "How does knowledge management influence innovation and competitiveness?", Journal of Knowledge Management, Volume 4, pp. 87–98.

Christensen, C.M. and Rosenbloom, R. (1995) "Explaining the attacker's advantage: technological paradigms, organisational dynamics and the value network", Research Policy, Volume 24, pp. 233–257.

Christensen, C.M. (1997) The Innovators Dilemma: When New Technologies Cause Great Firms to Fail, Harvard Business School Press, Boston, Massachusetts.

Danskin P., Englis B.G., Solomon, M.R., Goldsmith, M. and Davey, J. (2005) "Knowledge management as competitive advantage: lessons from the textile and apparel value chain", Journal of Knowledge Management, Volume 9 Number 2, pp. 91–102.

Brown, J. S., & Duguid, P. 2001. Knowledge and organization: A social-practice perspective. Organzation Science, 12(2): 198-213.

Chan, LL.M.; Shaffer, M. A.; Snape, Ed (2004) In search of sustained competitive advantage: the impact of organizational culture, competitive strategy and human resource management practices on firm performance, International Journal of Human Resource Management, 15 (1), pp: 17-35

Davenport, T.H. & Grover, V. (2001) General perspectives on knowledge management: fostering a research agenda. Journal of Management Information Systems, 18 (1), 5-21.

Denning, S. (2000) The Springboard: How Storytelling Ignites Action in Knowledge-Era Organizations, Butterworth Heinemann, Boston, London.

Gold, A., Malhotra, A. & Segars, A. (2001) Knowledge management: an organizational capabilities perspective. Journal of Management Information Systems, 18 (1), 185-214.

Gobadian A, O'Regan, N. (2002) The Link Between Culture, Strategy and Performance in Man facturing SMEs. Journal of General Management, 28 (1), pp: 16-35

Hamel, G. (2000) Leading the Revolution, Harvard Business School Press, Boston, Massachusetts.

Johannessen J., Olaisen J. and Olsen B. (1999) "Strategic use of information technology for increased innovation and performance", Information Management and Computer Security, Volume 7 Number 1, pp. 5–22.

Kim, D., Cameron, S. and Quinn R.E. (August 1998) Diagnosing and Changing Organizational Culture: Based on the Competing Values Framework (Addison-Wesley Series on Organization Development) by Addison-Wesley Pub Co; ISBN: 0201338718.

Kuczmarski, T. (1996) "What is innovation? The art of welcoming risk", Journal of Consumer Marketing, Volume 13 Number 5, pp. 7–11.

Kyriazopoulos, P. (2000) "The modern firm in the starting of the 21st century", Chapter 8, E-Commerce pp. 284–323, Sychrony Ekdotiki, Athens.

Panagiotis Kyriazopoulos, Denis Yannacopoulos , Athanasios Spyridakos, Yannis Siskos, Evangelos Grigoroudi (2007) " Implementing internal marketing through employee's motivation" POMS Conference 2007 Dallas Texas

Lorente A., Dewhurst F. and Dale B.G. (1999) "TQM and business innovation", European Journal of Innovation Management, Volume 2 Number 1, pp. 12–19.

Liebowitz, J. (2000) Building organizational intelligence- a knowledge management primer, CRC Press: Boca Raton, FL.

Lindsey, K. "Unmasking Barriers to Knowledge Sharing Using a Communication Framework," Ninth Americas Conference on Information Systems, 2003, pp. 3350- 3358.

Malhotra, Y. (2000) Knowledge Management for E-business Performance. Information Strategy: The Executives Journal, 16 (4), 5-16.

Nonaka, I. (1994) A dinamic theory of organizational knowledge creation. Organization

Neely, A., Filippini, F., Forza, C., Vinelli, A. and Hii, J. (2001) "A framework for analysing business performance, firm innovation and related contextual factors: perceptions of managers and policy makers in two European regions", Integrated Manufacturing Systems, Volume 12 Number 2, pp. 114–124.

Nonaka, I. (1994) "The dynamic theory of organizational knowledge creation", Organization Science, Volume 5 Number 1, pp. 14–37.

Penrose, E.T. (1958) The Theory of the Growth of the Firm. Wiley, New York

Polanyi,M. (1966), The Tacit Dimension, Routledge & Kegan Paul, London

Probst, G., Raub, S. & Romhardt, K. (2000) Managing knowledge: building blocks for success, John Wiley: Chichester.

Powell TC, Dent-Micallef A. (1997) Information technology as competitive advantage: The role of human, business, and technology, Strategic Management Journal, 18, pp:375-405

Szeto, E. (2000) "Innovation capacity: working towards a mechanism for improving innovation within an inter-organizational network", The TQM Magazine, Volume 12 Number 2, pp. 149–158.

Smircich, L. (1983) Concepts of Culture and Organizational Analysis, Administrative Science Quarterly, 28 (3), pp: 339-358

Thomond P. and Lettice F. (2002) Disruptive Innovation Explored, 9th IPSE International Conference on Concurrent Engineering: Research and Applications (CE2002).

Authors Bios

R. Todd Stephens is the Senior Technical Architect of the Collaboration and On-line Services Group for the AT&T Corporation. Todd is responsible for setting the corporate strategy and architecture for the development and implementation of the enterprise collaborative and metadata solutions. Todd has over 130 professional and academic publications including seven patents. Additionally, he has authored or co-authored eight books in the field of information technology. Todd holds degrees in Mathematics and Computer Science from Columbus State University, an MBA degree from Georgia State University, and a Ph.D. in Information Systems from Nova Southeastern University.

Kathrin Kirchner is a postdoc at Friedrich-Schiller-University Jena, Department of Business Information Systems. She works in the fields of (spatial) data mining, decision support and knowledge management. Her PhD work entitled "A spatial decision support system for the rehabilitation of gas pipeline networks" was finished in 2006 in Jena.

Liana Razmerita is Assistant Professor at Copenhagen Business School, Center of Applied ICT. She holds a PhD in computer science from University Paul Sabatier, Toulouse, France. Her PhD entitled 'User Models and User Modeling in Knowledge Management Systems: an Ontology-based Approach' has been awarded in December 2003. Her research work includes domains such as: User Modelling, Semantic Web, Knowledge Management, e-Learning and e-Government.

Frantisek Sudzina finished his studies in Economics and Business Management at the University of Economics Bratislava in 2000, in Mathematics in 2004, and in Computer Science in 2006. He finished his PhD with the title "Impact of Management Information Systems on Business Competitiveness" in 2003. Then he became an assistant professor at the University of Economics Bratislava and since 2007, he works as an assistant professor at Copenhagen Business School.

Christian Briggs is completing his PhD in Human Computer Interaction Design at the Indiana University School of Informatics, where his formal research focuses on digitally-augmented organizations and culture, new media and marketing. Prior to IU, Christian worked for Ziff Davis Interactive, Surfwatch, Walt Disney Imagineering, One to One Interactive and The Palladium Group. Within these roles, Christian has gained a deep understanding of digital culture, and how it dialectically interacts with individuals and with groups of people. In his free time, Christian has founded BigTreetop.com – a web platform for bridging customer interests with local business entrepreneurism to revitalize community marketplaces.

Margarida Cardoso is a Sociologist with a Master degree in Anthropology of Social Movements. She is a PhD student in Information Systems and Technologies, at University of Minho - School of Engineering. She has been a research grantee for the last two years at INETI, a Portuguese State Laboratory, where she worked among other things, on projects about CoPs and future centers & open innovation. She is now on the move for a new position in a national agency.

António João Vidal de Carvalho holds a degree in Informatics/Applied Mathematics, a Master Degree in Informatics for Management and is a PhD student in Information Systems and Technologies at the University of Minho. He is a lecturer at Instituto Superior de Contabilidade e Administração do Porto (ISCAP) since 1992. He is co-author of four books in the area of informatics for personal productivity edited by Centro Atlântico.

Isabel Ramos is an Assistant Professor at Information Systems Department of University of Minho, Portugal. She is the Chair of the Master Programmes in Information Systems. She coordinates a research group in Knowledge Management. She also has research work in the field of Requirements Engineering. Isabel Ramos is associate editor of the International Journal of Technology and Human Interaction and Secretary of the IFIP TC8 (Information Systems). Her research and teaching interests include: requirements engineering, knowledge management, open innovation, organizational theory, sociology of knowledge, history of science, research methodology. She is responsible for the user studies in two funded R&D projects and does academic consulting in knowledge management.
Isabel Ramos is author of more than two dozen scientific papers presented at international conferences and published in scientific and technical journals. She advises the work of several PhD and Master students.

Nicole Radziwill is co-chair of the innovation research group of the Network Roundtable at the University of Virginia, and serves as the Assistant Director (VP) of the National Radio Astronomy Observatory where she is responsible for broadening global access to diverse observatory resources using information technology. Nicole has an MBA and is a doctoral candidate in Technology Management and Quality Systems at Indiana State University, investigating practical ways to drive quality, innovation and business value through social networks and participative technologies.

Ron DuPlain is a Software & Systems Engineer at the National Radio Astronomy Observatory, where he applies agile development to web applications and telescope instrumentation. Ron has a B.S. in Computer Engineering from the University of Cincinnati, where he studied hardware systems, simulations, VLSI microchip design, and software engineering. Ron co-founded ThoughtView Ltd. to investigate emergent thought management tools in the context of participative networks.

Jose Luis Marín de la Iglesia serves as CEO in Gateway S.C.S., a Spanish consultancy firm. His expertise and multidisciplinary College education (University of Valladolid) in Technology (Telecommunication Engineer in 2000) and Business Administration (Graduate in 2006) provides him a deep understanding of both technical and managing issues involved in Web 2.0. He is currently undertaking PhD studies on Web languages and technologies, field in which he has leaded 6 research projects in the past few years. He is also a member of IEEE and writes about Web 2.0 in the Open Economy blog.

Jose Emilio Labra Gayo obtained his PhD in Computer Engineering at the University of Oviedo in 2001. He has been the Dean of the School of Computer Science Engineering of Oviedo since 2004. His research interests are Semantic Web Technologies and Programming Languages. He has been part of the Programme Committee of several International Conferences in those subjects. He is the leader of the WESO (Semantic Web Oviedo) research group at the University of Oviedo.

Senoaji Wijaya, B.Eng. is a post-graduate student and a teaching assistant at the Institute of Information and Computing Sciences of Utrecht University, majoring in Business Informatics. He is currently conducting a thesis research at Deloitte Consulting, the Netherlands, and has developed a Webstrategy Framework with regard to the emergence of web 2.0 and collaborative business model. His teaching assistance responsibilities include 'E-Business', 'Enterprise Architecture', and 'Strategic Management, Organization Development and ICT' master courses.

Marco R. Spruit is an assistant professor in the Organisation & Information research group at the Institute of Information and Computing Sciences of Utrecht University in the Netherlands. His research currently focuses on business aspects regarding Linguistic Engineering and Data Mining. Before, he had been a professional software developer for 14 years in the fields of Information Retrieval & Intelligence, and an independent product software vendor for SME's.

Wim J. Scheper is a professor in the business-IT alignment at the Institute of Information and Computing Sciences of Utrecht University, the Netherlands. His current interests are in the field of Business Model Innovation, especially on web 2.0 business models. He also actively works as a partner at Deloitte Consulting and has developed the Business Maturity Model.

Sagar Bhatnagar works at Yahoo! HQ in Sunnyvale (CA) in "My Yahoo" team. He has an MBA from SUNY Buffalo(MIS and Operations Mgmt), a Bachelor of Engineering (Computer Science) from Delhi Institute of Technology (now NSIT) and around 7 years work experience in telecom and internet software. His interests are web-based softwares, web2.0/3.0 and virtual worlds.

Tejaswini Herath is an Assistant Professor at Brock University, Canada. She got her PhD in MIS at SUNY Buffalo

Raj Sharman is an Assistant Professor in the Management Science and Systems Department at SUNY Buffalo, NY. He received his B. Tech and M. Tech degree from IIT Bombay, India and his M.S degree in Industrial Engineering and PhD in Computer Science from Louisiana State University. His research streams include Information Assurance, Extreme Events, and improving performance on the Web. His papers have been published in a number of national and international journals. He is also the recipient of several grants from the university as well as external agencies. He serves as an Associate Editor for the Journal of Information Systems Security.

H. R. Rao is a professor of management information system and science at the state university of New York at Buffalo. He has authored or co-authored more than 100 technical papers, of which more than 90 are published in archival journals. He is a associate editor of Decision Support Systems, Information Systems Research and IEEE Transactions in Systems, Man and Cybernetics, and , guest senior editor of MISQ special issue on cybersecurity and co-editor- in -chief of Information Systems Frontiers.

Shambhu J. Upadhyaya, Ph.D., is a Professor of Computer Science and Engineering at the State University of New York at Buffalo where he also directs the Center of Excellence in Information Systems Assurance Research and Education, designated by the National Security Agency and the Department of Homeland Security. His research interests are information assurance, computer security, fault diagnosis, fault tolerant computing, and VLSI Testing. He has authored or coauthored more than 200 articles in refereed journals and conferences in these areas. He was a guest co-editor of the book Managing Information Assurance in Financial Services, IGI Global, 2007 and was a guest co-editor of a special issue on Secure Knowledge Management in IEEE Transactions on Systems, Man and Cybernetics, May 2006. He is on the Program Committees of several international conferences and workshops. He is a senior member of IEEE.

Clif Kussmaul is Chief Technology Officer for Elegance Technologies, which develops software products and provides product development services, and Associate Professor of Computer Science at Muhlenberg College. Formerly, he was Senior Member of Technical Staff at NeST Technologies. He has a PhD from the

University of California, Davis, an MS and MA from Dartmouth College, and a BS and BA from Swarthmore College. His interests include agile development, virtual teams, and entrepreneurship.

Roger Jack is President of Elegance Technologies, Inc. Roger has experience in project management, and creating reliable and robust interfaces and architectures. He was Vice President of U.S. Software Operations for NeST Technologies, where he managed many offshore projects. He has an MBA from Duke University's Fuqua School of Business, and an MS in Computer Science from Villanova University.

Marie-Helene Abel passed the PhD from the university of Compiègne in 1994 (France). She worked during four years at the University of Amiens as associate professor before joining the University of Compiègne in 2000. She is in charge of: the specialization "Knowledge Engineering and Information Media" - University of Technologie of Compiègne, and the DoC research team (Document and Knowledge) - UMR CNRS Heudiasyc. She is leader of the Research Team ICI (Information, Knowledge, and Interaction). She has published numerous papers in Journals and Conferences in the e-learning or knowledge engineering domain. She was in the scientific committee of conferences on e-learning and knowledge management. She takes part to European research projects. She is a member of the Network of Excellence Kaleidoscope, the European Network Taconet, and the Web Intelligent Consortium.

Hak-Lae Kim received his PhD degree from the Dankook University in 2008. He is currently a researcher at the Digital Enterprise Research Institute at NUI Galway, and is researching semantically-enabled social spaces and social computing. He is also member of the Web 2.0 Working Group in Korea. He is founder of the SCOT (Social Semantic Cloud of Tags) ontology and project, aims to provide semantic relations for tagging data, and has implemented the int.ere.st web site for OpenTagging platform.

John Breslin received his PhD degree from the National University of Ireland, Galway in 2002. He is currently a researcher and adjunct lecturer at the Digital Enterprise Research Institute at NUI Galway, and is leader of the Social Software research group there. He is founder of the SIOC (Semantically-Interlinked Online Communities) initiative, which provides an open-data format for community description. He co-founded Ireland's largest message board site, boards.ie Ltd., in 2000. The Irish Internet Association presented him with Net Visionary awards in 2005 (for boards.ie) and 2006 (for adverts.ie).

Mariano Corso, PhD, is full professor of Organization and Human Resources at the School of Management, Polytechnic of Milano where he chairs the course of Management Engineering at the Cremona site. He is director of the Master in "Management and Organisation Development" and of the Observatory on Enterprise 2.0. He promoted and coordinated national and international researches on Knowledge Management and is author of 100 publications at the international level.

Antonella Martini, PhD, is assistant professor of management at the University of Pisa where she teaches Innovation Management and Business Economics and Organisation. Her main research interests concern Knowledge & Community Management, and Continuous Innovation: she is actively involved in national and international projects on the fields and member of the international board of the Continuous Innovation Network (CINet). She is author of more than 50 publications at the international level.

Andrea Pesoli is researcher at the School of Management, Polytechnic of Milano, where he is the project manager for the Observatory on Enterprise 2.0. His main research interests concern Intranet and Enterprise 2.0.

Vladlena Benson received her PhD in Computer Science from the University of Texas at Dallas, USA. She is an active researcher in the areas of Information Security and Semantic Web technologies. In 2004 Vladlena joined the Department of Informatics and Operations Management at Kingston University, London. Between 2001 and 2004 she held a Senior Lecturer post at the Department of Computing Science at Middlesex University, UK.

Barry Avery is a Principal Lecturer in the Department of Informatics and Operations Management at Kingston University, London. He is an active researcher in Web Technologies, in particular those applied to learning and teaching.

Wen-Chung Shih received a B.S. degree in Computer and Information Science from National Chiao Tung University in 1992 and an M.S. degree in Computer and Information Science from National Chiao Tung University in 1994. He received the PhD degree in Computer Science from National Chiao Tung University in 2008. He passed the second class of the National Higher Examination in Information Processing field in 1994 and in Library Information Management field in 2004, respectively. Since 2004, he has worked as an executive officer in National Chi Nan University library, Taiwan. In August 2008, he joined the faculty of the Department of Information Science and Applications at Asia University, where he is currently an assistant professor. His research interests include e-learning, ubiquitous learning, web 2.0, content retrieval, parallel loop scheduling, grid computing and expert systems.

Shian-Shyong Tseng received the Ph.D. degree in computer engineering from the National Chiao Tung University in 1984. Since August 1983, he has been on the faculty of the Department of Computer and Information Science at National Chiao Tung University, and is currently a Professor there. From 1988 to 1991, he was the Director of the Computer Center at National Chiao Tung University. From 1991 to 1992 and 1996 to 1998, he acted as the Chairman of Department of Computer and Information Science. From 1992 to 1996, he was the Director of the Computer Center at Ministry of Education and the Chairman of Taiwan Academic Network (TANet) management committee. From 1999 to 2003, he has participated in the National Telecommunication Project and acted as the Chairman of the Network Planning Committee, National Broadband Experimental Network (NBEN). Since 2003, he has been acting as the principal investigator of the Taiwan SIP/ENUM trial project and the Chairman of the SIP/ENUM Forum Taiwan. In Dec. 1999, he founded Taiwan Network Information Center (TWNIC) and was the Chairman of the board of directors of TWNIC from 1999 to 2005. Since August 2005, he is the Dean of the College of Computer Science, Asia University. He is also the Director of the e-learning and application research center at National Chiao-Tung University and is currently a science and technology consultant of Ministry of Education. His current research interests include expert systems, data mining, computer-assisted learning, and Internet-based applications. He has published more than 100 journal papers. Dr. Tseng is an editor of International Journal of Fuzzy Systems, Journal of Internet Technology and Journal of Computers, and a member of IEEE and Phi Tau Phi Societies. He is also a Co Editor-in-Chief of Asian Journal of Health and Information Science. He was named an Outstanding Talent of Information Science of the Republic of China in 1989. He obtained the 1992, 1994, and 1995 Outstanding Research Awards of the National Science Council of the Republic of China. He was the winner of the 1990, 1991, 1998 and 2000 Acer Long Term Awards for outstanding M.S. Thesis Supervision and the winner of 1992 and 1996 Acer Long Term Awards for outstanding Ph.D. Dissertation Supervision. He was also awarded Outstanding Youth Honor of R.O.C. in 1992

Jui-Feng Weng receieved his B.S. and M.S. degrees from the Department of Computer and Information Science, National Chiao Tung University Taiwan in 2000 and 2002, respectively. Currently, he is a Ph. D student of National Chiao Tung University, Taiwan. His current research interests include e-learning, knowledge engineering, expert systems, and data mining, etc.

Georgios G. Tziralis, Mech. Eng. is a Doctoral Researcher in the Section of Industrial Management and Operations Research of National Technical University Athens (NTUA). His research and teaching interests are highly correlated with the term 'forecasting' at large, ranging from statistics, time series and econometrics, to data mining and machine learning. His clear focus is now on prediction markets, which also comprise the core of his dissertation, aiming at some contributions of impact to the field. Lately, prediction markets also gave outlet to his entrepreneurial flair.

George Vagenas is a Mechanical Engineer of the National Technical University of Athens (NTUA), specialized in Industrial Engineering. He is also a Doctoral Researcher in the Sector of Industrial Management and Operational Research of the National Technical University Athens (NTUA). His research interests include among others Knowledge Management (see www.kminpractice.com) and Business Process Management and Information Technology.

Stavros T. Ponis is a Lecturer in the Section of Industrial Management and Operations Research of National Technical University Athens (NTUA) where he is teaching a number of courses in a graduate and post graduate level (Supply Chain Management, E-Commerce and Management of Information Systems among others). Dr. Ponis is also an expert reviewer for the European Community, the General Secretariat of Research and Development and the Greek Information Society S.A. His current research interests and publications move around the areas of Virtual Enterprises, Knowledge Logistics for Empowering Supply Chain Effectiveness and Performance, UML and Agent Modelling, E-Commerce and Supply Chain Management Systems.

Samanta Rounti received her Bachelor in Business Administration, from the Graduate Technological Education Institute of Piraeus, Greece. She continues with Post Graduate Studies in International Marketing (M.Sc. in International Marketing) and M.Phil. in e-Marketing Business to Business Relationships with the University of West of Scotland (former University of Paisley U.K.). She is a Research Fellow at the Graduate Technological Education Institute of Piraeus. Her current scientific research activities include e-marketing, B2B relationship, Marketing Communication, Innovation Culture. Her research has been presented in more than 16 European and global conferences with proceedings. In addition, she has published a number of articles in scientific Journals. She is member of the Editorial Committee in Strategic Outsourcing, an International Journal (EMERALD Group Publishing)

Index